AMERICAN CITY

MICHAEL P. WEBER
Carnegie-Mellon University

ANNE LLOYD
Temple University

WEST PUBLISHING COMPANY
St. Paul • New York • Boston
Los Angeles • San Francisco

TO PATRICIA AND ANTHONY

Library of Congress Cataloging in Publication Data
Main entry under title:

American city.

Includes bibliographical references and index.
1. Cities and towns—United States. I. Weber, Michael P. II. Lloyd, Anne.

HT123.A6618 301.36'0973 75-15882

ISBN 0-8299-0036-9

THE AMERICAN CITY

THE

A Project of The Curriculum Center, Carnegie-Mellon University
Managing Editor: Michael P. Weber Consulting Editor: Edwin Fenton

Acknowledgments

We gratefully acknowledge the following for materials reprinted within this book.

Text acknowledgments

"Postcard," © 1969 by Suzanne Ostro Zavrian; "The Culture of Urban America," from *Environment and Change: The Next Fifty Years,* edited by William Ewald Jr. © 1968 by Indiana University Press, Bloomington, reprinted by permission from the publisher; "Chicago," by Carl Sandberg from *Chicago Poems* (New York: Henry Holt, 1916); "May be Fair . . . But it Sho' is Hard," from *Ghetto Scenes* (Chicago: Free Black Press), pp. 219–220; "Dead End Street," Words and Music by Ben Raleigh and David Axelrod, © 1967, Beechwood Music Corporation, used by special permission; "The Invisible City," by Joseph Hudnut in *Architecture and the Spirit of Man* (Cambridge: Harvard, 1949); *The Human Community* by Baker Brownell (New York: Harper and Brothers, 1950), p. 327; "Events and Offerings," *Los Angeles Magazine,* 1974; "What's Wrong with Cities," abridged and reprinted with permission from *Senior Scholastic* © 1968 by Scholastic Magazines Inc.; Edward C. Banfield, *The Unheavenly City* (Boston: Little Brown and Co., 1969), pp. 3, 21; Homer Hoyt, *One Hundred Years of Land Values in Chicago* (Chicago: Univ. of Chicago Press, 1933); "Squeezing the Yahoos," © 1970 by Jimmy Breslin, reprinted by permission of the Sterling Agency Inc.; "How Fast Can You Get Out of Town," Courtesy of *Fortune* Magazine; Allan T. Demaree, "Cars and Cities on a Collision Course," reprinted from the February, 1970 issue of *Fortune* Magazine by special permission, © 1970, *Time* Inc.; Jack Rosenthal, "Large Suburbs Overtaking Cities in the Number of Jobs Supplied," © 1972 by the New York Times Company, reprinted by permission; Jane Jacobs, *The Economy of Cities,* © 1960, reprinted by permission of Random House Inc.; "Detroit Auto Worker," reprinted by permission of United Press International © 1972; "Charlie O," *Parade Magazine,* Jan. 28, 1973; "Ted Straight, Man on the Way Up," Text and Drawings by W.B. Park, © 1971, reprinted by permission of the author; "Four American Suburbs," reprinted by permission of *Time*, The Weekly Newsmagazine, Copyright 1971, *Time* Inc., Skybus Articles, *The Pittsburgh Post Gazette*, 1965–73; "The Dump Game," by Edward Martin and Martin Sandler, adapted from *Social Education*, Nov. 1971, reprinted with permission of The National Council for the Social Studies and the authors; "School Cancels Pacifist Movie," and "Academic Freedom," from Classroom Outlines, American Civil Liberties Union, reprinted by permission; Donald Parker, Robert O'Neil, and Nicholas Econopouly, "The Abuse of Power," in *Civil Liberties,* copyright © 1965 by the Lincoln Filine Center for Citizenship and Public Affairs, Tufts University, reprinted by permission of the publishers, Houghton Mifflin Co.; Gini Kopecky, "To Scoop or Not to Scoop," © 1972 by the New York Times Company, reprinted by permission; I. A. Gardner, "New York, Oh What a Charming City" (n.p., n.d.); "New York in the 1830's," adapted from John F. Watson, *Annals of Philadelphia* (Vol. II, Philadelphia, 1857); "New York, A City of Variety," adapted from: William James, *Talks to Teachers on Psychology* (N. Y., 1899); "Baltimore in the 1840's," adapted from: *The Life and Times of Frederick Douglas* (Hartford, 1882); *Eldorado* by Bayard Taylor (G.P. Putnam's, 1859); "New Orleans in the 1830's," adapted from: Thomas Hamilton, *Men and Manners in America* (New York, 1833);

"Boston in the 1820's," adapted from Shubael Bell, Letter to a Friend, 1817 in Whitehall, *Boston: A Topographical History* (Cambridge; Belknap Press, 1968); "Atlanta Residents Talk about Their City," adapted from: William Hanleiter, *Atlanta Directory,* 1871, courtesy of Atlanta Historical Society; "Richmond: Tobacco Processing and Trade," adapted from Bondurant, *Poe's Richmond* (Richmond:Garrett and Massie, 1942); Louden Wainright, "The Dying Girl No One Helped," *Life* April 10, 1964, p. 10; "Cincinnati: Commerce and Enterprising Citizens," adapted from: Michael Chevalier, *Society and Manners and Politics* (N. Y., 1839); "Manufacturing in the Walking City: Lowell, Massachusetts, 1845," adapted from: William T. Thompson, "The Exploits of Major Jones," in *My Native Land*, W. S. Tyron, ed. (Chicago: University of Chicago Press, 1952); "Pittsburgh: Trade and Manufacturing in 1826," adapted from: Samuel Jones, *Pittsburgh, 1826* (Pittsburgh, 1826); Michael Holt, *Forging A Majority* (New Haven: Yale University Press, 1969); Sam Bass Warner Jr., *The Private City* (Philadelphia: University of Pennsylvania Press, 1968); Octave Mirbeau, *The Epidemic* (1898), Translation Jacques Barzun, *Modern Repertoire Series II,* Eric Bently, ed. (University of Denver Press, 1952); "Yellow Fever in New Orleans," adapted from: "History and Incidents of Plague in New Orleans," *Harper's Monthly* (November, 1853); "Menu for Dinner Worthy of New York's Elite," from: Lloyd Morris, *Incredible New York* (New York: Random House. 1951); John Spargo, *The Bitter Cry of Children* (New York, 1906); George Maxwell, "Rural Homes Are the Safeguards of the Nation," *Maxwells Talisman* (May, 1908); Frederic C. Howe, *The City, The Hope of Democracy* (New York, 1905); Meridith Nicholson, "Indianapolis, A City of Homes," *Atlantic Monthly* (June, 1904); Elizabeth McCallie, "The Saga of a Business Girl in the 1890's," courtesy of the Atlanta Historical Society; "New Names for East Siders," *New York Herald Tribune* (July 3, 1898); Cook, Gittel, and Mack (eds.), *City Life, 1865–1900* © 1973 by Praeger Publishers Inc., New York, excerpted and reprinted by permission; George Rogers, "First Electric Streetcars," *Richmond News Leader* (Sept. 17, 1952); Walter Marshall, *Through America; Or Nine Months in the United States* (London, 1882); Howard A. Bridgman, "The Suburbanite," in *The Independent* (April, 1902); Adam Smith, *An Inquiry into the Nature and Causes of the Wealth of Nations* (London, 1802); William Stead, *Chicago Today* (London, 1894); *Horatio Alger, The Store Boy or the Fortunes of Ben Barclay* (N. Y., 1887); Michael P. Weber, "Patterns of Progress," adapted (Pittsburgh, 1972); "The District Messenger Boy," courtesy of The Pittsburgh Landmarks Society; Theodore Dreiser, *Twelve Men* (New York: Boni and Liveright, 1919); Frederick Howe, *The Confessions of a Reformer* (N. Y.: Charles Scribner's Sons, 1925); Carl Lorenz, *Tom L. Johnson* (N. Y.: A. S. Barnes Co., 1911); Tom L. Johnson, *My Story* (N. Y.: Columbus Sterling Publishing Co., 1911); *Rosina Meadows, The Village Maid,* adapted by Charles H. Saunders from the novel of the same name by William B. English; *Love of Life* adapted from Robert Shaw's script for *Love of Life*, American Home Products Inc., reprinted by permission; Cynthia Proulx, "Sex as Athletics in the Singles Complex," *Saturday Review* (May, 1973); Herbert Otto, "Communes, The Alternate Life Style," *Saturday Review* (April, 1971); Charlotte Saikowski, "The Adamses of Palos Verdes, California," reprinted by permission from: *The Christian Science Monitor* © 1967 The Christian Science Publishing Society, All Rights Reserved; "New Life in Retirement Communities," reprinted from the July 8, 1972 issue of *Business Week* by Special Permission © 1972 by McGraw Hill Inc.; Robert Lynn Adams and Robert Jon Rox, "Mainlining Jesus: The New Trip," published by permission of Transactions Inc., from *Society* (February, 1972) © 1972; "Coming of Age in Nueva York," adaptation by permission of G. P. Putnam's Sons from *Irrational Ravings* by Peter Hamill; *Report of the Committee of the Senate Upon the Relations Between Labor and Capital* (Washington, 1885) III; Ann Rivington, "We Live on Relief," *Scribner's* (April, 1934); Tom Buckley, "Poverty and Pride Trap City's Aged," © 1973 by The New York Times Company, reprinted by permission; Office of Economic Opportunity, *The Poor in 1970, A Chartbook* (Washington, D. C., 1971); Claude McKay, "If We Must Die–" *Liberator* (July, 1919); "Letters of Negro Migrants of 1916–1918 to the *Chicago Defender,*" reprinted in *Journal of Negro History* (July, 1919); Chicago Commission on Race Relations, *The Negro in Chicago* (Chicago: University of Chicago Press, © 1922); "Where Whites and Negroes Agree," *Newsweek* (Sept., Oct., 1963); Governor's Commission on the Los Angeles Riots, John A. McCone, Chairman, *Violence in the City–An End or a Beginning?;* Elijah Muhammed, *Muhammed Speaks* (July 2, 1965); Excerpt from "I Have a Dream," by Martin Luther King Jr., reprinted by permission of Joan Daves, copyright © 1963; Lyndon B. Johnson, "Address of the President," Howard University, Washington, D. C. (June 4, 1964); "Jesse Jackson, One Leader Among Many," "Other Voices, Other Strategies," "Fortress California," "The Women in Blue," all reprinted by permission from *Time*, The Weekly Newsmagazine, copyright Time Inc.; Theodore White, *The Making of the President, 1972* (New York: Atheneum, 1973); Thomas P. Benic, "A Night in a Police Patrol Car," Pittsburgh Post Gazette (Dec. 29, 1973); "Crime Surge Defies All Efforts," *U. S. News and World Report* (June 10, 1974); Safeplaces, Inc., copyright © 1974, all rights reserved; used with permission of the publisher, Arlington House Inc.; Interview with Inspector William Moore, Pittsburgh Police (November, 1973); "Gun Control," *Life* (June 30, 1972); Patrick V. Murphey, Police Commissioner of New York, "Certainty of Punishment," *U. S. News and World Report* (Jan. 31, 1972); Jane Geniesse, "Blockwork Orange," copyright © 1973 by the NYM Corp., reprinted with the permission of *New York Magazine;* "Safe with Harm," *Newsweek* (January 1, 1973); Bill Kovach, "Garbage Smothered Cities Face Crises in Five Years," © 1973 by The New York Times Company, reprinted by permission; "The Huttons of New Hope," *Environmental Action Bulletin* (Sept. 23, 1972); Linda Greenhouse "Garbage Recycling Helps Out a Village," © 1972 by The New York Times Company, reprinted by permission; William Allan, "Garbage Now Generates Electricity," *Pittsburgh Press* (April 13, 1973); "Environmental Quality," The Second Annual Report of the Council on Environmental Quality (Washington, D. C., August, 1971); Seth S. King, "City Downtowns Struggle Back," © 1973 by The New York Times Company, reprinted by permission; P. Arctander, "Dubious Dogma of Urban Planning and Research," Donald Canty, "What Could Make Hartford Tick?", Ellen Berkeley, "The New Process in Hartford's North End," all reprinted by permission from: *City, Magazine of Urban Life and Environment,* National Urban Coalition, 2100 M Street, N. W. Washington, D. C., All Rights Reserved; "Tomorrow's Cities," reprinted by permission from *Changing Times,* The Kiplinger Magazine (April, 1970) copyright © 1970 by the Washington Editors Inc., 1729 H Street, N. W., Washington, D. C.; "Columbia, Maryland," adapted from: *The Promises and Purpose of Columbia,* Howard Research and Development Corporation, reprinted by permission; *The Urban Design Plan,* San Francisco Department of Planning (May, 1971); "Community Development in Action: A Progress Report," reprinted courtesy of The Greater Hartford Chamber of Commerce (Feb., 1974); James Hudson, "We Can Build Space Age Cities Now," copyright © 1970 by the National Wildlife Federation, reprinted from the August/September issue of *National Wildlife* Magazine; "The World of Buckminister Fuller," *Architectural Forum* (Jan.–Feb. 1972), reprinted by permission of Informat Publishing Corporation, Architectural Plus; Walter Karp, "Soleri: Designer in the Desert," *Horizon* (Autumn, 1970); *The City in the Image of Man* by Paolo Soleri, reprinted by permission of the M.I.T. Press, 1972; Robert Silverberg, "The Throwbacks," *Galaxy Science Fiction* © 1970 by UPD Publishing Corporation, reprinted by permission of the author.

Art acknowledgments

"Ode to a Freeway," © 1973 by the New York Times Company, reprinted by permission; "Steel Valley," Louis Lozowick, lithograph, Associated American Galleries; "Home for Christmas," Norman Rockwell, *Saturday Evening Post,* © 1944, Curtis Publishing Co., Philadelphia; "The Bowery," Reginald Marsh, The Metropolitian Museum of Art, Arthur H. Hearn Fund; "Spring in Central Park," Adolf Dehn, The Metropolitian Museum of Art, Fletcher Fund, 1941; "Night Hawks," Edward M. Hopper, Art Institute of Chicago, Friends of American Art Collection; "The Street," Richard M. Lindner, 1963, Collection Mr. and Mrs. I.M. Pei, Katonah, New York; "City Scape," Louise Piper Zinner, reprinted by permission of the author; "First day of May in New York – A General Move," The J. Clarence Davies Collection, Museum of the City of New York; "Market in a Southern City," *The Great South,* Edward King, American Publishing Co., Hartford, 1875; "Cotton Baling, Galveston, Texas"; *The Great South*; River Front of Cincinnati," original entitled "Cincinnati, 1848" by Charles Fontayne and William Porter daguerreotype, courtesy Cincinnati Public Library; "View of Union Stockyards," Courtesy Chicago Historical Society; "McCormic Reaper Factory," International Harvester Company; "Woolen Mills, Rockville, Conn.," Harry T. Peters, American on Stone Lithography Collection, Smithsonian Institute; "The Custom House, New York, 1845," lithographed by Robert Kerr, Library of Congress; Iron Factory, Pittsburgh, 1839," courtesy Carnegie Library Pittsburgh; "Pittsburgh in 1845," Carnegie Library Pittsburgh; "Labor Day, Buffalo, New York, 1905," Library of Congress; "The Grain Movement from the West," Library of Congress; "The War of Wealth," Library of Congress; "The Working Man's Mite," *Harper's Weekly,* May 20, 1871; Ad for Cleaning Fluid, 1896, Library of Congress; "Woolworth Building, 1913, The Museum of the City of New York.

All contemporary photographs, unless otherwise cited, were taken by: Joseph Dicey, Pittsburgh, Pennsylvania.

We gratefully acknowledge the cooperation of the academic staff of the several institutions of higher learning who participated in testing these materials. Testing and suggestions for revision were conducted by the following: Barbara W. Thomas, Caldwell Community College and Technical institute, Lenoir, North Carolina; Robert Ziegenfus, North Hampton Community College, Bethlehem, Pennsylvania; Jean Hunt, Loop College, Chicago, Illinois; Lester Hunt, Southwest College, Chicago, Illinois; Steve Herzog, Moorpark, California. The authors also tested the materials at Allegheny Community College, Allegheny Campus, Pittsburgh, Pennsylvania; Ms. Lloyd tested the materials at Temple University, Philadelphia, Pennsylvania.

We also wish to offer a special thanks to the following persons for assistance, suggestions, and, above all, encouragement: Ted Fenton and Joel Tarr of the Department of History, Carnegie-Mellon University; Randy Kelley, Community College of Allegheny County; Ms. Dorothy Kabakeris, Ms. Ethel Strasser, Ms. Katherine Dudas, Ms. Irene Yourgas, and Mr. T. William Bolts. To the students and administrative staff at the Community College of Allegheny County, Allegheny Campus, we are also grateful.

Contents

To the student

This is a new kind of textbook about the American city. Most urban texts were written by one or two authors who organized material in a chronological fashion. These textbooks, usually ten or twelve chapters long, told a continuing story of urban growth. The authors illustrated these books with pictures, maps, charts, and graphs, each with a caption underneath it to explain the illustration. Students read and discussed this material to learn facts and generalizations about city life.

This book contains thirty-six assignments, organized into four units. Each assignment includes one or more articles or pieces of historical material taken from a book, magazine, newspaper article, journal, or other source, or written especially for this book. An introduction and study questions, which help to identify what to look for in the readings, precede each assignment. A study question for further thought, and two individual and small group activities appear at the end of each assignment.

Numerous illustrations, maps, charts, and graphs appear throughout the text. Each has been carefully chosen to help you understand American urban life. Your instructor will probably refer to these illustrations frequently throughout the semester.

The materials within this book have been selected or written with great care. Rather than memorizing facts, you will use the materials to identify problems, develop tentative answers to questions (hypotheses), gather information, and arrive at your own conclusions.

This course concentrates on urban life in three time periods. In Part I, you will examine the American city as it exists today. The materials in this part provide a framework for analyzing cities in other times and other locations. The assignments include ideas from the fields of geography, economics, sociology, and political science. You will use these ideas in Parts II and III to study urban life during two nineteenth century time periods. By studying cities in each of these periods you can learn how to analyze any city that has ever existed. Part IV discusses the problems and opportunities of the modern American city. Your ability to analyze cities will enable you to suggest solutions to these problems and help make the city a better place to live.

How to use this book

Each of the thirty-six assignments follows this pattern:

1. *The Introduction.* Each introduction relates an assignment to other assignments in the course and provides essential background information.
2. *Study Questions.* A few study questions precede the materials within the assignment. The questions highlight the most important parts of the readings. You may wish to write brief answers to the questions in preparation for class discussion.
3. *The Article or Source Material.* Each assignment contains one or more readings, or graphs, pictures, tables, or other forms of written material.
4. *A Thought Question.* One question designed to provoke further thought appears at the end of each assignment.
5. *Individual and Small Group Activities.* Suggestions for activities to be completed at home or within your city conclude each assignment.

THE AMERICAN CITY

SANTA
MONICA
10
LOS
ANGELES
STREET
EXITS
13

INTRODUCTION
to the unit on the automobile city

We live in an urban age. In 1972, nearly 152 million Americans lived in or near cities. Each year the number of Americans living in urban areas continues to grow despite complaints about the declining quality of life in cities. Most people, however, know little about the city in which they live.

Historians often call the modern American city the "automobile city." Since World War I Americans have become increasingly dependent upon their cars. Most Americans commute by automobile to shopping and recreational areas. They also use cars to travel to work and school. The automobile has created what some Americans call "urban sprawl." Cities, and their surrounding towns, continue to spread farther and farther from the downtown section. Many urban residents commute ten or fifteen miles, driving from an outlying suburb to the city each day. The automobile has influenced the geographic, economic, social, and political patterns of modern American cities.

Assignments 1 through 10 examine the automobile city. In Assignments 1 and 2 you will analyze attitudes toward life in the automobile city. Assignments 3 through 10 use ideas (concepts) from the fields of geography, economics, sociology and political science to explain the organization of the modern city. Each of these concepts suggests questions which will help you to analyze the automobile city. Your ability to use these questions will enable you to examine both modern and historical cities.

*

Images of the contemporary city

Assignment 1

How do you feel about the quality of life in the American city? Ask American citizens that question and their answers will range from glowing praise to outright condemnation. Few Americans remain neutral about life in the city. City planners talk about an urban crisis that cannot be solved without drastic action. Inner city residents complain of rundown housing, poor schools, lack of jobs, and a variety of other shortcomings. On the other hand, young professional people point to the cultural, intellectual, and recreational advantages of urban life. The suburban businessperson-commuter, however, speaks of job opportunities while decrying morning and evening traffic jams, pollution, and crime in the streets. Yet, all of these people, along with 150 million other Americans, continue to live and work in urban areas.

What is the lure of the American city, and why does it prompt these diverse reactions? In Assignment 1 you will examine attitudes of people such as artists, poets, songwriters, and scholars toward the American city. To help you organize information about these attitudes, you should keep a chart of the most significant ideas. The chart should contain three columns. Label the columns Positve Images of the American City, Negative Images of the American City, and Other Images. On the left-hand margin of your paper write the following words: artists, poets, songwriters, and average Americans. Enter specific notes in each column as soon as you finish studying a section of the assignment. This chart will provide a summary of Assignment 1 and will serve as an analytical tool to help you examine the images of the city.

Art and the American city

The seven paintings which follow illustrate artists' conceptions of the American city. As you examine each painting, think about the following questions:

1. How do these paintings make you feel about city life?
2. How do you account for the different images portrayed in the paintings?

The Bowery, by Reginald Marsh
The Metropolitan Museum of Art,
Arthur H. Hearn Fund, 1932.

Home for Christmas, by Norman Rockwell

Steel Valley, by Louis Lozowick Associated American Artists.

Spring in Central Park,
by Adolf Dehn
The Metropolitan Museum of Art,
Fletcher Fund, 1941.

City Patterns, by Eloise Piper Zinner
Reprinted by permission.

The Street, by Richard M. Lindner
Collection: Mr. & Mrs. I.M. Pei, Katonah, N.Y.

Night Hawks, by Edward Hopper
Courtesy of The Art Institute of Chicago

Poets write about the American city

American poets frequently turn to the city as a source of inspiration. More sensitive and perceptive than most of us, poets often find beauty, love, loneliness, or despair in urban life. Often, however, poets express feelings that many of us recognize and experience.

As you read the following selections, answer these questions in your own mind:

1. What are these poems saying about urban life?
2. What images of the good life in the city do these poems reveal?

Postcard

Suzanne Ostro Zavrian resides in New York City where she writes poetry and co-edits Extensions, *a magazine of poetry and fiction. A power blackout, a garbage strike and other similar annoyances in the mid-1960's prompted her to write the following poem. From: ©Suzanne O. Zavrian, 1969.*

What can I tell you?

The subways stopped
and we couldn't use the tunnels;
the buses broke down, fell apart
  a few went
out of
    control
     into

    the power failed
and we ran out of candles.
(do not go out during New Moon)

I am writing this to you
on top of sixteen feet of garbage,
taking a sunbath as I watch
the Saint Patrick's Day parade.

Chicago
by Carl Sandberg

Born in Illinois in 1878, Carl Sandberg experienced first-hand, the growth of urban America. Beginning at the age of thirteen he worked as a driver of a milkwagon, a worker in a brick yard, a dishwasher in hotels, and a department store advertising manager before turning to poetry. In 1914 he earned his first acclaim as a poet with a series of "Chicago Poems." Often known as the "Poet of Industrial America," Sandberg presents an exciting image of the industrial city.

Hog Butcher for the World,
Tool Maker, Stacker of Wheat,
Player with Railroads and the Nation's Freight Handler;
Stormy, husky, brawling,
City of Big Shoulders

They tell me you're wicked and I believe them, for I have seen your painted women under the gas lamps luring the farm boys,
And they tell me you are crooked and I answer: Yes, it is true I have seen the gunman kill and go free and kill again
And they tell me you are brutal and my reply is: On the faces of women and children I have seen the marks of wanton hunger.
And having answered so I turn once more to those who sneer at this my city, and I give them back the sneer and say to them:
Come and show me another city with lifted head singing so proud to be alive and coarse and strong and cunning.
Flinging magnetic curses amid the toil of piling job on job, here is a tall bold slugger set vivid against the little soft cries.
Fierce as a dog with tongue lapping for action, cunning as a savage pitted against the wilderness

Bareheaded,
Shoveling,
Wrecking,
Planning,

Building, breaking, rebuilding
Under the smoke, dust all over his mouth, laughing with white teeth,
Under the terrible burden of destiny laughing as a young man laughs,
Laughing even as an ignorant fighter laughs who has never lost a battle,
Bragging and laughing that under his wrist is the pulse, and under his ribs the heart of the people
Laughing!
Laughing the stormy, husky, brawling laughter of Youth, half-naked, sweating, proud to be Hog Butcher, Tool Maker, Stacker of Wheat, Player with Railroads and Freight Handler to the Nation.

May be Fair . . . but It Sho' Is Hard

The poetry of black Americans reveals a dramatically different image of the American city than that held by most white urban dwellers. The following poem, by an unknown black writer illustrates the frustration and despair felt in the black urban ghetto.

Living in the slums
is a pain in the ass.
Mostly dirt and concrete–
Very little grass.
Come home late–
No place to park,
Just like Noah
Up in that Ark.

Rats play tag
all through the night,
Catch me sleep
And take a bite
Out of a toe,
Or arm or ham–
Daley's poison's
not worth a damn.

Rats tote land deeds
in their vests,
Some smoke Hedges'
Cigarettes.
It's obvious why
Rent's so high
On these slummy flats–
We playing extra
For the rats.

I don't forget
the roaches man!
They strut around
Like they own the land!
Bold as Batman
high on pot!
As soon walk off
With your plate
as not.

Sometimes . . .
Don't wait 'til you

through cookin'–
They liftin' up
The lids and lookin'–
to see if the menu
meets their taste,
Ghetto Roaches
are the super race!
Stone gourmets!
Our roaches are!–
They'll eat soul food,
but prefer caviar,
Or filet Mignon,
Or other high-
falutin' stuff,

. . . .

Another thing's
the food we buy.

I get so mad
I damn near cry–
Seeing picked-over garbage
Brought here for us.
It's enough to make
A Boy Scout cuss.

Third-Class food
at first class prices
left after white folks
buys the nicest.
Leftovers sent
for us to buy,–
And we do–
But I can't see why.

Meat so tough–
Only acid cuts it.
But with Accent and Adolph's
We thrive off of it.
Using plenty of gravy–
to slide it down–
While white folks on
their side of town
Are laughing at
we silly clowns.
Eating stuff
that they've rejected–

But . . .
That's life in the slums–
Until we wreck it.

Songs of the city

Song lyrics often reflect the attitudes of the society in which they were written. Through them we may view the hopes and concerns of people living in that society. Songs about the city illustrate the importance of music as an historical document. Their words often reveal deep feelings, both positive and negative, and express important concerns about urban life. In this section of Assignment 1, two contemporary lyricists provide their images of the city. As you read the words to this song, think about the following questions:

1. What are the major concerns of the songwriters? How does this song make you feel?
2. Can you think of other songs which illustrate a writer's image of the city? Bring one to your next class.

The song in this section was popular in the late 1960's. It illustrates the author's image of the American city. As you read the words to this song think about your own city.

Dead End Street
Chicago's the town they call the windy city
They call it the windy city because of the hawk
The hawk, the almighty hawk
Just the wind
Takes care of plenty business

The place that I lived in was on a street
That happened to be one of the dead-end streets
Where there was nothing to block the wind, the elements
Nothing to block the wind
To keep it from knocking my pad down
I mean really sockin it to me.

When the boiler was bust and the heat was gone
I had to get fully dressed for I could go to bed
'Course I couldn't pull on my gouloshes
Cause they had buckles on
My folks didn't play that, They said
"Don't you tear up my bed clothes with them gouloshes on"

But I was fortunate!
Soon's I was big enough to get a job
To save money. Get a ticket. Catch anything
I split
I said one day I'm gonna return
Then I'm gonna straighten it all out
I'm about ready to go back now
So I thought I'd tell you about it

They say this is the big rich town
I live in the poorest part
I know I'm on a dead-end street
in a city without a heart

I learned to fight before I was six
only way I could get along
When your raised on a dead-end street
You gotta be tough and strong
All the guys I know getting in trouble
Life's always been when the odds are all against you
How can you win

I'm gonna push my way outta here
Even though I can't say when
Well I'm gonna get off of this dead-end street
I ain't never gonna come back again
Never!

I ain't gonna come back to this dead-end street
No more. No!
Cause I'm gonna get me a job
I'm gonna save my dough
get away from here
I ain't gonna come back no more
I'm tired of a dead end street
I wanna get out in the world and learn something
Tired of breaking my back
I want to start using my mind

The scholar and the city

American intellectuals frequently criticized American urban life. Thomas Jefferson's happiest moments occurred when he was on his rural estate in Virginia. Thoreau counseled Americans to escape the brutality of the city and return to a simpler way of life. Different scholars, however, often hold different images of the city. The two excerpts which follow, written by men with similar professional backgrounds illustrate these dramatic differences. As you read, answer in your own mind, the questions listed below.

1. What images of the good life does the article by Joseph Hudnut reveal?
2. What, according to Baker Brownell, is wrong with city life? Do you agree that an urban dweller cannot be a whole person?

Joseph Hudnut talks about the city

Perhaps because I was born and brought up in the country I have always wanted to live near the heart of a great city. Even now I look forward to the day when I can live again in New York; in a little flat, say, at the corner of Broadway and Forty-Second Street. I should like to be clothed again in the strength and space of that city; to taste again the diversity of its fashions and humors; to feel about me the encompassment and drift of its opinion. I am not alone in New York even when I am alone. The city furnishes and fortifies my mind . . . .

Baker Brownell discusses rural life

Some may say that small communities are dull, monotonous. They do indeed lack the artificial coloration of New York. They lack the shocks, . . . , the displays, the fictions of significance and attention-getting, that make so much in the city that is called interesting. They express more often the continuities of living, the lifelong drama with its beginning, its middle, and its end, and the deep stability and balance of movement that human life sometimes can attain.

If we are interested mainly in human beings, the little places are the most interesting areas of experience in the world .... The statement is made in the belief that human beings, not parts of human beings, ..., are the most important to us of all things. Not solely hands to work, or feet to dance, or brains to direct a bank or a laboratory; not solely athletic skill, or beauty of face and body, or sex lure, not solely this perfected skill or that narrowly limited job, or some other specialized functional relation; these are not human relations in any full or complete sense, nor can they be substituted for them. They are fragments, and in spite of scientific codes and philosophies designed to put them together again, in spite of over-all organizational efforts and totalitarian plans, they remain—so far as human beings are concerned—fragments. They lack essential human wholeness. Human beings, I believe, are found in this enormous world only in the small community ....

Urban residents talk about their city

Artists, poets, songwriters, and scholars hold definite opinions about urban life. Many urban residents also feel strongly about the quality of life in the American city. Recently, a reporter for a large San Francisco newspaper stopped a number of people on the street asking them, "What is your opinion of contemporary American urban culture and its future?" As you read their responses, think about your own city.

1. What did each of the persons interviewed think of the city?
2. How do you account for the variety of opinions given by residents of the same city?

A young man with a green carnation in his buttonhole: "Nothing but Roses. Did you catch Margo and Rudy the other night in their exquisite Romeo? Did you notice how the hippies tossed them flowers—anti-establishment flowers? Did you hear how much the Ford Foundation and the National Humanities Foundation are going to give to support dance next year? Soon we will teach dance in all the schools, and everyone will learn about ballet and crave to see it. And we will dance and dance and dance and spend and spend and spend. I don't go so far as to look for a choreographer President - but oh my!"

A balding taxi driver: "Lousier every day. It isn't only the traffic jams and the well dressed muggers and the group riders who won't tip. The wife and I look at a lot of television, and it's getting weaker every night. There's practically no wrestling anymore, or prize fights; the things you could count on regularly like *Perry Mason* and *Have Gun Will Travel* are disappearing. The other week they shelved a lot of good stuff for nights to spiel about the Warren Commission. Who cares? And all those Ebans and Goldbergs at the UN! Phooie!"

A prosperous subdivider: "How could it be better? The population's growing, isn't it? And all those babies have to live somewhere, don't they? We have some trouble with the conservationists, but we can handle them. And we're getting more professional all the time. Have you seen any of our late-model purple-tiled bathrooms, or our cookouts, or our front door bell that plays Annie Laurie, or the new little green plaza in Sunshine Acres with sculpture, yet?"

A resident of Mill Valley; a suburb north of San Francisco: "I see nothing but threats to the Marin County way of life. It isn't only the subdividers. We know how to keep them down to our standards of not more than 3-½ families per acre. But there are all those other people who want to come in here and leave us a lot of unused land but increase our density with high-risers. Imagine that! What will happen to our way of life if we have a lot of old people and childless families around here, even if they have managed to stay married for forty years? We've got to stop all this immigration, that's all. And if the San Franciscans think they are going to get any of our money to get them out of their troubles, they are crazy . . . . Oh, of course we all go over there every day."

An engineer carrying blueprints and a black box: "I'm glad you asked. A lot of people have been clobbering us with the accusation that we don't care what we do to the countryside. Well let me tell you that is not the attitude of the Highway Department. Of course, our main job is to give the people what they want at a cost they can afford. What they want is more lanes going more places. Most of them don't want all this prettification that the planners and the architectural nuts write about. And if they did, they couldn't afford it. I'm a bird watcher myself. If there were money for it, I'd be glad to specify beauty in. For instance, we can't do much planting because we can't afford to maintain it. Today I picked some plastic flowers. Look at them, mister. Highway beauty's on the way."

A Ford worker who had just bought his second General Motors car: "This is a great culture, and it's getting better. I turn up bolts on an assembly line. They've got an automatic machine about ready to do it, but I can arrange to watch the machine. And Walter's going to get us all $25,000 a year guaranteed annual wage. How can you beat that? Of course, there'll be a lot of spare time, but let the writers worry about that. I can probably find another job to keep from being bored. Maybe I won't be bored anyway, what with beer and bowling. Maybe I'll even invent a machine."

A young black drop-out: "It never has been any good, and it ain't about to get better. I never had much of a job, and I haven't got any now. Nobody's talking about paying me $25,000 to sit on my fanny. The only fun I get is to burn something, and the only way for me to get anywhere is to burn it all down and then maybe something will happen."

For thought and discussion

Examine carefully the chart you constructed while studying Assignment 1. What relationships can you find between the positive and negative images of the city? Can you think of other ways to look at the American city?

Individual and small group activities

1. Write a poem, paint a picture, make a collage, or draw a cartoon that best illustrates your image of the American city.
2. Organize a group of four to six of your classmates and write a few questions about urban life. The questions you select should measure perceptions of life in the city. Using a portable tape recorder, interview several groups of people passing by on the streets of your city. Compare the answers and organize them into groups. Report your findings to the class in a way which you and your instructor agree upon.

The pros and cons of city life

Assignment 2

The 1970 federal census showed that thirteen of America's twenty-five largest cities had decreased in population since 1960. The suburban areas of twenty-four of these twenty-five cities, however, increased in population during the same ten years. This census information suggests that a large number of people left cities between 1960 and 1970, but few fled to rural areas. Those leaving the city did not go far. The rapid growth of suburbs shows that a growing number of people prefer to live close to, but not in, the American city. In Assignment 2 you will examine some advantages and disadvantages of city life in order to find reasons for this population movement.

Pictures of the city

The pictures which follow illustrate various pros and cons of city life. As you examine the pictures, try to answer these questions:

1. Which pictures make you want to live in the city? Which pictures make you want to escape urban life?
2. What hypotheses about urban life do these photographs suggest?

EVENTS & OFFERINGS

THEATRE

"Finishing Touches," Ahmanson Theatre, Music Center, 626-7211. Through Jan. 12: Jean Kerr's sensible comedy about a marital crisis in the family of a suburban professor continues, featuring original New York stars Barbara Bel Geddes and Robert Lansing. Eves. at 8:30, mats. Sat. at 2:30. Dark Sun.

"Saint Joan," Ahmanson Theatre, Music Center, 626-7211. Opens Jan. 29-Mar. 9: GBS explores the Maid of Orlean's intricate confrontations with church and state, aided by Sarah Miles as Joan and Richard Thomas as the young Dauphin. Eves. at 8:30, mats. Sat. at 2:30. Dark Sun.

Marlene Dietrich, Ahmanson Theatre, Music Center, 626-7211. Jan. 29: An evening of song and nostalgia with the Living Legend. 8:30.

"That Championship Season," Shubert Theatre, 2020 Avenue of the Stars, Century City, 553-9000. Through Jan. 19: Jason Miller's highly acclaimed study of five men recreating their 20-year-old basketball championship, only to have to face the unavoidable truth of life's passage. Tue.-Sat. 8:30, Sun. 7:30, mats. Wed., Sat. 2:30. Dark Mon.

"The Sunshine Boys," Shubert Theatre, 2020 Avenue of the Stars, Century City, 553-9000. Opens Jan. 29-Mar. 23: A quarrelsome pair of retired vaudeville comics match wits with riotous results when they come back for one last reprise of their act on TV. Neil Simon in top form. Tue.-Sat. at 8:30, Sun. at 7:30, mats. Wed., Sat. at 2:30. Dark Mon.

"Will Rogers," Mark Taper Forum, Music Center, 626-7211. Through Jan. 20: James Whitcomb returns with his more-than-reasonable facsimile of the gum-chewing cowboy who laughed at Presidents and made them love it. Evenings at 8, except Sun. at 7:30, mats. Sat. and Sun. at 2:30. No performance Jan. 1.

ART MUSEUMS

Los Angeles County Museum of Art, 5905 Wilshire Blvd., 937-4250. Through Mar. 3: "Islamic Art: the Palevsky-Heeramanec Collection," 500 works from one of the finest private Islamic collections in the world including paintings, glassware, bronzes and textiles covering a period of Islamic history from 700 to 1900 A.D. Through Jan. 6: "If the Crinoline Comes Back," 19th c. costumes, accessories, furniture and photographic materials primarily from the collection of the Museum's Textiles and Costume Dept. Hours: Tue.-Fri. 10-5, Sat., Sun. 10-6. Closed Mon.

Pasadena Museum of Modern Art, 411 W. Colorado Blvd., 449-6840. Through Jan. 13: A retrospective exhibition of sixty works by Jules Olitsky; Jan. 15 through Mar. 10: an exhibition of wood carvings in the tradition of the American Northwest Indians by Don Lelooska Smith; Jan. 15 through Mar. 3: 76 works of painting and sculpture by the noted American colorist Ellsworth Kelly; Jan. 8 through Feb. 17: "New Directions in Photography: 3M Images"; Jan. 28-Mar. 25: an exhibit of works by Kasimir Malevich organized by the Guggenheim Museum; Jan. 6, 13, 19, 27 and 29: dates for lectures at Crossett Auditorium, including the fourth lecture in the "Specimen '73" series on Jan. 13. Hours: Tue.-Sat. 10-5, Sun., noon-5. Closed Mon.

The Los Angeles Municipal Art Gallery, Barnsdall Park, 485-2433. Jan. 16-Feb. 10: A large collection of outstanding Huichol Indian wool paintings, free. Hours: Tue.-Sun. noon-5, closed Mon.

MUSIC

Los Angeles Philharmonic Orchestra, Dorothy Chandler Pavilion, Music Center, 626-7211. **Jan. 1:** Zubin Mehta conducts PDQ Bach; **Jan. 10, 11 and 13:** James De Priest conducts with John Browning, piano; **Jan. 15:** Rudolph Serkin, piano; **Jan. 17, 18 and 25:** Joseph Krips conducts with Rudolph Serkin, piano. Generally Tues., Thurs., Fri. at 8:30, Sun. at 3, Jan. 18 at 1:30.

Wilshire Ebell Music Events, Wilshire Ebell Theatre, 4401 W. 8th St., Los Angeles, 939-1128. Jan. 16: American mezzo-soprano Anne Ayer joins forces with baritone Michael More in a program of highlights from the 18th c. opera "Thesee" by Lully. Wed. at 8:30.

UCLA Music Events, Royce Hall, 825-2953. **Jan. 5:** Rey de la Torre, classical guitarist; **Jan. 11:** Contemporary Chamber Ensemble; **Jan. 12:** Leonard Rose, cello; **Jan. 13:** Paul Hersh and David Montgomery, duo pianists (8); **Jan. 18:** Leo Smit, piano, and Eudice Shapiro, violin; **Jan. 19:** Claudio Arrau, piano; **Jan. 20:** Chamber Orchestra with Stanley Plummer, violin, and Ralph Grierson, piano (8); **Jan. 25:** La Salle Quartet; **Jan. 26:** James Galway, flute; **Jan. 27:** Vasso Devetzi, piano. 8:30 pm unless otherwise noted.

SPORTS

Basketball: Los Angeles Lakers. Jan. 4: Golden State; Jan. 6: Kansas City; Jan. 22, Cleveland; Jan. 25: Capital; Jan. 27: Milwaukee, 8. (Forum)

Basketball: USC. Jan. 11: Stanford; Jan. 12: California, 8. (Sports Arena)

Basketball: UCLA. Jan. 11: California (8); Jan. 12: Stanford (3); Jan. 25: Santa Clara (8); Jan. 26: Notre Dame (8:40). (Pauley Pavillion)

Thoroughbred Racing: Winter season continues with the Jan. 26 San Fernando Stakes; Wed.-Sun. from 12:30. (Santa Anita)

Quarter Horses: The night-owl ponies continue doing their best this season every night except Sun. from 1:45. (Los Alamitos)

Tennis: The Davis Cup North American Zone Finals, Sunrise Country Club, Palm Springs, 475-2029, noon to dark.

Auto Racing: Riverside International Raceway. Jan. 19: 8th Annual Permatex 200, 1:00. Jan. 20: Winston Western 500, 11:00.

SKI HOTLINE

Call 393-6721 for local snow conditions, 24 hours.

FASHION SHOWS

Helft's. Informal modeling of 'Round the Clock fashions at the Wilshire Hyatt House, 3517 Wilshire Blvd., 381-7411. Tues.-Fri., 12:30-1:30.

Beverly Hills Hotel, 9641 Sunset Blvd., 276-2251. Friday showings. Jan. 4: Lanz Junior Styles; Jan. 11: Helft's, Jan. 18: Alvena Tomin Ward; Jan. 25: Ferguson's West.

I. Magnin, 3240 Wilshire Blvd., Los Angeles, 387-4111. Bridal fashion show with personal appearance by designer Christos of Galina, Jan. 24, 6:00 pm.

Boutique Allee. Daily informal modeling, 12-4 pm, of leisure wear fashions, during luncheon in all restaurants. Century Plaza Hotel, Ave. of the Stars. (277-2000).

AFTER DARK

Dancing & Entertainment

Abruzzi, 7800 Sunset Blvd., West Hollywood, 876-0030. Arthur Hanko, concert pianist-stylist nightly exc. Sun.

Athenian Gardens, 1835 Cahuenga Blvd., Hollywood, 469-7038. Bouzouki music, grape leaves and belly dancers. No Mon.

Bantam Cock, 634 N. LaCienaga, Los Angeles, 652-0323. The Bantam Violins play for elegant dining and late supper.

Beef Barron, Los Angeles Hilton, 930 Wilshire Blvd., Los Angeles, 629-4321. Sandy Hathaway, guitarist-singer entertains Mon.-Sat. Luncheon fashion shows on the Verandah Mon.-Fri.

Bel-Air Hotel, 701 Stone Canyon Rd., Bel Air, 472-1211. Bud Herman plays for listening Tue.-Sun. Ann Richards' vocals join him Wed.-Sat.

Cabaret, 834 N. Highland Ave., Los Angeles, 462-6501. Ann Weldon, back from TV and recording dates, Tue.-Sat. Dahle Scott heads Guest Night on Mondays. Closed Sun.

Chadney's, 13620 Ventura Blvd., Sherman Oaks, 783-5594. Ken Larson, jazz organist Tue.-Sat. Terri Bishop, guitarist singer on Sun., Mon.

Chicago Speakeasy, 13562 Ventura Blvd. Sherman Oaks, 872-1689. New restaurant has entertainment every night: Sam Alessi, his guitar and Italian songs, Ceci Grant, Danny Costello, etc.

Cinegrill, Hollywood Roosevelt Hotel, 7000 Hollywood Blvd., Hollywood, 469-2442. Harry Hellings and his Orchestra play for dancing Mon.-Sat.

Comedy Store, 8433 W. Sunset Blvd., West Hollywood, 656-6225. Thru Jan. 5: Jack Farrell, comedic astrologist; Jan. 7-12: Liz Torrez; Jan. 14-19: Gabriel Kaplan.

The Cove, 3191 W. 7th St., Los Angeles, 388-0361. Concert violinist Shony Alex Braun right at your table, gourmet dining. No Sun.

The Daisy, 326 N. Rodeo Dr., Beverly Hills, 273-3786. Possibly the only formal dining, dancing in the County, elegant room. Borrow a member's card.

SING YOU SISTERS

If you're wondering whatever happened to supper club chanteuses, the **Weldon Sisters** can help . . . individually. Both offer a smoky, knowing ballad style. Ann warbles Tues.-Sat. at the Cabaret on Highland while sister Maxine holds the fort at the etc. club until Jan. 8.

SALES & BARGAINS

Barker Brothers. 10% to 50% savings in all departments during this largest sale of the year. All fifteen Barker Brothers stores, including the newly remodeled Downtown store at 7th and Figueroa (624-3355).

Helft's. Big once a year sale at all locations. Complete selection of fine apparel and accessories. Hyatt House Wilshire, Los Angeles Hilton, Beverly Hills Hotel, Arco Plaza, Tishman Plaza.

Glabman Furniture. Mid-Winter sale. Baker, Henredon, and White furniture; Karastan Carpeting specially priced. Los Angeles: 8765 W. Pico Blvd. (278-1174). Woodland Hills: 20011 Ventura Blvd. (340-7677). ■

1122
HECKLER DRUG CO
1122

Advantages and disadvantages of urban living

Some of the photographs on the previous pages illustrated the disadvantages of living in the city. Other photographs illustrated some of the benefits of urban life. The three essays which follow expand upon these themes, enabling you to examine further the pros and cons of city life.

In the first essay a long term urban resident explains why, despite all of New York's problems, he continues to live there. As you read his statement keep this question in mind:

1. Do cities present more opportunities to live the good life than rural areas?

The good life in New York City

Name a problem, almost any one, and chances are that you will find it here. Crime, poverty, congestion, pollution–we've got them all. But we also have the bright lights, theatres, museums, and planetariums and the greatest parades around. I wouldn't want to live anywhere else, no matter what. There's always something happening in this city. Take a look around you. Did you ever see such a collection of different people in one place before in your life? Why I can meet people from all over the world right here in the city. I can have breakfast in a French restaurant, lunch in an Italian one, dinner at Chan's, and go watch the Mets play tonight. Try that in your small town!

Besides, look at it this way. Most of the major industries in the country have offices or factories here. Do you realize what that means? Any job you want is located right here in the city. Laborers, engineers, clerks, executives, and specialists from all over the nation come here looking for work. And most of them find what they're looking for. Where do your artists, musicians, dancers, actors, and writers live? Certainly not in small towns. It's too humdrum there. Talk about opportunity and diversity, man, we have it.

It isn't just jobs and people either. Cities provide the greatest services in the country. Our hospitals use all the latest methods and can treat almost any illness you can think of. If you have to get sick, the city's the place to be. Our recreation program runs all year long, giving instruction in everything from basketball to scuba diving. We also have the best trained fire and police forces around. Nothing amateur about those men.

Another thing, have you ever gone shopping, tried to watch TV, or tried to buy a newspaper in a small town? Why there's no such thing as choice. We have dozens of major department stores here? And the specialty shops,–they're the most fun. Sometimes my wife and I spend all day just looking at all the exotic things they sell. Last week we saw a necklace made out of real sharks teeth. As for newspapers and TV. We still have four daily newspapers,–we used to have seven,–and we have a choice of eleven different television stations. Of course, a lot of them show nothing but old movies but you can't really complain. After all it's free.

You know, on a clear day I can see the Empire State building from my bedroom window. I guess I wouldn't trade city living for anything else. Besides, we can always drive up the Connecticut Valley if we want to get away for a while.

What's wrong with cities

In 1968 the editors of *Senior Scholastic* devoted one entire issue of the magazine to an analysis of the American city. Some sections of that issue praised the city and suggested that urban dwellers lead a fuller, more exciting life than rural inhabitants do. The editors of *Senior Scholastic*, however, devoted the largest portion of that issue to the problems of the city. The following selection, taken from part of that analysis, discusses several serious urban problems. As you read this selection look for evidence to support, revise, or refute your original hypotheses about urban life.

Just about anyone who lives in a U.S. city these days could come up with a long list of answers to our "what's wrong" query. If it isn't the traffice snarls, it's the air pollution. If it isn't the fear of being mugged, it's the reality of being burglarized. If it isn't another tax increase, it's a strike that stops another vital municipal service. If it isn't the growing burden of welfare costs on every taxpayer, it's rentals so high that even men with good jobs can't afford decent housing.

These stresses and pressures aren't so acute in the medium-sized cities of the U.S.—though these, too, have their problems. But everything grinds together in a seething urban caldron in the giant cities—the Detroits, Chicagos, Los Angeles.

Take New York City this fall. For a warmup there were the "routine" crises such as high crime, miles and miles of slums, stifling air pollution, jammed airports, smelly rivers, racial antagonisms, antiquated subways, and a seemingly endless rise in the numbers of those on public welfare . . . .

It's been said that being mayor of New York City is the second most difficult job in the U.S. (No. 1 being the Presidency). But mayors of other major cities are quick to line up for Numbers 3, 4, and 5.

Detroit's Mayor, for one, says his job is impossible. The reason, he argues, is that mayors have all the problems to solve and none of the resources and authority to solve them.

Most cities are desperately short of two indispensable items: money and power. Without a good portion of each, tackling even one major city ailment on a scale likely to cure it becomes a near-impossible task. With all the problems interlocked, and with money desperately short, it's a wonder anyone even applies for the mayor's job . . . .

While the specifics may vary a little from Chicago to Baltimore, or from Los Angeles to Pittsburgh, few of the big cities could cross off even one of the following items from their own list of major problems:

Decay. City after city is blotched with acres of deteriorated housing.

Despite a boom in private building and more than a decade of federal urban renewal programs, slums remain a prominent feature of every single U.S. city. For the cities, slums are a double-edged problem. Because they harbor and foster more crime, more disease, more welfare clients, more unemployment, more drug addiction, they require proportionally more city services and more expenditures than other areas. Yet they produce far less in taxes.

Though experiments abound and some partial successes have been chalked up, no city has wiped out its slums. Federal urban renewal programs (aimed at eliminating slums) have actually destroyed more low-cost housing than they have replaced. One result: as one slum is bulldozed, bigger slums grow up in another area as the dispossessed take over new quarters.

Crime. In every recent year, FBI crime statistics have shown a consistent rise in serious crimes. The rise is a nationwide phenomenon, but it gets the most attention in the cities. One result is a rising belief among many city dwellers that neither they nor their property is safe. This very fear helps keep many law-abiding people off the streets and behind locked doors after dark. That, too, helps make the city unsafe. Repeatedly there are stories of passersby who refused to help a person being mugged or attacked—or even refused to telephone the police.[1] This "I-don't-want-to-get-involved" attitude seems to be an outgrowth of modern urban life. Many people just don't want to accept responsibility for the urban community they live in. It is just too big for them to identify with.

The simplest answer to the crime problem, some say, is to hire more police, pay them more, train them better. But even the partial solution runs into economic reality: it costs money to hire more men, and most cities are up against the wall financially.

Congestion. Getting from here to there can be the most frustrating part of living in a city. Whether you use a car, a bus, or a subway, it is likely to be a slow, utterly nerve-wracking trip at rush hour—the time when most people need to go from here to there. Better build more subways, say the problem solvers. But where is the money to come from? Well then, run more buses. But buses add to air pollution and to traffic snarls. All right, so build more roads. But on whose land and through whose front yard? Won't this just encourage more traffic and lead to newer-and bigger—traffic snarls? And by the time a highway is planned, approved, and built (sometimes a 20-year process), will it be able to handle the additional traffic arising from population increases?

Garbage. Out in the country, you can burn your own debris, or haul it to a dump, or pay someone to take it away. In big cities, such "do-it-yourselfing" isn't feasible—or legal. Usually, the city government itself as-

[1] To what degree, if any, are individuals responsible for the well-being of others?

sumes the job of collecting and disposing of the millions of tons of refuse that city dwellers each day heave into their trash cans.

Just collecting it is a headache in the city. When will the big and noisy garbage trucks clatter down those already clogged streets? During business hours? Or perhaps at night when the natives like to sleep? Then where to put the stuff? Burning trash thickens the already gray haze that separates the sunlight from most metropolitan areas. Put it in a big hole? Many cities have already filled all the convenient big holes.

Water and sewage. The urban household with its garbage disposals, dishwashers, and two bathrooms, uses prodigious amounts of water. That same water then drains away, full of detergents and human waste. Where to dump it without polluting the source of drinking water? The old answer was to pipe sewage to the nearest river or lake. But most of these are now so dirty that they aren't fit to supply fresh water that hasn't first undergone extensive (and costly) treatment. So why not build plants to treat the water? Fine, but such plants cost millions, and city taxpayers are already moving to suburbia because they believe their tax bills are too high.

Race. As whites hurry to suburbia, the inner cities become blacker. For the cities, it is a social and economic upheaval of major importance. In the 10 years between the 1950 and 1960 federal censuses, only eight of the 20 largest cities gained in white population. But black population increased in all 20. By 1960, 17 per cent of the North's inner city population was black. Many of these Negroes were not city-born. In 1960 two thirds of the adult Negroes in Northern cities were born in the South.

In other words, while the inner cities have been losing middle-class whites to the surrounding suburbs, these cities have been gaining poorly educated rural Negroes who had lost their agricultural jobs in the South as machines replaced human labor. The city beckoned to these newcomers as a place to find a job, to make a better life. Unfortunately, many found that they lacked the education needed to crack the urban job market. In 1950 five out of every six Negroes who migrated to Northern cities found jobs. By the 1960's the figure was down to four out of six. That means two in six did not find a job.

Crowded into the ghettos, unable to find meaningful work, subjected to discrimination many thought they were leaving behind, some blacks have given up all hope. Others have just become angrier. The very successes of the civil rights movement of the early 1960's fanned hopes that sometimes turned to bitter anger when the Promised Land didn't arrive for everyone. Four summers of urban riots have painted a vivid picture of how deep that anger lies.[2]

Welfare. Cities have traditionally beckoned to those in rural America

[2] Are violence and rioting ever justifiable? If so, under what conditions?

down on their luck. In recent years, however, the kind of jobs undereducated rural people could find have been disappearing. But rural people continue to move into cities. Caught in this technological squeeze, millions have turned to public welfare. The cost to cities forced to pay a large share of the welfare bills has reached major proportions—and has spurred a major reappraisal of the entire welfare system.

What this shift can mean to the city is again vividly clear in New York. A recent study showed that by next June one million people, or one out of every eight New Yorkers,[3] would be fully or partially supported by public welfare, a whopping 26 per cent of the city's budget.

Lack of power. With power, all the other problems might seem a little more soluble, but the city is just a little sister when it comes to governmental authority. "The basic local governmental structure in the United States was designed primarily for a rural agricultural society whose inhabitants had a basic distrust of all governments," says the National League of Cities. Most cities do not have the legal authority for a frontal assault on their problems. City boundaries are often haphazard, not really reflecting where the real city begins and ends. Special districts and authorities carve up the power to tax and make decisions.

State legislatures, which have total authority over their cities (and which are usually controlled by rural interest), have consistently been unwilling to give the cities broad and continuing power to run their own affairs or even to decide for themselves what taxes to levy on their citizens. It all adds up to a system of buckpassing when the time comes to assess the blame for urban failures . . . .

Money. At the start of this century, local governments spent more per person than did state and federal governments combined. In 1902 local governments spent 54.8 per cent of all government monies, compared with just 34.5 per cent by the federal government.

In the following six and a half decades, local government responsibilities have multiplied, population has soared, and so has government spending at all levels. But the local government's share of the fiscal pie has dwindled. Local governments now spend about 20 per cent of all government money. Where cities once collected more than 70 per cent of all taxes, they now collect only about 15 per cent while trying to provide services for most of the population.

The one big source of local revenue is the property tax, which provides about 88 per cent of all locally raised revenue. In most places, this tax is about as high as it can go, and no other source has proved particularly[4]

[3] Should we provide welfare assistance to persons who are unemployed but physically able to work? Why, or why not?

[4] Should suburban residents be expected to contribute financially to the upkeep and renewal of urban areas? Why, or why not?

workable for raising large sums.

The problems list could go on and on. Whether the cities created the problems or simply inherited them is debatable. But it seems increasingly clear that most of the serious domestic problems in the U.S. today are focused in the city. What is worse, many people are coming to the conclusion that the problems aren't going to be solved . . . .

It's a depressing picture—particularly for those millions who live in cities because that's where the action is and they don't want to be anywhere else. But whether by choice or by circumstance, millions of city dwellers are each day made aware that plenty is wrong in the cities and each day hope against hope that more can be made right.

A different view of the urban crises

In the final essay of Assignment 2, Edward C. Banfield suggests that we re-examine our attitudes about the nature of the urban crisis. Mr. Banfield, a Harvard professor, argues that urban conditions are getting better, but we fail to recognize these improvements. He further suggests that we make serious mistakes and actually create an urban crisis by acting as if the crisis were real. As you read, think about the following issues:

1. Have urban conditions actually improved in the last several decades? If so, why have we failed to recognize the areas of improvement?
2. Do you agree with Edward Banfield's conclusions? If you do, what evidence can you add to support his position? If you do not, what evidence leads you to reject his ideas?

That we face an urban crisis of utmost seriousness has in recent years come to be part of the conventional wisdom. We are told on all sides that the cities are uninhabitable, that they must be torn down and rebuilt or new ones must be built from the ground up, that something drastic must be done—and soon . . . .

There is, however, another side to the matter. The plain fact is that the overwhelming majority of city dwellers live more comfortably and conveniently than ever before. They have more and better[5] housing, more and better schools, more and better transportation, and so on. By any conceivable measure of material welfare the present generation of urban Americans is, on the whole, better off than any other large group of people has ever been anywhere. What is more, there is every reason to expect that the general level of comfort and convenience will continue to rise at an even more rapid rate through the foreseeable future . . . .

To a large extent, our urban problems are like the mechanical rabbit, which is set to keep just ahead of the dogs no matter how fast they may run. Our performance is better and better, but because we set our standards and

[5]Do such things as "more and better" schools and housing mean a better life? Why, or why not?

expectations to keep ahead of performance, the problems may get (relatively) worse as they get (absolutely) better.

Some may say that since almost everything about the city can stand improvement, this mechanical rabbit effect is a good thing in that it spurs us on to make constant progress. No doubt this is true to some extent. On the other hand, there is danger that we may mistake failure to progress as fast as we would like for failure to progress at all and, in panic, rush into ill-considered measures that will only make matters worse . . . .

For thought and discussion

What can you as an individual do to improve the quality of life in your own city?

Individual and small group activities

1. Take a walking tour through your own city photographing such things as buildings, people, and events which represent the pros and cons of urban life. Arrange the photos in a scrapbook or for a display in your classroom.
2. With a group of your classmates find out what you, as a group, can do to help solve one of your city's problems.

The physical structure of the contemporary city

Assignment 3

In the first two assignments, you examined reasons why people live in cities and discussed several of the advantages and disadvantages of urban life. A thorough understanding of the American city, however, requires a more sophisticated method of analysis than simply examining pros and cons. Geographers, economists, sociologists, and political scientists all apply the techniques of their various fields of study to examine urban life. The next eight assignments will employ methods of analysis from each of these social sciences to help you broaden your understanding of the American city.

According to the Bureau of the Census, the United States contained twenty-five cities in 1970 with populations ranging from one-half million to nearly eight million. Another 125 cities had more than 100,000 but less than one-half million inhabitants in 1970. These 150 cities, of course, are not evenly distributed throughout the United States. The 1970 census map shows heavy concentrations of population in Northeastern United States, the Northern Midwest, and the Far West. An examination of earlier maps shows that some of these cities grew rapidly in recent years. Others were important urban centers over a century ago.

A number of complex and often interrelated factors influenced the location and growth of American cities. For example, New York City, Boston, Philadelphia, and Charleston became the first major cities in the United States. All of these cities had good harbors which provided ideal locations for overseas trade. Moreover, people living in these colonial cities felt safe from raiding Indians.

City location

Where were the cities in 1840?

As Americans began to push westward following the Revolutionary War, other cities soon developed. By 1840 eight cities with more than 10,000 persons each were located in the interior of the United States. The map below shows rivers and lakes of a portion of this region. Examine this map and place numbers at five places where you think early cities might have developed. Then answer the following questions:

1. What are your reasons for choosing each location? What other information would help you make a better choice?
2. Using an atlas locate the places where actual cities did develop in the Midwest. How do you explain any differences from your own choices?
3. What hypotheses can you develop about the location of early American cities?

Figure 3.1

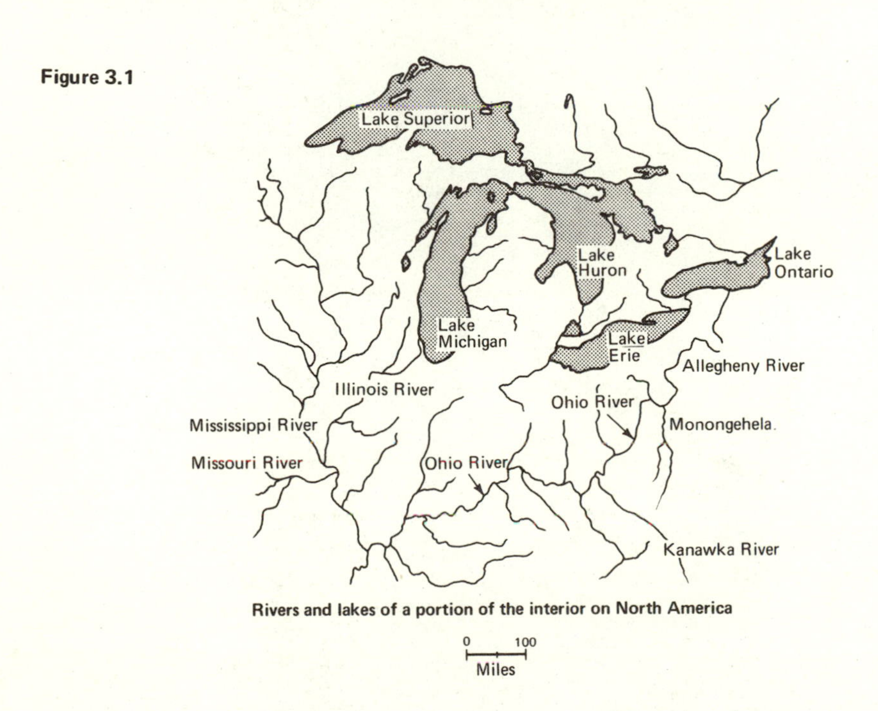

Rivers and lakes of a portion of the interior on North America

Where were the cities in 1890?

In the thirty-five years following the Civil War America went through a period of great industrial and urban growth. The population of the United States, fed by the arrival of immigrants, grew dramatically. Technological development and the demand for industrial and consumer goods spurred the growth of new towns and cities. By 1890 there were more than two dozen cities of over 25,000 persons in the interior regions of the United States. The map on page 28 shows the location and size of each of these new cities. As you look at this map answer the following questions in your notebooks:

1. How did geographical factors influence the location of these cities?
2. What other factors seem to have influenced the location of cities? Does your answer cause you to revise your previously stated hypotheses? In what ways?

3. What accounts for the number of small cities near Pittsburgh and Cleveland? Why do you think a city developed at Duluth, Minnesota?
4. How can you explain Chicago's phenomenal growth? Why didn't a major city develop where the Ohio and Mississippi river join?

Figure 3.2

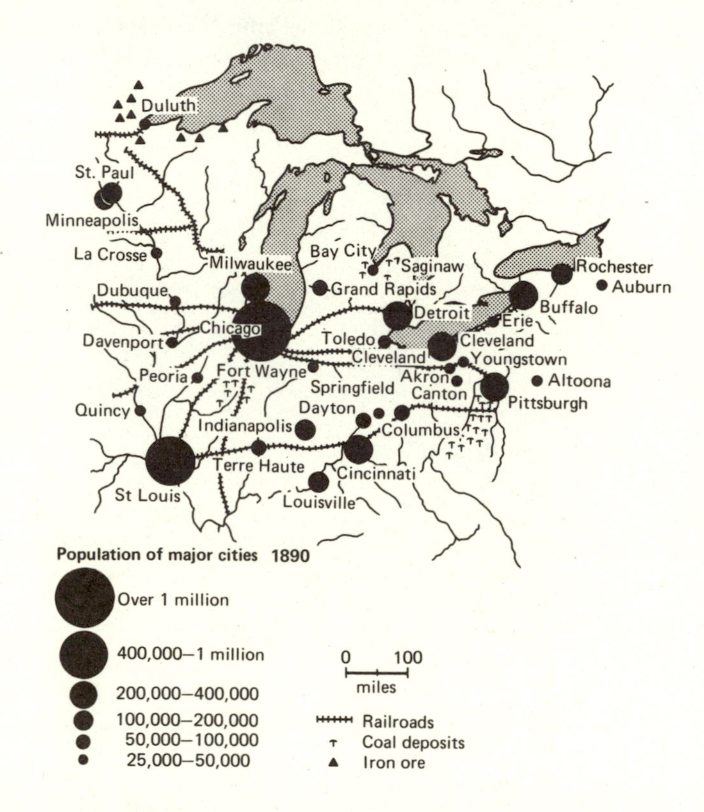

Theories of urban structure

We can determine the sites of cities and reasons for the selection of these sites. We can also determine and explain the location of zones within the city. Many urban communities contain distinct zones, such as areas of residence and areas of commerce and industry. The pattern of zones, often called the structure, of the modern American city results from many geographical, economic, social, and cultural factors. The location of these specialized zones, however, frequently follow similar patterns from city to city.

Knowledge of a city's pattern of zones can help us understand the nature of the city. It can also help us to find our way around the city, much as we do through a supermarket. After a few trips to the supermarket we begin to notice certain patterns. We expect to find the frozen goods, milk, and dairy products along the side walls. Meat products are often cut and displayed at the rear of the store. Separate areas have been set up for canned and fresh fruits. We do not find items grouped together so that they form menus—breakfast here, dinner items in another area. Some of the zones in the supermarket have geographical reasons for their location; others do not. For example, refrigerated items, located along the wall require expensive electrical wiring. Locating these units in the center of the store would demand additional wiring, thus increasing the cost of operation. Similarly, fresh meats are located near the rear of the store to provide the butcher with a private work area to cut and prepare products for display. Bread, on the other hand, might be located anywhere in the store.

Similarly, knowledge of urban zones can help us find our way about the city. We know, for example, not to look for city hall on the outskirts of town. We rarely expect to find high cost homes next to factories. The center of the downtown nearly always contains major commercial businesses. Thus, a pattern of zones provides a rough guide to most American cities. When we go to a strange city we know approximately what to expect.

In 1925, urban ecologists Ernest W. Burgess and Robert Park developed the first modern explanation for urban structure and growth. Burgess hypothesized that as a city grows it expands outward from its center, to form a series of concentric circles or zones, each with distinct characteristics. Beginning in 1939, a number of urban social scientists developed alternate theories of city structure and growth. Homer Hoyt, for example, argued that once zones had developed near the center of a city, they would expand as the city expanded outward. Distinctive zones, then were likely to grow out from the center rather than in concentric circles around the center. In 1945, geographers Chauncy Harris and Edward Ullman suggested that the concentric and sector models were too simple to describe urban growth. Cities, they argued, usually have several centers or nuclei, and that distinctive urban zones develop around each of them. The diagrams on page 30 illustrate these three well known models of city growth. Examine carefully each of these models and think about these questions:

1. Which patterns seems most logical? Why? What conditions might have caused a city to develop along the lines of each model?
2. In what ways might the geographic features of a city influence its structure and growth?
3. What relationship can you see between one sector of the city and those sectors next to it?

Zones in Pittsburgh, Pennsylvania: A case study

The three models of urban structure that you have just examined illustrate two important geographic concepts. The first concept, known as spatial distribution, attempts to explain the location of cities in a geographic area or the placement of certain specialized zones throughout the city. For example, many cities were originally built along major rivers to take advantage of cheap water transportation. Similarly,

Figure 3.3
Theories of urban spatial structure

Key:
1. Central Business District
2. Wholesale Light Manufacturing
3. Low-cost Residential
4. Medium-cost Residential
5. High-cost Residential
6. Heavy Manufacturing
7. Outlying Business District
8. Residential Suburb
9. Industrial Suburb

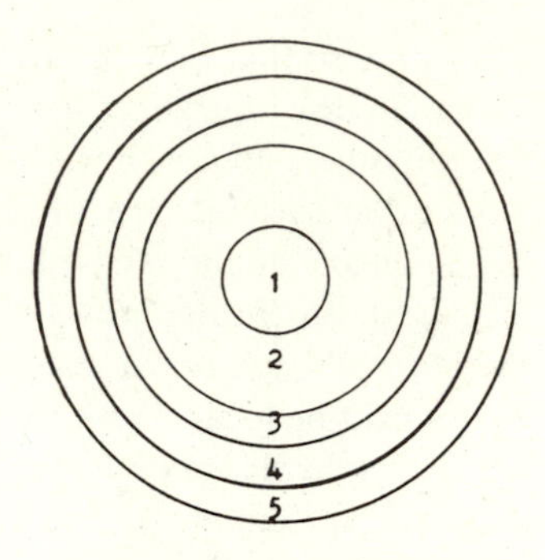

Concentric zone theory
(Robert Park, E.W. Burgess)

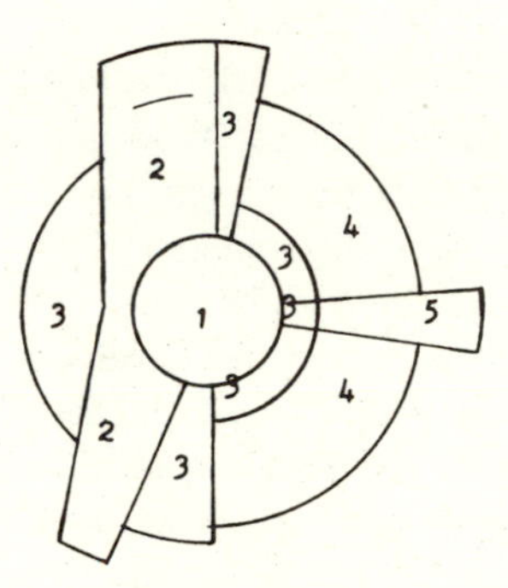

Sector theory (Homer Hoyt)

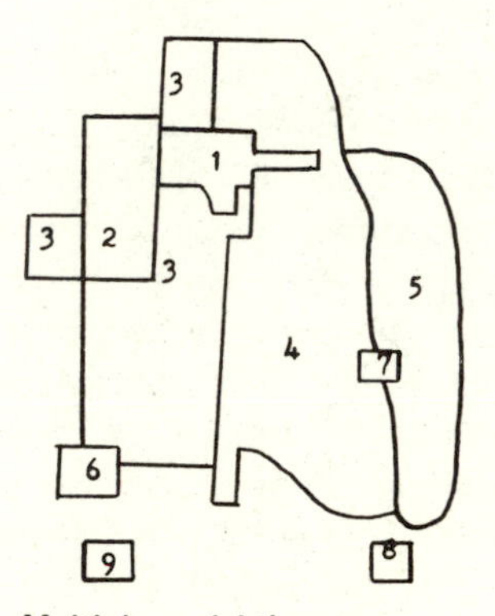

Multiple nuclei theory
(Chauncy Harris, Edward Ullman)

Figure 3.4

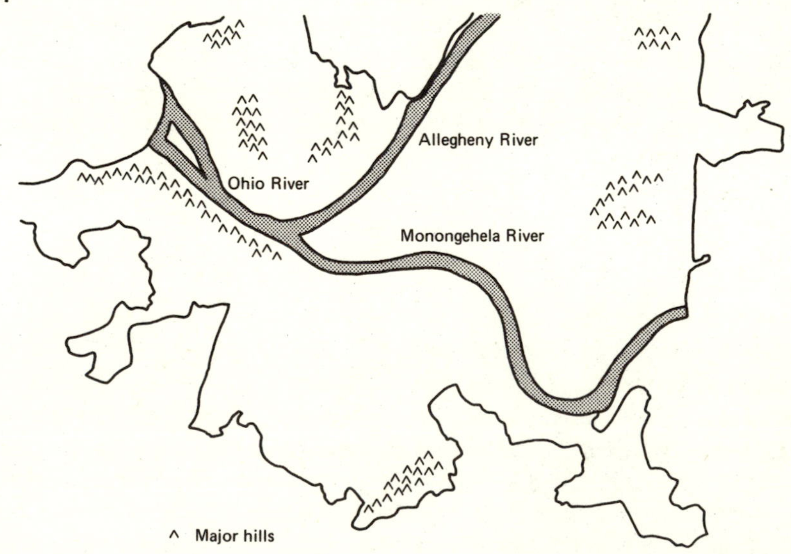

the industries within these cities were frequently built as close to the river banks as possible. In both cases river transportation helps to explain the location of cities and the placement of the industrial zone within those cities. Of course, river transportation is only one factor influencing spatial distribution.

The second geographical concept, spatial interaction, refers to the relationships that exist between one region and other regions. City 'A,' for example, may produce automobiles, while City 'B' produces rolled sheet steel used in the production of automobiles. The growth and welfare of each city depends to some degree upon the activities carried on in the other city. Within each city a similar relationship may exist between certain regions or zones of that city. For example, the homes of industrial workers might be located near the factory zone. The workers depend upon the activities in the factory zone while the success of those activities depends primarily upon the workers. Each zone then relies upon another for its growth and welfare.

To help you understand the concepts of spatial distribution and spatial interaction, the final part of Assignment 3 includes information about one major American city, Pittsburgh, Pennsylvania. The city of Pittsburgh, founded in 1794 where the Allegheny and Monongehela Rivers meet to form the Ohio River, became a major steel producing center. Pittsburgh grew rapidly during the latter half of the nineteenth century, reaching a population of more than 300,000 by 1900. Today Pittsburgh ranks as the 25th largest city in the United States with a population of slightly over 500,000. In addition to its reputation as the steel capital of the world, the city provides a home for the corporate headquarters of Gulf Oil, Westinghouse Electric Co., H. J. Heinz Co., The United States Steel Corporation, and ALCOA aluminum.

The outline map on page 30 shows several important physical characteristics of the city of Pittsburgh in the 1970's. Examine the map and the ten recent photographs of Pittsburgh on pages 32-34. Then determine the most likely zone or zones on the map for the area pictured in each photograph. After you have concluded this exercise answer the following questions:

1. How did Pittsburgh's location on three rivers influence the distribution of the various zones within the city? What other factors might have influenced the development of sectors within Pittsburgh?
2. What relationships can you determine between the zones you identified?

Spatial zones in Pittsburgh

The second map of Pittsburgh on page 35 shows the correct placement of the cities various zones. Compare this map with the decisions you made about spatial distribution in the previous exercise. Then answer the following questions in your notebook:

1. How are the sectors of Pittsburgh different from your placement? How do you account for these differences?

Photographs of Pittsburgh

COTTON

Gulf

2. Do any of the three models of urban structure noted on page 30 explain Pittsburgh's sector pattern? If so, which one?
3. What generalizations can you make about the location and interaction of urban zones?

Figure 3.5

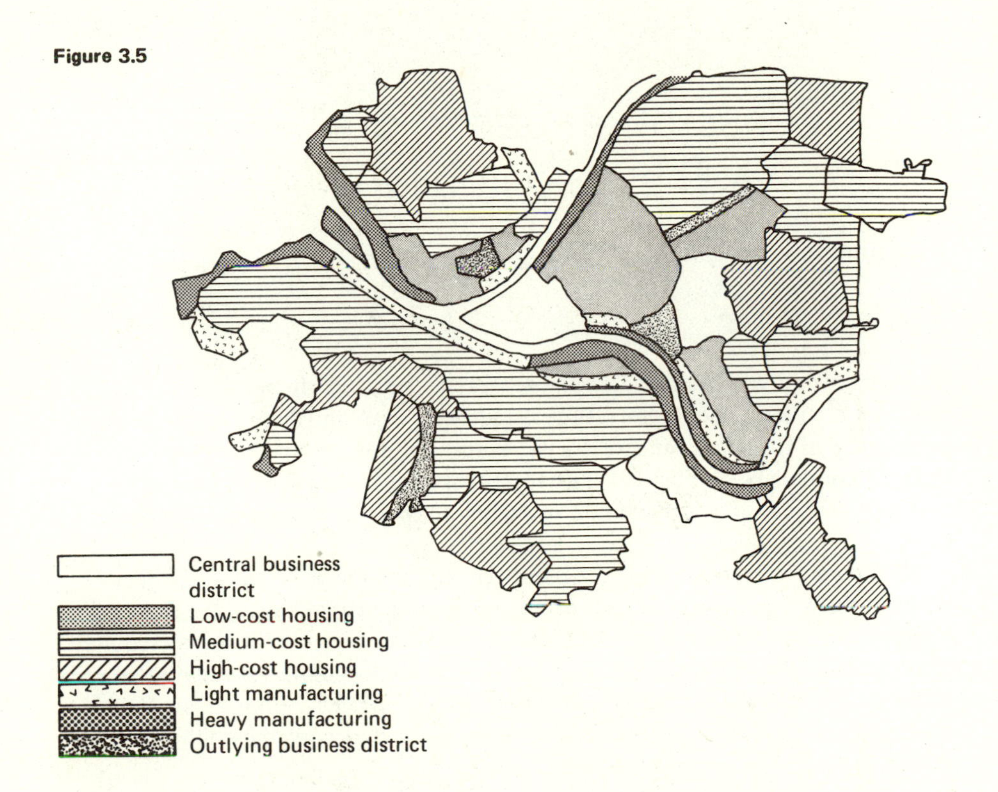

For thought and discussion

What effect do you think the development of technical innovations such as railroads, streetcars, automobiles, highways, bridges, and tunnels, had on the pattern of growth of American cities?

Individual and small group activities

1. Board a bus at the outskirts of your city and ride downtown. Look out the window and make a list describing the structures and activities you see as you pass them. Can you detect the various zones through which you passed? Which urban pattern discussed in Assignment 3 most resembles your city?
2. With a group of your classmates try to plot the sectors of your city on an outline map. To gather your information, consult zoning maps or census income distribution maps, ride through the city, or visit your local city planning office. Use a large map or overhead projector to report your findings to the class.

Zones of residence and work: The automobile city

Assignment 4

In Assignment 3 you examined several geographic features which influenced the structure of cities. Other factors, such as railroads, also contributed to the physical makeup of the American city. City structure has not remained static but has changed continually throughout the nation's history. During the last century changing methods of transportation strongly influenced the reshaping of American cities.

A common feature of the pre-industrial city was the close relationship between residence and work. In fact, people often worked and lived in the same building. As industrialism progressed new forms of energy and technology required the concentration of large numbers of workers in one location. Soon industrial activities dominated certain regions within the city. The central business district quickly spread to form a specialized city zone. Areas unoccupied by either industry or commerce became residential zones.

Factory workers, forced to leave their homes to secure work, settled as close to the industrial zone as possible. Unable to afford the luxury of horse-drawn vehicles, most urban dwellers walked to work. The distance one had to walk, the time involved in the journey, and the cost of housing became crucial factors in the choice of a homesite. Thus, zones of low-cost housing, inhabited mostly by factory workers, spread rapidly around the industrial area of the city. Factory owners and other wealthy families, on the other hand, could avoid the unpleasant environment associated with the factory. These more fortunate people moved some distance away and travelled to work each day by carriage.

In the latter half of the nineteenth century the introduction of the streetcar made it possible for some middle-class urban dwellers to move away from the industrial zone. These new commuters rented or purchased modest homes along the street rail lines, creating a zone of middle-cost housing. For most workers, however, the location of their jobs remained the most important factor in choosing a place to live. Many people who worked long hours did not wish to spend time travelling to and from work each day. Others could not afford either the higher-cost housing in the middle-residence zone or the streetcar fare.

Since the 1920's the widespread use of the automobile has provided even greater freedom to American workers. They may now choose where to live with less regard to work site than ever before. In 1970 the Federal Highway Administration reported that automobile registrations exceeded 108 million. These cars travelled on more than three-and-a-half million miles of paved roads and highways. In addition, in 1969 alone Americans rode nearly 25 million passenger miles in buses within city limits.

The continued unchecked growth of automobile traffic, some observers insist, will eventually destroy the American city. They point to Los Angeles as an example. In time these critics predict, Los Angeles will have to cover so much land with roadway that there will be little taxpaying property left to maintain the basic community services. The remainder of this assignment describes the ways in which automobiles have changed—and will continue to change—the structure of American cities.

The automobile and city structure

The automobile changed the American way of life in the twentieth century. It also helped to reshape city structure during the last fifty years. The seven maps of the city of Chicago on pages 38, 39 will help you to determine how transportation technology affected spatial distribution and spatial interaction within American cities. After looking at the maps answer these questions:

1. What specific changes in the five zones of residence and work occurred in each of the three time periods? (1857 to 1899, 1899 to 1930, 1930 to 1970)
2. Which changes in urban structure appear to be related to highway construction in Chicago?
3. What general statements can you make about the relationship between auto transportation and city structure?

The journey to work: Public or private transportation?

As you probably noticed in your examination of the maps of Chicago, American cities have spread farther and farther from their original center. In fact most urban areas now include not only the territory with the city limits but miles of surrounding suburbs as well. Commuting via private or public transportation has enabled millions of Americans to live some distance from their place of work. Unfortunately commuting to work, particularly by private automobile, brought with it a number of serious problems. Lack of parking space in the central business district, air pollution, traffic congestion, and leisure time lost in the journey to and from work are only a few of the problems faced by urban commuters. Yet, as the editors of *Fortune* magazine pointed out in 1958, people continue to reject public transport-

Figure 4.1
The growth of residential areas, Chicago

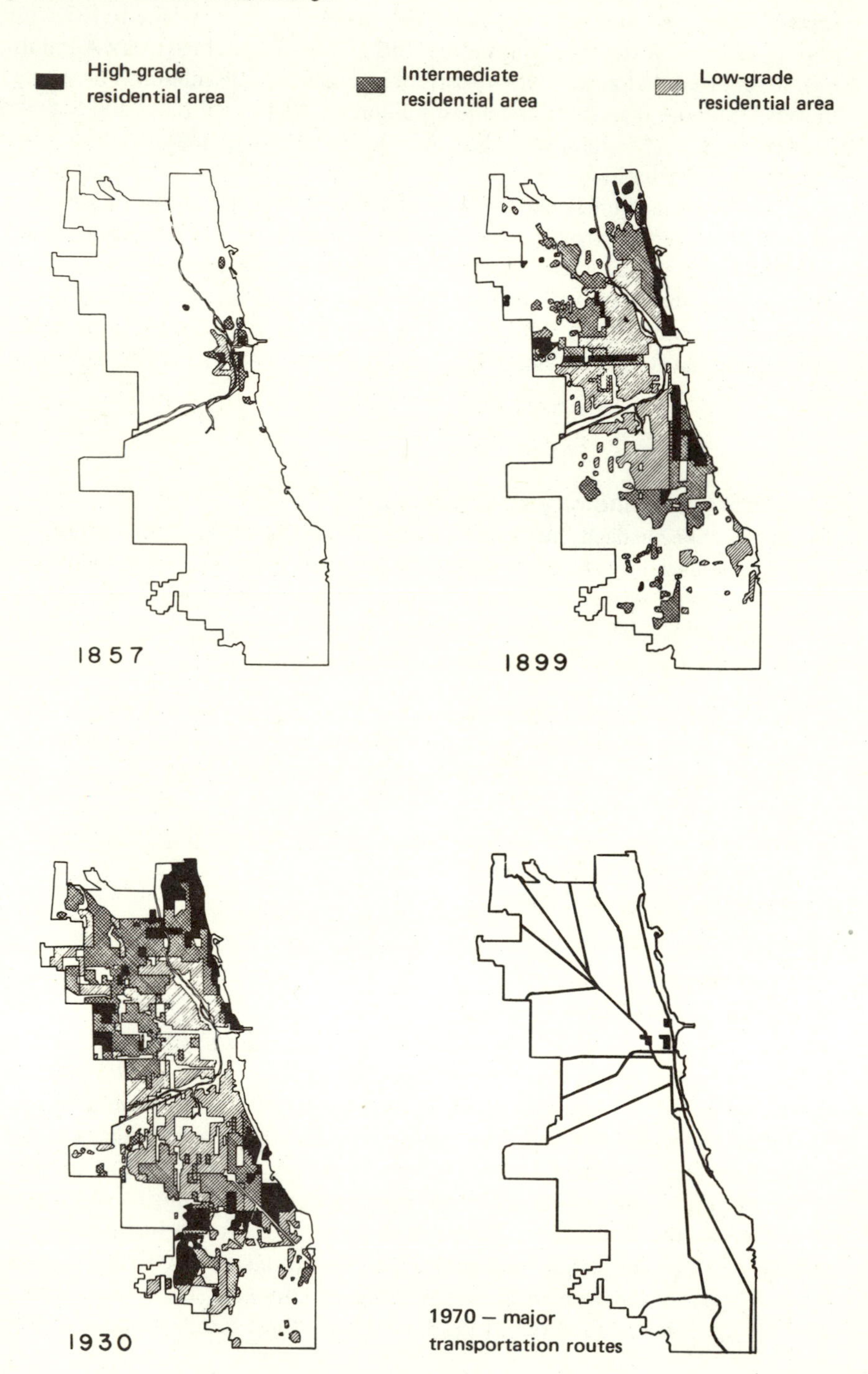

Figure 4.2
Growth of central business and manufacturing areas, Chicago

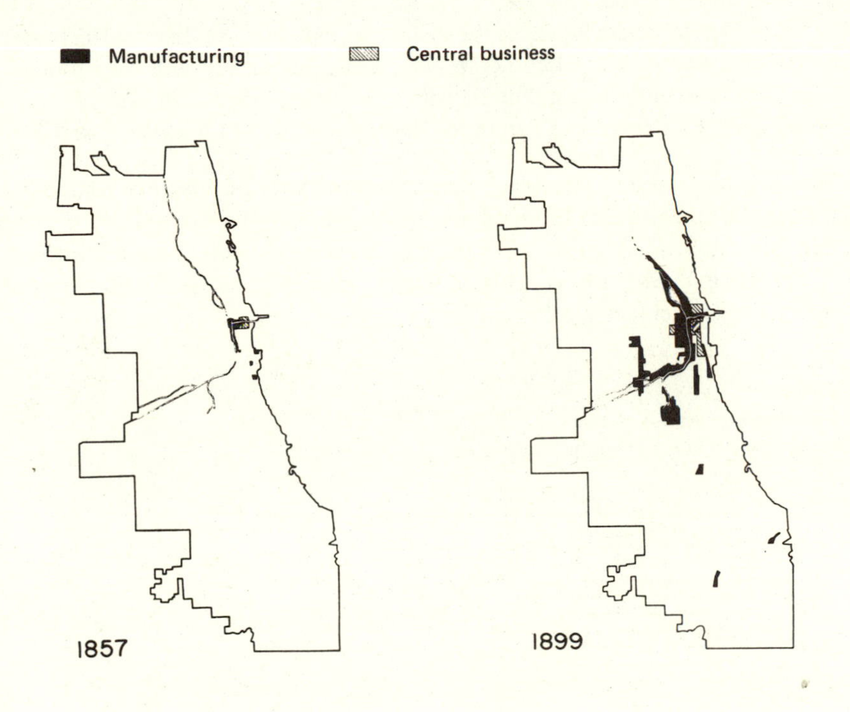

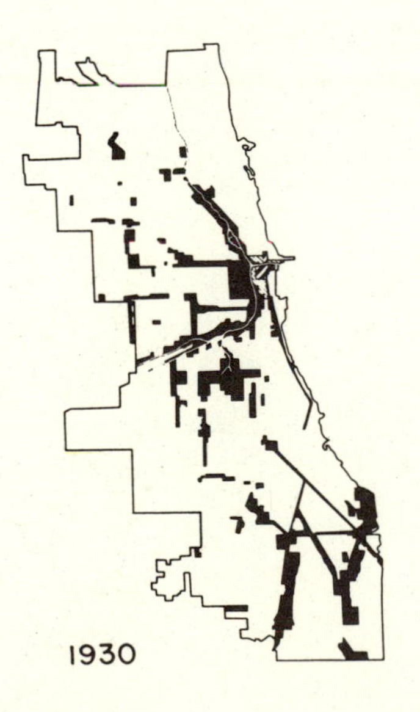

Source: Homer Hoyt, *One Hundred Years of Land Values in Chicago* (Chicago University Press, 1933), p. 319.

ation in favor of the private automobile. In that year in fifteen of the nation's twenty-five largest cities, over 60 per cent of all riders entering the downtown business district arrived by automobile.

The following chart indicates the distance a motorist can drive in thirty minutes, starting from the busiest corner in town along the busiest outbound route, compared with an outbound public transit rider under similar circumstances. As you look at these comparisons determine the answers to the following questions:

1. What hypotheses can you suggest about the popularity of private automobile transportation? Can you find evidence in the chart to support your hypotheses?
2. Can you think of any reasons why New Yorkers might prefer public to private transportation? Does this conclusion suggest any solutions for the problems of traffic congestion facing other cities?

Figure 4.3
How fast can you get out of town?
(Distance covered at rush hour in 30 minutes)

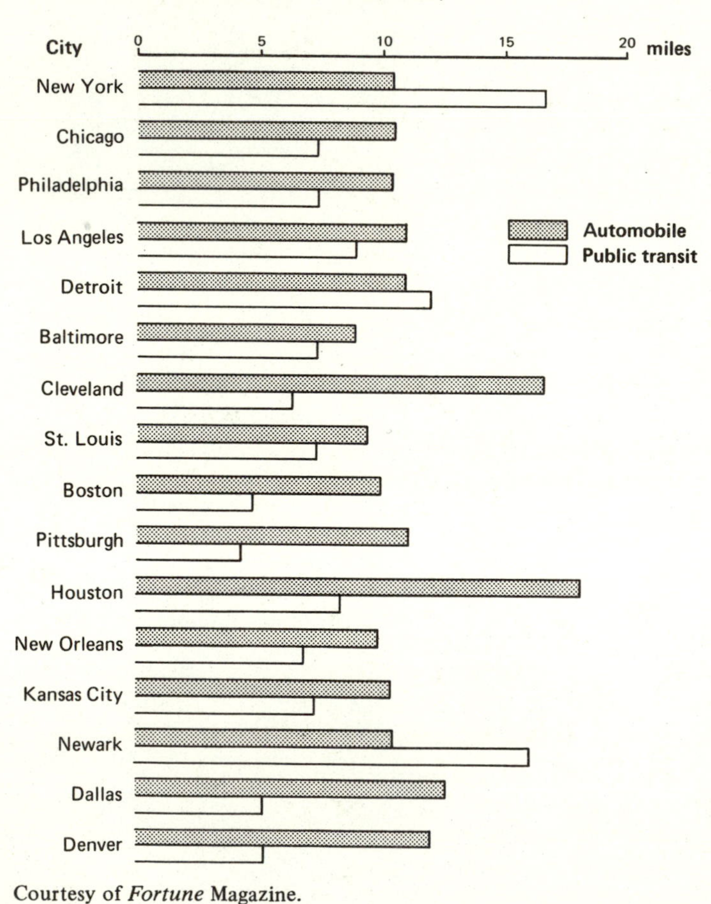

Courtesy of *Fortune* Magazine.

Public transportation in New York City

Each day millions of commuters ride the train, subway, or bus into New York City. Many of these people complain bitterly about the service they receive, yet they continue to patronize the New York Public Transit System. In the following article, a well known author, Jimmy Breslin, angrily denounces public transit but also explains its importance to the well-being of New York City. Breslin wrote the following article in January 1970, shortly after the New York Transit Authority raised fares from 20 to 30 cents. For a short time, thousands of New Yorkers threatened to refuse to pay the increased fare. As you read this article think about public transportation in your own city.

At 8:05 on a gray Tuesday morning, I stood on the back of a line of 11 people at the bus stop on 210th Street and Linden Boulevard in a part of Queens called Cambria Heights. The area, like almost everyplace else in Queens, is something less than its name. The only height in Cambria Heights is a curb. There is a smallish elm tree at the 210th Street bus stop. On this morning, two sparrows rattled the bare branches and chirped into the damp air. The foot of the tree was covered with a clot of dirt-blackened ice. Pepsi-Cola cans and used Kleenex were imbedded in the ice. The bus, bouncing through potholes that looked like shell craters, pulled up. I shuffled with the line, arms held up against the ribs, taking the first of these tense little quarter-steps that brush against your energy so much more than full strides. The great Archie Moore used to boast, "I am still a champion during my old age because only I know the secret of all energy, the way to force a man to tensionize himself into exhaustion." Archie's secret was to make the other guy fight with constricted movements, as if he were going to work in the morning in Queens.

When I got on the bus and put my 30 cents into the till, I had the good luck to find one empty strap left. I grabbed it and the bus began to sway and bounce through potholes to the next stop and the stops after that on the way to Jamaica and the subway ride to the city, as people in Queens refer to Manhattan . . . . Once, I looked out the window and saw the main entrance to St. Albans Naval Hospital. The brick buildings, with clean snow covering the lawns, seemed almost pleasant. It did not work that way inside the bus. By now, there was a spreading discomfort in the small of the back and I began pulling my shoulder up to relieve it. I asked the fellow next to me for the time. He held out his watch. It was 8:27. If he had told me the time himself, he would have been the only person on this crowded bus to speak during the entire ride. In silence, with diesel fumes starting to thicken in the rear of the bus, the people swayed and bounced for the rest of the trip to Jamaica and the subway.

It was 8:31 when the bus passed Broadway Joe's restaurant on the corner of 168th Street and Jamaica Avenue. . . . The small of my back was aching now, and the fumes in the bus were making me sick. I pushed out of the bus at the last stop, Hillside Avenue, and took deep swallows of the damp air and then started quarter-stepping my way toward the subway entrance. At 8:35 a.m., body tense, feet shuffling, I pushed onto a filthy, crowded E. train and pulled my shoulder up for the ride to the city.

A woman who had been on the bus with me, Mrs. Margaret Steinlein, nodded hello.

"How's the new fare?" I asked her.

"My daughter-in-law lives in Bellrose—it's only 15 minutes away by car, but when she doesn't have the car she takes three buses to come and visit me. They're short bus rides but she still takes three of them. That costs 90 cents one way now. Think if you make the trip with two kids you have to pay for, I mean, you can't do it anymore."

Of course that is the story of the transit fare raise. The buses and subways of this city were meant to bring it together. Particularly the subway. Without the subway, there is no City of New York. The subway is the thing that takes a father and two children from Flatbush to the Hayden Planetarium. It is what a kid rides from the Bronx to Madison Square Garden. One of the thrills of growing up was to press your forehead against the front window of the train and see the dark tunnel dissolve into white tile and the first sign saying MADISON SQUARE GARDEN flash by. Upstairs was the rodeo, or the Rangers, and you would leave the window and rush to the door and press against it so you would be the first out onto the platform when the train stopped. It took a nickel and then a dime to ride the subway then, and it made Queens close to the Museum of Natural History and Brooklyn close to the Central Park Zoo. But the other week, when the politicians and labor leaders sat down and came up with the 30-cent transit fare, they started to push the city apart. In a family of five, with a workingman's take-home pay, you do not casually tell three of the kids. "Yes, you can go to the zoo if you don't feel like staying here today." Not if you live in Cambria Heights and the round trip costs a total of $6.40. Instead, you might tell them, "Oh, the zoo is too far. Why don't you stay around here today?" Once this process starts, it is not the City of New York anymore. It is just another sprawling place.

I don't think the people who sat in on the transit fare rises really understood this. And I don't think they understood something else: the simple draining act of riding in this subway car I was in from 168th Street station in Jamaica to Fulton Street in downtown Manhattan. The small of the back aches; each time the doors open, more heads push into the car, and directly above the heads comes this movement of air, soot-filled air from the station and the trash baskets and the tracks and the tunnels. Nobody reads, nobody talks. Everybody just seems to sway on his feet and arch his back and stare numbly at the windows. Once in a while a man pulls his head back from the perfume smell of a woman's hair. That is the closest thing to a sex move I ever saw on the E train during rush hours. The crowding and swaying and thick air is enough to disgust even the worst degenerate. *Hey, Lady! Stop rubbing against me–you got me leaning on my heels now and my knees are killing me.*

From 8:35 a.m. until 9:20, I rode this way. There was not even the hint of simple human dignity. The people who use the subways to go to work in the mornings might as well be handcuffed and naked. And at 9:20, one hour and 15 minutes after I got on the bus in Cambria Heights, I was through with the trip and I came upstairs and went into a coffee shop and sat down. I thought about the people who took the ride with me. I was through. They were only starting. Wilted and humiliated, they went into buildings and to a day's work. And at night, there would be another hour-and-15-minute ride, under the same conditions, back to Cambria Heights. In the newspaper, which I was unable even to open until getting to the counter of the coffee shop, I noticed a story about New York City's welfare costs reaching $2 billion a year. I thought about the guy in Cambria Heights who has just put in a day's work, and those two bus-and-subway trips, reading that story at night. Reading it and going berserk. And I thought about all the people I've known in charge of things in Manhattan and Washington and Albany, the ones with chauffeurs and diplomas and known family names, who shake their heads: "These yahoos in Queens, can you tell me how a decent human being can *reach* them? Those right-wingers, hell, they don't care if people starve . . ."

Thirty cents is a lot of money to pay for the instrument which makes the city what it is. The late Mike Quill was closest of all to this. "The subways should be free," he always said. But money is just one part of the problem. The other part is the one that the people in charge never seem to think of because the people who get to be in charge of things never really have had to experience it. That is the one-hour-and-15-minute ride from Cambria Heights to a day's work in Manhattan and the one-hour-and-15-minute ride back to Cambria Heights. Not just once, as I did it to write this. But every day, and the days run into each other and become weeks and the weeks turn to months and then years and people spend a lifetime of indignity, and you wonder what it does to them.

The journey to work:
Problems and answers in three cities

The following article, taken from a 1970 issue of *Fortune* magazine discusses the problems created by the automobile in urban America. The author, Allan T. Demaree, examines the plight of three cities–Boston, Milwaukee, and Houston–and concludes that while many problems continue to exist, imaginative planning may one day solve the conflict between the car and the city. While reading this article answer these questions:

1. In what ways has the automobile contributed to the decline of the central business districts of our cities?

2. Considering the reluctance of Americans to use mass transit, should we build more or fewer highways into the city?
3. Which of the solutions to urban transportation suggested by the following article seem most promising to you? Why?

Do you favor restrictions on commuting by private auto to prevent traffic congestion and pollution? Why, or why not?

As a blessing, the automobile is far from pure. In many U. S. cities, motor vehicles contribute as much as 75 per cent of the noise and 80 per cent of the air pollution. They consume great quantities of land for parking and highways, breaking up neighborhoods, uprooting residents, and displacing businesses. They clog downtown streets and freeways until, as one British observer put it, "buildings seem to rise from a plinth of cars." They browbeat pedestrians and jangle nerves. They abet that homely, unplanned urban growth called sprawl, which some fear will permanently turn America into an endless string of Tastee Freezes. They kill and injure more Americans annually than a hundred Vietnam wars. One transportation expert, Wilfred Owen of the Brookings Institution, wonders "whether it is possible to be urbanized and motorized and at the same time civilized."

Many Americans are familiar with—even support—these indictments. Yet individually they cling devotedly to their cars, cherishing the independence and convenience that comes from owning their own wheels. And therein lies a dilemma that threatens to become far more painful. For the great factories in Detroit are adding to the car supply at a rate of 22,000 a day, and the men who make cars confidently predict that production will climb to 41,000 a day by the end of the decade—the greatest ten-year increase in history. Even after allowing for the junking of old vehicles, the American Automobile Association expects the number of autos, trucks, and buses to climb to 170 million by the year 1985, over 60 per cent more than are on the road today. To handle traffic requirements by then, state highway officials estimate more than 40,000 additional freeway miles will be needed . . . .

The impact of the growing flood of cars will be felt most keenly in America's bustling cities. By the end of this decade, metropolitan traffic volumes are projected to increase roughly 40 per cent in Pittsburgh, 50 per cent in Boston, 90 per cent in Detroit, and 100 per cent in Los Angeles.

For cities, cars are not only ugly and disruptive, but wasteful as well. Between 250 and 300 square feet of space is needed for every car that commuters park in the city. Cities typically devote 10 to 20 per cent of their downtown land solely to parking cars these days. A single lane of city freeway carries approximately 3,000 people an hour in cars. By contrast, buses and rail rapid transit using the same amount of space can transport as many as 30,000 and 40,000 persons respectively. Most highway interchanges built to accommodate auto commuters take up at least forty acres of land and sometimes twice that much. Mayors rankle at seeing freeways push taxpaying properties off the tax rolls.

How to repel an invader

One obvious way for a city to defend itself is to fight off new highways. A series of freeway revolts began in 1959 when San Franciscans rebelled at the ugly intrusion of the double-decked Embarcadero Freeway and forced the road builders to discontinue it, leaving the highway literally suspended in midair. Since then San Francisco has turned down hundreds of millions in federal highway in Washington, D.C., Indianapolis, Cleveland, Philadelphia, New York, and elsewhere. In Boston last December, Mayor Kevin H. White cited the "anguished objections of neighborhood residents" and urged the governor of Massachusetts to order "an immediate halt to any land taking, demolition, or construction . . . for new highways."

But there is a price to pay for such blocking tactics. The traffic keeps coming on relentlessly, and in the absence of freeways to handle it, the jams worsen. The root cause of all the trouble remains untouched. Few possessions have become so intricately entwined in the fabric of American life. The same car that has proved awkward and ill-mannered in the city made possible the single most important movement in postwar living, the massive migration to the suburbs. And, for those who can afford it, the car serves suburban living well. It frees the driver from reliance on fixed schedules, from waiting for buses or trains in cold or rainy weather, from lugging packages in crowded, uncomfortable public conveyances, and from annoying transfers from one form of travel to another.

America's fierce allegiance to the automobile was strikingly revealed by two nationwide surveys in 1967 that posed this question: "The auto pollutes air, creates traffic, demolishes property, and kills people.[6] Is the contribution the auto makes to our way of life worth this?" Four out of five respondents answered yes, even in metropolitan areas where the adverse impact of the auto is greatest.[7]

[6]Is the right to own and drive an automobile an inalienable freedom of Americans? Why, or why not?

[7]Should commuters into the city be forced to use public transportation or join car pools to preserve fuel? Why, or why not?

A tale of three cities

Equally perplexing is the fact that transit systems must be hand-tailored to the communities they serve. Consider, for example, the problem of carrying commuters into the central cities of Boston, Milwaukee, and Houston. Practically the only thing the three cities have in common is that they all face the threat of growing congestion unless mass transit is provided to complement the automobile.

Boston, an old city whose narrow streets were laid down more than two centuries before the advent of the auto, built the first subway in the U. S. (in 1897) and has a long history of heavy transit patronage, both rail and bus, although this patronage has been declining in recent years. Peak-hour travel into the already congested core city is expected to increase about 10 per cent. The downtown street system cannot be altered to accommodate this volume in cars. The number of people that would have to be dislocated, the heavy investment in existing buildings, the very history of the place foreclose that possibility.

So Boston's civic leaders hope that the number of peak-hour transit riders will increase 20 per cent while auto travel edges up only 3 per cent. The city is expanding and improving its rail system, which seems a wise choice under the circumstances. Boston's population density, among the highest in the nation, generates enough patronage to employ efficiently rail's high hauling capacity. Moreover, the fact that the city already has large investments in the subway, . . . makes improving that system more sensible than building a new rail line would be in a city of comparable density.

"No city left to go to"

Houston is at the opposite pole. While Boston houses more than 14,000 persons per square mile, Houston's residential densities are less than 3,000, hardly enough to support a rail commuter system. While 45 per cent of the travelers to and from Boston use public transit, in Houston only 4 per cent do, and a glance at the queues at bus stops shows that 4 per cent to be predominantly the black and the poor. The local bus company was so scantily used that it went into receivership in 1966 and has since been taken over by National City Lines. That company has put the line back in the black, but has been unable to increase ridership despite innumerable experiments. Two new routes, a dime-a-ride shopper's special and a twenty-mile run to the Houston Intercontinental Airport, both lose money and the latter will probably be discontinued.

So the task of getting Houstonians out of their cars and onto public transportation is a particularly vexing one, though the city leadership sees it must be solved if downtown isn't going to be swamped with cars. Traffic in and out of downtown is expected to triple by 1990 and, as city planner Roscoe Jones puts it, "When you start putting freeways between freeways, there's no city left to go to." A recent study recommended that Houston adopt some form of rapid transit to downtown. Some experts think nothing short of a futuristic "personal transit" system carrying passengers over a net of automated guideways would induce Houstonians to give up the car.

Milwaukee falls between the extremes of Houston and Boston. Early in the century it was well served by a network of electrified interurban rail lines so snappy that when commuters lit their cigars, they struck their matches on serrated German silver pieces mounted by the windows. As elsewhere, however, the auto's siren song was heard: in 1951 the railroad ceased passenger operations. Now the local bus company is losing ridership to the point where the county is talking seriously about a government take-over.

One bright sign runs counter to the general decline in transit. In 1964 Milwaukee's bus company began an experimental service that sped suburban riders nonstop over freeways into the city, cutting a fifty-six minute ride down to thirty-three. This service has grown and prospered. Two out of every five riders formerly drove their cars into Milwaukee. Now they park in fringe lots provided free by suburban shopping centers where the "freeway flyer" routes begin. The Milwaukee region is planning to build an exclusive two-lane busway along the most densely traveled corridor to the city, probably by paving over an east-west right-of-way that was formerly used by the electrified rail line. The busway is expected to be congestion-free, carrying 47,000 riders each weekday by 1990, or 25 per cent of the rush-hour travelers who commute along that busy corridor. This would mean a reduction of about 6,000 in the numbers of cars that might otherwise be driven into Milwaukee and parked.

Zones of residence and work: Looking toward the future

The 1970 federal census revealed that some interesting, if not dramatic, changes occurred in urban structure during the last decade. Many of the old statistics about urban working and living patterns no longer held true. For example, in its analysis of the 1970 census, *The New York Times* reported that half of all the jobs in the fifteen largest metropolitan areas are now loctated outside the city limits. The article from *The New York Times* summarizes some of the findings of the 1970 federal census and raise a number of questions about change in the American city. As you read the article, list the questions about spatial distribution you would like to have answered. Then reread the article to find evidence to answer your own questions. Where else might you find information to help answer your questions?

The mushrooming suburbs of America's major metropolitan areas, which already have more population than the cities that produced them, are fast approaching an even more striking milestone in urbanization.

They have equaled, and perhaps by now surpassed, the central cities as providers of jobs . . . .

And of all the enormous number of workers who live in the suburbs, only one in four still commutes from a suburban home to a city job. The others both live and work in the suburbs . . . .

It is a time of the suburbanization of almost everything. Potato fields and tract developments have been joined by poverty and wealth; by crime and culture; by pro-football and French cuisine.

In 1960, the suburbs of these areas (among 15 largest metropolitan areas), contained about seven million jobs and their cities contained about 12 million. That is, the central cities provided nearly two-thirds of the jobs in their metropolitan areas.

But during the nineteen-sixties, the suburbs of these areas gained more than three million jobs—a rise of 44 per cent. Meanwhile, the central cities lost 836,000, a 7 per cent decline.

By census day, April 1, 1970, the central cities had only 52 per cent of total metropolitan area jobs. And if, as is likely, the rates of change of the last decade have continued, one day in the next month or two the suburbs will draw ahead . . . .

The second major finding of *The Times'* analysis is of a massive increase in the number of workers who both live and work in the suburbs.

There was a rise in the number of conventional . . . commuters—from suburb to city. They increased 13 per cent, to 3.3 million. But meanwhile, the number of people who commuted from a home somewhere in the suburbs to a job somewhere in the suburbs shot up 40 per cent, to 8.7 million.

Over-all in the 15 metropolitan areas, 72 per cent of workers who live in the suburbs also work in the suburbs. For some areas, the figure is significantly higher. In the New York suburbs, for example, it is 78 per cent. In other words only 22 per cent of suburban workers commute to the city.

The pull of suburban employment is evident also from a sharp rise in reverse commuters, those who travel from homes in the city to jobs in the suburbs. Over-all, the number rose from 845,000, or 4 per cent of metropolitan employment, in 1960 to 1,460,000, or 7 per cent.

Moreover, the suburbs accounted for three-fourths of all new manufacturing and retail jobs that developed during the last decade. As a result, by 1967, they had 45 per cent of all metropolitan area manufacturing jobs and 41 per cent of all those in retail trade.

By now, as with other measurements, the suburbs may have pulled even and perhaps gone ahead. For all these measures are reflections of an "outward movement" in this century that ranks in importance with the Westward movement of the last . . . .

For thought and discussion

What factors, other than public and private transportation, might produce changes in the spatial distribution of our cities?

Individual and small group activities

1. Examine a number of current magazines from your college or local library and gather information on ideas for future urban transportation. Prepare a photo or slide report for class.
2. Organize a group of your classmates to visit your local planning office or department of transportation. Find out where the majority of your city's population lives. Also determine the major areas of morning and evening traffic congestion. Devise a plan to lessen these areas of congestion. Would you build additional highways? Where? How much does a mile of four lane highway cost today? Could you make public transportation more attractive to riders? How? (Note: One city increased its ridership on streetcars and busses simply by painting them bright lively colors.) Your instructor will inform you about how to present your information to the class. (Two groups with different recommendations may wish to present a panel discussion defending each position.)

Producing and distributing goods

Assignment 5

As Assignments 3 and 4 illustrated, geographic features strongly influence the location and structure of American cities. Geography alone, however, does not explain the reasons why people have clustered together in cities. The early medieval city, surrounded by high walls, provided protection for its inhabitants. Fearing both barbarian invaders and highway bandits, people often joined together in cities for mutual secutity. People also clustered together for economic reasons. Many early cities began as trading centers or depots at convenient sites where merchants established themselves to buy and sell goods produced in other cities and towns.

Most American cities began as trade centers exporting and importing food, raw materials, or manufactured goods. New York, Boston, Pittsburgh, Detroit, and Chicago all started as trade depots. Trading activities alone, however, could not sustain large populations or insure continued growth. Many early trading centers did not industrialize and failed to become cities. Most modern cities which began as import-export centers soon added manufacturing to their list of economic activities. Some items manufactured there became trade goods to sell elsewhere. Others filled the needs of the residents of the city itself.

The city of Detroit, for example, began its growth in the 1820's, exporting flour to ports along the Great Lakes. Waterfront shops built small ships to carry the flour. By the 1840's some of the shipyards had begun to sell locally manufactured steamboats to other port cities. Eventually as the shipyards expanded, engine and parts manufacturers were needed to fill the constantly growing markets. By the Civil War, ship engines and copper, originally used in engine production were among the leading exports of the city of Detroit. As Detroit grew from a depot center to a depot-manufacturing center, other industries grew to service local needs. Businessmen produced and supplied equipment to the large export industries. They also supplied clothing, housing, and other locally consumed goods. Thus, the original export economy of Detroit expanded to include the manufacture and export of new items as well as the production of items for local use.

New Obsidian

Many urban economists believe that most cities, both ancient and modern, grew in a fashion similar to that of Detroit. To illustrate this hypothesis about urban economic growth, urbanist Jane Jacobs created an imaginary ancient city, New Obsidian. (Obsidian is a hard, black, natural glass produced by volcanoes.) Born in Scranton, Pennsylvania, Ms. Jacobs now lives in Toronto. From 1952 to 1962 she was an associate editor of *Architectural Forum*. Jane Jacobs has written a number of books and articles about cities. As you read the description of New Obsidian, the following questions will help you test the accuracy of Jane Jacobs' hypotheses about urban economic growth:

1. What was the original economic basis of New Obsidian? What did its people export and import?
2. What manufactured items were added to the original economy? Which were produced for export and which were consumed locally?
3. Do you agree or disagree with the hypothesis of Jane Jacobs? Why or why not? Can you suggest any other hypotheses about urban economic growth?

In 8,500 B.C., New Obsidian's population numbers about two thousand persons. It is a mixture of the original people of the settlement and of the obsidian owning tribes, much of whose population is now settled within the city because of the trade and the various kinds of work connected with it. A small outlying population, to be sure, still works at the volcanoes and patrols the territory around them. Every day, parties from New Obsidian traverse the route between, bringing down treasure. The people of the city are wonderfully skilled at crafts and will become still more so because of the opportunity to specialize. The city has a peculiar religion because not one, but several, tribal gods are respected, officially celebrated and depended upon; these gods have become changed like the population itself.

The system of trade that prevails runs this way: The initiative is taken by the people who want to buy something. Traveling salesmen have not yet appeared on the scene; the traders, rather, regard themselves, and are regarded as, traveling purchasing agents. Undoubtedly, they take trade goods of their own to the place of purchase, but this is used like money to buy whatever it is they came for. Thus, the traders who come to New Obsidian from greater and greater distances come there purposely to get obsidian, not to get rid of something else. For the most part, the barter goods they bring consist of the ordinary produce of their hunting territories. When the New Obsidian people want special treasures like copper, shells or pigments that they themselves do not find in their territory, parties of their own traders go forth to get these things from other settlements. With them they take obsidian, as if it were money.

In this way, settlements that possess unusual treasures—copper, fine shells, pigments—have become minor trading centers for obsidian too. They exchange with nearby hunting tribes some of the obsidian that has been brought to them in barter and are paid in ordinary hunting produce. And New Obsidian, similarly, is a regional trading center for other rare goods besides obsidian.

New Obsidian, in this fashion, has become a "depot" settlement as well as a "production" settlement. It has two kinds of major export work, not one. Obsidian, of course, is one export. The other export is a service: the service of obtaining, handling and trading goods that are brought in from outside and are destined for secondary customers who also come from outside.

The economy of New Obsidian divides into an export-import economy on the one hand, and a local or internal economy on the other. But these two major divisions of the settlement's economy are not static. As time passes, New Obsidian adds many new exports to those first two, and all the new exports come out of the city's own local economy. For example, the excellently manufactured hide bags in which obsidian is carried down from its sources are sometimes bartered to hunters or traders from other settlements who have come to purchase obsidian but, after seeing the bags, wish to carry their obsidian back in one. Fine, finished obsidian knives, arrowheads, spearheads and mirrors of the kind that the workers in New Obsidian produce for their own people are also coveted by those who come for raw obsidian. The potent religion of prospering New Obsidian becomes an object of trade too; its common local trinkets are bought. Trinkets of personal dress also go into the export trade . . . .

To understand why New Obsidian has become a trading center of such importance, the goal of people from great distances, it is necessary to understand the enormous value of obsidian to hunters. Obsidian is not merely a substance that catches the eye or carries prestige; it is a vital production material. Once possessed, it is regarded as a necessity, both by the hunters in every little trading city and by the rural hunting tribesmen. Obsidian makes the sharpest cutting tools to be had . . . . Obsidian is not steel, but it is the nearest thing to it in the world of New Obsidian . . . .

A large proportion of the food of New Obsidian is imported from foreign hunting territories. This is food that is traded at the barter square for obsidian and for other exports of the city. Food is the customary goods brought by customers who do not pay in copper, shells, pigments or other unusual treasures. Wild food of the right kind commands a good exchange. In effect, New Obsidian has thus enormously enlarged its hunting territory by drawing, through trade, upon the produce of scores of hunting territories . . . .

Because of New Obsidian's unusually voluminous and extensive trade, large quantities of live animals and seeds flow into the city. The animals are trussed up or carried in pole cages if they are dangerous. They are hobbled with fiber rope and alternately carried and driven on their own feet if they are not dangerous. Nonperishable plant food is easier to handle than animals, and traders carrying it can travel more swiftly. Thus, especially from the greater distances, beans, nuts and edible grass seeds pour into New Obsidian.

The imported food promptly enters New Obsidian's local economy and there it comes under the custody of local workers who specialize in its protection, storage and distribution. They are, in effect, stewards: stewards of wild animals and stewards of edible seeds . . . .

Some people *within* the city trade seeds to others. That is, they make a business of handing out seeds in return for trinkets. Possibly this trade is confined to the women. It is not as radical an arrangement as their ancestors would probably have thought it, because the people inside the city who engage in this practice are modeling their transactions upon the barter that has long gone on in the city square . . . .

Gradually, New Obsidian grows more and more of its own meat and grain but it does not, as a consequence, wallow in unwanted surpluses of imported food. First, the very practice of growing foods in new ways requires new tools and more industrial materials. The population of New Obsidian grows and so does the work to be done in New Obsidian.

The city's total food supply is made up of its own territorial yield of wild animals and plants, its imports of wild animals and seeds, and its new home-grown meats and grains. The total increases but the imports decrease as the new city-made food greatly increase . . . . The city, in short, is now supplying itself with some of the goods that it formerly had to import. In principle, this is not much different from importing baskets and then manufacturing them locally so they need no longer be imported. Since New Obsidian had formerly imported so much wild food—in comparison to baskets or boxes, say—the substituted local production makes a big difference in the city's economy.

In place of unneeded food imports, New Obsidian can import other things—a lot of other things. The effect is as if the city's imports have increased enormously, although they have not. The city, instead, has shifted its imports from one kind of goods to other kinds. This change radically changes the economies of the people with whom New Obsidian trades. Now people from ordinary hunting tribes who come for obsidian find that ordinary industrial raw materials from their own territories—furs, hides, bundles or rushes, fibers and horn—are much welcomed in barter, while pouches of grass seeds and exhausted, scrawny live animals do not command the obsidian they once did.

Now too the traders of the city itself go forth ever more frequently to points ever more distant in search of exotic materials for the city's craftsmen. And the things that the craftsmen make of the new wealth of materials pouring in amount to an explosion of city wealth, an explosion of new kinds of work, an explosion of new exports, and an explosion in the very size of the city. The work to be done and the population both increase rapidly—so rapidly that some people from outlying tribes become permanent residents of the city too. Their hands are needed. New Obsidian has experienced a momentous economic change peculiar to cities: explosive growth owing to local production of goods that were formerly imported and to a consequent shift of imports.

The traders of New Obsidian, when they go off on their trips, take along New Obsidian food to sustain themselves. Sometimes they bring back a strange animal, or a bit of promising foreign seed. And the trader of other little cities who come to New Obsidian sometimes take back food with them and tell what they have seen in the metropolis. Thus, the first spread of the new grains and animals is from city to city. The rural world is still a world in which wild food and other wild things are hunted and gathered. The cultivation of plants and animals is, as yet, only city work. It is duplicated, as yet, only by other city people, not by the hunters of ordinary settlements.

Modern urban economics

In your analysis of the economy of New Obsidian, you probably noticed the relationship between export trade and manufacturing, both for local use and for export. As one element of the economy grew, so did others. If one element, such as manufacturing goods for export, failed to grow, the other elements might also fail to expand. The economy of the Appalacian area of the United States provides an example of this principle. Appalachia remains dependent upon the exportation of raw materials, mainly coal. Few cities of the area manufacture export items in large quantities. Today, large numbers of workers in Appalachia remain unemployed, and its cities suffer from economic depression. Many workers leave the area to seek work elsewhere.

Your examination of New Obsidian may have also led you to develop this hypothesis: in expanding urban areas we might expect to find substantial export trade, along with manufacturing of products both for export and local use. The final part of Assignment 5 consists of a number of tables to help you test this hypothesis. Each table contains current economic information about the city of Chicago. Examine the data carefully and answer the questions below each table. When you have completed your examination of all the tables, be prepared to defend, revise, or refute your hypothesis.

Which of the businesses pictured here, if any, shows an industry that is likely to sell most of its goods in another city? Which shows an industry that produces goods mostly for local consumption?

Table 5.1
Number of persons employed in all Chicago industries (to the nearest thousand)

Industry	*No. of persons employed*	*Industry*	*No. of persons employed*
Agric., forestry & fisheries	4,000	Wholesale trade	63,000
Mining	1,000	Food, bakery & dairy stores	33,000
Construction	51,000	Eating & drinking places	39,000
Manufacturing (total)	444,000	General merchandise retailing	54,000
Furn, lumber, wood prod.	16,000	Motor vehicles retail, ser. sta.	15,000
Metal indus.	74,000	Other retail trade	74,000
Machinery, equip.	114,000	Banking & credit agencies	29,000
Motor vehicles, trans. equip.	14,000	Ins., real est. other financial ins.	59,000
Other durable goods	60,000	Business services	36,000
Food products	42,000	Repair services	26,000
Textile products	16,000	Pvt. households (maids)	9,000
Printing, publishing	46,000	Other personal services	50,000
Chemical products	16,000	Entertainment & rel. services	8,000
Other non-durable goods	51,000	Hospital, health services	68,000
Railways & railway exp. ser.	18,000	Education	77,000
Trucking, service, warehousing	26,000	Welfare, religious & non-profit	23,000
Other transportation	28,000	Legal, eng. & other professions	41,000
Communications	18,000	Public administration	77,000
Utilities & sanitary services	23,000		

1. Which industries and how many workers probably produce goods for export? Which industries and how many workers probably produce goods or services for local use?

Table 5.2
General statistics of major Chicago industries: 1967

Industry	*Establishments* *Total no.*	*All employees (rounded)* *Number (1000)*	*Payroll (million $)*	*Value of shipments (rounded) Million $*
Food & kindred products	645	58.0	417.0	2,955.0
Apparel, textile products	562	22.0	106.0	379.0
Lumber & wood products	172	5.0	30.0	89.0
Furniture & fixtures	300	11.0	66.0	212.0
Paper & allied products	235	17.0	112.0	419.0
Printing & publishing	1,501	67.0	545.0	1,653.0
Chemical products	433	18.0	134.0	908.0
Petroleum & coal products	29	1.0	11.0	76.0
Rubber & plastic products	213	14.0	83.0	263.0
Stone, clay & glass products	188	9.0	57.0	220.0
Primary metal industries	210	36.0	284.0	1,394.0
Fabricated metal products	1,177	58.0	415.0	1,359.0
Machinery, except electrical	1,106	58.0	460.0	1,477.0
Electrical equip. & supplies	468	73.0	441.0	1,802.0
Transportation equipment	103	13.0	95.0	686.0
Instruments & related prod.	178	17.0	115.0	365.0
Misc. mfg. industries	503	22.0	132.0	407.0

1. In terms of employment and income, which three industries are most important to the Chicago economy? Which three are the least important?
2. Compare this table with the one in Figure 5.4. What is the relationship between manufacturing for export and manufacturing for local consumption in the Chicago economy?

Table 5.3
Occupation of all employed persons in Chicago: 1970
(to the nearest thousand)

Occupations	*No. of persons employed*
Professional, technical & kindred workers	175,000
Managers and administrators	72,000
Sales workers	81,000
Clerical and kindred workers	336,000
Craftsmen, foreman & kindred workers	177,000
Transport equipment operatives	60,000
Other operatives	236,000
Laborers (except farm)	70,000
Farmers, farm managers, farm laborers	2,000
Service workers (except pvt. households)	167,000
Private household workers	11,000

1. What do Chicagoans do for a living? Do you think that most workers produce goods and services for local use or for export?
2. Does the large number of clerical and service workers suggest any revisions to your original hypothesis?

Table 5.4
Retail trade by selected Chicago industries: 1967

Industry	*Number of business*	*Number of employees*	*Number of proprietors*	*Value of sales*
Building materials	832	3,784	767	$ 15,730,000
Gen. mchdse, dept. store	818	39,539	571	1,029,644,000
Food stores	4,616	27,458	4,460	1,241,079,000
Auto dlrs, gas stations	668	10,869	454	825,615,000
Apparel stores	2,517	19,456	1,862	534,905,000
Furniture, home furn.	1,295	7,495	990	322,431,000
Eating & drinking places	7,788	45,269	7,660	659,645,000
Drug stores	1,078	9,408	661	267,604,000
Misc. retail stores	6,320	16,010	NA*	NA*

1. In what ways are the businesses above dependent upon Chicago's export industries listed in Figure 5.2? What would happen to the businesses listed above if Chicago's export industries increased or decreased substantially?
2. How does the evidence you examined influence the original hypothesis stated on page 55? What additional evidence might strengthen your hypothesis?

For thought and discussion

What kind of measures could be undertaken within your own city to strengthen or stimulate its economy?

Individual and small group activities

1. Examine 1970 census data for your own city to determine the nature of the relationship between manufacturing for local consumption and manufacturing for export. What can be done to strengthen this relationship.
2. What is your city doing to attract new industry? Visit your local Chamber of Commerce to find out. Ask for any pamphlets, brochures, or pictures they may use for this purpose. Prepare a report for class, using any materials you receive, illustrating the activities of the Chamber of Commerce.

Occupational opportunities in the contemporary city

Assignment 6

During the next few years you will make one of the most crucial decisions of your entire life. Your choice of occupation may influence to a great degree both your life style and your future happiness. Millions of Americans find their jobs stimulating, challenging, and rewarding. A number of recent studies, however, suggest that many Americans dislike their occupations. Some workers consider their jobs boring drudgery—work which provides neither inspiration nor a sense of fulfillment. Others find their jobs too demanding of both time and energy. These studies imply that people often choose their occupations with little investigation or knowledge of alternative careers.

Moreover, few people have examined the future trends of their particular occupational choice. For example, what are the future prospects of the occupation you are now training for? Will the needs for your particular skill expand or decline during the next thirty years? Does the occupation you select provide opportunities for advancement into other interesting positions. Will you perform essentially the same work task for the next thirty years? Does that possibility make you happy?

Employment opportunities in the next decade

In 1973 nearly 83 million people were employed in thousands of occupations throughout the United States. The Department of Labor estimates that the number of employed persons will climb to 95 million by 1980. Most of these people will work in or near large cities. Unfortunately, not all occupations will expand at the same rate. Jobs in some industries, such as computer operations, electronics, communications, and photographic equipment will expand rapidly during the next ten years. On the other hand, few new occupational opportunities are expected in industries such as agriculture, mining, and steel.

The graph and table on the next two pages with help you determine the areas of greatest occupational opportunity in the next few years. Examine the evidence carefully and answer the questions which follow the table on page 63. When you have finished your investigation, list the occupation you will qualify for at the conclusion of your education and then evaluate your occupational future realistically.

Figure 6.1
Employment trends in goods–producing and services–industries, 1947–1980

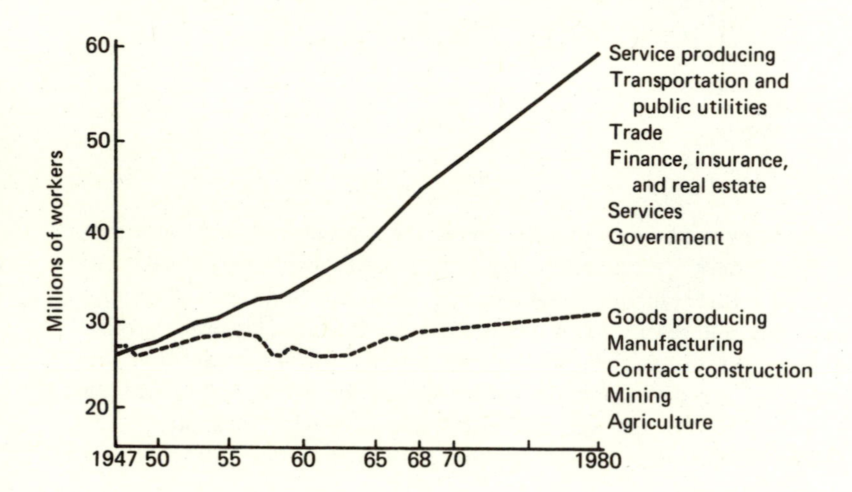

Table 6.1
Total national employment and projected average annual job openings, selected occupations

Occupation	*1970 employment*	*Projected 1980 employment*	*Projected annual job openings 1970–1980*
Secretaries, stenos and typists	3,504,000	4,580,000	215,000
Elementary and secondary school teachers	2,275,000	2,330,000	200,000
Private household workers	1,588,000	1,980,000	180,000
Sales people	4,845,000	5,760,000	165,000
Truck drivers	1,855,000	2,150,000	129,000
Bookkeeping workers	860,000	970,000	80,000
Hospital attendents	830,000	1,500,000	77,000
Engineers	1,081,000	1,408,000	65,000
Waiters and waitresses	1,040,000	1,240,000	64,000
Registered professional nurses	688,000	983,000	61,000
Cashiers	847,000	1,110,000	60,000
Cooks and chefs	740,000	930,000	44,000
Carpenters	830,000	1,075,000	32,000
Assemblers	716,000	854,000	30,000
Licensed practical nurses	370,000	670,000	29,000
Telephone operators	420,000	480,000	28,000
Bank clerks	225,000	337,000	26,000
Construction laborers	3,724,000	3,700,000	26,000
Office machine operators	565,000	860,000	25,000
Accountants	491,000	800,000	25,000
Welders	535,000	675,000	23,000
Auto mechanics	830,000	1,020,000	20,000

1. Which occupations will grow the fastest during the current decade? Which will grow the slowest?
2. Which occupations seem to provide the greatest opportunities for you?
3. What can you do to improve your occupational future?

Seeking a job

Every day the American city provides hundreds of job opportunities for qualified people. All of the occupations listed on the above table may be found in every large city. People get these jobs in a variety of ways. Some write letters to prospective employers asking for employment. These letters usually include detailed summaries, called a resumé, of one's educational and work experiences. Other people examine the want ads in the classified section of the daily newspaper and apply in person for those jobs that appeal to them. Some people secure employment through professional agencies. They provide the agency with information about their background and occupational interests. When the agency has found a likely occupational opening for the applicant, it will arrange for an interview between the employer and the prospective employee. Upon accepting a position, the employee pays a fee, usually some percentage of the first year's salary, to the employment agency.

Finally, many people secure employment through a state or federal employment agency. Nearly all cities maintain branch offices of a state employment agency. These offices provide computerized up-to-date records of the hundreds of jobs available within the city. These records describe each occupation. They also list educational or experience requirements, hours, wages, working conditions, and special fringe benefits.

The information on the following pages, taken from one city's "jobbook" illustrates the wide variety of occupational opportunities in the contemporary city. As you read, make a list of the jobs you will be qualified for at the conclusion of your education. For each occupation you list, note several reasons why you might or might not want the position. Include such characteristics as hours, wages, prospects for advancement, and the nature of the work. Finally, eliminate all those occupations which you would not be interested in applying for. Then answer these questions:

1. How many occupations are you qualified for? How many appeal to you?
2. What can you do to expand your list? Can you think of other desirable occupations you might qualify for?

```
    COMPUTR OPER  11   0106  2
TYP-        SRTHD         LIC       ZONE-
VIET VET PRFRRD  GRAD OF COMPUTER SCHL
MIN 2YRS HANDS ON OPERATIONS EXP  FAMILI
AR WITH IBM 360 50 7090 AND 1401
HARDWARE ROTATE SHIFTS  APPLY  DIREC MON
DAY THRU THURSDAY 9 TO 4PM
WK/WK-FULL  PAY-  566.00-  762.00/MONTHLY
                  HRS/WK-40 PAY PD-BI-WEEK
DURATION-PERM   TST/RQ-N/A   TST/BY-N/A
JOB REQUIRES-EDUC-13 MTH/EXP-12  AGE-00-00
PHY/DMD-290 WK/COND-1   MAR/SIN.MALE/FM.

                 MAND
BENEFITS-INS       .HOSP.SCKLV.VAC..PENS
```

CONTACT LENS TECH
TYP- SRTHD- LIC
WILL OPERATE CONTACT LENS LABORATORY
MINIMUM 1 YRS EXP IN CONTACT LENS
MAKING APPLICANT CALL WALK TO
INTERVIEW DOWNTOWN ZIP 15222

WK/WK-FULL PAY- 2.50-4.00/PER HR
**CALL FIRST HRS/WK-40 PAY PD-WEEKLY
DURATION-PERM TST/RQ-N/A TST/BY-N/A
JOB REQUIRES-EDUC-13 MTH/EXP-12 AGE-00-00
PHY/DMD-180 WK/COND-1 MAR/SIN.MALE/FM.

BENEFITS-.VAC.

BILINGUAL SECRETARY
TYP- SRTHD- LIC
JOB SITE GUINEA W AFRICA 2YR CONTRACT
BILINGUAL FRENCH ENGLISH SECRETARIAL TR
AINING TYPE 65 WPM SHORTHAND 100 WPM
HANDLE ALL SECRETARIAL WORK FOR MANAGER
SET UP OFFICE FILING SYSTEM PREFER PREV
OVERSEAS EXPERIENCE ZIP CODE 15212
WK/WK-FULL PAY- 700.00- 750.00/MONTHLY
**CALL FIRST HRS/WK-40 PAY PD-BI-WEEK
DURATION-PERM TST/RQ-PROF TST/BY-EMPLR
JOB REQUIRES-EDUC-12 MTH/EXP-04 AGE-00-00
PHY/DMD-290 WK/COND-1 MAR/SIN.MALE/FM.
ORFT/EX.US/CIT. PHYSICAL

BENEFITS-INS. HOSP.SCKLV.VAC.BONUS

ELECTRONIC TEST TECH NEWPORT NW
TYP- SRTHD- LIC
JOBSITE NEWPORT NEWS VA ZIP 23607
ASSOCIATE DEGREE IN ELECTRONICS ENGINRNG
TECHNOLOGY OR MARINE ELECTRONICS TEST OR
DESIGN EXPER EXPER IN MK 114 INSTALATN
MAINTENANCE OR SIMILAR SYSTEM
EXTREMELY HELPFUL
WK/WK-FULL PAY- 150.00- 250.00/WEEKLY
**CALL FIRST HRS/WK-40 PAY PD-SEMI-MO
DURATION-PERM TST/RQ-N/A
JOB REQUIRES-EDUC-14 MTH/EXP-00 AGE-00-0
PHY/DMD-290 WK/COND-1 MAR/SIN.MALE/FM.
US/CIT. SEC/CLR.PHYSICAL

BENEFITS-INS. HOSP.SCKLV.VAC..PENS

DENTAL HYGIENIST DRUMS
TYP- SRTHD- LIC
JOB SITE DRUMS PA NEAR HAZLETON 15222
PA CERTIFICATION AS DENTAL HYGIENIST
RECENT GRAD ACCEPTABLE
ADMINISTER AND TEACH PREVENTIVE
DENTISTRY PROGRAM TO JOB CORPS
TRAINEES
WK/WK-FULL PAY-10000.00/YEARLY
**CALL FIRST HRS/WK-40 PAY PD-SEMI-MO
DURATION-PERM TST/RQ-N/A TST/BY-N/A
JOB REQUIRES-EDUC-14MTH/EXP-00 AGE-00-00
PHY/DMD-290 WK/COND-1 MAR/SIN.MALE/FM.

BENEFITS-INS. HOSP..VAC..PENS

STAFF THERAPIST
TYP- SRTHD-
MUST BE TRAINED IN REGISTERED
RESPIRATORY THERAPIST TO CARE FOR
PATIENTS N EQUIPMENT MUST BE
REGISTERED INTRVUR CALL AT BUS
61 ABC ON FORBES AVE
ZIP 15213
WK/WK-FULL PAY- 576.00/MONTHLY
**CALL FIRST HRS/WK-40 PAY PD-BI-WEEK
DURATION-PERM TST/RQ-N/A TST/BY-N/A
JOB/DMD-380 WK/COND-L8 MAR/SIN.MALE/FM.
US/CIT. PHYSICAL

BENEFITS-INS.HOSP.SCKLV.VAC..PENS

MINE EQUIPMNT INSTCTR 70 09
TYP- SRTHD- LIC
JOB SITE GUINEA 2 YR CONTRACT
BILINGUAL FRENCH ENGLISH LEARN INDIGENOUS
LANGUAGE INSTRUCT LOCAL PERSNNEL IN
OPERATION OF MINING EQUIP NO MAINTENANC
TEACHING EXP NO OPERATING EXP
INTERVIEWER CALL CLEARANCE
WK/WK-FULL PAY- 1100.00- 1150.00/MONTHLY
**CALL FIRST HRS/WK-40 PAY PD-SEMI-MO
DURATION-PERM TST/RQ-N/A TST/BY-N/A
JOB REQUIRES-EDUC-14 MTH/EXP-00 AGE-00-00
PHY/DMD-2 WK/COND-1 MAR/SIN.MALE/FM.
DRFT/EX.

BENEFITS-INS. HOSP.SCKLV.VAC.BONUS

SALES MANAGMT TRAINEE
TYP- SRTHD- LIC
VET OR DRAFT EXEMPT PFD COLLEG
GRAD OR 2 YRS COLLEG PLUS 2 YRS BUSNS
EXP MUST HAVE OWN CAR N VALID
DRIVERS LICENSE 3 YR TRAINING
APPLY IN PERSON 9AM TO 4PM EMPLYR
MAY GIVE APTITUDE TEST ZIP 15222
WK/WK-FULL PAY- 500.00- 800.00/MONTHLY
HRS/WK-40 PAY PD-MONTHLY
DURATION-PERM TST/RQ-OTHR TST/BY-EMPLR
JOB REQUIRES-EDUC-14 MTH/EXP-24 AGE-00-00
PHY/DMD-1 WK/COND-1 MAR/SIN.MALE/FM.
US/CIT

BENEFITS-INS. HOSP..VAC.BONUS

MACHINIST
TYP- SRTHD- LIC ZONE-
JOB IN NEWPORT NEWS VA TRDE SCH 2YRS EXP
ALL GENRL MACH SHOP WRK INCLUDING REPAIR
OF SMALL MACH PARTS OPS DRILL PRESS
LATHE ETC USE MEASURING INSTRUMENTS SUCH
AS MICROMETER HT GAGES N GAGE BLOCK HON
DISCHARGE
WK/WK-FULL PAY- 3.96- 4.42/PER HR
**CALL FIRST HRS/WK-40 PAY PD-SEMI-MO
DURATION-PERM TST/RQ-N/A TST/BY-N/A
JOB REQUIRES-EDUC-14 MTH/EXP-00 AGE-00-00
PHY?DMD-478 WK/COND-18 MAR/SIN.MALE/FM.
US/CIT. SEC/CLR.PHYSICAL

BENEFITS-INS. HOSP..VAC..PENS

REAL ESTATE MANAGER 70
TYP- SRTHD- LIC ZONE
WILL OVERSEE OPERATION OF VARIOUS APT
COMPLEXS IN CINN SUPERVISE ACTIVITIES OF
RENTAL AGNTS EXP PRF N SIMILAR POST
CPM CERT DESERABLE MUST HAVE OWN CAR
WILL BE ON CALL RESUME ONLY TO PRES

WK/WK-FULL PAY- 8000.00-12000.00/YEARLY
HRS/WK-40 PAY PD-BI-WEEK
DURATION-PERM TST/RQ-N/A TST/BY-N/A
JOB REQUIRES-EDUC-14 MTH/EXP-12 AGE-00-00
PHY/DMD-19 WK/COND-1 MAR/SIN.MALE/FM.

CONTROLLER
TYP-   SRTHD-   LIC   ZONE
50 PERCENT TRAVEL THROUGHOUT PA NEW YORK
NEW JERSEY HOME OFFICE PHILA
DIRECT FINANCIAL AFFAIRS OF A CHAIN OF
MOTELS IN PA NY AND NJ ESTABLISH ECONOM
IC OBJECTIVES PREPARE GOVT REPORTS OF
TERMIN DEPRECIATION ARRANGE FOR AUDITS
WK/WK-FULL PAY-15000.00-16000.00/YEARLY
**CALL FIRST HRS/WK-40 PAY PD-SEMI-MO
DURATION-PERM   TST/RQ-N/A   TST/BY-N/A
JOB REQUIRES-EDUC-14 MTH/EXP-12 AGE-00-00
PHY/DMD-290 WK/COND-1 MAR/SIN.MALE/FM.

BENEFITS-INS. HOSP..VAC.

DRAFTSMAN   70
TYP-   SRTHD-   LIC   ZONE
MDTA OR TECHNICAL SCHOOL GRAD DRAFTS
DETAILED ENGINEERING DRAWINGS USING
TRIANGLE T SQUARE ETC UTILIZES NOLEDG
OF ENGNRNG PRACTICES AND MATH TO COM
PLETE DRAWNGS MON THRU FRI 8 TO 5 APPL
CALL EMP DIRECTS ZIP 15222
WK/WK-FULL PAY- 350.00/MONTHLY
**CALL FIRST HRS/WK-40 PAY PD-BI-WEEK
DURATION-PERM   TST/RQ-N/A   TST/BY-N/A
JOB REQUIRES-EDUC-13 MTH/EXP-00 AGE-00-00
PHY/DMD-180 WK/COND-1 MAR/SIN.MALE/FM.

SR SECTY 0012   3
TYP-   SRTHD-   LIC   ZONE-
VIET VT PFD BES TSTO TYP 6K WPM SHTHND 100
BUS SCHL GRAD OR 2 TO 1 YRS GEN OFC EXP
COMPOSE GEN OFC CORESPNDNC TRANSCRIBE FROM
DICTAPHONE MAINTAIN MONITR INVENTRY LEVLS
ARANG APTS MAKE TRAVL RESERVATIONS INTR
VUS MON THRU THUR 9 TO 4 61 ABC ZIP 15213
WK/WK-FULL PAY- 453.00- 580.00/MONTHLY
HRS/WK-40 PAY PD-BI-WEEK
DURATION-PERM TST/RQ-PROF TST/BY-E.X.
JOB REQUIRES-EDUC-13 MTH/EXP-0-25 AGE-00-00
PHY/DMD-19 WK/COND-1 MAR/SIN.MALE/FM.
DRFT/EX.

BENEFITS-INS. MAND HOSP.SCKLV.VAC..PENS

```
    INSTRUCTOR JUDO
TYP-     SRTHD-
ZIP 15146  OLYMPIC KARATE STUDIOS
HOURS 200 TO 1000PM MON THRU FRI
DUTIES: TEACHES KARATE
WILL BE MOTIVATED OTHER OFFICE 1782N HIGH
LAND AVE 15214 PHONE 3449297

STS-    CO   CLS-RL/DATE=                CANC
WK/WK-FULL PAY-   2.00/PER HR
**CALL FIRST  HRS/WK-40 PAY PD-WEEKLY
DURATION-PERM   TST/RQ-N/A  TST/BY-N/A
JOB REQUIRES-EDUC-12 MTH/EXP-12 AGE-00-00
PHY/DMD-93 WK/COND-1    MAR/SIN.MALE/FM.
DRFT/EX.US/CIT.

BENEFITS-INS.HOSP..VAC.BONUS
```

Work satisfaction

On the following pages urban workers in several different job classifications discuss their occupations. Some of these workers enjoy their jobs; others do not. As you read each of these selections answer the following questions:

1. What do these workers seem to like most about their jobs? What do they like least?
2. Which occupation is most similar to the one you are presently training for? What predictions can you make about your future satisfaction with your occupational choice?

Three blue-collar workers

Blue Collar Blues, ©Newsweek Inc., 1971, reprinted by permission.

Willie Sanders was taking a day off. In a waterfront bar called The Hatch, across the street from the Todd Shipyards in San Pedro, Calif., Willie, a 37-year-old riveter, sipped his beer. "You get to the point," he said, "where you stare at the rivets and to make the job mean something you start counting them like counting sheep. When you do that, you better watch out. Some guys tell you that means you're going crazy. So when it happens to me, I just go home and watch television until I can come back and face it again. My kid looks at me and says, 'Dad, what're you doing home again?' I tell him, 'Listen, kid, you're going to college one day. You just won't understand it.' I can never explain to him. You just can't get the feeling of what it's like there until you get behind a riveting gun and begin blasting away. Some guys like to think they're fighting a war. It makes them feel good."

In the fluorescent-lit office of UAW Local 1364, across from the GM assembly plant in Fremont, Calif., half a dozen younger workers smoked and drank beer. "The problem with our job," said 32-year-old Chuck Cline, "is that psychology hasn't kept up with technology. It's a gold-plated salt mine. People get bored. We don't have any pride in our work." The work takes its toll of their private lives, too. "Everybody likes money," said Tony Navarette, a 30-year-old assembler and father of two, "but who has the time to enjoy it? By the time you get off an assembly line you're like dunce." Added 30-year-old Mike Lilley (who had just been fired for failing to repair a loose bolt), "GM is one of the biggest causes of divorce. What am I gonna do now–walk in and show the wife the pink slip? I wish I'd never heard of General Motors. Eighty per cent of the men are dissatisfied, but you gotta feed your family." Would he want his children to work in the factory? "Would you want yours to be in prison?"

In The Hatch, George Watson finished his beer. "People like me have dreams too, you know," he said. "If I had the chance I would have liked to be a lawyer. I ain't kidding myself that I could make it but it's nice to think about. But with this job, hell, man, you're going nowhere fast. So what if you've just made a great weld of a tough angle bend? No one gives a damn. I once suggested [at a union meeting] we should have some kind of recognition program like the boys in business do when they sell a million dollars' worth of insurance. You know, something like 'George Watson made a great weld this week' or 'George Watson was working with this apprentice and now the kid is coming along just fine.' I made that suggestion in a regular meeting and people just laughed at me. 'Sit down, George,' someone yelled, 'What the hell do you care? You get good pay.' I thought that was worth smashing somebody's fat nose in. But I didn't. I went out and got drunk. There was nothing I could do."[8]

Willie Carolina, auto worker

For most men, choosing a career is one of the most difficult decisions of a lifetime–and often the most regretable.

For Willie Carolina, it was easy.

As a black man coming of age in the years immediately preceding World War II, there was little choice for him. It was simply a matter of finding a job that paid well.

This was not all that easy in Baltimore. So after Carolina did his time in the Army, he headed for the green pastures of Detroit. Now 47, he's been an auto worker ever since.

[8]What, if anything, can people like George Watson do to increase their job satisfaction?

"I went where I could make some money," the short, but muscular die truck driver said. "They weren't paying enough in Maryland for me."

Like many who migrated here after the war to work for the giant car makers Carolina considered Detroit "a booming city," and still does for that matter.

"I wanted to go to a manufacturing plant and get a job," he said. "I put in three applications and I got a job on the third one."

He started with the Briggs Manufacturing Co., which made car bodies for Chrysler Corp., on April 1, 1946, as a $38-a-week sweeper. For three years, he did nothing but push a broom.

"When I first went in the plant, for black man all he could get was a job as a laborer, a janitor, or a sweeper. If he had enough experience, he would get a job on the sandlines," Carolina said.

"Now they got'em everywhere," he said. "Now a black man can go as far as he wants . . . if he's qualified."

Carolina can remember when there was no such thing as a black foreman. And the first black men to become foremen, he said, had only black men working under them. Now, he said, "a black foreman might have more white guys under him than black guys."

Carolina has been a die truck driver for the past 12 years, most of which he has spent at the Chrysler stamping plant on Detroit's northeast side, and is now in the $10,000-a-year bracket, a wage he rates as good for a man without a high school diploma.

He considers himself a professional, doing the best he can at the job he's best qualified for.

"I like my job. I see a lot of jobs out there that I like and a lot that I don't like. But this is the job I think I'm best qualified for," he said.

"I consider myself as much a professional at my job as you are at yours," he told the reporter interviewing him.

At leisure, Carolina comes across as a pretty typical middle-aged man. An avid sports fan, he spends much of his weekend in front of the television if he's not out fishing or having a drink with the boys. Not having any children, his only financial goal is to buy his own home—something he could afford to do now.

His home, located in one of many of Detroit's blighted neighborhoods, belongs to his wife's family and costs him nothing as far as mortgage or rent payments go. He's waiting for urban renewal to take it over before he puts down any money on a house of his own.

He said he's satisfied with his current wage, less than $200 per week without overtime, "as long as the rapid rate of inflation doesn't continue."

"What good is it to make $300 a week when it costs $5 or $6 to buy a steak?" he asked. "Houses are going for $25,000 that aren't worth any more than $12,000."

Well aware of the changes time has brought, Carolina is optimistic about the future of the black worker, but he places a certain amount of responsibility with the black man himself.

"Once we start moving, we'll get any job as long as we're qualified," he said.

Lisa Watkins, computer programmer

Lisa Watkins works for a large corporation in the city of Dallas. As a computer programmer she first determines what information is needed to prepare documents for the company. She next makes a flow chart or diagram showing the order in which the computer must perform each operation. Lisa then prepares detailed instructions for the computer's control unit to tell the machine exactly what to do with each piece of information. Finally, she prepares an instruction sheet for the computer operator to follow when running the program.

Following graduation from a Houston, Texas community college, Lisa applied for several positions in both Houston and Dallas. She received job offers from one company in each city. The position in Dallas seemed more promising to her, so she left her family and friends and moved the 250 miles from Houston to Dallas.[9] According to Lisa, the decision to move was difficult at first, but she has no regrets. "I must admit when I first thought about moving away from home I was plenty scared. I wondered if I'd miss my family and friends. You know, be homesick. I did miss home for the first month or so, particularly my old boyfriend, but then I met some new friends and everything worked out fine. I've been here for seven years and I consider Dallas my home now." When Lisa first began her job she joined a pool of five other computer programmers at the company's computer center. "At that time," she explained, "I handled mostly routine jobs. I worked on the company payroll, accounts receivable, and accounts payable."

Gradually as some people in the computer pool left the company and Lisa gained valuable experience, she received more important assignments. Six months ago she became director of the programming staff. Five other men and women now work for her. "I have my own office now," she says, "As you can see it's a bit small but I really don't mind. It's mine! Of course, I have more responsibility now too. If something goes wrong it's my job to determine the problem and make sure it's corrected. I also have to keep the staff happy and prevent small problems from interfering with their work. Time is an important element in our work. The company must meet production schedules, shipping schedules and so on. This means that all of our work must be completed on time or we will slow down the whole process. I often take home work or work evenings at the office. I guess that's the only thing

[9]Would you be willing to move 250 or more miles from your home to secure a good job? Why, or why not?

I don't like about my new promotion. Sometimes it interferes with things I want to do. Like two weeks ago, for example, I had tickets to a new play in town but we had a program due for completion Friday morning. One of the staff was off sick all week and the program wasn't finished by quitting time on Thursday. Two of us worked Thursday evening until ten o'clock to make sure it would be ready on time. I missed the play but we met the deadline. I felt good about that. Besides the pay is good, I make $13,000 a year and I meet many nice and interesting people. I really can't complain, but that three weeks vacation this summer really looks good to me."

Harold Miller, advertising designer

Hal Miller works for an advertising firm in the city of Chicago. In the past ten years since graduating from Illinois Community College with an Associate degree in design he has worked for three different companies in three different cities—Peoria, Illinois, St. Louis, Missouri, and now Chicago. Hal considers himself a typical man on the "way up." As he explains, "As soon as I had a year's experience in my first job I began to look for something better. Each time I changed jobs I moved to a position with more authority and responsibility. And I might add, a better salary. Ten years ago I was making around $600 per month and now I'm up to $14,500 a year. I'm not finished either. Right now I'm beginning to send letters to advertising firms in New York City. Of course, it's a lot more difficult to break into the New York firms. In advertising that's where it's at and everyone wants to go there. Sometimes just thinking about the competition frightens me. But it's exciting and I'll make it sooner or later. I just have to keep working here and trying to build up the proper reputation."

Hal and his wife Maryanne, recently purchased a new home in a fashionable section of the city. "It's a bit more than we can afford," he confessed, "but I look upon it as a kind of investment. I frequently entertain company officials and prospective clients from out-of-town and the house provides a suitable environment. You would be surprised how important it is to make the right impression on prospective advertisers. I also do a lot of my work right here at home. I would guess that I work on the average around twelve hours per day. Sometimes more, sometimes less, but I always bring a couple of hours of work home with me." According to Hal much of his success is due to his willingness to work longer and harder than others who work with him.

The Millers have not taken a true vacation in the eight years they have been married. Two vacations they spent moving from one city to another. One year Hal's company conducted a large advertising campaign during his scheduled vacation. Hal felt he should be a part of the campaign, so he took his vacation one day at a time that year. The company showed its appreciation by awarding him a substantial bonus at the conclusion of the campaign.

Maryanne doesn't complain, but Hal knows she thinks he works too hard. During the interview she remarked several times, "I know that Hal really enjoys his work but I do wish he could get away from it for awhile. We have taken several week-end vacations but it's almost impossible to get him away from the office for more than four days at a time. But, of course, it has paid off in advancement. Look at us now. We have a lovely home, two cars and our children are well-dressed. Eight years ago when we were married we had nothing. Besides, we won't always have to work this hard. Once Hal gets that position in New York we can slow down a little.[10] Then we'll get that vacation and Hal can spend a bit more time with the children."

Charles O. Finley, insurance executive

Charles O. Finley operates a Chicago based insurance firm, named after him. "Charlie O," as he likes to be called, also loves sports. During the spring and summer he runs his championship baseball team, the Oakland A's. In the fall and winter he's concerned with two other professional teams he owns, the Memphis Tams of the American Basketball Association and the California Golden Seals of the National Hockey League. Today Charles O. Finley is worth well over one million dollars but he wasn't always wealthy. In the following article Finley discusses what work means to him and outlines his formula for success.

Charlie Finley is an unconventional folk-hero. A shrewd, industrious businessman, he's known to the public as probably the most flamboyant and unpredictable sports magnate on the American scene. His zany promotions brought fame to the A's—a ragtag aggregation he picked up in 1961 when they were playing in Kansas City—before anybody took them seriously as athletes.

To get people to pay money to see them, he ran a "Bald-Headed Day" and a "Hot Pants Night." He put on sideshows like greased-pig chases and cow-milking contests. He promised every man on his team a $300 suit for growing a moustache, thus making the A's the most hirsute ball club since the Gay 90's. He got rid of the traditional white and gray uniforms, and garbed his minions—the hockey and basketball squads as well as the baseball players—in bright green and gold.

"They're a good pick for Charlie," mutters one detractor. "Both of them are the color of money."

For all his far-flung sports and insurance interests, Charlie O. has been a confirmed Midwesterner for 40 years. Born in Birmingham, Ala., on Feb. 22, 1918, he came with his family to Gary, Ind., at the age of 15. During World War II, he tried to enlist in the Marines, was turned down because of an ulcer history, and took a job as an ordinance plant foreman in nearby La Porte.

Finley's work in a defense plant lasted through the war, but while he was there he developed a lucrative sideline in selling insurance. Finally, he went into insurance full time, setting a sales record in his first year with the

[10]Do you think the Miller's will ever "slow down a little?" Why, or why not?

Travelers Insurance Company. But also at the end of that year he landed in a sanatorium with a case of pneumonic tuberculosis. Although he'd been an ace insurance man, he hadn't written a policy on himself. His wife had to take a job with the local newspaper, the *Gary Post-Tribune*, to support the family.

"The 27 months I was confined changed my philosophy of life," says Charlie Finley. "I was determined not to die . . . I'd gone down from 160 to 97 pounds during my illness, but I walked out of that hospital weighing 209 pounds. Today I keep my weight around 180.

"The illness turned out to be a blessing in disguise. I learned two big things the average person doesn't learn. First, if you have your health and your happiness you have everything in the world. Money is secondary.

"People say to me, 'Yeah, you can say this now because you've made your money.' But I say all you have to do is to lose your health or your happiness and you'll find out what a poor man you are."

"The second thing I learned is that the most beautiful things in life are free–literally free–the air, the sunshine, water, flowers, friends, love–I mean the happy-marriage kind of love."

Also while in the hospital, Finley was struck by his discovery that most doctors carried no health insurance of their own. When he came out after his long siege he and Shirley, operating out of their home, began contacting professional medical organizations to sell them group insurance. The climax came in 1962 when he landed a contract with the American Medical Association. Today premiums from Finley's insurance business amount to $43 million a year.

In building his insurance empire, Charlie O. says he followed a simple, sure-fire formula: S + S = S.[11]

"It stands for 'Sweat plus Sacrifice equals Success,'" he explains. "I preach it to my ballplayers and my children. I had it engraved on the World Series rings I made up for the team members.

"If any one will pay the price for success, he can attain it. But the price is high. You have to do more work than your competitor, and sacrifice some of your competitor's enjoyments.

You ask a thousand young people about success, and you'll find that 95 per cent of them have only desire. Desire is in the head. The other 5 per cent have determination. And determination is right here." And Charlie places his hand over his heart.

Finley's success has been reflected in the growth of his beloved farm. It started out at a relatively modest 300 acres, but has quadrupled in size with the buying up of two adjacent farmsteads. Charlie keeps a herd of steers and raises enough grain "to feed the cattle and pay the taxes."

Showing a visitor around the farm, Charlie is especially proud of the warm, cozy "family room" that he added to the original house, built in 1931. The room, which has its own separate kitchen, was designed by Shirley,

[11] Do you agree with Finley's formula for success? Why, or why not?

whose talents extend to oil-painting and who has had exhibitions in La Porte and Chicago.

Charlie, who runs his insurance and sports operations firsthand, usually manages to get to the La Porte farm over weekends, on holidays, and for special occasions. "I don't spend as much time there as I'd like," he says ruefully. "My wife will tell you I'm like a bad penny—I'm liable to show up anytime."

Shirley spends most of her time in La Porte where, in addition to supervising the farm and family, she's involved in a variety of community affairs. She's especially active as a fund raiser for the community's charities. Largely through Charlie's and her efforts, La Porte has a new Salvation Army building. Remembering his long bout with illness, Charlie served as national chairman for the National Tuberculosis Association in 1961, raising a record total for that time.

When the Oakland A's won the pennant last season, Shirley and the whole family (except for Sharon, who was pregnant) traveled with Charlie to the playoffs and the World Series games. No "board of directors" ever rooted harder.

During the tense seventh game of the Series, with the score tied in the ninth inning, Charlie O. turned to Shirley and said: "Listen, baby, if we win this game, as soon as it's over I'm going to pick you up and stand you on that dugout and give you the biggest damn kiss you've had since we got married."

That's just what he did, right on national television. As far as Shirley Finley is concerned, he can do it again this year.

For thought and discussion

What can be done to increase the job satisfaction of both manual and non-manual workers in America today?

Individual and small group activities

1. Arrange a tour for yourself and several of your classmates to visit a number of offices or corporations where you might eventually seek employment. Prepare a list of questions about the job conditions, opportunities, salaries, etc., to ask employees during the tour.
2. Prepare a collage showing some of the occupations engaged in by recent graduates from your school. Your school's employment counselor can help provide you with accurate information.
3. Prepare a typed letter of application and a resume outlining your experience and educational preparation for a job of your choice. Ask your English instructor to examine it and make suggestions for revisions. Your finished copy will serve as a useful guide when you begin to seek employment.

Urban social structure

Assignment 7

In every American school, college, or university certain students seem to receive more praise or admiration than others. These "in" students belong to the elite of the school. Class officers, outstanding athletes, and honor students often have more influence and receive more respect from teachers and peers than typical students do. You would probably have little difficulty in classifying the student body of your college into groups. You could rank students into higher, middle, and lower classes.

This type of organization, known as social stratification, exists in nearly all American institutions. In some organizations such as the Army, certain religions, and the police department, members wear symbols or insignia so that all will know their rank order. One's position is clearly defined. In other organizations, outsiders might have difficulty detecting the system of stratification. Nevertheless it exists. In corporations, for example, executives receive more respect, authority, privileges, and greater salaries than do secretaries. In turn secretaries receive greater respect than office boys. The executive, the secretary, and the office boy all play a particular occupational role which the corporation ranks according to its perceived importance of the role. Sociologists call this ranking of roles into different levels status. Assignment 7 deals with status and social classes in American cities.

Social class in America

In American society some roles receive high status while others are given lower status. Bank presidents, doctors, and national politicians usually receive high status, while the skid row wino and the tramp are placed at the bottom of the status ladder. This ranking, of course, varies from nation to nation. In some societies, for example, educated people and the elderly receive higher status than they do in the United States.

An analysis of the American urban community suggests that many large stratified groups exist in the city. These large groups known as social classes share many things in common and are classified by other members of the community as belonging together. Sociologists frequently disagree on exactly how many classes exist in American society. Some list only three American classes while others place the number as high as nine. But all agree that social classes do exist.

If you attempted to rank students within your own college, you would probably notice that personal qualities, such as friendliness or athletic ability, played an important part. Recent sociological studies have noted that in small towns personal qualities such as family background, length of residence in the community, or membership in local clubs play an important part in determining one's social standing. Urban social classes, however, are usually rated along more impersonal lines. One group of sociologists feel that the following six items represent the most important criteria in determining social class in urban societies:

1. *Income:* How much is there and from what source is it derived?
   Although, in general, the rich have greater status than the poor, source of income is an important factor. A doctor with a medium income receives more status than a millionaire who heads a crime syndicate.
2. *Occupation and skill:* How much skill and learning is required by an occupation?
   In an occupational prestige rating, Americans ranked lawyers above accountants. They believed that practicing the law required more skill and learning than did accounting.
3. *Education:* Amount of schooling and type of school attended.
   Among urban Americans, college graduates receive greater prestige than non-college graduates. Whether a person graduates from a well-known private college or from a newer public institution also influences prestige.
4. *Residence:* Place of residence and type of housing.
   Urban residents who live in the zone of higher cost homes generally receive greater status than those who live in the zones of medium or low cost homes.
5. *Authority in the community:* How much influence does a group or person wield in the community?
   Influence or power is best measured by the number of persons' lives which an individual affects. Such power may be direct, by actually occupying political office, or indirect, through pressure which can be applied to politicians.
6. *Life style:* How much does an individual's life style reflect the accepted values and customs of the society?
   In general a hard-working medium income businessman receives more status than a wealthy playboy.

No single item in the above list determines the social class of a particular individual. Usually all of these factors combined form the basis of judgment. Finally, at certain times other criteria, such as religion and place of birth, help to determine a person's social class standing. For example, at one time many Irish Catholics found themselves at the bottom of the social scale no matter what other characteristics they possessed. Today most Americans no longer consider religion and place of birth as important characteristics which determine social class.

Five urban social classes

Pages 80–89 of Assignment 7 contain a graph and five photographic essay's. Each series of pictures in the essays depict the roles and activities of five urban social classes. Examine each set of photographs carefully to determine the nature of the American urban social class system. To help you organize your thoughts construct the following chart. Arrange the chart into five vertical columns, one for each social class, ranging from the lowest to the highest. Along the left-hand margin, place the following categories: Income, Education, Occupation, Residence, Type of Social Activities, and Life Style. As you examine each set of photographs write a sentence or two for each of the above categories. You may not be able to discover information about every category. When you have completed the chart write an essay of several paragraphs describing the social classes of urban America. The following questions should assist you in completing this assignments:

1. What criteria seem to be the most important in determining a person's social standing in America? Why?
2. How do people's social class seem to influence their life style?

In 1971 approximately sixteen million families lived within the boundaries of cities in the United States. The bar graphs below show the distribution of income among inner city black and white families. Each graph is divided into five sections corresponding with the five sets of photographs on pages 80–89. As you examine each set of photographs refer to these graphs to determine approximately what per cent of each urban social class falls within each income group? Remember that income is not the only determinant of social class.

Figure 7.1
Per cent of inner city families in each income group, by race - 1972

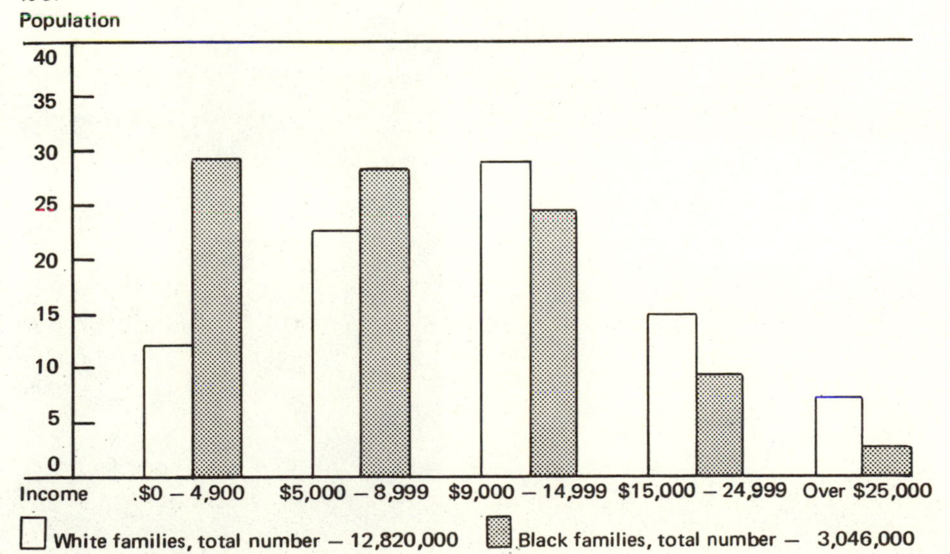

Table 7.1
PICTORIAL ESSAY
Social class A–1974 monthly budget for urban family of four

Item	*Amount spent*
Food	$232
Housing and utilities	$240
Transportation	$ 88
Clothing and personal care	$110
Medical care	$ 56
Other family consumption	$ 62
Savings, ins., contributions	$ 90
Personal taxes	$123
Total per month	$1001

1

2

3

4

Table 7.2
Social class B—1974 monthly budget for urban family of four

Item	*Amount spent*
Food	$466
Housing and utilities	$678
Transportation	$231
Clothing and personal care	$346
Medical care	$137
Other family consumption	$444
Savings, ins., contributions	$753
Personal taxes	$1,125
Total per month	$4,180

1

2

3

4

5

Table 7.3
Social class C—1974 monthly budget for urban family of four

Item	*Amount spent*
Food	$112
Housing and utilities	$110
Transportation	$ 38
Clothing and personal care	$ 15
Medical care	$ 34
Other family consumption	$ 22
Savings, ins., contributions	$ 14
Personal taxes	$ 34
Total per month	$379

1

2

3

4

Table 7.4
Social class D–1974 monthly budget for urban family of four

Item	*Amount spent*
Food	$292
Housing and utilities	$365
Transportation	$114
Clothing and personal care	$160
Medical care	$ 59
Other family consumption	$103
Savings, ins., contributions	$124
Personal taxes	$240
Total per month	$1,457

1

2

3

4

5

Table 7.5
Social class E–1974 monthly budget for urban family of four

Item	*Amount spent*
Food	$180
Housing and utilities	$138
Transportation	$ 49
Clothing and personal care	$ 78
Medical care	$ 56
Other family consumption	$ 34
Savings, ins., contributions	$ 68
Personal taxes	$ 57
Total per month	$660

1

2

3

4

5

Social structure in American cities

An understanding of the criteria for determining social classes in America tells us much about our system of values. You probably discovered, for example, that in American society one's occupation and income seem to play the most important roles in assigning status. This conclusion suggests that Americans seem to value these elements over such things as education or age. Social classes, however, do not tell us how the population is distributed. Suppose, that only a few of the workers in the five social classes you examined fell within the three middle classifications. Moreover, suppose that nearly 70 per cent of urban workers belonged in the lowest classification. We could then say that a few people in the society controlled most of the wealth while most of the population lived in poverty. If we were to diagram this type of social arrangement it would resemble a pyramid. ▲ Other social structures consisting of a large number of wealthy families with few poor or middle class families might resemble an inverted pyramid. ▼ Some exclusive American suburbs fit this model.

In general, social structures of larger cities in the United States have different shapes than the structures of smaller towns. The largest cities contain greater numbers of upper and lower class people. The bar graph you examined on p. 79 contains information about both white and black inner city social structures. Reexamine the graph and construct models representing each social structure. Then answer these questions:

1. In your opinion which model represents the most favorable social structure? Why?
2. Considering what you know about urban spatial distribution and social class, how do you account for the differences between the two racial groups?

For thought and discussion

What effect does educational opportunity for all have on class structure? How much opportunity exists in urban America for individuals to move upward from one social class to another?

Individual and small group activities

1. Draw up a list of occupations familiar to people in your community, and ask residents to rank them on a scale of status. Then construct a graph for your classroom bulletin board showing the occupational structure within your community.
2. With a small group of your classmates, make a collage depicting the diverse social classes which exist in your community. To insure accuracy in your representation first determine the percentage of families in each income group by consulting the current U. S. Census, "characteristics of the population," for your community. The number of pictures for each social class on your collage should roughly approximate the existing social structure.

People in city and suburb

Assignment 8

Before 1950, the United States Bureau of the Census classified any place with a population of more than 2,500 persons as a city. This classification presented several serious problems as cities grew in size. Classifying a place with over one million people in the same way as a small village of 2,500 people seemed to make little sense. Moreover, the many small communities which border large American cities often remain independent only in a political sense. Most of these surrounding communities and their residents are in reality an important part of the larger city.

To eliminate this confusion, the Bureau of the Census began in 1950 to use the term Standard Metropolitan Statistical Area (often called SMSA) to describe cities of at least 50,000 residents and those heavily settled areas surrounding them. For example, in 1970 the city of Atlanta had a population of 497,000, but the population of the Atlanta SMSA was 1,390,000; Detroit's population totaled 1,511,000 while the Detroit SMSA reached 4,200,000.

The suburban portion of the SMSA's grew dramatically during the decade of the 1960's. By the end of the decade, for the first time in the nation's history, the people living in the suburbs outnumbered those living in central cities. Moreover, the data revealed by the 1970 census suggests that white Americans leaving the central city contributed heavily to this suburban growth. Between 1960 and 1970 the white population of suburbia increased by nearly 19 million while the black suburban population grew by only one million.

People who live in the suburbs are similar, in some respects to those who live in the central city. Many suburbanites work and shop in the central city. They often commute to the city for entertainment and educational activities. In general they think of themselves as belonging to the city. Recent studies, however, suggest a number of important differences between people who live in the city and those who live in the suburbs. The materials in Assignment 7 will help you to explore the similarities and differences between the city and suburb.

Who lives in the suburbs?

Considering your own urban area make a list of the similar and different characteristics between the city and its suburbs. Then use the data on the following pages to test your list.

Table 8.1
1971 urban and suburban family population—by race

Location of families	*White*	*Black*
Central cities	13,000,000	3,000,000
Suburbs	19,000,000	900,000
Rural areas	15,400,000	1,200,000

Which area, the central cities or the suburbs, contains the greater racial imbalance?

Table 8.2
1972 educational attainment of urban and suburban residents
(25 years of age or older)

Grade attained	*Urban residents*	*Suburban residents*
Less than 4 yrs. high school	42.8%	34.3%
High school graduate	33.3%	38.5%
College –1–3 yrs.	11.0%	12.6%
College –4 or more yrs.	12.8%	14.5%

Which area contains the greater percentage of college trained residents?

Table 8.3
1971 ownership of real estate and personal property

Item	*Urban*	*Suburban*
Home ownership	49.0%	70.0%
One car	67.7%	87.9%
Two cars	20.8%	39.5%
Color t.v.	38.6%	51.6%
Washing machine	60.9%	80.0%
Colthes dryer	33.6%	57.5%
Freezer	20.0%	32.2%
Dishwasher	17.1%	30.5%
Central air conditioning	13.7%	16.1%

In which area do the residents appear to be more affluent?

Figure 8.1
Distribution of income in suburbia, by race—1972

(For urban-suburban differences compare this chart with the urban income distribution chart, Figure 7.1, Assignment 7.)

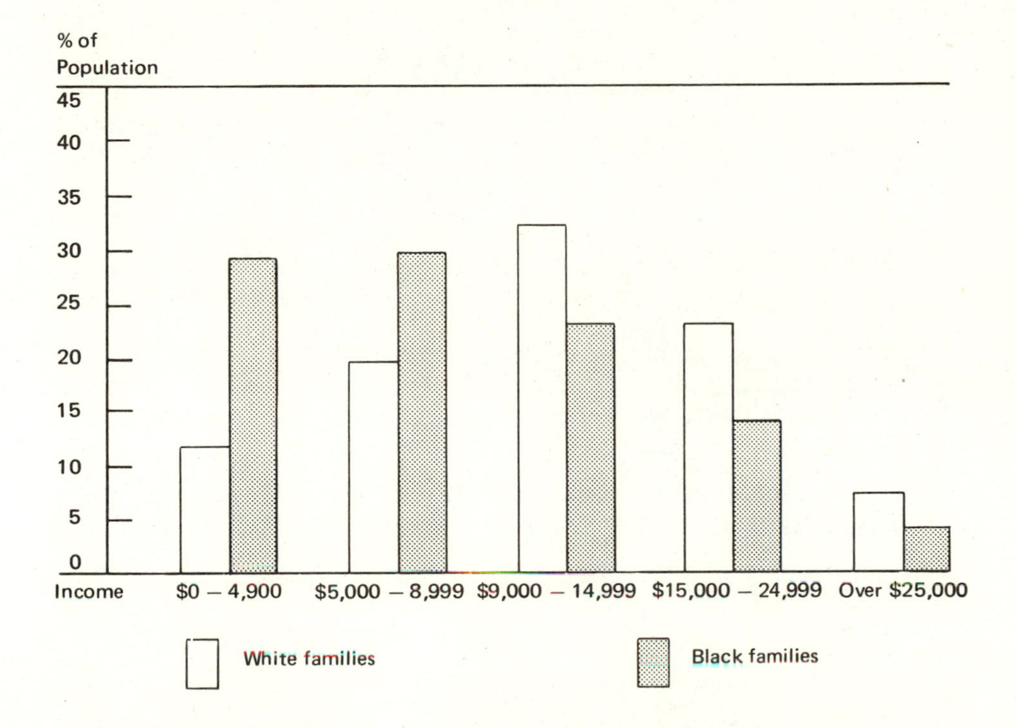

Which group of suburban residents, white or black, contained the greater percentage of poor persons?

Suburban life styles

Many critics of the American suburb complain of its sterility and lack of diversity. They see suburbia as a world of split level and ranch houses, backyard barbecues, station wagons and conservative political views. In 1962, Malvina Reynolds captured this stereotype of suburbia with the following words from her song "Little Boxes":

LITTLE BOXES

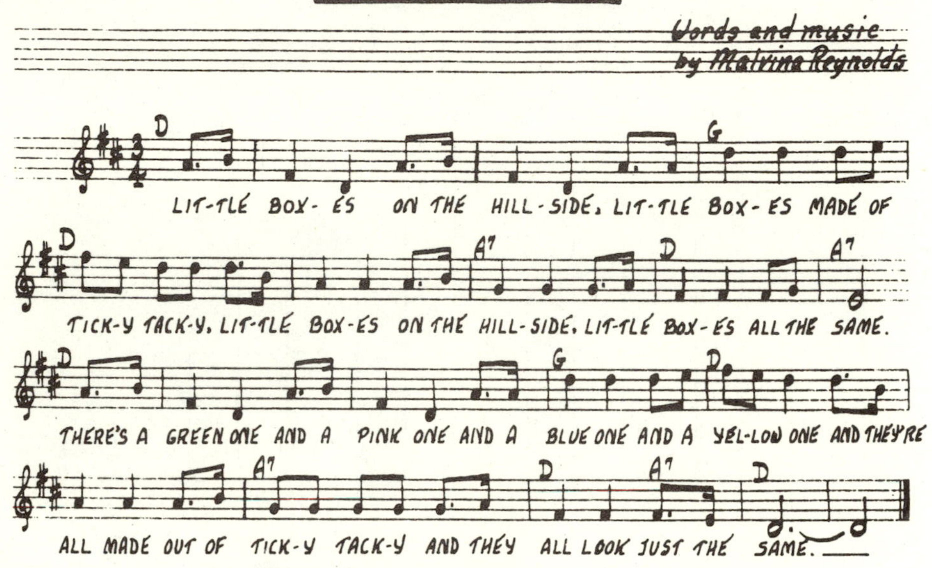

2. And the people in the houses
All went to the university,
Where they were put in boxes
And they came out all the same,
And there's doctors and lawyers,
And business executives,
And they're all made out of ticky tacky
And they all look just the same.

3. And they all play on the golf course
And drink their martinis dry,
And they all have pretty children
And the children go to school,
And the children go to summer camp
And then to the university,
Where they are put in boxes
And they come out all the same.

4. And the boys go into business
And marry and raise a family
In boxes made of ticky tacky
And they all look just the same.
There's a green one and a pink one,
And a blue one and a yellow one,
And they're all made out of ticky tacky
And they all look just the same.

Nine years after Malvina Reynolds wrote "Little Boxes" the stereotype of suburbia continued to exist. W. B. Park drew the following cartoon depicting a "typical" suburban dweller for *Look Magazine* in 1971.[12]

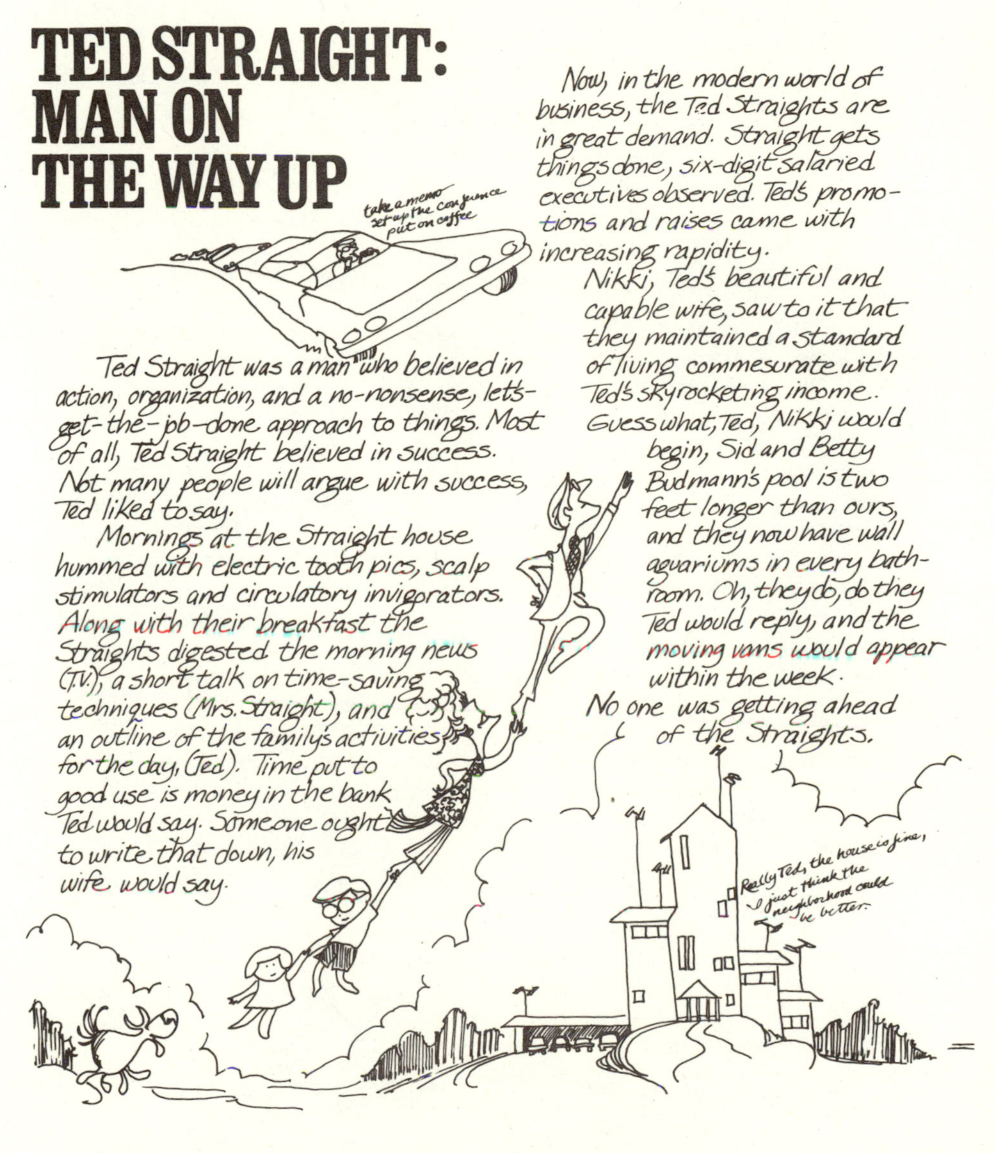

[12]Do you think the Straights were happy? Why, or why not?

The only ill-fitting, non-productive cog in the Straight machinery was the dog, Fuddles. The animal was unbelievably devoid of coordination, energy, obedience, and all the other virtues Man has come to expect of his Faithful Companion. Fuddles not only CAN'T, angrily cried Mr. Straight after an attempt to teach the dog discipline and useful skills, Fuddles WON'T! The dog has no desire to improve, he said, staring severely at the embarrassed animal. Several days later, over the passionate objections of the children, Fuddles was given to a family which lives in the country, where Fuddles will have lots of room to run and play. Of course, we'll go and visit Fuddles. Stop crying.

Time passed, and the Straight's fortunes continued to rise. They graduated into the multi-residence concept, and went from two to three to four cars. The children's playthings were hydroplanes, air-jet pogo sticks, and a four-foot robot they named Milhous. Ted and Nikki amused themselves with weeknight jet hops to various restaurants around the world. Work hard, play hard, Ted always said.

Life was good to the Straights. Maybe it was too good. Haven't we dined here before, Nikki asked Ted one evening as they sipped saki in Tokyo. Not another 200 pound teddybear, Ted's daughter pouted one Christmas morning. Deep sea diving bells were in last year, not this year, her brother Larry explained with impatience on his 12th birthday. A deadly sameness was creeping into their lives, and Ted began to notice it in his work. Every thousand dollar bill has the same picture on it, he would say.

One night, as they sat at dinner, mechanically picking at the gourmet food, one of the children asked, Does anyone remember Fuddles? Fuddles. How could anyone forget Fuddles, asked Mrs. Straight fondly. That ridiculous dog certainly had its own lifestyle, said Ted, more than a shade of admiration in his voice. Soon everyone was happily recalling all the absurd things Fuddles used to do. I loved Fuddles, Lem said. Couldn't we get Fuddles back, begged Larry.

But it was just too late—they had gone too far. They all knew that happy, playful foolish loveable Fuddles could never ever fit into the world of the Straight's.

Fuddles was a loser.

Text and drawings by W.B. Park

Four American suburbs

In 1971, the same year that Park produced the caricature of "Ted Straight, Man on the Way Up," Time Magazine *sent correspondents to four American suburbs with instructions to observe and report on the life styles of these communities. The reading selections on* *pp. 97-103* *describe each of the four suburbs. As you read these accounts determine the following:*

1. Do any or all of these communities fit the picture or life in suburbia presented by Malvina Reynolds or W. B. Park? Which ones? In what ways?
2. Turn to the list you developed of similarities and differences of urban and suburban dwellers. Revise or modify your list where necessary in the light of the evidence presented in these accounts.

Leawood, Kansas

More than a decade ago, a bridge over a ravine carried heavy traffic outbound from Kansas City to Leawood and points west. Then the bridge collapsed under the weight of a truck. Though insurance money was available, the bridge was never rebuilt. The street now stops at one edge of the ravine, then starts on the other; it takes a two-mile detour to get across.

That is the way they like things in Leawood. A local editor and publisher, Tom Leathers, says that he has been trying for years to get West 95th Street, one of the main thoroughfares, widened. "It's inconvenient and dangerous even for our own people," he says, "But I haven't made any headway. It's as though they think improvements would bring in a lot of riffraff from Kansas City . . . After their day's work in K. C., the people of Leawood obviously want nothing more than to come home to their handsome houses in their manicured suburb and slam the door. They might as well put up a sign reading Private–Keep Out.

Some of the houses in Leawood are more than 40 years old, but the town only began to blossom in the late 1930's when the Kroh Bros. real estate company undertook a major development. Now there are nearly 11,000 residents in just over 3,000 houses–ranch-styles and split-levels with a good sprinkling of two-stories. The lawns are spacious, and there is often a paddock with two or three horses gamboling about. Some of the original houses that once sold for less than $25,000 would probably be worth twice that today; newer houses range from $65,000 to $125,000–and up.

About 90 per cent of Leawood's working population, including a growing number of housewives, commute by car to Kansas City. They are heavily Republican, many of them professional people, lawyers and doctors. A majority of the newer, more transient residents are often-transferred executives of major U. S. corporations. In many cases, their company helps foot the homeowner's bill just for the prestige of having a Leawood address for its man in Kansas City. As soon as a family settles, the wife is recruited into the Leawood Welcomers Club; for the next two years she meets other newcomers and learns the local ropes along with them. The men join neighborhood associations that meet weekly or monthly to talk over questions like the status of garbage collections before they adjourn for a hand of cards.

Leawood has three Protestant churches (Baptist, Methodist, Presbyterian), one Roman Catholic church and no synagogues. Perhaps 3 per cent of the population are Jewish. There are few Black families. Once deeds in Leawood forbade resale to Negroes, Jews–or Arabs. Now Leawood gets nearly the same results by defter means: a local ordinance bars For Sale signs on houses, and Leawood brokers can easily avoid showing a house to someone they consider undesirable. Tom Leathers remembers that a couple of years ago, Bobby Bell, the Kansas City Chief's great linebacker, wanted to buy in Leawood. Bell is black. Leathers telephoned a member of the Kroh family and appealed with all the eloquence of a dedicated Chiefs fan: he was told that nothing was up for sale at the time, so Bell went elsewhere.

Of those who can and do settle in Leawood, Mayor V. M. Dostal says: "At least 85 per cent of them are the salt of the earth." Maybe so, but Police Chief Martin ("Jack") Kelly says that his two major problems are booze–with adults–and drugs–with kids. (Kelly is the only member of his 18-man force who can afford to live in Leawood, and only because he has a retired Army officer's pension on top of his salary.) Leawood's two country clubs have private liquor lockers for members, and things tend to get lively on Saturday night. The teen-agers face what everyone agrees is a serious drug problem, though it is probably no worse than it is, say, at Mamaroneck High School in New York's Westchester County or at New Trier East High School near Chicago.

There are other threats to the community. Because the suburb is so rigidly residential, it has no industrial tax base; one result is inadequate public services, including a wretched sewer system that would cost at least $1,000,000 to modernize. In a heavy rain the sewers back up into the prosperous residents' basements. In addition, there is what Mrs. Margaret Jordan, lawyer and city council-woman, calls "the spector of Tomahawk Creek Reservoir"–a proposed federal flood-control project that would create recreational facilities open to nonresidents. Another city council member puts the dilemna of Leawood's future neatly: "We know that change is inevitable, but we want to keep things the way they are."

Evanston, Illinois

Many Chicagoans talk of the suburb of Evanston as the straitlaced capital of the North Shore–national headquarters of the Woman's Christian Temperance Union, the stodgy bastion of proper matrons and upright WASP gentlemen . . . In fact, as City Planner Richard Carter says, Evanston is "a microcosm of a larger city, diversified in income, ethnically, racially and every other way." It ranks high in affluence: a $12,200 a year median income in 1968. Yet Evanston's 80,000 population includes over 1,600 on welfare, as well as top-salaried executives and professional men. The ethnic majority is still basically Northern European–English, German and Scandinavian–but there are Poles, Luxembourgers, Russians, Canadians, Armenians, Orientals, blacks.

The new ethnic groups have combined with another new kind of migrant to change Evanston from a Republican stonghold into a city, that Nixon barely carried in 1968, and Adlai Stevenson III won last November. Throughout the 1950's and 1960's, younger, activist families have moved in, attracted by Evanston's lack of resemblance to a caricature suburb. Nancy Sheck moved with her husband, a printing executive, and two young sons from Chicago's South Side to Evanston four years ago. "It is the only suburb that allows for individuality," she says. "There aren't the same pressures for conformity here. There are so many kinds of people and kinds of circles to choose from." Republican Alderman William Nott, 61, who represents established northwest Evanston, says scornfully: "These independents and liberals want to change things. I'll tell you that a lot of oldtime Evanstonians resent them."

The momentum of change built in Evanston until it nearly split the town in two last year. Evanston has a black population of 16 per cent; some are fourth-generation Evanstonians, descendants of Blacks who moved there as domestic servants a century ago. The blacks were at the center of a battle over school integration, allied with liberal whites behind School Superintendent Gregory Coffin's implementation of a plan to distribute blacks equally among the city's 16 elementary schools.[13] Coffin was forced out after integration was completed. Evanston's grammar schools survived, however, as a model of quality and racial integration.

One reason that black-white relations in Evanston are relatively calm is that the black community has a strong middle-class orientation. Its members like to boast: "In Evanston, the Black ghetto is black owned." But there is a growing black consciousness. "Blacks can't find a better place to live" than Evanston, says Mrs. Jesse Smith, a welfare mother. But she adds: "We don't want to be pushed down any more." Whites complain of black-white student friction in Evanston Township High School, and there is a tinge of race in rising local taxes. Says Alderman Nott: "Every year more services are demanded for the poor and the blacks. It seems there's no end to it."

State Farm Insurance Man Tom Martin, a South Evanstonian, says: "We don't have suburban problems here. We have big-city problems." They do: race, rising crime rates (burglaries up from 594 in 1969 to 842 last year), low-income housing, downtown business stagnation, taxes, traffic, student unrest of Northwestern (which has a 21-year-old black woman as student body president). Evanston's acting city manager, Edward Martin, 27, finds the scene far from dismal. "We have all the problems of a major city," he says, "but on a manageable level. I feel we're a great laboratory in that sense." One thing that helps enormously is the high level of citizen involve-

[13]Do you consider busing to achieve racial integration a positive solution to urban racial problems? Why, or why not?

ment in everything from antiwar rallies through school board meetings to Fourth of July block parties. "I like the fact that the town gets aroused over issues," says James Lytle, vice president of the State National Bank, which is housed in a 21-story building that looms large in Evanston's downtown business district . . .

Evanstonians consider themselves city dwellers: then again, they feel like suburbanites. Evanston is a city with the virtues of a suburb, or a suburb with the virtues of a city. Either way, it seems to be working.

El Monte, California

Even its defenders admit that El Monte is an eyesore, a blur of suburban sprawl 14 miles from downtown Los Angeles. Its boundaries meander without obvious aim or purpose. Tiny houses, usually stucco and rarely worth more than $30,000, are jumbled together with tacky businesses along its dismal streets. Some 70,000 people call it home, but only a city father could love it. "This is a lower-middle-class workingman's community," says City Administrator Kenneth Botts. Unnecessarily, he adds: "We will never be a Beverly Hills."

Within its 15 sq. mi., there is no college, no symphony orchestra, no art gallery, no country club, no good bookstore. There is one cinema. The bars run to beer, the churches to fundamentalism, there was a synagogue once, but it closed about ten years ago. Western music flourishes in popular nightspots like Nashville West. The stores are mainly cutrate (Crawford's: The Biggest Country Store in the World). The citizens for the most part are unskilled or semiskilled workers from the South and the Midwest. They find jobs in places ranging from the Clayton Manufacturing Co., a valve-making concern with more than 1,000 employees, to hundreds of small, ten-to twelve-man machine shops.

There are no Blacks in El Monte, in fact, Blacks call it "whitey's town." The prejudice against Blacks is unspoken, but it is well understood. During a public meeting, a former city employee spoke of their absence in the community; he was ignored by city officials and later privately chewed out by them. El Monte calls itself the first "all-American" community in Los Angeles County. Ironically, it is now fast becoming a Mexican American stronghold, with a Chicano population estimated at between 35 per cent and 50 per cent. There are increasing strains . . .

For the Mexican-Americans, El Monte is a step up out of East Los Angeles. Explains Richard Mendez, 31: "We moved here from East Los Angeles because it is a better neighborhood. Life is better here. The schools are cleaner. There is not so much trouble." For others, El Monte is a way station en route to something else. "We get them coming both ways," says Dick Naumann, 56, who runs a women's clothing store. "Those who are coming from other parts of the country and those who are leaving. Those who are going up in life and those who are going down." The transients move into cheap clapboard weekly rentals around gloomy Garvey Avenue, then land a job in one of the little machine shops. They stay a month or a year; some schools report a 100 per cent annual student turnover. "I don't live here, I exist," says Earl Vetter, 43, a machinist recently arrived from the East. "As soon as I find something I can afford I'm getting out."

For those who grew up in El Monte, the present scene is all a bit unreal.[14] Police Chief Orval Davis, a member of the force since 1938 remembers that there were only 3,600 residents and six policemen in El Monte when he was a rookie. (There are 77 cops today.) "Those are the people I identify with," he says. "Those are the people I know. We've grown so fast. I hardly know any of the new ones." Ray ("Tex") Rickerd, an oldtimer who owns the weekly *Mid Valley News*, does not think much of the newcomers. "To be honest, I wish most of them would go back where they came from," he says.

Despite its staggering growth, El Monte oddly manages to retain a smalltown atmosphere . . . The pace in El Monte is just a bit slower than in Los Angeles, the people are just a bit friendlier. Hands dirtied by honest work are still a badge of honor. Few people drink at lunch; television is the usual evening entertainment. The merchants run their own stores, and when they talk, city hall listens.

Much of the small town atmosphere is deceptive, however, The downtown mall area contains the local headquarters of the Office of Economic Opportunity's neighborhood action program, which is pressing for low-cost housing over old-line opposition. On the 1st and 15th of every month, long sad lines of weary mothers and scraggly children stand on the street all day to collect food stamps. The young are displaced persons in El Monte. "There is nothing to do here," says goodlooking Tina Chassi, 25, "If I go out on a date, we go out of town."

Some El Monte residents moved in to stay, and they look at it as a place to put down roots. Joseph Hermes, 50, an insurance salesman, found in the late 1950's that a house that would cost $20,000 in the San Fernando Valley went for $5,000 less in El Monte. "I like the people here," he says. "I think they are good. They work hard." He has only one complaint: "They are used to being kicked around a little bit, so they don't take as much interest in the city as they should."

East Orange, New Jersey

On the map on the ground, they mix into patterns of dense urban settlement on the rim of the New York Metropolitan area—Newark and East Orange and Orange and Maplewood and Irvington and Bloomfield and Glen Ridge. There are no green belts, no distinct borders; instead, there are parkways, railroads, and political boundaries that may run through the middle of a block. Main Street in East Orange becomes Main Street in Orange, and except for the

[14]What, if anything, can communities do to prevent physical deterioration?

change in house numbers, one town melts into another. Near the center of East Orange is a giant cross formed by the interchange between the Garden State Parkway and still incomplete Interstate 280. "Crossroads of New Jersey," they call it. Some crossroads.

East Orange has many faces: the tree-lined streets and substantial houses of the well-heeled First Ward, the old, rundown frame houses of the Fifth Ward, the modern apartment buildings that tower over both. The citizens of East Orange lead parallel but unlinked lives. Some 55 per cent to 60 per cent of them are black, and black-white contacts are guarded. "I have the feeling that people don't quite trust one another," says Mrs. Dorothy Scull, a school board member. But there is more to their isolation from one another than race. Many of the homeowners feel that the high-rise dwellers take little interest in the community. Says one white housewife: "Sometimes I get the impression that the only thing they are interested in is their personal safety—more street lights, getting from the front door to the parking lot in one piece." The lines also divide have from have-not, black middle class from black working class.

"I can still have breakfast in my own backyard," says Mayor William Hart, 45, who is black. "In that sense we are not the city. But we are just a few bricks removed from it." For many of the blacks, East Orange has been the first step out from the city, from Newark or New York, a reach for a suburban hinterland of open space and green grass and fresh air. Once it was that for wealthy whites. Long before World War II, it was a gracious, self-contained suburb with some mansions, imposing apartment buildings, a Baptist seminary, and Upsala College.

Most of that changed after the war. Black families moved in, looking for better housing and better schools. Whites drifted away toward the shore or to the mountains, either because they felt uncomfortable among the newcomers or because their houses were now too large to manage. For short periods, parts of town were integrated, but in the long run blocks with some black families almost invariably went entirely black. The white middle class thinned out: The black middle class moved in. The racial ratio in the schools changed quickly: 21 per cent black in 1952, 49 per cent in 1962, around 90 per cent today. Most white children switched to private or parochial schools if their parents chose to stay in East Orange.

The schools are short of classroom space, and there is a drug problem among the young—though no one agrees on its proportions. Several East Orange High students have been hospitalized with drug overdoses. Says Mayor Hart: "What's hurting is that the children have little in terms of recreation. There is no swimming pool, no bowling alley, no dance pavilion, no roller-skating rink." The housing shortage is acute. Some 800 families are on the waiting list for public housing. Construction of single-family houses is almost at a standstill—partly because the city's property tax rate is among the highest in the state.

Once, branches of elegant New York City stores lined Central Avenue;

now East Orange has little to offer its residents commercially. It has no shopping center of its own. The people of East Orange do their business either in New York or Newark, or at the shopping malls and plazas that have sprung up in other suburbs. Central Avenue is not dead, but it is decaying.

Despite its problems, East Orange has quite a bit going for it. It is compact, if overcrowded. Unlike neighboring Newark, it has a history of capable, efficient government. It has a stable white and black middle class. There are some extreme views on both sides of the racial fence, but tensions are far lower than in some other Jersey towns—a fact that the mayor attributes to East Orange's high percentage of homeowners. It is still a town in search of itself. As one white resident put it: "We haven't had soul here in 20 years." East Orange used to be middle-to upper-class, Staunchly Republican, predominantly white; now it is middle-to lower-class, Democratic, predominantly black. Says Mayor Hart: "This town can go up or down. What we need is money, resources. We have the people—good people who will back you when you call them."

For thought and discussion

What, if anything, should be done by city leaders to reverse the flow of affluent middle-and upper-class citizens to the suburbs.

Individual and small group activities

1. Prepare a questionnaire dealing with current political, social, and economic issues. With a group of your classmates administer the questions to a group of urban and suburban residents. Then compare the results. In what ways are they alike? Different? Report your findings to the class.
2. Write a poem, a song, or draw a cartoon for the class bulletin board depicting how you feel about either the city or suburbia.

City government in action: A case study

Assignment 9

Each day throughout the United States city governments make hundreds of decisions which directly or indirectly affect our lives. Most people feel that local government should provide services that individuals can not provide for themselves. Few of us, for example, could provide our own education, parks, or fire and police protection. We rely on our government to do these things for us. City governments must, therefore, make decisions about education, utilities, highways, public welfare, health care, sanitation, urban renewal, parks and hundreds of other things. All of these services cost money. In 1972 New York City alone spent more than seven billion dollars to provide needed services to the people of the city. Obviously city governments must make hundreds of decisions about budgeting and taxation. How are these decisions made? For example, what factors cause a government to support one project and not another? Assignment 9, *City Government in Action*, should help you analyze decision-making in one large American city.

Forms of city government

Three forms of city government exist in the United States to make and implement decisions. They are the mayor-council, the commission, and the council-manager. Nearly half of all cities in the United States use the mayor-council form of government.

Adopted from the English model of urban government, the mayor-council consists of an elected mayor and an elected council. The council, usually made up of from five to twenty members, makes decisions and passes laws. The mayor, at least in theory, is the chief executive. The mayor appoints the heads of the various departments, such as fire, police, and sanitation, and executes laws enacted by the council.

Mayor-council governments fall into two groups depending upon the powers of the chief executive. They are the "strong-mayor" type and the "weak-mayor" type. In the strong-mayor form, the mayor's administrative powers dominate the council, making the council a legislative body only. A strong council controlling most of the administrative as well as legislative power characterizes the weak-mayor plans. Nearly all large urban governments use the strong-mayor plan.

The commission form of city government provides for a board of five to seven commissioners, the only elected officers of the city. They hold responsibility for making and carrying out the laws of the community. In addition, each commissioner serves as the head of one major administrative department. One commissioner usually serves as mayor but he exercises no more power than the other elected officials.

The council-manager form of city government includes an elected council, usually five to seven persons, and an appointed professional city-manager responsible to the council. Under this plan the council makes all the laws. The city-manager chooses the department heads, supervises their activities and makes recommendations to the council. Many small cities use the council-manager plan because it provides the services of a professionally trained expert to run the day-to-day activities of the city.

Political scientists who study urban governments know that despite different governmental forms, each city's political system can be analyzed in similar ways. In Assignment 9 you will examine the decision-making process in one major American city. Some of the concepts used by political scientists will help you to analyze this decision.

In previous assignments you used concepts from geography, economics, and sociology to examine aspects of city life. Your ability to use political science concepts will enable you to analyze political systems in your own as well as in other cities. The concept of decision-making will guide your analysis of the political system in Pittsburgh in the 1970's. As you examine each of the readings in the following pages you should attempt to answer these three analytical questions.

1. What are the formal and informal rules for making decisions?
2. What factors help shape the decision?
3. Who are the decision makers? (What are their characteristics, beliefs, attitudes and skills?)

As you read each article in Assignment 9 keep a set of notes answering each of the above questions. Your notes should include specific evidence to substantiate each answer. For example, you might say that public opinion plays an important role in shaping the decision. As evidence you could note that article five said that 5,000 citizens signed a petition to support a particular position, and the governmental body subsequently adopted that position.

Skybus: A political decision

Since World War II the city of Pittsburgh, like most other American cities, has faced serious transportation problems. Lacking a system of subways or rapid transit, commuters in or out of the city brave long, tiresome traffic jams each day.

In 1964 in an attempt to improve public transportation Allegheny County authorities—Allegheny County surrounds the city of Pittsburgh—consolidated 33 independent bus companies into one county wide system known as the Port Authority Transit or PAT. Commuters, however, continued to shun public bus transportation in favor of private automobiles. By the mid-1960's most Pittsburgh transportation experts agreed that only a system of rapid transit traveling along private roadways could solve the city's transportation dilemma.

The articles which follow illustrate the complex nature of decision-making in the modern urban metropolis. Some decisions made by city governments involve only the city council and the mayor. Major urban questions, however, frequently demand participation by a number of governmental bodies and other interested parties. For example, the Pittsburgh decision to experiment with an above ground type of rapid transit, skybus, involved city, county, suburban, and national governments as well as private corporations and municipal authorities. As you examine each of the following accounts of the skybus decision use the three analytical questions listed on page 105 under the concept of decision-making, as a foundation for your analysis. You may think of additional questions to put to the data.

An innovation in rapid transit

On December 11, 1963 Westinghouse Electric Corporation announced plans to test and develop a completely automated, electronically operated overhead mass-transit system. According to the developers, this plan, if successful, could revolutionize modern urban mass transit. Assisted by a $2,872,000 grant from the federal government, the Pittsburgh based firm constructed a two mile experimental roadway at a county park near the city. On September 1, 1965 county fair visitors received their first look at the new transportation system. In the following account a *Pittsburgh Post-Gazette* staff writer described the first voyage of skybus.

The Skybus
in operation

The Skybus works!

The experimental railway in South Park proved this yesterday as Westinghouse Electric Corp. officials demonstrated their $5,000,000 creation to newsmen.

The Skybus will be in full-time operation beginning tomorrow as visitors at the County Fair will be taken for rides—at 10 cents a head—around the two-mile track circling the fairgrounds.

Although the Skybus had proved its operability in earlier test runs, there was momentary doubt yesterday whether the official maiden trip would be a success.

Doubts arise. The doubt arose as the shiny, aluminum and glass car, instead of smoothly picking up power and speed, jerked hesitantly out of the station along Corrigan Drive.

In about 50 yards the car drew to a near halt, but Robert Sedlock, Port Authority technician who was at the controls, jiggled a few levers and the car surged ahead at normal speed.

The difficulty was later traced by John K. Howell, project engineer, to an open power connection in the computer control center. Howell pushed one button and the trouble was eliminated.

Once en route, the rubber-tired car provided a smooth, silent ride which was marred only by the slight side-to-side swaying motion common to trains and trolleys.

Raymond H. Fields, manager of the Westinghouse transportation systems department, assured the passengers that this motion would be eliminated by adjustments in the guide rail between the two concrete wheel tracks.

"We didn't have enough time to smooth the ride out—good as it is," Fields said.

All-weather tests. Shortly after the Fair ends, Fields said, the system would go on full computer operation and would be open to the public on weekends through the winter to test all-weather operation.

The major question to be answered now is: Will the system sell itself to cities interested in establishing rapid transit systems?

Fields said the response to date was enthusiastic and that a Westinghouse system similar to the Skybus would soon be in operation at the Tampa, Fla. airport.

"There has been worldwide interest, from Rome, Mexico City, South America, Sweden, and Australia," he said. "As soon as we flash the signal they'll be here to see it." (Sept. 1, 1965)

City and county officials support Skybus

Following a two year period of experimentation the Port Authority of Allegheny County, PAT, proposed to install a ten mile $60 million demonstration skybus system to run from the center of the city of Pittsburgh to a southern suburb. If the system proved successful the Port Authority hoped to eventually construct a sixty mile, $739,000,000 system to serve all sections of the city and county. At first the decision appeared to be a simple one authorized by a branch of the county government, the Port Authority. On September 20, 1967, the county commissioners and the former mayor of the city of Pittsburgh, Joseph Barr, issued favorable opinions on the plan.

It's "Go" on Skybus

Dr. William D. McClelland, chairman of the county commissioners, said yesterday that the proposal to build an experimental Skybus from Downtown into the South Hills is "worthwhile, logical and will probably necessitate a tax increase."

Dr. McClelland was joined by Mayor Joseph M. Barr plus Democratic and Republican public office seekers in wishing the $60 million proposal well.

The recommendation to build the second-stage Skybus and to temporarily set aside all current studies on a rapid transit system for the entire county was outlined Monday by Leland Hazard, chairman of the Port Authority's rapid transit committee.

Leonard C. Staisey and Thomas J. Foerster, Democratic candidates for county commissioners, summed up their feelings over the new Skybus project in a joint press release.

"We consider rapid transit a major key to expansion and we hope to see Allegheny County become the nation's headquarters for the rapid transit industry," they said.

Study time important. "After it has been presented to PAT's board of directors and we have had time to study it, we will comment further. However, if the federal government will pay the bulk of the cost, we certainly favor it in principle."[15] (Sept. 20, 1967)

Opposition to Skybus

Immediately after the announcement by the Port Authority, opposition to the Skybus demonstration proposal began to form. Between 1967 and 1969 various suburban groups and one county commissioner, Dr. William Hunt, used various methods to block the South Hills proposal. The following articles illustrate the methods used to delay the Skybus proposal and suggest the specific complaints of the dissident groups. While all of these articles are negative in context they play a crucial part in the decision-making process. As you read these articles continue to answer the analytical questions listed in the introduction to Assignment 9.

[15]Should the federal government use taxpayers' money to support urban rapid transit programs? Why, or why not?

Suburbia demands information

The Port Authority Transit's proposed Skybus experiment slated for the South Hills met with opposition from suburbs yesterday . . . .

David Horvath, a member of PAT's advisory committee, said he had been instructed by the Allegheny County Supervisors Association to ask for a delay of the Skybus proposal.

Horvath said he, as a member of the advisory committee, had never been consulted about any planning regarding rapid transit.

He said the only thing he, and a lot of those he represented, knew was what they had read in the newspaper.

"There are a lot of unanswered questions," he told the board members.

Horvath said unless boroughs, townships and cities in Allegheny County are consulted "you are going to have a difficult, if not impossible, time getting support."

He was critical of the sudden stoppage of two rapid transit studies with the announcement of the Skybus proposal, asserting the people should be told why they were stopped.

Leland Hazard, chairman of the Rapid Transit Committe, told Horvath he "will be glad to sit down with somebody and talk this thing out." Horvath said, "We will take you up on that." (Sept. 29, 1967)

Hunt blasts PAT's plan on transit

County Commissioner Dr. William R. Hunt vowed yesterday that the county commissioners will give no blanket approval to a $150 million "early action" transportation program recommended by the Port Authority Transit (PAT) last month.

Hunt called cost estimates of the program—designed to supply the Greater Pittsburgh area with a fare-producing Skybus into the South Hills plus paved bus rights-of-way to the south and east—"a pie in the sky."

"They have been underestimated by 50 to 100 per cent," he said.

The GOP minority commissioner ripped portions of the program following a closed meeting between the commissioners and PAT's board of directors yesterday afternoon.

"They suggested that we not discuss what was said here," said Hunt, "but I think the taxpayers have a right to know what's going on."

Besides cost estimates of the program Hunt attacked the plan to send the Skybus underground after it reaches the Downtown area . . . .

"They are talking of building a $10 million station which in itself is too expensive," he said. "This is supposed to be an experiment."

$30 million to tunnel. The station, he said, would mandate the demolition of two buildings. He added that it will cost $30 million to tunnel the Skybus from Market Street to the courthouse but only three million to do the same thing on or above the ground.

Hunt said he thought the Skybus could run along the river fronts without destroying the setting of the Downtown area.

Hunt said he thinks the Authority is trying to "do too many things at the same time . . . ." (Sept. 6, 1968)

Public hearings

In repsonse to the public opposition to the Port Authority's Skybus plan, county officials conducted the first of three public hearings on the controversy. For three days during the month of August, 1969, political candidates, city, county and suburban government officials along with other interested parties all presented opinions. The following articles summarize these conflicting opinions.

Peter H. Flaherty, Democratic city councilman and later mayor of the city of Pittsburgh

"Whatever the background reasons are for this commitment I am realistic enough to believe that nothing is going to change the plan already on file in Washington."

Flaherty gave his scathing attack—along with seven suggestions—as the commissioners concluded the first of three days of hearing into mass transit . . . .

"One of the questions I must raise," Flaherty said, "is that regardless of the sincerity and executive ability of the PAT board they are not people oriented to and do not adequately represent the values of the people of the city of Pittsburgh or of Allegheny County."

He noted that two-thirds of the PAT members are tied to the Pittsburgh corporate community and added:

"Their tone is not one of 'the public be damned' but rather 'we know best.'"

One of Flaherty's suggestions to the commissioners was a further expansion of the board so taxpayers would be truly represented. The PAT board was increased by four members last year. (August 21, 1969)

Frederick J. Close, member of PAT and ALCOA board chairman

"Why are we here? What brings us together in common concern? That great philosopher Yogi Berra said it well: 'If you don't know where you're going, you sure as hell will end up in some other place.'"

The hearings are not only about rapid transit. Close said: "What we are really seeking is to improve the quality of living for all who call this their home."

Close recalled his childhood in Highland Park where, he said, the gas lights had to be turned on at noon because of the smoke.

His father made him carry drinking water in a bucket from a long distance, Close said, because he distrusted tap water.

Pittsburgh solved these problems and can solve its transit problem, he said, "But we have to get excited. We have to move. If we fail, what will our children say when they bury us?" he asked. (August 23, 1969)

Mrs. Donald B. Bierwerth, chairman of the county council, League of Women Voters

"The argument about skybus has been primarily on cost with little attention to the benefits of a comprehensive rapid transit system or the economic penalty of no system."

Transit can stimulate new buildings, business, industries and revitalize declining areas, Mrs. Bierwerth said.

She also commented on what psychology professors call the decision-making process. "We are wondering how the city fathers of 1860 ever managed to decide to construct a horsecar line without getting bogged down over whether the cars should be drawn by black or white horses.

"After all," she said, "a black horse can be seen in the winter but doesn't take the summer heat too well." (August 23, 1969)

Joseph M. Barr, mayor of the city of Pittsburgh, 1962–1970

Mayor Joseph M. Barr also touched on these issues: "Whether job producers will seek to invest here in the future, whether people will choose to live here, whether we can even keep what we have in this county—all this may become an academic exercise unless we get a rapid transit system into operation here soon."

They were saying, in effect, that a city's rapid transit system can't be measured by its profit and loss. It should be considered the way good schools or a fire department are.

"I am prepared to endorse the Early Action Program today because I see great merit to PAT's proposals and because I see no realistic or more attractive alternative which is appropriate for this area," Mayor Barr said.

"I reject the notion that Allegheny County needs a rail system to handle its day-to-day commuter operations because it is a 'proven' technology or because 'other cities have it.' " . . . .

"I am convinced that if we are ever to succeed in luring people from their private autos—at least in their journeys to and from work—then we have to offer something more attractive than 'shake-rattle-and-roll.' "

Leonard Staisey, chairman of the board of county commissioners

"Isn't the real question, not which system is cheaper, but which one can compete successfully with the automobile? Its rider-pulling power is the crucial question." (August 23, 1969)

The opposition mounts

The public hearings over the Skybus controversy apparently settled few questions in the Pittsburgh metropolitan area. Following the hearings the Board of County

All of the pictures on this page illustrate characteristics of political decision-makers. Which characteristic do you consider most important? Which one is least important? Why?

Commissioners voted two to one to proceed with the construction of the demonstration project into the South Hills. The Pittsburgh City Council also voted to approve the project. The dissenting county commissioner, William Hunt, was joined by the newly elected mayor in his opposition to Skybus. In February of 1970, Commissioner Hunt demanded that the question of Skybus be placed on that years ballot to be voted on by the citizens. A majority of the commissioners ignored this request.

The County, meanwhile, proceeded to hire contractors to begin construction. Skybus was to become a reality! or so it seemed. On September 21, 1971, six years after the announcement of the successful Skybus experiment, Mayor Flaherty began new moves to block Skybus. As you read the following account determine whether the Mayor is using formal or informal methods to influence the Skybus decision.

The Mayor attempts to block Skybus

Mayor Peter F. Flaherty apparently is prepared to do everything that he can to block Skybus from entering the City of Pittsburgh . . . .

In doing so, the mayor has put his administration on a collision course with City Council, Allegheny County Commissioners Leonard C. Staisey and Thomas J. Foerster, and the Port Authority of Allegheny County.

It is a situation that has been developing for more than a year and during the summer reached the critical point. It can add tremendously to the cost of rapid transit and delay or even prevent its achievement . . . .

Right now, Flaherty holds the upper hand, through city ownership of property, or certain rights to properties, that the Port Authority must have in order to bring rapid transit into the city. The Flaherty administration simply has ignored Port Authority requests for the transfer of those properties or property rights.

On June 2, Robert McKenzie, real estate manager for Port Authority Transit (PAT), wrote Stephen A. George, then director of the city's Department of Lands and Buildings, requesting deeds for whatever rights the city may have within the old Wabash tunnel through Mt. Washington . . . .

The city so far has ignored the request. Nevertheless PAT has received a low bid, for renovation of the tunnel. The contract may be awarded this week.

On Sept. 2 PAT announced the purchase of 63.7 acres of land, in Bethel Park and Upper St. Clair township, for $2,605,000, for the erection of a Transit Expressway Car Storage Building, a maintenance building and the South Hills Village Station.

PAT's determination to go ahead and the mayor's determination to stop the program may make Pittsburgh the only city in the nation whose transit stops at the city line.

On June 28, McKenzie wrote to Samuel Marsh, acting city engineer in the Department of Public Works, requesting the vacating of two streets, in the vicinity of the Monongahela portal of the tunnel.

"The Port Authority is in the process of acquiring 100 per cent of the adjoining property," McKenzie wrote, "I would appreciate it if you could start the necessary procedures in order to vacate these streets."

So far, that request has been ignored; no "yes," no "no," no answer.

But in the interval between the two requests, and without addressing himself to them specifically, Mayor Flaherty made his position quite clear, in a letter written June 24th.

"In view of the fact that the proposed Early Action Program is unacceptable to this community, it is folly to insure further costs or to attempt to implement the project," the mayor's letter said. (Sept. 21, 1971)

The mayor takes action

On November 11, 1972, in an attempt to get the Skybus project moving the Pittsburgh City Council approved, by a seven to one vote, two bills decided to supply the Port Authority with land along the controversial transit system. The mayor vetoed the bills, but council overrode the veto. Prior to the initial vote the mayor pleaded for more than an hour with council. He asked council to deny the land to the Port Authority. The following article illustrates the position of the mayor and the tactics he employed to halt the Skybus project. As you examine these articles determine what formal or informal methods he used to influence the decision.

Arguing that neither council nor the public has been given the true facts behind the Early Action Program, Flaherty attacked the Skybus basically from an economic viewpoint. He said the system, if it is built, could cost as much as a half-billion dollars—almost 100 per cent more than the projected $228 million price tag for Skybus and the rest of the program.

He added that he didn't think the Skybus would meet the transit needs of Allegheny County and called it the "slowest alternative" to mass rapid transit in the Pittsburgh area.

He also charged that use of public money to "experiment with the Skybus constituted a shirking of responsibility on the part of elected officials for their constituents."

"You're in effect subsidizing another SST," said Flaherty to the council members. "The costs [of Skybus] are tremendously out of proportion."

To support his claims, Flaherty used some of the Port Authority's own studies and reports in hammering away at alleged economic drawbacks of the Skybus.

He quoted from a preliminary engineering report done by the Westinghouse Electric Corp. in 1970 which put a $2.8 million price tag on rehabilitation work for the two tunnels that Skybus will need to get into the city—the Penn Central and the Wabash.

He then reminded the city lawmakers that the Port Authority since then has signed a contract for the rehabilitation of the Wabash Tunnel alone with the cost now at $4.5 million.

He then referred to the Port Authority's progress report which asserted that an updated cost analysis of the entire Skybus project would be performed by Kaiser Engineers—the company receiving millions from the authority to perform the final design work for the Skybus.

"You're not being told what the updated costs are," he said. "The public is still under the impression the project will cost $228 million. PAT itself must know that figure is wrong. Not only because it's old but because they have Kaiser involved."

The mayor charged PAT with being "afraid" to show the public any updated costs for Skybus for fear that a complete cost analysis of an entire rapid transit program would create the need for a referendum. "And they know the referendum might lose," he added.

In summing up this plea to council to refuse the Port Authority access to the tunnel, Flaherty told council members:

"I know you're going to get heck for it. I know that this thing is being steamrolled. But remember, we represent the guy who elected us."

When Flaherty had finished, Councilman George Shields moved that the two ordinances be given committee approval and his motion was seconded and passed by a seven to one vote.

The final act?

The decision by the Pittsburgh City Council once again appeared to remove all road blocks to the construction of the Skybus demonstration project. The majority of the county commissioners and the city council agreed that the project should proceed at once. However, two months later Mayor Flaherty, dissenting County Commissioner Hunt and twelve suburban borough and township mayors filed suit in the Allegheny County Court of Common Pleas to prevent the building of Skybus. Judge Anne X. Alpern granted a temporary injunction until the court could hear arguments for both sides. Following a two month hearing in which more than 8000 pages of testimony were recorded Judge Alpern ordered a permanent injunction against Skybus. The forces in opposition to Skybus had won this important round. Ten days later, however, the supporters of the project asked the State Supreme Court to provide the final answer. On January 20, 1973, the Pennsylvania State Supreme Court returned its decision on Skybus. The final step in this long complex decision-making process was completed.

When you have completed reading the results of the Supreme Court case complete your list of formal and informal rules for decision-making. This list should assist you in analyzing the process of decision-making in your own class in the exercise on p. 117.

The state Supreme Court yesterday put Skybus back on the track by overturning a lower court ruling that had halted further spending on the $228.5 million Early Action Program in Allegheny County.

The decision, released simultaneously here and in Philadelphia, was 6-to-1, with Justice Michael J. Eagen dissenting.

The Supreme Court ruling was handed down one year and nine days after Mayor Flaherty, minority County Commissioner Dr. William R. Hunt and 12 suburban borough and city mayors filed the "stop-Skybus" lawsuit.

The 26-page opinion was written by Chief Justice Benjamin R. Jones.

It invalidates the Allegheny County Common Pleas Court permanent injunction issued by Judge Anne X. Alpern, and it means that the county may proceed with the Early Action Program, including a 10.6-mile Skybus line and two bus-only Patways.

Justice Jones' opinion stated that the plaintiffs had waited too long to start legal action after Port Authority Transit (PAT) and the county commissioners already had spent or had committed themselves to spending millions of dollars.

The Supreme Court reversed Judge Alpern's decision in three basic areas, ruling that:

Neither PAT nor the county commissioners abused their discretion in planning the transit system and approving the Early Action Program.

Westinghouse Electric Corp., which developed the Skybus, was not guilty of any conflict of interest by serving as a systems manager in Skybus development in a contract with PAT which expressly allowed Westinghouse to compete in later bidding on the Skybus line.

PAT was not required by the Port Authority Act to submit to the county commissioners an amended plan of an over-all transit operation before they launched the Early Action Program. (January 20, 1973)

For thought and discussion

You have just examined the long and often frustrating process of decision-making in the city of Pittsburgh. Based on the arguments presented by Pittsburghers in Assignment 9 can you think of any other ways to implement this decision that would have avoided the long and costly delays.

Individual and small group activities

1. Observe a meeting of your city council to analyze the decision-making process in your own community. Are decisions based upon evidence presented at the council meeting or do councilors appear to have reached their decisions prior to attending the meeting? If the latter is the case interview a councilman or the mayor to determine how they arrive at their decisions. Your instructor may wish to have you report your findings to the class.
2. Write a letter to the editor of your local newspaper either protesting a decision or urging action on some issue which you feel strongly about.

The dump game—town of Middleboro (Optional Exercise in Decision-Making)

The town of Middleboro has a rubbish disposal problem. Until now, everyone has taken care of his own trash, with the result that the town lands, the marsh, the quarry, pond, stream, beach, and forest have become quite littered, polluted and unattractive. The store areas are dirty and infested with rodents. Individual burning of trash is becoming a health hazard.

Money has been appropriated for the construction of a town incinerator. A town meeting is to be held to decide where it will be built, and its location must have the approval of a majority of three-fifths of the members of the community.

Each member of the class should assume ownership of one of the properties lettered A to Z (the dairy, golf course, garage, lumberyard, or gas station) or represent the school or the church. Keeping in mind your own interests as property owners, determine the best location for the incinerator.

After each property owner has selected a site for the incinerator, a town meeting will be held to determine whether the residents can agree upon a single solution. Agreement by three-fifths of the property owners is necessary for a decision.

At the conclusion of the simulation you should answer the following questions:

1. What were the formal and informal rules for arriving at your decision?
2. What factors helped shape the decision?
3. Who were the decision makers?
4. What similarities, if any, do you see between the decision-making process used in this simulation and that employed in the city of Pittsburgh? What differences?

Figure 9.1

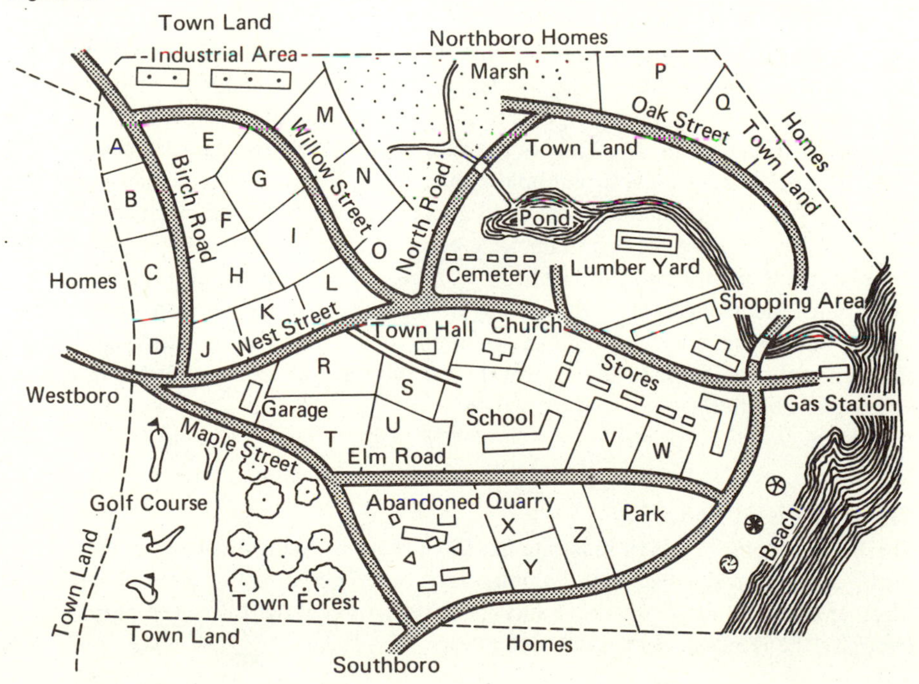

The urban citizen: Rights and responsibilities

Assignment 10

Citizens in urban America have many rights. They also have a number of responsibilities. For example, the Constitution of the United States guarantees all adult citizens the right to vote in local elections. On the other hand, urban residents must pay taxes to support the activities of their government. Not all rights and responsibilities are as obvious as voting and paying taxes. Political scientists, lawmakers, and concerned citizens often disagree about whether a certain activity is a right of a citizen or an obligation to be fulfilled.

Assignment 10 examines three kinds of rights, and the responsibilities implied by these rights, in urban America. Social rights refer to the welfare of members of a community. These rights include the right to a free education and a minimal standard of living. Social rights also imply certain responsibilities including respect for the property of others and willingness to obey school attendance laws. Political rights refer to one's right to influence the actions and make-up of government. They include the right to vote and hold public office. Political responsibilities include working for the candidates of one's choice and accepting the results of free elections. Civil rights refer to certain basic personal freedoms such as freedom of the press, freedom of assembly, and freedom of speech. Civil responsibilities implied by these rights include respecting the privacy, religious beliefs, and opinions of others.

The cartoons and readings in Assignment 10 will help you to classify activities as social, political, or civil and help you to clarify your own values about your rights and responsibilities.

Three kinds of rights

The five cartoons on p. 119 illustrate the three types of rights discussed in the introduction to this assignment. Examine each one. Then in your notebook indicate whether each cartoon represents a social, political, or civil right. In a sentence or two, give the reasons for your decision in each case.

JOIN
WOMENS
LIBER-
ATION!
AMENDMENT
32
32
FREEDOM
NOW
NOW
VOTE ★ VO
VOTE!

Making a choice: Rights or responsibilities

The remaining part of Assignment 10 contains a number of case studies about the rights and responsibilities of urban Americans. As you read these studies, determine whether each one deals with a social, political, or civil issue. Then answer the questions which preceed each case study.

The right to life: Obligations of citizens

At 3:25 A. M. on the morning of March 13, 1964, a man attacked 28 year old Catherine Genovese as she returned from work to her New York apartment. He stabbed her. She screamed for help and the man fled. Twice in the next half hour the man returned to stab her. Her calls for help went unanswered and she bled to death on the sidewalk. Investigators found that at least 38 of Kitty Genovese's neighbors heard her screams, but none of them helped her or even bothered to call the police. The article which follows contains the explanation of one neighbor. As you read his account try to determine the answers to these questions:

1. What rights did Catherine Genovese have?
2. What were the obligations of her neighbors? Did any of them fulfill those obligations? Were the neighbors justified in not coming to her aid?

Later, in one of the apartment houses, a witness to part of Kitty Genovese's murder talked. His comments–agonized, contradictory, guilt-ridden, self-excusing–indicate the price in bad conscience he and his neighbors are now paying. "I feel terrible about it," he said. "The thing keeps coming back in my mind. You just don't want to get involved. They might have picked me up as a suspect if I'd bounced right out there. I was getting ready, but my wife stopped me. She didn't want to be a hero's widow. I woke up about the third scream. I pulled the blind so hard it came off the window. The girl was on her knees struggling to get up. I didn't know if she was drunk or what. She staggered a little when she walked, like she had a few drinks in her. I forgot the screen was there and I almost put my head through it trying to get a better look. I could see people with their heads out and hear windows going up and down all along the street."

The man walked to the window and looked down at the sidewalk. He was plainly depressed and disappointed at his own failure. "Every time I look out here now," he said, "it's like looking out at a nightmare. How could so many of us have had the same idea that we didn't need to do anything? But that's not all that's wrong." Now he sounded betrayed and he told what was really eating him. Those 38 witnesses had, at least, talked to the police after the murder. The man pointed to a nearby building. "There are people over there who saw everything," he said. "And there hasn't been a peep out of them yet. Not one peep."

Academic freedom

The two essays which follow present case histories of recent events at two urban high schools. In each case officials acted in behalf of the city's residents to prevent teachers from imposing their ideas on students in the school. As you read each article try to determine which teacher, if either, violated any rights or failed to carry out the responsibilities implied by these rights. Then answer these questions:

1. What obligations do teachers have to their students? To the community?
2. Do you agree with Mrs. Foxe's statement "the teacher has the right to decide on what's significant and what she teaches in her area?
3. Should either teacher have been fired? Which one? Why, or why not?

A history teacher at Southwestern High School yesterday was forbidden to show a pacifist film strip on war to four of her classes. "I don't think parents have the slightest conception of the way teachers are controlled," declared the teacher, Mrs. Juli Foxe.

Mrs. Foxe met yesterday morning with city school officials but declined to discuss details of the meeting before a conference next week with Dr. Laurence Perkins, city school superintendent.

Mrs. Foxe said she was prevented from showing her students a film strip on American policy in Vietnam which was produced by the Student Nonviolent Coordinating Committee, a civil rights organization, and which was distributed by the American Friends Committee, a pacifist group associated with the Quakers.

"I don't see why anything should be swept under the rug," she argued. Mrs. Foxe, a 28-year-old graduate of Goucher College, has a teaching degree from the Johns Hopkins University and has taught history in Baltimore public schools for 7½ years.

Mrs. Foxe said she returned from her meeting with school officials yesterday morning to find Robert DePaul, head of the history department, teaching her class. He had not shown the film strip that she had scheduled. Mrs. Foxe said Mr. DePaul told the class that "we don't want students to be swayed by radical opinions." He explained the class could view a film strip prepared by a local newspaper which supported United States government policy but could not watch a film offering dissenting opinions.

"The first two classes were really incensed," Mrs. Foxe declared. She said they asked when they could "run down and scream and complain?"

Mrs. Foxe remarked that she doubted many teachers would speak out openly for freedom in the classroom. "There's a great deal of fear about losing your job," she observed. She said she was hesitant to discuss her plans with the school administration "because I felt anything I suggested would be rejected."

Commenting on restrictions on teaching, she stated: "The teacher has to decide on what's significant and what she teaches in her area."

* * *

John F. Kennedy High School was located in one of the liberal, integrated suburbs which on rare occasions are found outside our major cities. The people of the area were largely middle to upper middle class, 70 per cent white (many Jewish), doctors, lawyers, professors, and executives; and they prided themselves on being socially concerned, active in liberal Democratic politics, contributors to progressive causes, and readers of *The New Republic* . . . .

JFK High reflected the attitudes and concerns of the parents. The teachers were liberal in outlook, the student government had considerable influence over rules and discipline, and a student Bill of Rights was established and respected. A progressive structure prevailed at JFK—a wide variety of electives, examinations given only at the discretion of the teacher, most courses graded on a pass/fail system, standing permission for students to leave campus when they had no classes, and outside projects permitted as substitutions for regular course work.

And into this little haven of bliss (as most residents saw it) walked Hamilton Calhoun. Calhoun had taken over half the sections of the state-required senior Problems of Democracy course when the regular teacher left to care for her invalid father. Because he was obviously intelligent and had an excellent educational background (Phi Beta Kappa and graduation with honors from Yale, similar honors in graduate work at Harvard), the school hired him as a permanent teacher. The principal felt that Calhoun's moderate, realistic conservatism would be a useful addition to a generally liberal-left faculty.

Students found Hamilton Calhoun's tendency to lecture lengthily on abstract political points a bit stupefying, and a number squirmed under the biting questions which always seemed to buttress his own views, but many respected his grasp of history and vigorous intellect. However, few appreciated his insistence on an A to F marking system and his refusal to "dilly-dally" with outside projects.

After his third year at JFK, Calhoun shifted strongly to the right in his political, social, and religious views. Always a stickler for discipline in his classes, he became a regular policeman in the halls; spontaneous noise, roughness and gaiety fell to a dignified murmur in his presence. Many students (and faculty, at their monthly meetings) heard his lectures on the lack of responsibility and discipline among modern youth. Problems of Democracy became, much to the dismay of students, a combination of American history and political science. The teacher frequently drew lessons from history on man's "inherent rottenness" and corresponding need for strong authority . . . . An intense patriot, Calhoun damned a number of leaders and movements of the past forty years as subverters of American values, and he was particularly caustic about the civil rights, peace and youth movements of the 1960's. Conservative spokesmen were often invited to class, and most bulletin board displays came from conservative organizations and publications.

Class time was on occasion used to condemn the progressive atmosphere of the school; he found it detrimental to "real learning" and felt that students should be graded, examined, and disciplined in traditional academic subjects. Student rights and self-government were denounced as laughable for immature children who had little knowledge or self-control. Attacks on the "soft-minded" liberalism of teachers, administrators and people in the community won him the alienation of many on the faculty; he was frequently accused of violating professional ethics for his criticisms. Few confronted him directly, for his savage wit and systematic view of the world made him an opponent not easily bested in a public duel . . . .

Enraged parents, black and white, finally descended on the school in a fury of protest. Virtually all of them called for the firing of Hamilton Calhoun. . . . Even few conservative parents could be found to defend Calhoun—many were unhappy that their children were becoming too active and militant in the "right" causes.

The superintendent of schools, already disturbed by Calhoun's performance, was more than glad to avoid community rebellion by summarily firing the teacher. In his letter relieving Calhoun of his duties, the superintendent quoted the list of complaints in the petition as grounds for the termination of Calhoun's services. He gave as further reasons "your attacks on teachers, administrators and local leaders; lack of sympathy with the goals of the community; disregard for student feelings; over-dependence on the lecture method; general negativism about humanity; introduction of personal religious views; misuse of influence with students, causing them to disrupt the community; disruption of school activities; formation of an unauthorized campus publication; and your inability to conduct yourself with restraint and with respect for standards of civilized, orderly discussion."

A man's home is his castle, but what about his neighborhood?

The following article illustrates a dilemna present in many urban communities. As you read this account of a conflict over zoning and open housing, try to determine what you would do if you were in Al Langford's place. Answer these questions in your own mind:

1. Do Al Langford and the Community Protective Association have the right to prevent low-income groups from moving into their neighborhood? Do they have any obligations to these persons?
2. What are the rights of the low-income groups? Do you see any rights being violated in this account?

Al Langford grew up in the area of low-cost homes in St. Louis. His father had worked as a part-time janitor in a local department store. His mother stayed home and cared for Al's six younger brothers and sisters. The family never had enough money, and Al dropped out of school to go to work at the age of 16. When World War II came Al was one of the first in his neighborhood to enlist in the Army. He finished high school in the service. Following the War Al went to college on the G.I. Bill. All the while he helped to support his family and his new wife by working nights. In 1951, at the age of 28 Al graduated and accepted a job selling insurance in the St. Louis area. Today he is one of the top insurance salesmen there.

In 1968 Al and his family found their dream home in an all white suburb just 15 minutes from his office. The house cost more than the Langford's could afford but they decided it was too good to pass up. The neighborhood and the schools were perfect. As Al explains it, "All my life I wanted a home and a neighborhood like this. I was determined that my children wouldn't have to live in an area like I did when I was a kid. I hated it there. Now this new housing project might ruin it all."

The new project Al refers to is an application to the Zoning Commission to erect low-income condominiums within his subdivision. According to the contractor the condominiums will fit in with the existing architecture of the community. Al and a number of his neighbors formed the Community Protective Association to fight the zoning change. At a recent meeting in Al Langford's home, the Community Protective Association explained their opposition to the low-income housing. "We understand that these people need decent housing and we're not against the idea in principle. It's just that we object to what will happen to our neighborhood. Our school will become overcrowded because most of the people who move will have large families. Also we will need more fire and police protection, better sanitary facilities, and things like that. Who do you think will pay for these improvements? We will. People who live in low-income houses couldn't afford the taxes to support the added services. And what do you think would happen to the re-sale value of our homes if we let this project go through? Who do you think would give us a fair price then? Most of us have put our life's earnings in these homes. We have a right to expect a reasonable return if we decide to sell don't we? Really we wish there was some other solution. You can see our position, can't you?

Rights and responsibilities of voters

In the 1972 Presidential election less than 60 per cent of the eligible voters bothered to go to the polls. In most city elections less than half of the eligible voters cast a ballot for the man or women of their choice. The following account illustrates the results of such voter apathy. As you read this account try to determine whether the mayor's view of city politics is an accurate one. Then answer the questions listed below.

1. What are the rights and responsibilities of public office holder? Is "Big Jim" living up to these in your estimation?
2. Do citizens have the right to be apathetic? What responsibilities toward good government do citizens have?

Actually, the reason for the interview was to get material for a term paper on big city politics. But Jane looked forward to the visit for another, more personal reason. She smiled to herself as she thought back to the Sunday family dinners, to Uncle Jim's hearty laughter, to the glow of his undisguised love for children—a love which they had returned, just as openly. Jane wondered why Uncle Jim's visits had become less frequent, why people seemed to act with greater reserve when he was there. She assumed it was because they were all growing older and that age in some way was changing everything.

Now she was about to see Uncle Jim—"Big Jim" to the newspapers—in another world, his world of politics. She had no doubt it would be a visit she would long remember.

Big Jim Jackson also looked forward to the visit. He had always enjoyed the enthusiasm of his favorite niece. Next to battling in the jungle of big city politics Jim Jackson most enjoyed talking. He loved an audience—small or large.

He shoved aside some old campaign posters, ordered his assistant out of the room, and puffing fiercely on his cigar, turned to his niece. "Well, young lady, it's good to see you. I know you're here to find out about practical politics. So I'm going to speak 'straight from the shoulder.'

"Some people think that all political bosses are unpopular, even hated, and that they stay in power only because they're ruthless in dealing with the opposition."

This opening comment brought forth a look of astonishment from Jane. It was exactly the effect Jim intended.

"Well, isn't it true? Aren't all political bosses really just small-town dictators?" returned his niece, who had needed only a moment to recover.

"The trouble with so many of you college kids is that you don't know what makes people tick. You think a project on politics will teach you that? I learned it as a kid along the docks off River Street, where you had to act fast to stay alive. I learned about the carrot and the stick down by the waterfront when I was half your age. Haven't you ever heard about the carrot and the stick?"

"The stick? Do you mean the stick that some governments use to keep people under their control?"

"Of course! But you've ignored the carrot!" Beaming, Big Jim leaned back, studied the girl's face, and waited for the inevitable question.

"Are you saying, Uncle Jim, that bosses are popular, that they stay in power because they are loved and admired by the people, in spite of—"

"Did you ever see pictures of the crowds that came out to hear some of them talk?" asked the uncle. "Or what about the Communist bosses? Do you think the people were *forced* to come out? Or forced to cheer until they were horse? Or forced to hang the dictator's picture in their homes?"

"Well, weren't they?"

"That's one reason dictators are still in business," roared the uncle—"your fool notion that dictators use force and *only* force. Of course they use force, without hesitation, without concern for anybody's rights. But when a dictator resorts *only* to force, depends only on his secret police, firing squad, and his prisons, then that dictator's days are probably numbered, his time is almost up. You want examples?

The discussion was suddenly disrupted by the loud jangling of the telephone. Big Jim reached across the desk for it.

"Jackson speaking. Oh hello, Dan. How are you? Hmmm. Too bad. Well, you can get damages for that, you know. Sure. I'll be right over and tell you how to do it. O.K. That's all right. Always glad to help."

He put the receiver down and smiled across the phone at the girl. "Dan MacNamara just broke his toe getting on to a bus. Glad that happened. Dan hasn't been supporting the party the way he used to in the old days. He probably hasn't even been voting with us. This changes everything especially when I get him a good lawyer. Some of these people aren't in need of a job; they just want some good advice."

"Will you pay for the lawyer, Uncle Jim?"

"Sure. At least until the case is settled."

He spread his hand out. "I'll get it back and," he held up five fingers, "five votes too—his whole family."

"Is that what you mean by the carrot, Uncle Jim?"

Big Jim smiled, said nothing. His niece felt perhaps she had pursued the point far enough.

"You were saying, Uncle Jim, that the crowds were cheering the dictator because they wanted to, that there was no opposition—"

"I didn't say *no opposition.* There is always *some* opposition. But an able leader has ways of handling it—if need be, through the 'strong arm' of the law."

"And the rest are brainwashed?" asked the girl.

"Brainwashed sometimes. But more often, simply distracted."

"Distracted? Distracted from what?"

"Distracted from their idea of freedom. Distracted from democratic government. Distracted by something which looks very good, or which people need desperately," said the uncle.

"Like food?"

"Like food. Or highways in a place where there are none. Or hospitals. Or jobs. Or homes. *Anything*—as long as people want it badly enough." The uncle leaned back and waited for the next question, which he anticipated even before it was uttered.

"What's wrong with people wanting food, roads, jobs, and homes?" Jane queried.

"There's *nothing* wrong with wanting the things people need to lead comfortable lives. That's what governments are for—to help them get the things they need. A smart politician can help them do it faster—although the people may have to give up some of their personal liberties in the process. But if people are distracted or they don't know much about their democratic rights to begin with, they won't mind. Not even if the man in power muzzles the legislature, takes control of the press, and puts his brainwashing machinery into full gear."

At that very moment the girl decided to face her uncle squarely—come what may. She interrupted his thoughts with a question that had come to her mind earlier while he had been speaking.

"What about that bridge deal, Uncle Jim?" Jane had never really taken seriously the rumors about kickbacks and bribes in the Public Works Department. She had dismissed them quickly as part of the meaningless baggage of city politics. Now, for the first time, she was beginning to see the issue in a somewhat different light. "Is there any truth in those nasty rumors, Uncle Jim? People have been talking about it for some time."

"People always talk—but I don't mind. What counts is that they *vote* for me. They know me and I know them. I don't bother them with political arguments. If they need something I get it for them. They pay me back in votes. No nonsense. I try to make every man, woman, and child in this district think of Big Jim Jackson when they're in trouble. Then they remember me at the polls.

"So you build a superhighway for them, you get them jobs—"

Big Jim nodded. "What's wrong with that? I help them out. They want me because I see that they get jobs, that their rent gets paid, that they get legal advice if they want it—a thousand things that add up to what they need. You can't beat the personal touch."

"How about you, Uncle Jim? How far do you expect to go in politics?"

"As far as I can. As long as people here are willing to go along with me when I pat them on the head, see to it that they are well-fed, hand out jobs, and build a few highways—as long as they do that then I'll go running the place the *way* I think it should be run, and for as *long* as I want to run it. People know they can count on me to give them the kind of government they ask for."

To scoop or not to scoop

Like most other Americans, New Yorkers love their dogs, In fact, more than one-half million people living in New York City own dogs. Owning a dog in a city, however, presents a serious problem: What to do with dog litter? The Chief of New York's Environmental Protection Agency thought he had an answer. In May of 1972 he announced a new proposal requiring dog owners to pick up their pets' droppings or face a $25 fine. The article which follows illustrates the various reactions of New Yorkers. After you have finished reading the article. answer the questions listed below.

1. Do people who live in cities have a right to own pets? Does this right imply any obligations?
2. Can you think of any circumstances that might justify denying this right to city residents? What are they? What are the rights of non-pet owners?

To most nondog-owners, including Jerome Kretchmer [Head of the Environmental Protection Agency], whose own thing is turtles, the measure seems perfectly reasonable. But to those who will have to do the shoveling, it is outrageous, and they had turned out in force to show their opposition: groups with beautifully appropriate names like PAWS (Pets Are Worth Safeguarding) and DOG (Dog Owners' Guild) and, of course, the father of them all, Pet Owners' Protective Association (POPA), led by that old gentleman, Max Schnapp . . . .

In 1970, Max organized POPA to aid tenants who were being forced to get rid of their pets. "They would call me and say, 'Max, what should I do, I'm going to be evicted.' " And drawing heavily upon labor organizing tactics, Max would help them, either by negotiating with the landlord or, if necessary, packing a courtroom . . . .

Max's group was invited to speak at a meeting organized by the founders of the Dog Owners' Guild of Brooklyn Heights. Even before Kretchmer's legislation was announced, Robert and Sheila Angus had been disturbed by a local drive against dog dirt and, they feared, against dog owners. In an April letter to their local newspaper, the Anguses expressed their anxieties: "Like the Jews in Nazi Germany, we citizens, including the old and infirm, are to be humiliated by being forced to pick up excrement from the gutter." That night's meeting had been called as a defensive maneuver, and the speakers had been carefully selected for their prodog, antiscooping sentiments. "Let there be no mistake about it!" orated writer Cleveland Amory, who had made his debut at the April 26 meeting. "Kretchmer's scooping legislation is a carefully planned first step toward the banning of dogs from New York City!" . . . .

Other dog owners insist that cleaning up simply is not their responsibility; that's what the Sanitation Department is paid to do. But according to Sanitation Commissioner Herbert Elish, who owns a poodle, cleaning up after dogs is not the Sanitation Department's duty. "First of all, we are paid to clean the streets, not the sidewalks. Second of all, to clean up after dogs, we would have to sweep both sides of every street two or three times a day instead of twice a week as we do now. The cost would be astronomical." Well, what about flushing the streets once a day? "We did a study of that proposal last year and discovered that it would cost the city $18.5-million a year in additional equipment and manpower." And besides, should the dog dirt be flushed down the city's catch basins, the chances are good that it would proceed untreated right out into the river, whereas if it is picked up in plastic bags and placed in the garbage, it will probably end up by being used as landfill . . . .

At present, the Council seems evenly split, with the proscooping faction holding a slight edge. But even if the amendment does pass, the city will still be faced with the monumental problem of enforcement. It won't be easy . . . . In the beginning, the burden will fall upon the policemen, health inspectors and sanitation inspectors who are empowered to issue summonses.

According to Commissioner Elish, at least one sanitation inspector already takes the problem seriously. And when on a recent occasion he saw a well-dressed East Side woman allowing her pet to defecate on the sidewalk, he immediately approached her and began to write out a violation.

The woman became understandably flustered and, in her confusion, stepped back directly into the warm, soft deposit. At that the inspector flipped shut his book and said, "Lady, on second thought I won't give you a summons. I guess that's punishment enough."

For thought and discussion

Under what circumstances, if any, can you justify not fulfilling a social, political, or civil responsibility?

Individual and small group activities

1. How well do you know your rights? Suppose you were walking home one night when suddenly you were stopped by a policeman. Suppose the officer told you that you were being arrested for a crime committed earlier that day, and must go down to the station with him for questioning. What would you do once you got to the station. What legal rights do you have. Contact the American Bar Association or the American Civil Liberties Union in your city to find out what rights an arrested person has. Report your findings to the class.
2. Prepare a slide show, series of cartoons, or a collage illustrating how people in your city either exercise their rights or fulfill their responsibilities. Your instructor will inform you about how to present your information to the class.

First Day of May The Clarence J. Davies Collection, Museum of the City of New York.

INTRODUCTION to the unit on the walking city

Between 1830 and 1860 the number of cities in America grew dramatically. In 1820 the United States had only twelve urban centers of over 10,000 people. By 1860, 101 cities had a population of over 10,000 and in eight cities the population exceeded 100,000. Some of these cities such as New York, Philadelphia, and Boston were important because of their advantageous seaport locations. Other cities such as Pittsburgh, St. Louis, and Cincinnati began as trading centers and gradually established industries of their own.

Historians often call early American cities "walking cities." Most people lived within a short distance of work, school, church, shopping, and recreational areas. Thus the majority of people traveled by foot. Even with the spread of horse-drawn buses in the 1850's people continued to walk. Living close to work and the ability to cross one's city easily influenced the economy, residence patterns, and social and governmental interaction.

Assignments 11 through 15 explore the walking city. In Assignments 1 through 10 you used several social science concepts to examine the contemporary American city. These same concepts will assist your analysis of the walking city. Assignment 11 examines images of the walking city. Assignment 12 views the geographical relationships in city growth and focuses on the relationship between work and residence. Assignment 13 discusses the economy of the walking city. Assignment 14 explores difference social roles and relationships resulting from work and residence patterns and the economy of the walking city. Assignment 15 views the government of the walking city.

*

Images of the walking city

Assignment 11

In Assignment 1 you analyzed poems, pictures, and essays to determine images of the contemporary city. Most of the statements about the city were either very positive or very negative. These images of contemporary urban life evolved from attitudes toward cities developed during the period of the walking city. Just as your parents may influence your attitudes about life, people of one generation may influence the next generation's attitudes about cities.

The songs, photographs and travellers' accounts in Assignment 11 will help you to develop a general image of the walking city. Songs and ballads about the walking city represent popular feelings. These songs usually illustrate the positive and negative aspects of city life. Photographs and travellers' accounts, on the other hand, offer more specific descriptions of the cities. They offer evidence of why certain songs were popular. After you have developed general images of the walking city you will be able to compare these images with those of the contemporary city.

Songs of the walking city

Songs and ballads are sung for generations. They offer an easy way to hand down history and feelings. The following two songs represent popular attitudes towards the walking city. As you read these songs answer the questions below.

1. In what ways are the images of the cities, portrayed in these songs, alike?
2. What advantages and disadvantages of city life do these songs express?

New York, Oh What a Charming City

Bow'ry, in Broadway, he rambl-d'd up and down.
In by-way, and odd-way, resolv'd to see the town;
And as he went he sang this song:
"Now isn't it a pity
I should have stay'd away so long
From such a charming city."

New York, New York, oh what a charming city,
New York, New York, oh what a charming city.

Here freedom and duty and truth and joy remain.
Here honor and beauty and love and valor reign,
And ev'rywhere he went he met the grand, the gay, the witty;
He said: "Henceforth I'll spend my days in this delightful city."

The Factory Girl in the City
No more shall I work in the factory
To greasy up my clothes,
No more shall I work in the factory
With splinters in my toes.

Chorus: It's pity me, my darling,
It's pity me, I say.
It's pity me, my darling,
And carry me away.

No more shall I hear the bosses say,
"Boys, you'd better hurry
No more shall I hear those bosses say,
"Spinners, you had better clean off."

No more shall I hear the drummer wheels
A-rolling over my head;
When factory girls are hard at work,
I'll be in my bed.

No more shall I hear the whistle blow
To call me up so soon;
No more shall I hear the whistle blow
To call me from my home.

No more shall I see the super come,
All dressed up so fine;
For I know I'll marry a country boy
Before the year is round.

No more shall I wear the old black dress,
Greasy all around;
No more shall I wear the old black bonnet,
With holes all in the crown.

Photographs of the walking city

Photographs present vivid images of a person, event, of object at a particular moment in time. They often capture a mood or convey a particular feeling. The following photographs illustrate life in three walking cities. Examine each photograph then answer the accompanying questions.

What hypotheses about life in the walking city can you suggest from these photographs?

Fulton Street and Market, New York City, circa 1834
The Museum of the City of New York, J. Clarence Davies Collection.

Boston, from the South Boston Bridge
Courtesy the Boston Athenaeum.

What, if anything, can you determine about the relationship between place of residence and work from this picture?

Baltimore Street looking west, Baltimore, Maryland about 1853
Lithograph by E. Sachse. The Maryland Historical Society, Baltimore.

In what ways does the walking city of New Orleans appear similar to or different from Baltimore, New York, or Boston?

The French Opera House, by A. R. Waud, 1877
Courtesy the Kemper and Leila Williams Foundation, The Historic New Orleans Collection.

Travelers' accounts of the walking city

The following accounts present different views of city life in New York, Baltimore, Boston, San Francisco, and New Orleans. These accounts illustrate why people held positive and negative opinions of city life in this period. Some accounts are mostly descriptions of the physical appearance of a city; others show attitudes of the residents. As you read the following accounts make a chart listing the characteristics of each city under the following categories: 1. physical appearance of city; 2. where people live and work; 3. type of work; 4. attitudes of people toward each other; 5. attitudes of people toward their city. Some accounts will not have information about each category. After you have completed your chart answer the following questions:

1. How are these cities alike?
2. What three general statements can you make about the walking city?
3. How are the images of the walking city like the images of the contemporary city in Assignment 1? (The chart you constructed for Assignment 1 will help you make these comparisons.)

Boston in the 1820's

Boston, one of the oldest of all American cities, became a major trading center before the revolutionary war. By the 1820's, Boston was one of the three major ports in America, shipping goods all over the world. The following excerpt, from a letter written in 1817, presents a vivid picture of a growing commercial city.

Broad Street was built a few years ago, and extends at right angles, from near the bottom of King Street South, to the head of India Wharf. This street is made on a place which recently was occupied by a few zigzag wharves and ordinary buildings, and is from eighty to one hundred feet in breadth. The buildings on either side are from four to five stories in height, and constructed in a uniform and elegant style. They are chiefly occupied as stores and warehouses.

India Street begins at the bottom of King Street and extends, fronting the harbor, to India wharf. The east side is crowded with vessels, which are protected from the violence of storms by the adjacent wharves. The proprietors of the India and Central wharves have a plan to convert the intermediate space into a wet dock. The buildings on this street front the water, and are constructed in a similar style with those on Broad Street.

The space between India and Broad streets, at convenient distances, is intersected by cross streets, the principal of which is called Custom-house Street.

The new Custom-house in this street is a spacious building with compartments suitable to the business of the different offices of the customs. It is the property of the United States.

In the course of the last year, Central Wharf, and the extensive range of stores which it supports, was begun and completed. The completion of this undertaking is unparalleled in commercial history, and is a proof of the enterprize, the wealth, and persevering industry of Bostonians. The number of stores are fifty-four, and the length of the tier nearly thirteen hundred feet, and four stories high. The wharf is considerably longer, and about one hundred and fifty feet in breadth, and enclosed by a strong stone wall. The buildings are supported on piles and have water-proof cellars. The wharf is already lined with vessels and crowded with business.

Under an elevated centre is an arch making a convenient passage-way from one side of the wharf to the other. Over this are three rooms nearly sixty feet square, calculated for public sales. From an octagon cupola you have a charming view of the harbor and neighboring towns. The liberal proprietors have furnished this with a telescope and other apparatus for the accommodation of the public.

New York in the 1830's

The Dutch founded New Amsterdam, later New York, in 1626. By 1840 New York was the largest city in the United States with a population of over 300,000. An excellent harbor, rapid commercial expansion, and immigration contributed to the growth of New York. In the following reading, Captain John Watson, a popular historian, describes New York in the 1830's.

New York is not deformed because it has narrow and winding lanes. I might prefer straighter and wider streets, but as a visitor I enjoyed winding through the unknown mazes of streets to suddenly break upon some unexpected street or buildings. I am entertained by the primitive Dutch taste for such streets. The Dutch settlers loved the narrow lanes for their social conveniences. When sitting on their front door stoops in the evenings, they enjoyed talking to each other. They were as close to each other as the people facing each other in the buggies now used for travelling up and down Broadway.

New York resembles London, and I would rather just visit than live in either one. New York is always exciting. The stir and bustle; the perpetual desire to excel in display;–the various signs and devices to allure and catch the eye;–are imitations of London and other foreign cities. We should not copy foreigners; we must maintain our republican manners and principles. Why do we want our cities dense with foreigners?

New Yorkers display many signs on their houses and businesses; every device and expense is used to make them attractive. The residents crowd signs upon every story and even upon the tops and ends of some houses. One small house has twelve signs advertising lawyers.

The buildings are changing quickly. The former good houses are so fast passing away, and taller structures are replacing the old houses. To my eye, the whole city is changing. It is indeed another city. A new city building on the top of the former one! The houses over three stories displease the eye, particularly where several buildings go up so high as to break the former line of equality and beauty.

Our cities are fast becoming "great deserts." In the old houses lived superior families, free from the care and bustling strife of business. These families were essentially refined because of education, affluence, and family background. Now we see showy houses of the new rich. They aim at show and grandeur and compete against each other. In the meantime, store-keepers buy and drive out the old respectable residences—leaving no place for retired people. The shop-keepers and businessmen are turning the whole city into a great city mart of trade, bustle, display, and rivalry.

New York, a city of variety

While Captain Watson preferred the old New York to a new and fast changing New York, others like Walt Whitman received inspiration from the bustling and crowded city. Walt Whitman, an important American poet, grew up in Brooklyn. Throughout his life he preferred the companionship of the uneducated crowds of the city to the company of the rich and educated. In the following reading Whitman describes his daily life style to a friend.

Shall I tell you about my life? I generally spend the morning in my room writing, then take a bath, dress, and go out about twelve. I loaf somewhere or call on someone downtown or do some business. If it is very pleasant and I feel like it, I ride with a driver friend on Broadway for about three miles. You know it is a never-ending amusement for me to ride a couple of hours on a pleasant afternoon on a Broadway stage. You see everything as you pass, a sort of living, endless panorama—shops and splendid buildings and great windows. On the sidewalks crowds of women richly dressed pass by, as well as men dressed in high style. I delight to see plenty of foreigners. In the streets are crowded carriages, stages, carts, hotel and private coaches, and in fact all sorts of vehicles. The splendor of such a great street and so many tall noble buildings, and the gaiety and motion on every side, offer much amusement to a great loafer like me. I enjoy so much seeing the busy world move by.

New Orleans in 1833

New Orleans, initially settled by the French, became a major commercial port because of its location at the mouth of the Mississippi River. After the War of 1812, New Orleans grew rapidly. Its population increased from 17,000 in 1810 to 168,000 in 1860 and different immigrant cultures mixed with the predominant Creole (mixture of French, Indian, and Black) culture. In the following reading, Thomas Hamilton, an occasional resident of the city, describes city life in New Orleans in the 1830's.

It would be absurd to call New Orleans a handsome city. It is not so. The streets are generally narrow, and always filthy. There are no outstanding public buildings with the exception of the cathedral. In comparison to other American cities, New Orleans may be called picturesque. The architecture of the older sections of the city is Spanish. The houses are generally one story, and the principal apartment opens on the street. They are built of wood, but here and there more expensive buildings, covered with stucco, adorned with verandas, give a pleasing variety.

The French and Spanish reside in this quarter of the city. The part occupied by Anglo-Americans has no attraction of any kind. The streets are wider, but unpaved; the houses larger, but bare and unseemly.

The location of New Orleans is admirably adapted for commerce. It is the great port of the South, as New York is the center of the North. The Western states enjoy a ready communication with both.

As in most Catholic countries, Sunday is the great day for amusements of every kind. The shops are open; the market displays unusual attractions, and the sounds of merriment and music are heard in every street. In the morning, three-fourths of the population run to hear mass. The cathedral is crowded by people of all colors, in their best and gayest attire. In a European city the cathedral probably would pass without notice. In New Orleans it is a prominent object.

But in Protestant churches a different rule prevails. People of color are either excluded altogether, or are put in some remote corner, separated by barriers from the body of the church. It is impossible to forget their degraded condition even for a moment. No white Protestant would kneel at the same altar with a black one.[16] He asserts his superiority everywhere, and the very hue of his religion is affected by the color of his skin.

Baltimore in the 1840's

Baltimore in the 1840's was a major shipping port for the cotton and tobacco of the South. In the following account Frederick Douglass describes the life of a slave in Baltimore before the Civil War. He comments on the relations between blacks and whites in the walking city. Douglass finally escaped to the North where he became a leader in the abolition movement.

Very soon after I went to Baltimore to live, Master Hugh succeeded in getting me hired to Mr. William Gardiner, a shipbuilder. I was placed there to learn to calk (repair boats), a trade of which I already had some knowledge. When I entered the shipyard, everyone was hurrying to complete two man-of-war vessels. There were in the yard about one hundred men; of these, seventy or eighty were regular carpenters—privileged men. There was no time for a raw hand to learn anything. Every man had to do that which he knew how to do. Upon entering the yard Mr. Gardiner directed me to do whatever the carpenters told me to do. This was placing me at the beck and call of about seventy-five men. I was to regard all these men as my masters. Their word was to be

[16]Do you feel that these people were living up to the ideals of their religion? Why, or why not?

my law. My situation was a trying one. I was called a dozen ways in the space of a single minute. I needed a dozen pairs of hands.

At the end of eight months Master Hugh refused to allow me to remain with Gardiner. The circumstance which led to this refusal was the committing of an outrage upon me, by the white apprentices of the shipyard. The fight was a desperate one, and I came out of it shockingly mangled. The facts, which led to this brutal outrage upon me, illustrate an aspect of slavery which was destined to become an important element in the overthrow of the slave system. That aspect was this–slavery conflicted with the interests of white mechanics and laborers. In the country this conflict was not so apparent, but in cities, such as Baltimore, Richmond, New Orleans, Mobile, etc., it was seen pretty clearly. The slaveholders, by encouraging the hatred of the poor laboring white man against the blacks, succeeded in making the white man almost as much a slave as the black slave himself.[17] The difference between the white slave and the black slave was this: the black slave belonged to one slaveholder, while the white slave belonged to the slaveholders collectively. Both were plundered, and by the same plunderers. The slave was robbed by his master of all his earnings, above what was required for his bare physical necessities. The white laboring man was robbed by the slave system of the just results of his labor, because he was flung into competition with a class of laborers who worked without wages. The slaveholders blinded them to this competition by keeping alive their prejudice against the slaves as men–not against them as slaves. The impression was cunningly made that slavery was the only power that could prevent the laboring white man from falling to the level of the slave's poverty and degradation. In the City of Baltimore there were frequent murmurs that educating slaves to be mechanics might, in the end, give slave-masters power to dispense altogether with the services of the poor white man.

San Francisco in the 1850's

San Francisco, an old Spanish trading center, underwent a phenomenal growth with the discovery of gold in California in 1848. With the news of the gold strike, thousands of people poured into San Francisco in search of quick riches. Bayard Taylor, a writer for the *New York Tribune*, journeyed to California and described life in San Francisco in 1850. His account, written to excite the newspaper reader, emphasizes the dramatic, sensational, and colorful aspects of San Francisco in the 1850's.

As we crossed the hills the view extended around the curve of the bay. We saw hundreds of tents and houses. A furious wind filled the streets with clouds of dust. Everywhere stood half-finished buildings; many of them were mere canvas sheds, covered with all kinds of signs in all languages. Great quantities

[17]Do you agree with Douglass that the poor white man was almost as much a slave as the black slave himself? Why, or why not?

of goods were piled up in the open air, for want of a place to store them. The streets were full of all kinds of people, hurrying to and fro. There were Yankees of every possible variety, native Californians in sombreros, Chilians, Hawaiians, Chinese with long tails, and other brown and bearded people of unrecognizable nationality.

Many of the passengers began speculation at the moment of landing. A most shrewd gentleman from New York took out fifteen hundred copies of *The Tribune* and other papers which he sold for one dollar apiece in less than two hours. Hearing of this, I remembered the dozen papers which filled the crevices of my suitcase. There was a newspaper merchant at the corner of the City Hotel and I asked him to name a price. "I shall want to make a good profit," said he, "and can't give more than ten dollars for the lot." I was satisfied with the price, a gain of four thousand per cent!

. . . . When I returned to San Francisco after three weeks I could not believe the changes. The town had greatly extended its area and the number of dwellings appeared to have doubled. High up on the hills, where I had seen only sand and bushes, stood clusters of houses. Streets which had been merely laid out, were hemmed in with buildings and thronged with people. New warehouses had sprung up on the water side, and new piers were creeping out to the forest of masts. The noise, motion, and bustle of business and labor on all sides were never ending. The place was a marvel . . . .

The rapidity with which a ready-made house is put up and inhabited, strikes the stranger in San Francisco as little short of magic. He walks over an open lot in his before-breakfast stroll. The next morning, a house complete with a family inside, blocks his way . . . .

San Francisco, however, lacked society. Think of a city of over thirty thousand persons, peopled by men alone! Every man was his own housekeeper, doing his own sweeping, cooking, washing, and mending. He who cannot make a bed, cook a beefsteak, or sew up his ripped pants is unfit to be a citizen of California.

For thought and discussion

Suppose that people in the 1840's and 1850's had been able to ride around cities in streetcars instead of walking. How might their images of the city have changed?

Individual and small group activities

1. Go down to your local Chamber of Commerce and pick up brochures and other literature they hand out about the city? How are their images of your city like or unlike your images of your city? If you lived in another city and read the Chamber of Commerce literature would you want to move to your city? Why or why not? Report your findings to the class.
2. How well do you know your city and how well can you give and follow direc-

tions? Pick an area or place a few miles away from you in the city. Do not give street names, but give a description of what you would pass in order to arrive at the place. Give these directions to another student. Do not tell the student the final destination. Next class period ask the person who had your directions where he arrived? Could he follow your directions? What changes would the student make in your directions? What changes would you make in the directions you received from another person? What kind of buildings did you name to give directions? Why did you choose, for example, gas stations instead of historical landmarks?

Work and residence patterns in the walking city

Assignment 12

In Assignment 3 you examined the major geographic factors which influenced the location and growth of urban centers in the Mid-west. Geographic factors consisted of nearness to water, land elevation, the availability of natural resources, and distance from other cities. These factors influence spatial distribution and spatial interaction. Geographers use the concept of spatial distribution to explain the location of cities in a geographic area or the placement of certain specialized zones throughout the city. Spatial interaction refers to the relationships that exist between one region or zone and other regions or zones.

Spatial distribution and interaction do not refer only to the location of cities. Spatial distribution and interaction also influence the internal patterns of cities. Distance between zones of work and residence (internal spatial distribution) help to influence the interaction of human beings within the city. In Assignments 3 and 4 you found that in the modern city, work and residence are seldom located near each other. Great distances between work and residence made social relationships between classes of people difficult.

This assignment examines both external and internal spatial distribution and interaction in the walking city. Part I explores the geographic factors involved in the location and founding of Atlanta, Georgia, in 1847. Part II of this assignment will help you to analyze spatial distribution and interaction in Atlanta. By looking at living and working patterns and reading personal accounts left by residents of this period, you should be able to explain the ways in which people related to each other and their attitudes toward each other.

The founding of Atlanta in 1847

Before the Civil War, many southern cities had similar patterns of urban life. You have already viewed urban life in two southern walking cities, Baltimore and New Orleans, and noted similarities as well as differences between them and northern and western cities. However, the growth of urban areas in the southern region lagged behind the rest of the country, particularly the Northeast. This lag resulted largely from economic differences. Northern cities developed manufacturing economies while the South relied on farming and trade.

In 1837, the State of Georgia designated Atlanta as the site for a railroad to connect the cities of Madison, Barnesville, Macon, Augusta, Charleston, and Savannah. Georgia needed additional transportation routes from which to ship cotton and tobacco, and to which the North could send needed supplies. In addition, the railroad could provide a passageway for northern and western trade.

Using the following topographical map of the southeastern United States, determine what geographic factors influenced legislators to place Atlanta where they did.

1. List four major geographic factors that engineers might have considered.
2. State whether there is a better location? Why? or why not?

Figure 12.1
Map of the Southeastern United States in the 1840's

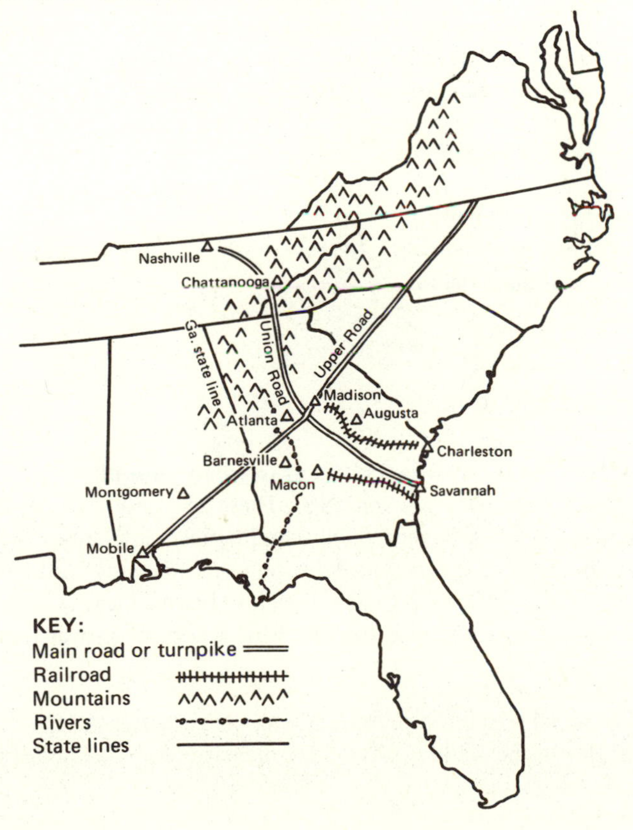

Atlanta: Work and residence patterns in a walking city

When state surveyors founded Atlanta in 1837, only three public roads met at the site where the railroads connected. The surrounding area was a wilderness where a few Indians traded as they passed through. Construction of the railroad began in 1838. Settlers immediately moved into the area to take advantage of potential commercial opportunities and to invest in land. In 1842, a crowd of five hundred people cheered the completion of the railroad lines. By 1845 several stores and a hotel as well as a jail, a school, a church, a weekly newspaper, and a Sunday school were established. During the 1850's Atlanta boomed, reaching a population of 10,000 by 1860. After the Civil War, Atlanta became the great marketplace and business exchange of the Southeast.

The map of Atlanta in 1850 on the next page will help you to determine the patterns of work and residence in the city. Examine the map and follow the instructions below.

1. Make a list of the places you would pass if you were:
   a. Mr. Norcross, local businessman and a mayor of Atlanta, and wanted to travel from your sawmill (4) along Whitehall and Peachtree Streets to the school (13).
   b. Mr. Loyd, local businessman, and wanted go go from your store (3) to Murrel's Row (7) to drink some beer and watch a cockfight.
   c. a citizen living in a small house on Broad and Mitchell (11) and wanted to mail a letter (8), buy some groceries at Thrasher's store (5) and go to Walton Springs (12) for a picnic.
2. List the people Mr. Norcross, Mr. Loyd, and the citizen might have talked to as they walked through the city.
3. Using your list as a guide, describe the relationship between work, residence, and social areas in walking Atlanta.

Atlanta residents talk about their city

Statements of residents about Atlanta help us to enlarge our picture of life in Atlanta during the period between 1840 and 1860. These accounts describe social relationships among residents of the community and indicate attitudes toward the city. The numbers in the following accounts correspond to locations on the map of Atlanta in the 1850's. You may wish to use these numbers to locate the places mentioned by the residents. As you read the following accounts, answer the questions below.

1. What kind of social relationships exist among the people in Atlanta?
2. What did people in the walking city do for recreation? What kind of work did they do?

Figure 12.2
Map of Atlanta in 1850's

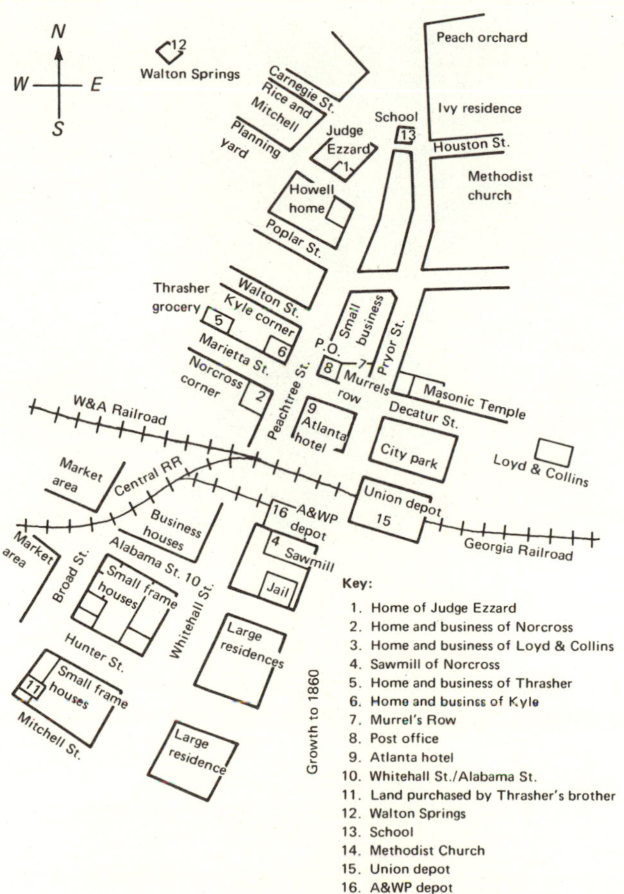

John Thrasher (5). When I arrived in this place in 1839, the country was entirely covered by forest. There was only one house then, and it stood where the post office is. I went to work building and fixing a store. First one person moved in from the country and then another, until we had a right smart little town. The people around here were very poor. Many women wore no shoes at all. We had dirt floors in our homes. My store was the only one at that time.

As the place grew up, the present Whitehall Street (10) was the place for drinking and fighting. After a while I sold out and went away for a few years. I came back in 1844 and went into business on Marrietta Street (5). At that time Mr. Norcross (2) had a horse sawmill (4), which was regarded as a curiosity. People came from the country on purpose to look at it.

Once, while I was absent from town, my brother-in-law, who was associated with me in the store, bought a piece of land between Mitchell and

Atlanta Scene, 1864
Oil painting by Wilbur Kurtz, Sr., from the collection of Beverly M. DuBose, Jr.

If you had a choice, would you prefer living in the walking city or the modern metropolis? Why, or why not? What can you do about it?

Hunter Streets (11) for sixty dollars. I was very much provoked when I heard of this. I had previously refused to give five dollars an acre for the same land, and he had given two dollars a foot for it. I told him if he made any more such trades I would dissolve partnership with him sure.

Decatur Street was called Murrel's Row (7) and was a great place for cock-fighting.

The first railroad engine that came here was called the "Florida." Before operating it, sixteen mules pulled it up from Madison. The people were nearly wild. They came from the country for miles to see it. I recollect when they started, the engineer got people to push it.

There was one particular piece of property that I wanted after the town got settled, and that was called Loyd's Corner (3). I tried for fifteen years to buy that property. The first time he asked me $3,000 and I offered him $2,500. After a while I concluded to give him his price, and then he asked me $4,000. I concluded to give him $4,000 and he asked me $5,000, and he went on in that way till he got up to $25,000 and I finally took it at that price. It went up from $3,000 to $25,000 before the trade was made.

William Ezzard (1). In 1856, people in Charleston began to call Atlanta the "Gateway City." It was given, I suppose, from the fact that this railroad had just been constructed through the mountains for the purpose of connecting the West with the Atlantic Ocean, and there was no other way to get to either place except to pass through Atlanta.

Mr. Norcross (2). At the time I was elected Mayor there was called an "orderly party" and a "rowdy party." The rowdy party hung out at Murrel's Row (7) and was very strong. They often broke the law and were very bitter against me because I was in favor of law and order and took active steps in that direction. The leaders of this party, the rowdies and ruffians and gamblers, swore that I should not be Mayor of the town. They said if I did not resign I would have to leave town. I concluded I would not do that. Two or three mornings after I was inaugurated I got up and found a cannon pointed directly at my store door. They said that they had fired it off, but there was no mark of any shot. They swore the cannon would remain there until I left. I went around and took counsel of the good citizens. I found that there were plenty of men who, when they could have the law to uphold them, were ready to enforce peace and good order. We organized about forty or fifty and drilled. The rowdy party saw the movement against them. They went to work and entrenched themselves. They swore they would not be arrested. But when they saw the force that was collected against them, they made no resistance. From that time to this the people of Atlanta have been peaceful and law-abiding.

When the Georgia Railroad was finished, a new kind of currency was used for change. The usual way of keeping accounts was by 6¼ cents, 12½ cents, 37½ cents, etc. I was the first man that commenced using accounts by the Federal money system–cents, dimes, etc.–and I believe that Atlanta was the first place in Georgia to inaugurate this change. The first merchants that came here were men of small capital–almost no capital at all–they were not able to give credit. Trade was always brisk. A good deal of trade always centered here, but our merchants never sold on credit. The consequence was that we only sold for cash at first.

The earliest merchants that came in after John Thrasher (5) were myself (2) and Collier & Loyd (3). When the first cars came here on the Georgia Railroad, there were only two stores that sold general merchandise–Collier & Loyd (3) and myself (2). Kyle (6) had a little grocery store but it did not amount to a great deal.

The first hotel here (9) after the Georgia road was completed, was started by a Dr. Joseph Thompson. That was all the hotel and all the boarding house there was in Atlanta. The postoffice was there, too (8).

I recollect very well the first train of cars over the Georgia Railroad. It was on the 15th of September, 1845. The train came in about dark. Judge King was on board and a great many others. There were a great many people out, and there was a great deal of excitement. There was a well in the square here, and such was the excitement, and it being dark, a man fell into the well and drowned. Judge King came very near falling in there, also. He was just on the brink of stepping in when someone caught and saved him. I suppose there were about twenty families here at that time.

The next great event in the history of Atlanta was the arrival of the cars on the Macon road in 1847. When it fell into new hands, the stock was bought up and they commenced to build it. They at first decided to run the track in up by the northern section of the city and to make the depot there. Those of us who lived in a different area of town and had bought property, went to work and held a meeting and brought all the influence we could to bear upon the company to get them to change the proposed location and bring it near us in the southern part of town. (16) We won, and that was a turning point in the growth of Atlanta.[18]

Mr. Thrasher. That was my ruin: I bought one hundred acres of land with the expectation that the railroad would run by the state road shops up north. When I found that the road was going down there, I was very enraged, and sold out my interest for one-half of what I gave for it. I sold out and went to Griffin.

Mr. Norcross. The reason why the streets are so crooked is that every man built on his land just to suit himself. The city charter provided for the appointment of commissioners to lay out a street plan, but no one supported this and built where they pleased.

Mr. Holcombe. I became a citizen of Atlanta in 1847. I then found a population of about two hundred and fifty or three hundred persons, counting all ages and colors, males and females. In September of that year the Methodist Episcopal Church (14) held its quarterly meeting under a cotton shed. There was not a church building in the place sufficiently large in which that assembly could convene. All of the lots now occupied by the church (14) were then in brush and forest. The grounds upon which now stands the depot of the State Railroads (15) were surrounded by forest, the immediate ground being a caney marsh. Cattle were frequently found mired in the marsh, having gone there to feed on the switch cane. There were but two houses on Whitehall and Alabama (10).

The first killing that occurred in Atlanta was the case of William Terrell killing one Mr. McWilliams by stabbing, which took place in 1847. Dr. N.G. Hilburn was murdered by Elijah Bird (his brother-in-law) who cut his throat, from which he died instantly. The first brick house erected in Atlanta was the Atlanta Hotel (9). I saw the "razor strap" man in 1847 on the corner of Whitehall and Alabama (10). He was crying off his razor-straps and saying that he had a few more left to sell. Then there were but a few houses in that part of the city.

For thought and discussion

What kinds of changes do you think have occurred in the central downtown areas of cities in the last one hundred years? Would you prefer to live in the downtown area today?

[18]In what ways, if any, do you prefer life in the walking city to life in cities today? Why?

Individual and small group activities

1. Examine the following 1973 map and key of Atlanta. Make a list of the buildings and activities you would pass if you were:
   a. Mr. Norcross and went from the new post office (12) to Underground Atlanta (13) and then to the Atlantan Hotel (2).
   b. Mr. Loyd and went from the Court House (14) to Massey Junior College (9) and then to the Carnegie Library (1).

   What kinds of changes have occurred in the central downtown area of Atlanta in the last one hundred years?

Figure 12.3
Map of Downtown Atlanta, 1973

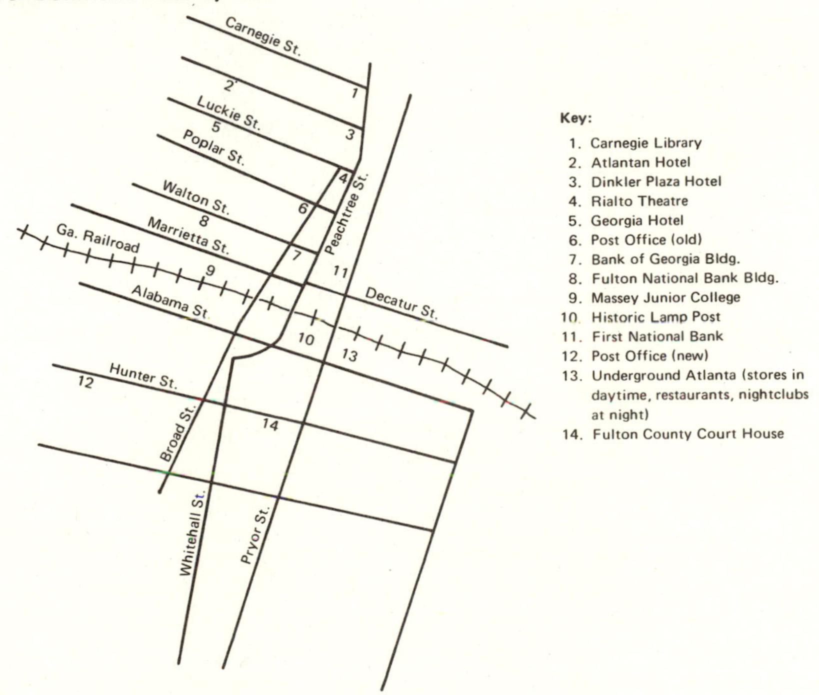

2. The railroad game in the city of Atlanta: Railroad speculators want to build another trunk line and depot into Atlanta. A town meeting will be held to decide where the people want the railroad line and depot to be built. A majority approval is necessary.

   Each member or group of members of the class should assume the role of one of the property holders in Atlanta, and decide what site would be most advantageous to him.

   After each property holder has selected a site for the railroad and depot, the town meeting is convened to determine whether the residents can agree upon a single solution.

List of property holders:

1. Judge Ezzard
2. Mr. Loyd
3. Mr. Norcross
4. Mr. Kyle
5. Mr. Collier
6. Homeowner on Broad and Hunter
7. Mr. Thrasher
8. Mr. Crusselle
9. Owner of Walton Springs
10. Owner of Atlanta Hotel
11. Owner of large warehouse in market area
12. Mr. Ivy
13. Minister of Methodist Church

At the conclusion of the simulation you should answer the following questions:

1. What factors influenced the location of the railroad?
2. What was the most important factor? Why?

Commerce and industry in the walking city

Assignment 13

Assignment 5 analyzed the production and distribution of goods and services in a contemporary city. The term goods includes all products which an economy makes, such as food, houses, automobiles, or submarines. The term services refers to such diverse activities as medical care, janitorial help, police protection, or trade. Assignment 5 used a description of an imaginary city, New Obsidian, to explain the kinds of trade and manufacturing involving goods and services necessary for urban economic growth. This assignment examines the economy of the walking city.

Three types of resources are needed in order for a city to produce goods and services. Economists call these types of resources, natural, human, and captial. Natural resources include land, water, forests, and minerals. All types of unskilled and skilled workers, entreprenurial talent, and other human creativity used in the economy are called human resources. Capital resources include any equipment such as tools, machines, and buildings used to produce goods and services. They include both a hammer and such sophisticated technology as a computer.

Before the development of manufacturing in the United States, cities were primarily trading centers which produced services rather than goods. They traded agricultural products, raw materials, and crafts among themselves and with European nations. American cities also imported and distributed European manufactured goods. Some of the production of goods in the early cities grew out of the needs of the part of the economy which provided services. For example, cities produced warehouses, ships, barrels, and wagons in order to supply services such as trade more economically.

Producing raw materials and agricultural products in the walking city required mainly natural and human resources rather than capital resources. Producing timber required extensive lands and many strong backs, and a few simple tools such as axes, saws, and wagons. Similarly, tobacco production required large quantities of land, much unskilled labor, and only a few relatively simple tools. The production of manufactured goods, however, required natural resources, more sophisticated and skilled human resources and extensive capital resources. Producing cotton cloth, for example, required raw cotton, water power, a large factory, many complicated machines, both skilled and unskilled workers, and the ability to organize and manage a large industrial enterprise.

Throughout its history, the walking city produced services for the American economy. At an increasing pace during the early decades of the 1800's, walking cities also began to produce manufactured goods. This assignment provides information about the nature of the economy in walking cities.

Visual images of economic resources of the walking city

Pictures can offer a much more vivid representation of the walking city than statistics do. The following pictures indicate the ways in which natural, human, and capital resources are used in the economies of various walking cities. As you look at these pictures answer these questions:

1. In what ways are natural, human, and capital resources used in the activities shown in each picture?
2. Which sorts of economic activities shown in the pictures require the most sophisticated technology and human resources?

Market in a Southern city, 1840

Cotton baling, Galveston, Texas, 1840

River front of Cincinnati, 1848
Courtesy of the Cincinnati Public Library.

View of Union Stockyards, Chicago, 1866.
Courtesy Chicago Historical Society.

"The Trading and Processing of Cattle"

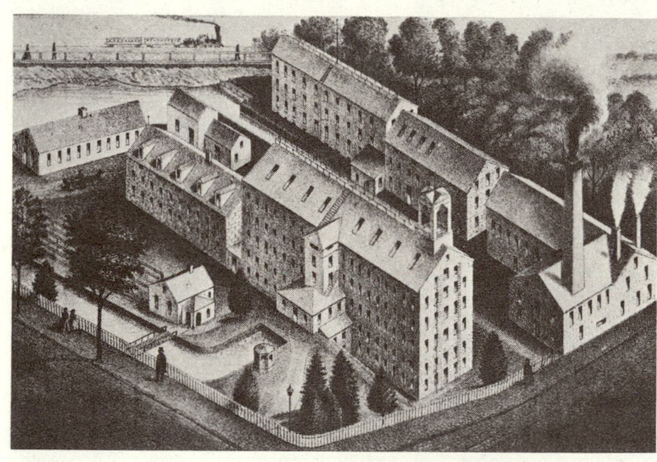

Woolen mills, with railroad in background, Rockville, Conn., 1841

From the Harry T. Peters *America on Stone* Lithography Collection, Smithsonian Institution.

McCormick reaper factory, Chicago 1847

Courtesy of International Harvester Company.

The Custom House, Wall Street, New York, 1845, "The Collection of Tariffs on Imports & Exports"

Courtesy of the Library of Congress.

Iron factory, Pittsburgh, 1839

Carnegie Library, Pittsburgh.

Accounts of trade and manufacturing in the walking city

The photographs probably suggested several hypotheses about the kinds of economic resources used in the walking cities. American cities grew, or failed to grow, partially because of the kinds of available resources. The level of development of natural, human, and capital resources also contributed to urban growth. For example, natural resources either increase, diminish, or remain the same. The development of natural resources usually depends on people. For example, people may irrigate their land, thereby developing their natural resources. Also, they may use up their coal, thereby diminishing their natural resources. Economists identify four factors which influence the adequacy of human resources. They are: educated manpower, adequate manpower, healthy manpower and willing manpower. The development of these four factors contributes to economic growth. Many immigrants came to Boston thereby increasing the supply of human resources. In addition, an enterprising businessman may invent a new way of mass-producing shirts. His creativity and business know-how are human resources as well. Capital resources may change depending on the money and equipment available and the desire of people to invest. For example, a growing economy produces new and better equipment. People reinvest some of their profits in new equipment and business.

The following accounts have information about the kind and level of development of resources in the walking cities. None of the four authors of these accounts viewed himself as an economist. However, all of them make assumptions about what the people in the walking city must do in order for the city to grow. As you read these accounts answer these questions:

1. Which cities are primarily trading centers? Why?
2. Which cities are primarily manufacturing centers? Why?
3. Which city's economy requires the highest level of development of natural, human, and capital resources? Which requires the least? Why?

Richmond: Tobacco processing and trading

The English settled Richmond primarily as a port for shipping raw materials such as cotton and tobacco. Richmond continued to grow because its good harbor helped to transport raw materials to foreign countries and to the North. Prior to the Civil War, Richmond had a large slave population employed as servants, and in the processing of raw materials. In the following account, William C. Bryant, poet-journalist, editor of the *New York Evening Post*, and a reformer, vividly portrays the processing of tobacco. As you read this account answer this question:

1. Do you think Richmond's economy depended primarily on natural, human, or capital resources? What evidence can you supply to defend your answer?

I went with a friend to see the inspection and sale of tobacco. Huge, upright columns of dried leaves, firmly packed and of a greenish hue, stood in rows, under the roof of a broad, low building, open on all sides. There were the bundles (hogsheads) of tobacco, stripped of the wooden staves. The inspector, a portly man, his white hair gathered in a tie behind, went very quietly through his task of determining the quality of the tobacco. Tobacco worth three million dollars is bought yearly and then sent to different nations.

Afterwards I went to a tobacco factory, the sight of which amused me, though the fumes made me cough. In one room a black man was taking apart the small bundles of leaves of each bundle of tobacco. He carefully separated each leaf. Other black men were sorting the leaves according to quality. Others were arranging the leaves in layers, and sprinkling each layer with extract of licorice. In another room were about eighty negroes–boys they are called, from the age of twelve through manhood–who received the leaves thus prepared. They rolled them into long even rolls, and then cut them into plugs of about four inches in length. These plugs were then passed through a press and became ready for market.

Cincinatti: Commerce and enterprising citizens

Distance from other cities and the expense of overland transportation, hampered the commercial growth of Cincinnati. However, the invention of the steamboat helped to increase Cincinnati's trade through New Orleans. The development of manufactured goods for export by local citizens also played an important role in the growth of Cincinnati. Both rich and poor Cincinnatians invested in industry. In the following reading Michael Chevalier, gives a favorable account of commerce and manufacturing in Cincinnati in 1835. Chevalier, a Frenchmen, came to American cities to study public works and manufacturing, and to make recommendations to the French government. As you read this account answer this question:

1. What actions taken by the citizens promoted the economic growth of Cincinnati?

Cincinnati has grown almost entirely without aid from other cities. Cincinnati's inhabitants, many of them poor immigrants, are mainly responsible for the city's growth. Other towns, such as Lowell, relied on outside investment to aid their economic growth.

Cincinnati was admirably situated on the river. However, other points along the river were just as advantageously placed. We can understand the growth of Pittsburgh. That city is situated where two rivers meet to form the Ohio River. Pittsburgh is also located near coal and iron. Thus, Pittsburgh is the central point for a vast system of roads, railroads, and canals. Pittsburgh was marked out by nature at once for a great manufacturing center and a great mart of trade. Another example, Louisville, is a natural central point for the commerce of the upper Ohio and that of the Mississippi and its tributaries.

From the beginning, Cincinnatians wanted to make their city the capital of Ohio, the great interior market of the West. In order to achieve their goal, they began to manufacture certain goods. The Cincinnatians make a variety of household furniture, agricultural and mechanical implements, machines, and wooden clocks. They also make many of the daily necessities of life such as soap, candles, paper, and leather. Western people always want these articles. Most of these articles are of ordinary quality. The furniture, for instance, would not meet Parisian taste. However it is cheap and neat, just what is wanted in a new country where people are poor. These people want quantity and comfort, not elegant workmanship.[19]

The prosperity of Cincinnati, therefore, rests upon the prosperity of the West, and upon the West's demand for basic necessary articles. Manufacturing centered around necessary goods is much more sensible than manufacturing centered around fashionable goods. Our (French) manufacturing should concentrate more on necessity and usefulness rather than on fashion.

The country trader is sure to find almost everything he wants in Cincinnati. He, therefore, comes here in preference to any other place. Cincinnati is thus in fact the great central mart of the West.

Manufacturing in the walking city, Lowell, Massachusetts, 1845

By the 1840's some walking cities contained factories which employed immigrants and unskilled and semi-skilled workers from the city and surrounding rural areas. Factory owners often established their industry near rivers for waterpower and transportation. Sometimes businessmen established factories in rural areas. Small cities usually sprang up around such factories. Lowell, Massachusetts typified such a factory city.

In the following account, William T. Thompson, a Georgia planter, newspaper owner, defender of slavery, and novelist, describes Lowell through the uneducated eyes of a southern farmer, Major Jones. Read this description then answer the following question:

1. Of the four factors which determine the adequacy of human resources—educated manpower, adequate manpower, healthy manpower, and willing manpower—which ones did Lowell have?

They poured into the mills by thousands, like bees into a hive. In a few minutes more, the noise of the machinery began to get louder and louder. Each factory sent out a buzzing sound; all sounds soon became mixed up. It seemed that we were in a city where men, women, children, water, fire, and light were all at work. The very air breathed the song of industry.

After breakfast we went to one of the mills. We went from one room to another and saw contraptions I never had seen before. The machinery made such a noise that we couldn't hear ourselves think, let alone say anything to one another. We were so completely dumbfounded by what we saw, that we couldn't find words to utter even if we could hear one another.

There were girls tending the looms and the spindles. They were mixed

[19]As a consumer are you more concerned with the quality or the quantity of goods you buy? Why?

among the cranks and wheels, and drum-heads, and crossbands, and iron fixings. The machine parts were going like lightning, and the girls' little white hands were flying like they were a part of the machinery. Busy as they were, though, they found time now and then to steal a sly glance at us green fellers who had never seen a cotton-mill before. I tried to get the hang of the machinery but it was no use. Everything I saw, from the ceiling to the floor, was whirling and whizzing and rattling and dashing as if it would tear everything to pieces. What was happening or what set them agoing was more than I could make out.

After going through three or four of the mills, which were pretty much alike, we went into one where they print calicos. We went into the dryingroom as they call it, but stayed there a very short time. If hell is much hotter than this dryingroom, it is not much misrepresented in the accounts we have heard.

The next place we went to was the whip factory. We saw a cover braided onto a whip-stalk, by machinery, in about two minutes. From there we went to another place where they made cotton and woolen cards. That machine banged like nothing I've ever seen. This little iron contraption took a piece of leather, and a coil of wire, and cut off the wire and bent it double, punched the holes in the leather, put the wire in the holes, and fastened them there quicker and better than five men could do it. I never dreamed of such a machine. The man that invented that machine could invent one so I could eat shad without swallering the bones.

The next place we went into was a machine carpenter's shop. The rough boards come into one door and go out another door as pine boxes. Saws and plainers and chissels and awgers were sawing, plaining, chisseling and boring in every direction by machinery, with men to tend them. For one that wasn't acquainted with the bearings of the place, it was necessary to keep a pretty sharp look out to prevent having a shaving taken off of himself.

Pittsburgh: Trade and manufacturing in 1826

Pittsburgh developed early as both a trading and manufacturing center. Because of its location, many people came through Pittsburgh on their journey westward. After traveling over the mountains, and arriving at the head of the Ohio River, settlers needed many goods such as tools, food, and household articles. Manufacturing in Pittsburgh grew to meet these needs.

Available resources of coal and water power spurred the growth of ironmaking and glassmaking in the city. In the following account, a local historian, Samuel Jones, describes trading in Pittsburgh and expresses his concern that Pittsburgh continue to sell more than she buys. Economists call this greater amount of exports than imports, a favorable balance of trade. As you read this account determine the following:

1. What resources should a city develop in order to insure a favorable balance of trade and future economic growth?

The commerce and trade of Pittsburgh in the last year surpasses that of any former period. The causes of prosperity are more people demanding more products, better transportation, better mineral resources and many enterprising merchants. We supply the West and South with iron, nails, glass, whiskey, paper, cottons, castings, etc. We supply the North with dry goods, groceries, and other merchandise. We supply the East with linen, feathers, beeswax, bacon, lard, flour, and a variety of domestic products. We trade with every part of the country and are the center for trade moving West.

Although we are progressing very rapidly in business, our increase is nearly balanced by the desire of our citizens for foreign luxuries and unnecessary consumption. Our favorable balance of trade is very small considering our resource advantages. I am concerned that five years from now that our residents overconsumption and imports will surpass our production and exports. The following figures indicate our current imports and exports.

Table 13.1

	Imports–1826	
Merchandise of various kinds		$1,232,000
Groceries and liquors		813,000
Drugs, stationary, etc.		74,000
	Total Imports	$2,119,000
	Exports–1826	
Iron		$398,000
Nails		210,000
Castings		88,000
Steam engines		100,000
Cotton yarns and cloths		160,324
Glass		105,000
Paper		55,000
Porter		18,000
Flour		10,500
Tobacco and sugars		25,800
Wire work		8,000
Axes, scythes shovels, sickles, etc.		49,000
Whiskey		29,832
Bacon		51,820
Dry goods, to north and west		480,000
Groceries and liquors to north and west		525,000
Saddlery and other leather goods		236,000
White lead		17,000
Miscellaneous		214,000
	Total Exports	$2,781,276

BALANCE OF TRADE	
Export	$2,781,276
Import	2,119,000
Favorable balance of trade	+ 662,276

For thought and discussion

Which of the four cities discussed in Assignment 13 would be most likely to grow in the future?

Individual and small group activities

1. Go to the local historical association and write a short one-page biographical sketch of an early industrialist in you city. How did he use and develop natural, human, and capital resources? Report to the class. Compare your biography to one of another industrialist. Do they have any similar characteristics?
2. In a group of 5 or 6 of the class members, meet outside of class and answer the following questions:

   Of the cities we studied in this assignment which one would you go to work in if you were:

   a. an unskilled immigrant from Sweden
   b. a business speculator looking for quick profit
   c. a skilled immigrant from Berlin, Germany
   d. a businessman dealing in the shipment of raw materials
   e. a farmer from rural Connecticut

What other information would you like to have in order to make your decision? Report your conclusions to the class.

Social structure in the walking city

Assignment 14

Like the contemporary city, the walking city had a system of social stratification. Income, occupation, education, place of residence, life style, and authority in the community all influenced one's place on the social ladder in cities in both periods of time. One's religion and place of birth also helped to determine social standing in the walking city. For example, the native-born Yankee or the English immigrant often received more status in his community than immigrants from other nations.

An examination of the criteria used for determining social classes tells us much about the system of values in the walking city. Place of birth, occupation, and amount of personal property, for example, were more important in assigning status than education or life style. These factors, however, do not explain how the population is distributed within the community. Assignment 7 suggested that social structure in some cities resembled a pyramid, with a few people at the top and many persons at the bottom. Social structure in other cities resembled an hour glass or an inverted pyramid.

Assignment 14 examines the social structure in Pittsburgh and Philadelphia during the 1850's. The ward map and census material in Part I will enable you to hypothesize about social class and social structure in Pittsburgh. The three tables on page 173 will provide you with information to test your hypothesis. In Part II of this assignment you should compare your conclusions about the walking city of Pittsburgh with an historian's analysis of social structure in Philadelphia during the same period.

Social structure and residence patterns in Pittsburgh in 1860

Social relationships in Pittsburgh in 1860 represent a mixture of the informal neighborhood street life of the early walking city and the formal community of the late 19th century industrialized city. By 1860 an increasingly industrialized Pittsburgh was densely populated. About 50,000 people lived and worked in a land area of 1.77 square miles.

Ward map of Pittsburgh in 1860

In the contemporary city poor people tend to live in the central areas, while the more affluent often live in suburbs. The following ward map and census data will help you to determine where the poor and rich lived in the walking city of the late 1850's. A ward map represents political voting units.

1. By examining the ward map indicating businesses, factories and institutions for Pittsburgh in 1860, what hypotheses can you suggest about where the rich and poor might have lived?

Figure 14.1
Ward map of Pittsburgh in 1860

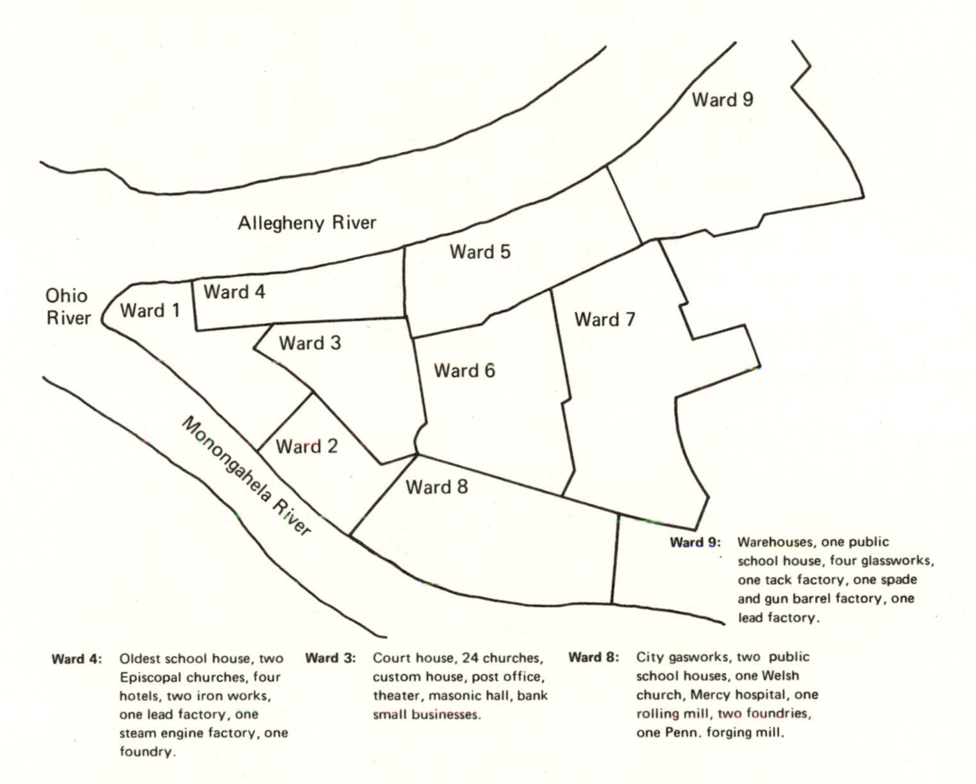

Pittsburgh census data in 1860

Manuscript census data provide us with information about a person's job, place of birth, and property holdings. Combined with the ward map, these data indicate where the wealthy and the poor lived in the city. Using all of this information we can hypothesize about social class and social structure in the walking city.

People went from door to door to collect manuscript census data. They recorded information about everyone living in the residence. In order to organize our evidence, make 5" x 7" index cards for each of wards three, four, eight, and nine, a total of four cards in all. Label the index cards: occupation, property, and place of birth. Then fill in the following information on the cards:

1. Under occupation list the occupation of every male over 18 years of age residing in that ward. (Try to label the type of occupation by unskilled, skilled, small manufacturer, clerks and shopkeepers, professional, large manufacturer, merchants, and bankers).
2. Under property, list the combined amount of real estate and personal property owned by every male and female over 18 years of age residing in that ward. (Round off each figure to correspond to one of the following categories: a) less than $100 b) $100–999 c) $1,000–4,999 d) $5,000–9,999 e) $10,000–24,999 f) $25,000–49,999 g) over $50,000)
3. Under place-of-birth, list the place of birth for every male and female resident over 18 years of age in each ward.

After completing the index card for each ward, list the following information:

1. The major type of occupation in each ward by unskilled, skilled, small manufacturer, clerk and shopkeeper, professional, large manufacturer, merchant, banker
2. The average value of personal property and real estate
3. The most common place of birth

Finally, use your index cards and ward map to answer these questions:

1. Where do certain occupation, nationality, and property groups live in the city?
2. What relationships exist among a person's occupation, place of birth, and ownership of personal property?

Figure 14.2

Page No. 218

SCHEDULE 1. --- Free Inhabitants in 3d Ward City of Pittsburgh in the County of Allegheny State of Penna. enumerated by me, on the 14th day of June 1860. J. K. Philips Ass't Marshal

Post Office Pittsburgh

Number of Dwelling	Number of Family	The name of every person whose usual place of abode on the first day of June, 1860, was in this family	Description: Age	Sex	Color	Profession, Occupation, or Trade of each person, male and female, over 15 years of age.	Value of Real Estate	Value of Personal Estate	Place of Birth	
111	106	George Reiman	36	M		Restaurant		4,000	Germany	
		Catherine "	21	F					Germany	
		Andy Bender	21	M		Barkeeper			Germany	
		Fred Kalf	15	M		Barkeeper			Germany	
		Henry Slip	15	M		Barkeeper			Penna	
		Cate Helpe	22	F		Servant			Germany	
112	107	Henry Jetty	14	M					Ger	
113	108	D.M. Egerton	25	M		Commercial Merchant		15,000	Ohio	
		Wm. Harrison	40	M		Clerk			Ireland	
		James Rafferty	31	M		Merchant		5,000	Ireland	
114	109	Wm. Cartwright	43	M					England	
		Mary "	31	F					Penna	
115	110	James Lindsey	24	M					Penna	
116	111	George Blair	28	M		Clerk			Ireland	
		W. G. Childs	27	M		Clerk			Penna	
117	112	John R. Epping	19	M		Whipmaker		200	Germany	
118	113	Hugh Gunngle	45	M		Driver			Ireland	
119	114	George Dickie	25	M		Upholster		200	Penna	
		Ellen "	23	F					Ohio	
		Jenette "	2	F					Penna	
	115	David "	55	M		Upholster		300	Scotland	
		Johanah "	35	F		Dressmaker			Penna	
		Mary "	12	F					Penna	
		David "	9	M					Penna	
		Nancy Gattons	23	F		"			England	
120	116	Hugh Gattons	48	M				300	Ireland	
		Charles "	28	M		Laborer	500		"	
		Ellen "	25	F		Leatherdresser			"	
		Francis Karr	28	M		Tailor			"	
							500	25,000		

Figure 14.3

Page No. 433

SCHEDULE 1. --Free Inhabitants in *the 4 Ward City of Pittsburgh* in the County of *Allegheny* State of *Penna.* enumerated by me, on the *5th* day of *June* 1860. *James G. Campbell* Marshal.

Post Office *Pittsburgh*

Number of Dwelling	Number of Family	The name of every person whose usual place of abode on the first day of June, 1860, was in this family	Description			Profession, Occupation, or Trade of each person, male and female, over 15 years of age.	Value of Real Estate	Value of Personal Estate	Place of Birth	
			Age	Sex	Color					
2588	4142	William Shaw	38	M		Corn Merchant	15,000	3000	Penna	
		Elza B. "	37	F					Md.	
		Elza	16	F					Penna	
		William	8	M					Penna	
		Mary Beattie	37	F		Cook			Ireland	
		Bell Hood	40	F		Housemaid			Ireland	
		Mary Dickson	40	F		Seamstress			Ireland	
		Barbara Sheets	16	F		Nurse			Germany	
		John Righn	25	M		Coachman			France	
2589	4143	Robert Beet	60	M		Private Gentleman	50,000	30,000	Penna	
		Adda "	92	F					Penna	
		Jane Ewing	55	F					Penna	
		Wm. H. Ewing	28	M		Oil Merchant			Penna	
		Adelina Garland	18	F		Housemaid			Penna	
		Catherine Bratton	17	F					Germany	
2590		James Laughlin	50	M		Iron Master	100,000	100,000	Ireland	
		Annie "	40	F					Penna	
		Henry A. "	21	M		Iron Merchant			Penna	
		Irwin "	19	M		Clerk			Penna	
		George M. "	17	M		Student			"	
		Eliza D. "	14	F					"	
		James "	12	M					"	
		James Steel	40	M		Clerk			"	
		Hanna While	16	F		Housemaid			Ireland	
		Grace Brice	25	F					Ireland	
		Hanna Berry	25	F					Ireland	
		Bartholomew Galliset	23	M		Coachman			France	
2591	4145	Sophia Grant	59	F				41,000	Tennessee	
		C.M. McCormick	28	M		Iron Manufacturer	30,000	30,000	Penna	
		Cecelia "	24	F					Penna	
							195,000	204,000		

Figure 14.4

Page No. *434*

SCHEDULE 1. --- Free Inhabitants in *the 4th Ward City of Pittsburgh* in the County of *Allegheny* State of *Penna.* enumerated by me, on the *5th* day of *June* 1860. *James G. Campbell* Marshal

Post Office *Pittsburgh* .

Number of Dwelling	Number of Family	The name of every person whose usual place of abode on the first day of June, 1860, was in this family	Description			Profession, Occupation, or Trade of each person, male and female, over 15 years of age.	Value of Real Estate	Value of Personal Estate	Place of Birth	
			Age	Sex	Color					
2592	4146	*Jane Little*	60	F		*Boarding House*	8,000	1,000	*Ireland*	
		Mary "	28	F					*Penna*	
		Harriet "	26	F					*Penna*	
		Lucienda "	22	F					*Penna*	
		Elizabeth "	18	F					*Penna*	
		David H. Gilman	37	M		*S. Boat Captain*			*Ohio*	
		Forest Miles	10	M					*Indiana*	
		Bridget McDonald	22	F		*Housemaid*			*Ireland*	
		Elizabeth Griffin	20	F		*Housemaid*			*Wales*	
		Thomas Might	23	M	B	*Waiter*			*Maryland*	
		Alfred Hood	25	M		*Salesman*			*Penna*	
		Isaac Towers	22	M		*Lawyer*			*Penna*	
		Chas. Peek	25	M		*Book Binder*			*Penna*	
		John Murray	23	M		*Bookeeper*			*Penna*	
		James Bradley	40	M		*Tinner*			*Maryland*	
		William Unger	18	M		*Student*			*Penna*	
2592	4147	*Elizabeth While*	30	F					*Ireland*	
		William While	8	M					*Penna*	
		John "	4	M					*Penna*	
		Mary Morgan	18	F		*Housemaid*			*Ireland*	
2593	4148	*William McKoen*	32	M		*Druggist*	1,000	500	*Ireland*	
		Harriet "	28	F					*Penna*	
		John "	5/12	M					*Penna*	
		Mary Jackson	18	F		*Housemaid*			*Penna*	
2594	4149	*Wm. Donaldson*	52	M		*Helmsman*			*Ireland*	
		Mary "	50	F					"	
		Harvey "	28	M		*Store Keeper*			*Penna*	
2595	4150	*Gabriel Mantson*	54	M		*Merchant*	1,000	500	*Penna*	
							10,000	2,000		

Figure 14.5

Page No. 21

SCHEDULE 1. --- Free Inhabitants in 8th Ward City of Pittsburgh in the County of Allegheny State of Penna. enumerated by me, on the 13th day of June 1860. R.O. Cummins Ass't Marshal

Post Office Pittsburgh

Number of Dwelling	Number of Family	The name of every person whose usual place of abode on the first day of June, 1860, was in this family	Description: Age	Description: Sex	Description: Color	Profession, Occupation, or Trade of each person, male and female, over 15 years of age.	Value of Real Estate	Value of Personal Estate	Place of Birth	
193	218	Thomas McClure	29	M		Carpenter		100	Ireland	
		Mary "	30	F					"	
		Margaret "	2	F					Penna	
		William "	8/12	M					"	
		Anne Gormley	15	F					Ireland	
		Patrick "	12	M					Ireland	
		James "	10	M					"	
		John "	5	M					Penna	
194	219	John Murphy	34	M		Coal Merchant		300	Ireland	
		Susan "	27	F					Penna	
		Francis "	5	M					"	
		Isabella	2	F					"	
195	220	James Mellon	45	M		Clerk	2500	300	Kentucky	
		Maria "	27	F					New York	
		James "	3	M					Penna	
		William	5/12	M					"	
196	221	Mary Hendspeth	50	F				300	England	
		Edward "	23	M		Marble Cutter		40	Penna	
		Anne "	19	F		Teacher			"	
197	222	Thomas Glinn	44	M		Blacksmith		50	Ireland	
		Frances "	37	F					Penna	
		Michael "	13	M					"	
		Bridget "	9	F					"	
		Mary "	7	F					"	
		Ellen "	3	F					"	
		Frances "	2	F					"	
		James "	1/4	M					"	
198	223	George Brooks	19	M		Laborer		65	England	
199	224	Thomas Rea	28	M		Laborer		40	Penna	
							2500	1195		

Figure 14.6

Page No. 484

SCHEDULE 1. --- Free Inhabitants in 9th Ward City of Pittsburgh in the County of Allegheny State of Penna. enumerated by me, on the 7th day of June 1860. Lawrence Mitchell Ass't Marshal

Post Office Pittsburgh .

Number of Dwelling	Number of Family	The name of every person whose usual place of abode on the first day of June, 1860, was in this family	Description			Profession, Occupation, or Trade of each person, male and female, over 15 years of age.	Value of Real Estate	Value of Personal Estate	Place of Birth	
			Age	Sex	Color					
124	124	Charles Bennett	28	M		Cooper		150	Germany	
		Mary "	28	F					"	
		Joseph	5	M					Penna	
		Margaret	3	F					"	
		old Mrs. Bennett	59	F		Dressmaker			Germany	
		Mary "	20	F		Dressmaker			Ohio	
		Leopold "	25	M		Machinist			Germany	
125	125	William Gray	30	M		Engineer	500	300	Scotland	
		Martha "	24	F					England	
		John "	2	M					Penna	
		Anne	1/2	F					Penna	
		Andrew "	18	M					Scotland	
126	126	William McGarvey	35	M		Glass Packer		270	Ireland	
		Margaret	35	F				10	"	
		John	11	M					Penna	
		Catherine	8	F					"	
		Elizabeth Miller	24	F		Farmer's Daughter		15	Ireland	
127	127	Anne Nichol	38	F		Engaged on Law		250	England	
		Sarah "	15	F					Penna	
		John "	13	M		Apprentice Moulder			"	
128	128	Harry Richards	35	M		Iron Roller		400	Penna	
		Elizabeth	33	F					"	
		Robert	11	M					"	
		Mary	10	F					"	
		John Richards	27	M		School Master			"	
129	129	David Wills	35	M		Blacksmith		75	"	
		Elizabeth	34	F					"	
		Martha	16	F					"	
		Barbara F. Neff	21	F		Farmer's Daughter			"	
130	130	Ellen Osetta Paisley	38	F			20,000	900	Ile of Man. British D.	
		Nancy	20	F		School Teacher			Pennsylvania	

Pittsburgh in 1859 Courtesy Carnegie Library, Pittsburgh.

In what ways, if any, did Pittsburgh's geographic features influence early residence and work patterns?

An historian tabulates census data

Michael Holt, an historian, used the census data from various Pittsburgh wards to determine the percentages of people in each category of occupation, property ownership, and place of birth. His summary data provide you with a means of testing your hypotheses about occupation, property, and place of birth in the walking city of Pittsburgh. Use the following three charts and your data from the index cards and ward map to answer this question:

1. Does Holt's data support your conclusions about social class and structure? If not how would you account for any differences?

An historian's interpretation of data

After collecting and analyzing census data, historians look to other social indicators to determine the social structure of a city. They use data such as club and church lists and political party affiliation in order to reconstruct the social structure of a particular period. Historians also look at work and residence patterns in order to discover the types of social interaction in a community. The following essay about

Table 14.1
Proportions of various economic groups in the adult white male population of Pittsburgh's wards in 1860

Ward	*Less Than $100*	*$100–999*	*$5,000–9,999*	*$10,000–24,999*	*$25,000–49,999*	*$50,000 plus*
First	63.8%	17.9%	3.6%	3.1%	0.8%	.5%
Second	52	18.5	5.9	6.5	2.2	1.1
Third	27.1	51.4	4.5	3.3	1	.13
Fourth	64.1	9.6	4.4	4.8	1.7	4.9
Fifth	43.1	37.8	3.5	2.1	0.8	0.23
Sixth	41	33.9	5.4	3	0.8	0.8
Seventh	45.8	28.6	2.5	1	1	0.66
Eighth	46.1	33.3	1.9	1.8	0.7	0.59
Ninth	45.5	37	3.3	1	0	0

Table 14.2
Proportions of ethnic groups in the adult white male population in Pittsburgh's wards in 1860

Ward	*Native*	*German*	*Irish*	*British*	*Other*
First	45.5%	19.7%	25.1%	5.7%	4 %
Second	53.7	11.1	23.8	11.4	
Third	32.9	23.1	40.4	3.6	
Fourth	46	13.7	25.3	3.9	11.1
Fifth	21.2	46.5	25.7	5.3	1.3
Sixth	41.3	15.5	36.3	6.6	.3
Seventh	39.2	25.6	30.2	3.4	1.6
Eighth	27.6	30	26.8	15.6	
Ninth	51.7	17.9	23.7	6.7	

Table 14.3
Proportions that men in various occupations constituted of the adult white male population of the wards of Pittsburgh in 1860

Ward	*Unskilled laborers*	*Skilled artisans*	*Small manufacturers*	*Clerks, shopkeepers*	*Professionals*	*Large manufacturers*	*Merchants*	*Bankers*
First	30.9%	31.6%	5.4%	22.8%	1.8%	1.6%	5 %	.8%
Second	22	26.1	5.5	28.2	6.3	3.4	5.3	3
Third	37.3	29.2	3.9	22.2	3.7	0.3	2.7	0.5
Fourth	23.6	20.9	4.4	28.8	7.4	4	9.4	1.4
Fifth	42.1	34.8	4.5	13.6	1.4	0.9	1.9	0.3
Sixth	32	30.4	7.8	20.5	2	1.6	4.9	0.7
Seventh	35.4	36.7	5.9	14.4	2.9	1.2	1.5	1
Eighth	45.1	32.7	6.3	11	1.1	1.9	1.7	0.1
Ninth	38	40.6	6.5	9.3	1.2	0.9	2.9	0.5

change Philadelphia from 1830 to 1860 analyzes the kinds of social indicators an historian must use to explain the social structure of a city. The historian, Sam Bass Warner, has written extensively about the development of cities. As you read this excerpt answer these questions:

1. Where did the different social classes in Philadelphia live?
2. How are Warner's conclusions about occupation, property and place of birth in Philadelphia similar to the ones you found in Pittsburgh during this period?
3. What groups have low and high status and class ranking? What reasons does Warner give for these rankings?

. . . . The social geography of the big city of 1860 was almost the reverse of the late nineteenth and early twentieth-century metropolis. Today's core of poverty and ring of affluence dates from the late nineteenth century and was not characteristic of the first wave of urban growth. Because Philadelphia grew so rapidly in the first half of the nineteenth century, and because it grew from such small beginnings, no large stock of old housing existed to absorb and to ghettoize the waves of poor immigrants. There were some run-down alleys adjacent to the wharves and south of Walnut Street, odd-lots not yet claimed for industry and commerce, but these pockets could not begin to hold the rush of newcomers. Philadelphians of all income levels had to locate in new construction. The shanties, shacks, backyard houses, and alley tenements . . . testify to the unpleasant meeting of low incomes with the costs of new construction. Segregated slums, however, did not result. Instead of large tracts of run-down houses occupied by Negroes or Italians or Jews, . . . Irish peasant immigrants flooded into every ward. The German immigrants . . . also lived in large numbers in most of the wards of the city. By 1860 Philadelphia's population was 30 per cent foreign-born; it included 95,000 immigrants from Ireland and 44,000 immigrants from Germany. Whatever accommodations had to be made within the city to incorporate this flood of newcomers into a new pattern of city life . . . took place in heterogeneous neighborhoods where almost every trade, nationality, and religion lived near every other. This was the pattern of the early big city, the way of the first era of the urban melting pot.

The scattering of immigrants through the wards of Philadelphia had been helped by the rapid growth of traditional occupations during the years 1774–1860. . . . Of the fifteen major occupations which together employed 30 to 40 per cent of all Philadelphia's adults, only two were new since the eighteenth century-machinist and factory operative . . . . In 1860, however, the big office had yet to come, and the big factories only manufactured locomotives, cottons, gas fixtures, umbrellas and parasols, clothing, trimmings, bricks, hosiery and iron machinery. Thus, the occupations of Philadelphia in 1860 remained much as they had in 1774. The city was still an agglomeration of old trades–laborers, clerks, carpenters, tailors, weavers, shoemakers, grocers, liquor dealers, butchers, tobacco dealers, cordwainers, blacksmiths, and cabinetmakers. The small size of the shops in which most of these trades were practiced had made the mixed wards of homes, workplaces, foreign-born and native Americans possible.

On top of this remarkably even grain of settlement the new industrial ways had begun to lay some of the patterns of the coming metropolis—especially the beginnings of a downtown, and some manufacturing sectors. The downtown had grown out of the expansion and differentiation of the old eighteenth century Delaware river importing merchant's district . . . . Manufacturers moved in next to these new dealers to supply some of their needs, and it was this manufacturing that gave the early nineteenth-century downtown its size and bulk. The downtown in 1860 was not, as it is today, a mere creature of offices and stores.

A quarter of all the city's manufacturing workers, 30,000 and more men, women, and children, worked in the principal downtown ward of Philadelphia. The garment industry in all its branches, boot and shoe makers, bookbinders, printers, and paper box fabricators, glass manufacturers, machinists, coopers, sugar refiners, brewers, and cigar makers especially concentrated here. The city's newspapers, banks, theatres, and restaurants, and many of its retail stores concentrated here too. Thousands of workers walked to the downtown every day, while omnibuses, and just before the Civil War, horse-drawn streetcars brought shopkeepers and customers. No tall office buildings yet outlined the downtown, no manufacturing lofts filled entire blocks, but the basic manufacturing-wholesale-retail-financial elements had already been assembled by 1860 for the future metropolis.

Beyond the downtown convenient transportation had encouraged additional manufacturing clusters. They took the common American pattern of radiating out from the original urban core like a crude spiderweb spun through the blocks of little houses. As the city grew along the Delaware shore, manufacturing sprang up behind its wharves and shipyards. To the north stood the leather and wool district, and the machinery and the textile mills. On the southside garment sweatshops scattered through the city's first slums. To the west, Market street, for many years the only road with a permanent bridge across the Schuylkill River, had become a manufacturing axis, especially for furniture, woodworking, and packing houses. On the northwest the new railroad yards there made that section the home of locomotive building and metalworking. . . .

These manufacturing concentrations introduced Philadelphia to some of the rhythms of an industrial metropolis. Work began to be separated from home. It is difficult today to estimate the number of commuting workers, as opposed to those employed within their own neighborhoods. Some estimate can be made, however, by comparing the residential information of the Street Directory of 1860 with the workplace information of the U. S. Census of the same year . . . .

By this very crude measure, the downtown and Market Street manufacturing clusters must have been the destination of thousands or workers. At least 20,000 persons, men, women, and children, must have come each day to staff the garment and shoe factories, printing plants, and furniture mills of the downtown. Market Street must have needed several thousand more workers. It seems most likely that the bulk of these early commuting workers came from the poor districts on the south side, while the skilled workers came from the northside residential concentrations. The northwest locomotive and metal-working center, the Kensington textile center, and the new Southwark mills must have been manned by workers living nearby. Altogether perhaps a third of Philadelphia's manufacturing workers were commuting to jobs in the manner of the majority of their successors in the twentieth-century industrial metropolis . . . .

By 1860 the combined effects of Philadelphia's rapid growth—the endless grid streets, the scattering of churches, stations, and factories, the flood of immigrants, the novelty, the sheer size, and pace of the big city—all its elements of change contributed to the thorough destruction of the informal neighborhood street life which had characterized the small-scale community of the eighteenth-century town. In response to these new conditions all Philadelphians, of every class and background, reacted in the same way to the loss of the old patterns of sociability and informal community. They rushed into clubs and associations . . . .

For thought and discussion

In what ways, if any, do you think one's race or religion might influence social class in the walking city? Why?

Individual and small group activities

1. In the older part of your city, find a residential block and snap several pictures or draw a couple of the houses. Take similar pictures in a new suburb of the city. Report to the class and show pictures of both kinds of houses. In which section did you find more interaction among the various people living on the block? Which houses seem to promote close social relationships among neighbors? Which kind of house do you prefer?
2. Find a very old person in your city. Ask him or her to describe the area of the city where he or she grew up. Did the person know all the nieghbors? Were they mostly native-born or immigrants? What were their occupations? Did they live long in the same house? Does the person know what happened to them? Report your findings to the class. You may wish to tape record the interview to form the basis of your report. How would you describe the kind of social structure in the city when the old person was young?

Government in the walking city

Assignment 15

During the period of the early walking city, private individuals and informal commities attempted to solve the city's problems. In Los Angeles, for example, each homeowner was required to sweep from the front of his house to the center of the road each day, and hang a lantern on his door from dusk to dawn. Volunteer fire companies and bucket brigades provided protection against fires in all early walking cities. Temporary committees raised money to aid the poor. They also regulated such things as the placement of horseracks and watering troughs within the town. Voluntary police guards protected the public order and banished beggars, drunkards, and loiterers from the city. However, as the problems of urban living became more complex, cities began to need a more formal governmental structure. Sanitation, canal and road building, and public order required the services of permanent legal bodies.

Gradually, city governments assumed responsibilities formerly held by individuals and temporary committees. Governmental leaders responded in a variety of ways to the growing problems of law and order, welfare, and the environment. Many city governments, however, proved inadequate to meet the growing list of serious urban problems.

In Assignment 9 you used the concepts of leadership and decision-making to analyze the role of government in the contemporary city. Assignment 15 deals with the attitudes of leaders and decision-makers as they fight against epidemics in the walking city. The concepts of leadership and decision-making will help you to understand the role of government in the early nineteenth century city.

Typhoid comes to the walking city

Epidemics hit the walking city. Government leaders and town councils often failed to act soon enough. When they did act, they usually used the wrong methods to stop the spread of disease. Lack of scientific knowledge and the unwillingness of people to eliminate filth and poor living areas hampered effective control of diseases. In the following play an imaginary city council attempts to cope with a typhoid epidemic. If possible act out this play in order that you might better understand the attitudes of the characters. After you have acted out this play, divide into groups of five or six and answer these questions:

1. What government agencies were available to combat the spread of disease?
2. What were the attitudes of the decision-makers? How did these attitudes affect the quality of the decisions?

The epidemic [20]

CHARACTERS
The Mayor
Leader of one faction of citizens
Leader of another majority faction
Doctor Fairweather
The very old member
Four members of the city council
The usher

PLACE
Around 1850, the meeting room of the City council in a large seaport. On the walls are paintings of several presidents, and copies of the Declaration of Independence and the Constitution. An American flag is prominently displayed. The city is very close to a navy and merchant marine camp. A long mahogany table stands in the middle of the room with each councilman's place marked by a blotter, inkstand and paper.

As the curtain rises, the Mayor is seen near the flag, talking to a group of city councilmen. Others are scattered around the room. Two are seated at the table writing. The secretary, with a pen between his teeth, is sorting out papers.

Mayor: (Rising as if for a great speech) And now, gentlemen, we shall take up the urgent and, I may say, very grave question for which I have called this special secret session.
(Surprise and alarm a sleeping member awakes.)
Second Councilman: What is it all about?
Voices: Quiet! Let him speak!
Mayor: Gentlemen, I have some news, unpleasant and unfortunate news, to impart to you. (Attention grows) But do not be unduly alarmed.
(Slow calming down)
Mayor: (Soothing, fatherly) Gentlemen, I implore you, in the name of patri-

[20](Adapted from *The Epidemic*, by Octave Mirbeau, 1898, trans. by Jacques Barzun, c. 1952 by Jacques Barzun from *The Modern Repertoire Series Two*, ed. by Eric Bentley, Univ. of Denver, 1952.)

otism! I appeal to your feelings of friendship and brotherly love. I call upon your devotion to our great city, upon your true inward municipal self. The matter I bring before you is not a matter of politics of our city, the city you love, the city that you represent and that you govern. Gentlemen! (With a catch in his voice) Within this city there has broken loose an epidemic of typhoid fever!

(The councilmen pale; they gaze at each other in silence)

Leader of the majority: (petrified) An epidemic, within the city?

Leader of the minority: (terrified) OUR city?

Mayor: You see right enough that it is not a matter of politics.

Leader of the minority and majority, together: In this city, an epidemic! In the city!

Mayor: When I say in the city, that isn't altogether accurate . . . Thank heaven, the epidemic is not inside the city. It is . . .

Leader of the minority: Well, where is it actually? Is it in the city or not? You must be more precise . . . Tell us the truth, we're not children. (With returning energy) We are men damn it! We've proved it in tighter corners than this. Where's the epidemic, speak up!

Voices: Yes, where? Speak up!

Mayor: You don't give me a chance. It is in the city, and yet not within it—or rather not quite. Let me explain.

(Murmurings)

Leader of the majority: Why don't you listen?

Mayor: (louder than the rest) The epidemic is in the navy and merchant marine camp.

Leader of the majority: Hear, hear!

Leader of the minority: (furious) Why couldn't you say so at once! Here we are, going through agonies—not that we're afraid of epidemics. We treat them with the manly scorn they deserve. But we have families—and friends, don't you know! And the camp is *not* in the city. The barracks are not within our city. Why, there are epidemics in that camp every year! It's not our affair. We can't help it.[21]

Mayor: No doubt you are right. In principle you are right. But you know how the Naval Commissioner is—rough, obstinate, wants his own way. He said he would move his men to another town. That means trade lost to us, gentlemen—and no band concert on Sundays—a serious blow to our beloved citizens. What he said was: "I'm not going to let my men croak like rats." His very words.

Leader of the minority: He's trying to scare us. Don't tell me he can move his men so easily, like a circus.

Leader of the majority: After all, it may be too bad. These people, when they decide on that kind of work expect sooner or later to die, don't they?

[21]What responsibility, if any, does the city have to the municipalities which surround it? Why?

Leader of the minority: That's what they're for!
Leader of the majority: It's their duty–
Very old councilman: Their honor!
Leader of the minority: At a time when the country is not at war, these epidemics are schools of heroism–a wonderful training place. Where else would our men learn contempt for death and sacrifice of self?
Mayor: Please allow me to add a word which may throw further light upon our discussions. Despite his rough manners, the Naval Commissioner is not an unreasonable man. I believe an understanding with him could be reached. I have the feeling that he is not so much concerned about the epidemic *as* epidemic–or at least. . . . I mean, what bothers him is public opinion. He fears the newspapers.
Leader of the minority: Well?
Mayor: Well, if my impression of his state of mind is correct, the commissioner would be prepared to consider his demands satisfied if we simply passed the appropriation for the specified requests. What he wants us to do is go through the formalities. He would not press us to carry them out. All he asks is that things should look right in the eyes of the press, the public, Congress. Isn't that, after all, perfectly reasonable–praiseworthy?
Councilman: But ticklish, risky, for us. What guarantee have we that he'll play fair, as regards the expense?
Mayor: I will guarantee it.
Councilman: That's not enough. Have you a written agreement?
Mayor: No.
Councilman: Have you his word of honor?
Mayor: No. I have something better than all that: his desire for a quiet life.
Councilman: We have to be careful just the same.
Councilman: I object. It would open a serious door, I mean create a dangerous precedent.
Very old councilman: (his voice shaking) Typhoid fever is a national institution. Let us not lay violent hands on our national traditions.
Doctor: The country can still boast hearts of oak. (All rise, talk and laugh as the formal business is put through by the Mayor and the secretary. In the midst of this, enter the usher, looking upset. He delivers a letter to the Mayor.)
Mayor: What is it? (Taking the letter) What's this?
Usher: I don't know, sir.
Mayor: Who brought it?
Usher: A man in mourning.
Mayor: A man in mourning Ah! (He turns the letter over, looking hard at each side) A city man?
Usher: I don't know, sir.
Mayor: You'd never seen him before?
Usher: No, sir.
Mayor: Ah! He left no word?
Usher: No, he did not say a word.

Mayor: (also upset) That's queer. I don't know why . . . I have a feeling . . . . Gentlemen, I think this letter brings bad news.
Councilman: Open it! Open it!
Mayor: I'm afraid to open it. (All are silent, staring at the Mayor. He opens the letter, reads a few words and turns pale as he lets out an exclamation.) Oh! God!
Councilman: Well, what is it?
(General confusion)
Mayor: God, oh God!
Councilman: (to the others) Be quiet! (to the Mayor) Tell us!
Mayor: Gentlemen–(he cannot go on)
Councilman: Are you ill?
Councilman: What makes you look so–?
Mayor: Gentlemen–
Councilman: Why you're shaking.
Mayor: (mastering his emotion) Gentlemen . . . Something terrible–unheard of–appalling!
All: Speak! Tell us! Out with it!
Mayor: Gentlemen! (The letter falls to the table.) One of our citizens has died!
Councilman: What's that you say?
Mayor: A citizen . . . a merchant . . . has died–carried off–by the epidemic!
A few voices: It can't be! Impossible!
Doctor: (screaming) Don't touch that letter! . . . . It's surely not been disinfected! Burn it! (He dashes forward, seizes it by one corner and throws it into the fireplace. He then pulls out of his pocket an atomizer with which he sprays himself and the whole room, striding swiftly.) Disinfection, gentlemen, dis-infection!
(Terror overwhelms the council who have suddenly become motionless, holding rigid poses. The Mayor continues speaking through the deathly silence, in a shaking, tearful voice.)
Mayor: We do not know his name . . . No matter, we are intimate with his soul . . . Gentlemen, he was a respected merchant, sleek, rosy-cheeked, blissful. His big somach was the envy of the poor . . . . Every day at the same hour, he took his constitutional walk in the city, with a smiling, contented look on his face. His double chin, his chubby hands were to everyone a living lesson in social welfare . . . . It seemed as if he should never die, and yet he has died. A merchant has died!
Councilman: (as if chanting a church hymn) A merchant has died!
All: (one after the other) A merchant has died!
(Silence–all the council stare at one another)
Mayor: It is not in my power, gentlemen, to render judgment on the life of a fellow merchant whose passing we all lament. He was the worthiest of merchants, friend and brother to us all.
(A few councilmen wipe away their tears)

Mayor: It will be to the merchant's lasting credit that he remained faithful to the national tradition of saving. For as was said on one occasion by a great philosopher, whose name escapes me, the Habit of Saving is the Mother of Virtue and the Safeguard of Law and Order. Let us lament and venerate our friend.

Councilmen: Long live our friend!

Mayor: He was a hero, gentlemen, our hero. A great statesman did say once that heroic times are a thing of the past, but he had forgotten the small investor. And so, our fellow merchant, farewell!

(General approval. Cheers.)

Doctor: And now, gentlemen, we must not allow ourselves to be bowed down by this unexpected disease, which is highly irregular and I daresay anti-scientific—don't you see? We must resist!

All: Yes, you're right.

Doctor: Up and at 'em!

All: Right! You said it!

Doctor: In the face of adversity, we must be men!

All: Cheers!

Doctor: When evil threatens, we gird our loins!

All: Hurrah!

Doctor: Are you game for the supreme sacrifice?

Council: We are!

Doctor: It will take money.

Council: We will get it. We will find it, we'll raise taxes!

Doctor: Use eminent domain!

All: That's it! We will!

Doctor: Destroy the slums, which are the seedbed of pestilence!

Councilmen: We'll raze them to the ground![22]

Doctor: And then rebuild!

Councilman: We will rebuild!

All: We will!

Councilman: We'll make room for public gardens!

Councilman: We'll plant avenues of trees!

Doctor: Pour light into dark corners, sanitate the sewers!

All: Yes, we will!

Doctor: We'll relieve the congestion in schools, convents, houses of prostitution and barracks.

Councilman: We'll tap new sources of pure water. The waters will spring!

Doctor: We will set up a committee for Health and Hygiene—a standing committee.

All: Cheers!

[22]If you were a member of the city council would you vote for this position? Why, or why not?

Doctor: Let us vote! It's for war against disease! Down with death! Long live science!
Councilman: Our friend will be avenged!
Doctor: A vote! A vote!
Mayor: Yes, gentlemen, we are about to vote. We are about to vote unheard of things—emergency measures—
Mayor: And now, dear friends to a vote!
Doctor: I ask for $100,000.
Councilman: (shrugging contemptuously) What can you do with $100,000? Don't be silly: $2,000,000.
Councilman: More! More!
Mayor: Let us settle for a round figure—5 million. We can always raise the ante.
All: Yes 5 million, 5 million.
Very old councilman: But where will we get it?
Mayor: (scornfully) We shall find it, sire, in our patriotism . . . .
All: Bravo! Well said!
Mayor: . . . our heroism . . .
Doctor: . . . in our will and our faith.
All: Yes, yes.
Mayor: To a vote, my friends, a vote!
All: Let's vote! Here is my vote! (They scramble about the table brandishing ballots, their faces flushed, their gestures uncontrolled.)

Yellow fever in New Orleans, 1853

Other frightening plagues like yellow fever and cholera descended upon American cities in the nineteenth century. Yellow fever results from mosquitos and stagnant water. However, many people in 1853 still believed that diseases came from either the sins of the lower classes or gases arising from filth. Great numbers of urban residents died from these plagues. These epidemics particularly ravaged the lower classes who lived in slumlike conditions and could not flee to the country as the wealthy could. Examine the following essay then answer these questions.

1. Who were the leaders in the fight against the epidemic?
2. What methods did the city leaders use to fight the epidemic? Were these methods successful?
3. In what ways were the attitudes and methods of the New Orleans council like or unlike the leaders and the methods used in the play?

. . . About the middle of June people whispered about some sickness among the shipping in the upper part of the city. The report was hushed up, or treated as a mere rumor of some panic-makers, or idle gossipers. The general cry was—"Hush up. Don't alarm people. You will frighten them into a fever. It is all humbug. A slight sickness among sailors and poor laborers, who eat bad food, etc." And so people determined to ignore and discredit the existence of the fever.

But the sickness would not consent to be ignored. All the while it was secretly and gradually spreading its poison—sowing the seeds of death, filling up the wards of the Charity Hospital, and thinning the crowds of laborers on the river. The small number of our citizens who examined the statistics of mortality became alarmed. But they were called panic-makers. The disease was just called shipfever which threatened only sailors. But what did the mortuary statistics show? On the books at the Charity Hospital the following cases were entered:

"James McGingan, laborer; native of Ireland; one week in the city; had just landed from a vessel direct from England; was taken sick on the 23 of May; entered the Hospital on the 27; and died the same day of black vomit.

"Gerhart H. Worte, a native of Germany; a sailor, last from Bremen, died on the 30 of May, of black vomit.

"Michael Mahoney, a native of Ireland—last from England; died June 7, of black vomit.

"Thomas Hart, a native of England—last from Liverpool; died on 10 of June, of black vomit.

"Margaret Runnel, fifteen days from Boston; died on 11 of June; of black vomit."

These were the first five cases which ended fatally. But these were ordinary occurrences, by no means justifying fears of an epidemic. Only five deaths from yellow fever in the Charity Hospital in twelve or fourteen days!

The first of July arrived. There had been but one death from yellow fever. But July was less satisfactory. The first week exhibited a result which created alarm. The deaths from yellow fever had doubled. Yet there were only 59 deaths out of a population of 80,000. "Let us hold on a little longer before we permit ourselves to be frightened," was the cry. The 16 of July arrives—204 deaths by yellow fever for one week. "That is serious, certainly." —"No, the fever exists among the shipping and very poor. It will not extend to the *more respectable* people." The Council was not alarmed, and the Mayor was not upset. Even the newspapers curbed their natural tendency for panics. However, at the same time the press criticized the Council for not cleaning the streets, or creating a Board of Health, or doing *something* to prevent the epidemic.[23] Alas! They knew well enough that the epidemic was already near the city . . . .

About the middle of June there was one ominous announcement understood by the old residents. It was the publication of the Program of the Howard Association. The association contained thirty gentlemen who had long organized to aid the poor sick *"during an epidemic."* This publication was loudly censured. It was equivalent to a declaration that an epidemic was

[23]**If you were a member of the New Orleans city council what recommendations would you make to prevent the spread of the epidemic?**

in the city. The doctors disputed this point. The disease was confined to the lower classes and the poor section of town. An "epidemic" must include all classes.

Finally the Council joined the forecast of the Howard Association. Meeting on the 27 of July it passed the following resolutions:

"Whereas, there now exists a general fear of epidemic among the good citizens of this city."

"And whereas, it is most imporant that every means be taken to prevent the spread of the disease and mass panic, we will now issue reports about the progress or decline of the epidemic."

Reports were not enough! The people were then dying at the rate of a hundred a day, in every part of the city. Fifteen hundred had already died of a disease many believed to be "sporadic and confined almost exclusively to the poorer sections of the city." Fifteen hundred in a few weeks–just one half the total number of the victims of the epidemic of 1847–which was considered the severest that ever visited the city. And the city government was only issuing reports!

The Council next created a Board of Health, placed $10,000 at its disposal, and then adjourned. Many of its members left the city. A few remained to perform their duties, like men and leaders.

The Board of Health set to work vigorously and earnestly. They established infirmaries in various parts of the city. It was too late to discuss preventive measures. Funeral processions crowded every street. No vehicles could be seen except doctor's cabs and coaches, passing to and from the cemeteries. Hearses, often solitary, moved toward those gloomy destination. The hum of trade was hushed. The streets, usually shining with fashion and beauty, were silent. The tombs–the home of the dead–were the only places where there was life–where crowds assembled.

To realize the full horror of the disease, you must go into the crowded areas of the laboring classes. Go into those miserable shanties which are the disgrace of the city. The poor immigrant class cluster together in filth, sleeping a half-dozen in one room, without ventilation. They have wet, filthy yards. When it rains these yards convert to green puddles–fit homes for frogs and sources of poisonous malaria. Here you will find scenes of woe, misery and death, which will haunt you. Here you will see the dead and the dying, the sick and the well in one bed. Here you will see the living baby sucking death from the yellow breasts of its dead mother. Here father, mother, and child die in one another's arms. Here you will find whole families swept off in a few hours. None are left to mourn or procure the rites of burial. Offensive odors frequently drew neighbors to such awful spectacles. This terrible disease gradually winds its folds around its victims, beguiles him, cheats his senses, and then consigns him to grim death.[24]

[24]Should citizens be willing to pay higher taxes to improve health conditions in the poorer sections of the city? Why, or why not?

The Board of Health began its operations about the 1st of August. Daily reports were then published of the burials in all the cemeteries. Beginning on the 1st of August with 106 deaths by Yellow Fever, the number increased daily, until on August 7, they amounted to 909 deaths by Yellow Fever. The next week showed a continued increase: 1288 by Yellow Fever. This was believed to be the maximum. There had been nothing to equal it in the history of any previous epidemic. No one believed it could be exceeded. But the next week the total deaths from Yellow Fever were 1346. On the 22 of August alone, 239 died of Yellow Fever. This proved to be the maximum mortality rate. From that point it began to slowly decrease. For the month of August alone 5122 died of Yellow Fever. The total number who died from the epidemic was 7439.

But do these figures include all the deaths? Alas! no. Hundreds have been buried of whom no note was taken. Hundreds have died away from the city, in attempting to fly from it. These figures do not include those who died in the suburbs. But even these figures need no additions to prove that the most destructive plague of modern times has just wreaked its vengeance upon New Orleans. Estimating the total deaths at 8000 for three months, we have ten percent of the whole population of New Orleans . . . .

For thought and discussion

Judging from the attitudes of governmental leaders portrayed in this Assignment, what predictions can you make about government in the street car city?

Individual and small group activities

1. Choose another classmate to work on this project. One partner should go to the Board of Health and find out what services are offered such as free shots, x-rays, dental care, and birth control information. The other partner should find out from the Board of Health what kinds of jobs are available in the local health department. What are the duties of these jobs? What kinds of personal requirements are needed in order to get these jobs? Combine your information and report to the class about the health services and health jobs available in your city.
2. Find out when a Board of Health or Sanitation Department was started in your city. Why did the city decide to start such an agency? Was it in response to a specific problem like an epidemic? Report your conclusions to the class.

INTRODUCTION
to the unit on
the streetcar city

Part II of this book analyzed the walking city, the name which historians have given to cities before the development of public transportation. The next five assignments, which make up Part III, will examine the American city from 1860 to 1910. The readings in this part illustrate how the walking city changed during the latter part of the nineteenth century under the impact of the streetcar.

In 1820 only seven per cent of the total population of the United States lived in urban areas. By 1910 urban areas contained forty-five per cent of the total population. People from rural areas and immigrants from abroad, as well as the children of city residents, contributed to urban population growth. Advances in transportation also helped cities grow in size. The introduction of the streetcar enabled persons to travel greater distances between work and home. In addition, the railroads connected urban areas, thus increasing trade, and passenger travel between cities. Changes in transportation had an enormous impact on the physical, social, and economic structure of late nineteenth century cities.

In the walking city residences, businesses, and social activities were located near each other. Your study of Pittsburgh's social structure in Assignment 14 indicated that the more affluent people lived near the center of the walking city while the poor lived on the outskirts. In the streetcar city, however, the poor lived increasingly near the center while many of the middle and upper classes moved to the suburbs. This movement foreshadowed the "flight to the suburbs" of our contemporary city.

The streetcar city also differed from the walking city in its economic and political structure. Manufacturing boomed and distribution methods grew and diversified. More factories, skyscrapers, and a great influx of people contributed to growing problems for city governments. The loose, informal form of government of the walking city could no longer effectively cope with these new problems. Rapid change brought increased frustrations to the residents of cities. These residents increasingly looked to their city governments for help. The study of the streetcar city should demonstrate that the roots of current urban problems lie buried deep in the cities of the latter part of the nineteenth century.

THE TOONERVILLE TROLLEY THAT
MEETS ALL THE TRAINS

Cartoons, by Fontaine Fox.
Harper, N. Y., 1918.

Images of the streetcar city

Assignment 16

Images of the streetcar city are both different and more diverse than the images of the walking city. Many technological and economic advances occurred in late nineteenth century cities, along with changes in the attitudes and expectations of the residents. Cities continually expanded, making an accurate picture of the total city more difficult for one person to grasp. Residents both praised and damned the streetcar city. Rapid change in all aspects of residents' lives brought both hope and despair.

In Assignment 16 you will use pictures and written accounts to make a chart indicating the physical, economic, social, and political images of the streetcar city. This chart will help you to make general hypotheses about life in the late ninteenth century. Assignments 17 through 20 provide information to help you test your hypotheses and to form conclusions about life in the streetcar city.

Visual images of the streetcar city

Many photographs and other visual images exist of the streetcar city. They offer a vivid picture of life in the American city in the late nineteenth century. The two menus and twelve photographs which follow illustrate both physical and attitudinal characteristics of the streetcar city. Prepare a chart to guide your analysis of images of the streetcar city. Your chart should include these categories: physical, economic, social and political. Under each category list the images presented by the menus and photographs. In Part 2 of this assignment you will use the chart to list other characteristics. You will use the completed chart at the end of this assignment to form some general hypotheses about the characteristics of the streetcar city.

MENU

Little Neck Clams
Montrachet
Potage tortue verte à l'anglaise
Potage crème d'artichauts
Amontillado
Whitebait, Filets de bass, sauce crevettes
Rauenthaler
Concombres
Timbales à la milanaise
Filet de boeuf au madère
Pommery sec
Selle d'agneau de Central Park, sauce menthe
Moët et Chandon Grand Crèmant Impèrial, Magnums
Petits pois, Tomates farcies, Pommes croquettes
Côtelletes de ris de veau à la parisienne
Cèpes à la bordelaise
Asperge froide en mayonnaise
Sorbet au Marasquin
Pluvier rôti au cresson
Chateau Margaux
Salade de laitue
Fromages variès
Old Madeira Charleston and Savannah
Bombe de glace Fraises Pêches Gâteaux
Raisins de serre
Cafè
Cognac et Liqueurs

Menu for a dinner worthy of New York's elite.

MENU

Family	*No. of school children*	*Breakfast*	*Lunch*	*Supper*
1	2	Bread and tea only	None	Bread and tea
2	1	None	Soup from charity	Coffee and bread
3	1	Coffee and rolls (no butter or jam)	Coffee and bread	Tea and bread
4	3	Bread and tea only	None	Bread and tea only
5	2	None	Soup with the soup-meat	Piece of bread
6	1	Bread and jam with coffee	None	Tea and bread with jam

Daily menu for poor, six families
From: John Spargo, *The Bitter Cry of Children* (New York, 1906).

Madison and Franklin Streets, Chicago, 1906

Courtesy
Chicago Historical Society.

The Woolworth Building
Museum of the City of New York.

The tallest skyscraper in New York in 1913, called "the dimestore king's monument."

Tenement housing circa 1900
History Division, Natural History Museum of Los Angeles.

Labor Day, Buffalo, New York, 1905
Courtesy Library of Congress.

The Jacob A. Riis Collection, Museum of the City of New York.

Fifth Street, New York City
Before the appointment of the sanitation commissioner in 1895.

Fifth Street, New York City
After the appointment of the sanitation commissioner in 1895.

Sears, Roebuck catalogue, Fall, 1897
Courtesy Sears, Roebuck and Company.

Westinghouse Electric Company, 1910
Courtesy Carnegie Library, Pittsburgh.

The grain movement from the West, 1877
Courtesy Library of Congress.

Poster for popular melodrama, ***The War of Wealth*****, 1896**

Courtesy Library of Congress.

The workingman's mite, 1871,
Beginning of Labor Unions

Ad for American-made cleaning fluid, 1896,
The Chinese Must Go

Courtesy Library of Congress.

Accounts of life in the streetcar city

Unlike the travelers accounts of the walking city, the following six accounts do not attempt to describe the entire streetcar city. Each account presents a different fragment of urban life in the late 19th century. When you combine these accounts with data from the pictures, you will have a mutli-dimensional image of the streetcar city. Read each account and continue to list the physical, economic, social, and political characteristics on your chart. At the conclusion of this assignment use your chart to develop some general hypotheses about life in the late nineteenth century city.

Rural homes safeguard the nation

George Maxwell, newspaper editor and professional government bureaucrat, wrote the following article after a series of riots broke out in Chicago. While Maxwell was active in urban reform, he viewed the city as a growing evil.

The people of this nation are at the forks of the road. We must now choose the way we will go.

On the one hand, we may take a course which will continue to pile up millions of mere wage-earners in our cities and towns. These millions are nothing more than day-laborers, mechanics, factory workers. They receive a bare subsistence wage. They have no roots, no rural soil to insure their patriotism.[25]

On the other hand, we may choose to spread our people out over the land in homes, suburban homes, or garden farms. Every family would be self-supporting. Economic depressions would not affect these rural people. These patriotic rural people would stand like a granite wall against communism and anarchy. Communism and anarchy are products of the cities.

Let us now lay aside all differences and unite in one grand and harmonious effort to turn the people from the cities and move them back to the country.

The city, the hope of democracy

Frederic Howe was a lawyer, politician, essayist, and reformer. He was active in reform movements in New York and Cleveland. Howe believed that real and lasting political reform required a reorganization of the economic system based on the "natural advantages" of the city.

The city is the hope of the future. Here life is full and eager. Here the major industrial problems will first be worked out. Democracy is organizing in the city. As time goes on, the powers of democracy will eliminate the bad conditions that modern industrial life has created. To those who fear reform and

[25]In what ways, if any, was Maxwell's pessimistic outlook of urban life justified?

greater government power I answer: "There is only one cure for the evils which newly acquired freedom produces. That cure is more freedom."

Many doubt the ability of democracy to solve the problems of city life. For the common man, it is easier to rely on the political boss, the political party, and the System which has been elected. However, history shows that society has constantly improved because of political activity from the common man. The great advances in government have been achieved because the common people slowly broke down privilege after privilege in the movement toward liberty.

The great problem before the American people is how to keep opportunity open. How can industry be saved from privilege? How can talent and ability instead of privilege be made the criteria for election? These are the problems which the city must solve, for the city is the life of the future.

Already too many costs burden the ordinary citizen. This burden arises in large measure from the increased cost of living. You can trace this increased cost of living to the monopolies of rent, transit, light, heat, and water.

We should socialize rents and services. Socialism would raise the standard of living. Cooperative agencies would make the city like an enlarged home, offering its members many of the comforts and conveniences that only a few have now. With greater opportunities and services, the citizen's love for his city would increase. This love would in turn purify our politics. Politics will remain corrupt as long as the rich and privileged classes are united against the community.

With such a program achieved, democracy would cease to be a class struggle. People would be united. The merit system, the party, and the ballot, would insure democracy. No longer would the privileged use government to maintain the status quo.

Indianapolis: A city of homes

This article about Indianapolis reflects the quickly changing urban lifestyle of the late nineteenth century. Continue to list the characteristics of the streetcar city as you read.

Indianapolis was a town that became a city against its will. It liked its own way, and its way was slow paced. But when the calamity could no longer be averted, it had its trousers creased and its shoes polished. Indianapolis accepted with good grace that its population was approximately two hundred thousand and that it had crept to a place near the top in the list of bank clearances. A man who left Indianapolis in 1880, returned in 1900—the Indianapolitan always goes back; he cannot successfully be transplanted—to find himself a stranger in a strange city. Once he knew all the people who rode in buggies. But on his return he found new people in smart vehicles. Once he had been able to talk on topics of the day with a passing friend in the middle of the street. Now he must duck and dive, and keep an eye on the policeman if he wanted to make a safe crossing. He was asked to luncheon at a club. In the old days there were no clubs: they were looked on as wicked things. He was taken to look at factories which were the largest of their kind in the world. At the railroad yards he saw machinery being loaded for shipment to Russia and Chile. He was told that books published at Indianapolis were sold in New York, Boston, Toronto, and London. He was driven over asphalt streets to parks that had not been dreamed of before his term of exile.[26]

The saga of a business girl in the 1890's

In this account Elizabeth McCallie recalls her experiences as a young business girl in Atlanta in the 1890's. While she achieved moderate success, many others did not.

The first attempt to teach commercial subjects in any public school in the United States was undertaken in 1888 by the city of Atlanta.

When I entered Girls' High School, the new department had been in operation only a few years. On first entering school I enrolled in the regular course and remained in it for a year. Having been born with a passion for independence, the opportunities offered by the new course urged me to change. My second year saw me a student in the commercial department. In the 1890's, a woman's opportunity to make a living was limited to teaching, sewing, working in a factory, or becoming a practical nurse after a long apprenticeship. Many people thought that working in a man's office was neither desirable nor quite respectable. Thus to enter a field so new and so supposedly fraught with danger took courage and determination. For myself, I wanted work—the sooner the better.

I found stenography far more difficult to learn than Latin or any subject I had taken in the regular course. The girls in the regular course looked on those taking the business course as inferior. There was and has been a snobbery in Atlanta dating back to the 1870's. Before that time the citizens were so busy building a city, only to have it destroyed in the 60's, that snobbery had little chance to grow. With the re-birth of the town, money became the yard-stick by which people were measured. Some, having little money, sewed for others, or sold milk, or flowers. My family and I worked openly and were not ashamed of the fact. We had no aspirations to join the so-called socially prominent or the newly rich. We had many friends of our own choosing.

Mrs. Douglas, my teacher, suggested that I work after graduation for a short time, without pay, for practical experience. She sent me to a jeweler's to assist the bookkeeper. I reported for work at 8 a.m. and had an hour off

[26]How do you account for the different attitudes of urban life presented by Maxwell, Howe, and the citizen from Indianapolis?

for the midday meal. I worked until 6 o'clock six days a week.

After working for no wages for two months, I was offered a place in the office of a collection agency. The office occupied half of the upper floor over Lynch's store on Whitehall Street. Lynch always had jugs of liquor on display by his door and heaven only knows what for sale inside.

The credit company had two dingy windows overlooking Whitehall and two overlooking Broad. (If you look back at your map of walking Atlanta in Assignment 12 you can find exactly where Mrs. McCallie worked.) A partition for a private office for the grand muck-a-mucks took up a great amount of the space. The rest of the space was occupied by the girls who worked there. A table extended down the middle of the room where some helpers sat. I had a typewriter against the wall. A narrow passage permitted movements to and fro. Several single gas fixtures, high up near the ceiling, shed feeble rays of light on the workers. There was one very unsanitary toilet for the whole upstairs. The salary paid was twenty-five dollars a month. The hours were from 8 a.m. to 6 p.m. with one-half hour for lunch. There was not time to go home so we brought sandwiches. There was no place to eat the sandwiches, so we walked up and down the block.

When I got influenza and finally recovered, I vowed I'd get another job. I found one in a dry goods store, but all the office workers were men. They did not like the intrusion of a woman in their field. [27] Little by little, I found myself forced behind a counter, or when shipments of new coats came in, I was asked to model them for the well-to-do customers. I received $30 a month. As I had not been trained to be a clothes horse or to sell merchandise, I was delighted when I was recommended for the position of secretary to the Superintendent of Public Schools and clerk of the Atlanta Board of Education.

I got the job and was paid forty dollars a month and thought that a fortune. Salaries in grammer schools ranged from forty dollars a month to one-hundred-and-twenty dollars a month for the principal. The Board had a unique and expedient way of balancing their budget each year. They deducted anywhere from 9 per cent to 15 per cent from the salaries of all teachers.

Girls' High School in the 1890's was the center of the culture of the city. The school brought lecturers on art, music, etc., to the city. When something worthwhile was to be sponsored, Girls' High was called upon.

New names for East Siders

The following account reveals how many of us got the names we have today. Changing a name often meant that a new immigrant could more easily blend into the new culture and would face less discrimination.

The directory-makers are experiencing less difficulty every year with the names

[27]Do you think women should be permitted to work in any occupation they choose? Why, or why not?

of the Russian and Polish Jews on the East Side of New York. Their unpronounceable old country names are made pronounceable by the children or the teachers when the second generation goes to school. While in some instances the new names sound like the original, they are written differently. In most cases the new names bear no resemblance to the roots from which they were taken. This is true not only of the family names, but of the "front" names. A long-bearded pushcart man was asked in court recently, "What is your name?"

"Yaikef Rabinowski," he answered.

The magistrate evidently thought that was the man's family name, and asked: "What's your Christian name?"

The man became indignant at being suspected of having anything "Christian" about him, and "front name" has been used for "Christian name" ever since.

Yitschok, the Hebrew of Jacob, has been made Hitchcock, and an old man whose neighbors know him as Checkel has assumed the easier name of Elwell. There are many similar cases of evolution. There are more American, English and even French names among the dwellers in the ghetto which are the result of accident as much as anything else. Children are sent to school and their names are placed on the records by the teacher. The child does the best he can with the unpronounceable thing. After the children have been in school a short time, they and their parents become known by the name given to them by the teacher.

An example of this kind was mentioned recently by a young woman who had been a teacher in a school where many Russian children were pupils. "A man came one day," she said, "with two boys who could not say a word in English. Their names were impossible except for those who had acquired the East Side jargon. When the man was gone I made one understand that his name would be John. The other would have to answer to the name William. In some way or other their family name, which was full of twists and turns, and ended with a 'witch,' became Holz. Within a few weeks John and William Holz made themselves understood in fair English. Within a year they were star pupils. One day the father called at the school to see me about his boys, and introduced himself as Mr. Holz! He seemed to be as much at home with the name as though he had been born with it. Many immigrants quickly become used to their new names.

In many instances a sign bought at a bargain has caused men to assume a new name. Sometimes the changes are made without the least feeling in the matter. One East Side patriarch said, "We honor our fathers just as much, even if we drop their names. Nothing good ever came to us while we bore them, possibly we'll have more luck with the new names."

But there are cases where men changed their names because they wanted to hide their foreign origin.[28] Thus a family came to New York with the name

[28]Would you consider changing your name? Why, or why not?

of Neuberger. Presently the name became Newburger. Then it was changed to Newburg. Now the two remaining brothers are known, one as Mr. New and the other as Mr. Berg.

"It does some people good to change their names," said an East Side observer." I doubt whether Mr. Gladstone would ever have been the great man he was if his ancestors had not dropped the Freudenstine for Gladstone, or whether other German names would have been as well received as their Americanized substitutes." The man could not be convinced that Gladstone was originally Freudenstein.

One group of names on the East Side is always recognized as "Bohemian." To this class belong the names Yeiteles, Abeles, Karpeles, Kakeles, and a number of other names ending with "les." When the owners of some of these names outgrow the East Side and move uptown they drop one of the e's in their name and then blossom forth as Karpels, Kakels, etc.

One Bohemian said that his countrymen were proud of the "les" names, because they show that Aristoteles, Sophocles, Pericles and Hercules were all Bohemians.

For thought and discussion

What were three of the most major problems facing the resident of the streetcar city? Are these problems similar to the problems of urban residents in the walking and contemporary cities?

Individual and small group activities

1. Get a partner and interview ten different people from various age groups. Ask them what their ethnic background is and whether their names have been changed. If their names were changed, ask them when and why? What differences exist in pride in ethnic backgrounds among age groups. Report your findings to class. Ask each class member if his name was changed and when it was changed?
2. Go to your local historical association and find out if and when your city began streetcar transportation. Write a brief historical sketch of the history of the streetcar in your city. Report to class. If possible illustrate your report to class with photographs or drawings of streetcars in your city. (If your city never adopted streetcars report to the class why streetcar transportation never came to your city.)

From walking city to streetcar city

Assignment 17

In Assignment 12 you examined work and residence patterns, spatial distribution, and spatial interaction, in early Atlanta. People lived close to their work, sometimes in the same place as their work. Residents could walk to most work and social activities. The necessity of traveling by foot or horse and buggy limited the size of the urban area, and encouraged communication and interaction among all members of the city.

In the latter half of the nineteenth century, increasing population coupled with the growth of business establishments caused congestion and overcrowding in the city. Advances in transportation such as the omnibus (a horse pulled bus), the commuter railroad, and the streetcar enabled residents to move to the suburbs and commute to work in the central city.

The omnibus and commuter railroad were rather expensive to ride. The streetcar, however, introduced in the late 1850's, cost less. City governments and private companies installed miles of streetcar tracks in the 1880's. More people could travel faster and cheaper. This development increased the separation of home and work. The following assignment will explore the impact of technology on the city and examine the effect of this new technology on attitudes about life in the city.

City growth, 1875–1900

With the introduction of the streetcar the urban area expanded tremendously. Real estate developers saw quick profits available in the building of suburban homes. The following maps and advertisements from Chicago in the late nineteenth century indicate the impact of the streetcar on city growth. As you examine the maps and advertisements answer these questions:

1. How does the map of the streetcar lines in Chicago correspond to the map of the area of Chicago in 1893?
2. In what ways did the installation of streetcar lines in Chicago influence the pattern of city growth?
3. Why would the more affluent inner city residents sell their homes and move to homes in the suburbs?

Figure 17.1
Growth of Chicago, 1871–1915

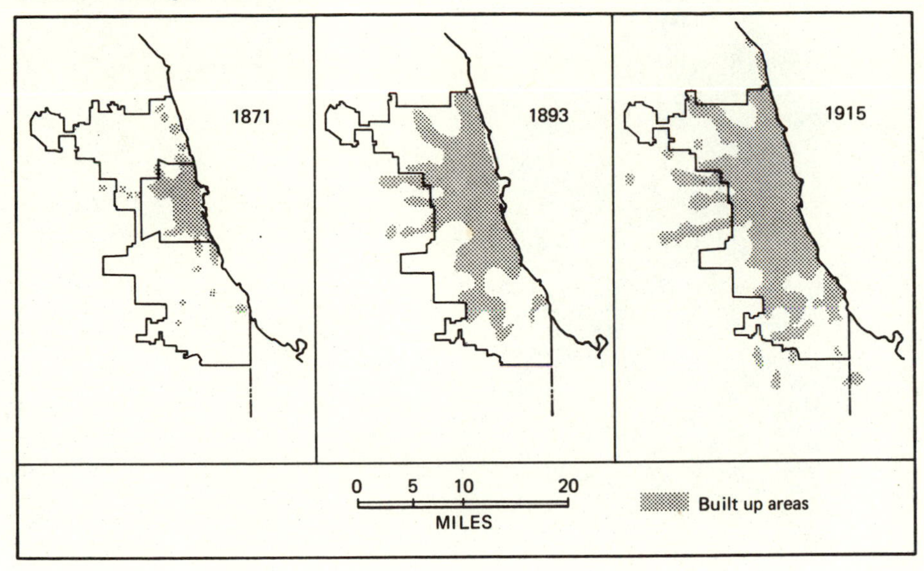

Figure 17.2

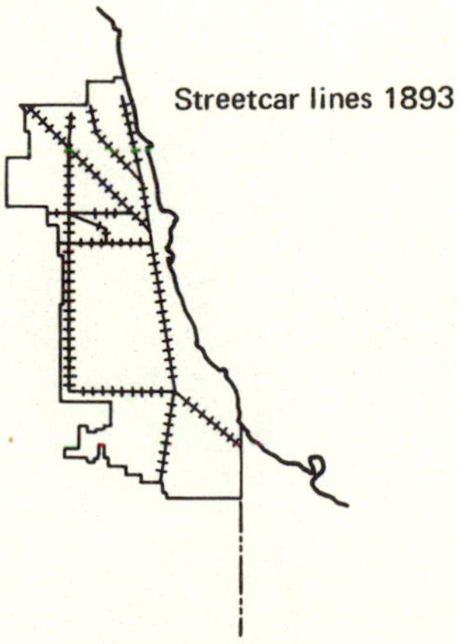

Streetcar lines 1893

1883. Courtesy Chicago Historical Society.

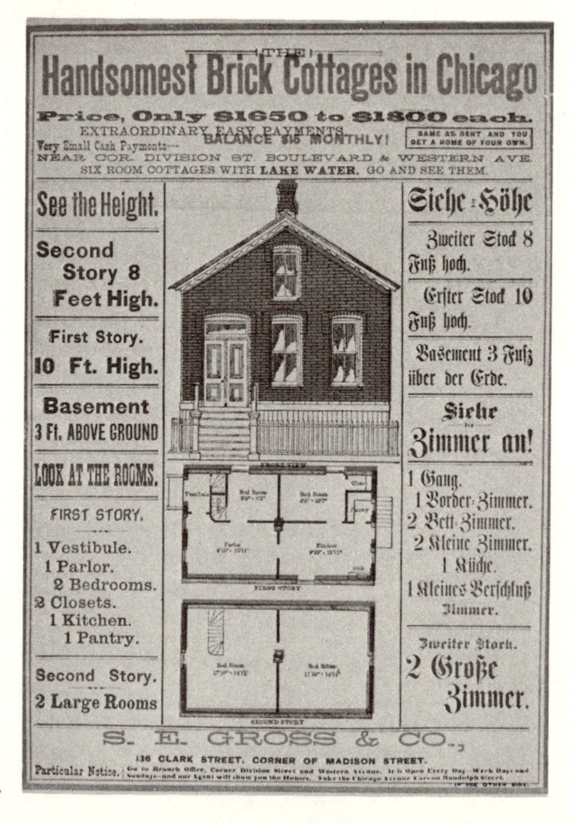

1883. Courtesy Chicago Historical Society.

The era of the streetcar

On May 4, 1888, Richmond, Virginia, became the first city to successfully operate a commercial electric streetcar system. This new method of transportation completely changed the patterns of work and residence in the city. As you read the statement about the impact of the streetcar on Richmond, match the suburban areas that the author names with areas on the map of Richmond on this page. Answer the questions below:

1. According to the author, why did people support the building of streetcar lines?
2. How do these data about the impact of the streetcar on Richmond support or refute your hypothesis about the streetcar's impact on Chicago?

About this time (circa 1888) Richmond began to spread her skirts, becoming the city of homes. The population increased thirty per cent during the decade, expanding in three directions. A marathon contest between the seekers of new franchises (licenses to streetcar companies) and the sellers of acreage created the era of suburbs. The barrier between Manchester (1) and her only sister, Richmond was partly removed by connecting the horse car lines of

Figure 17.3
Map of Richmond in the late 19th century

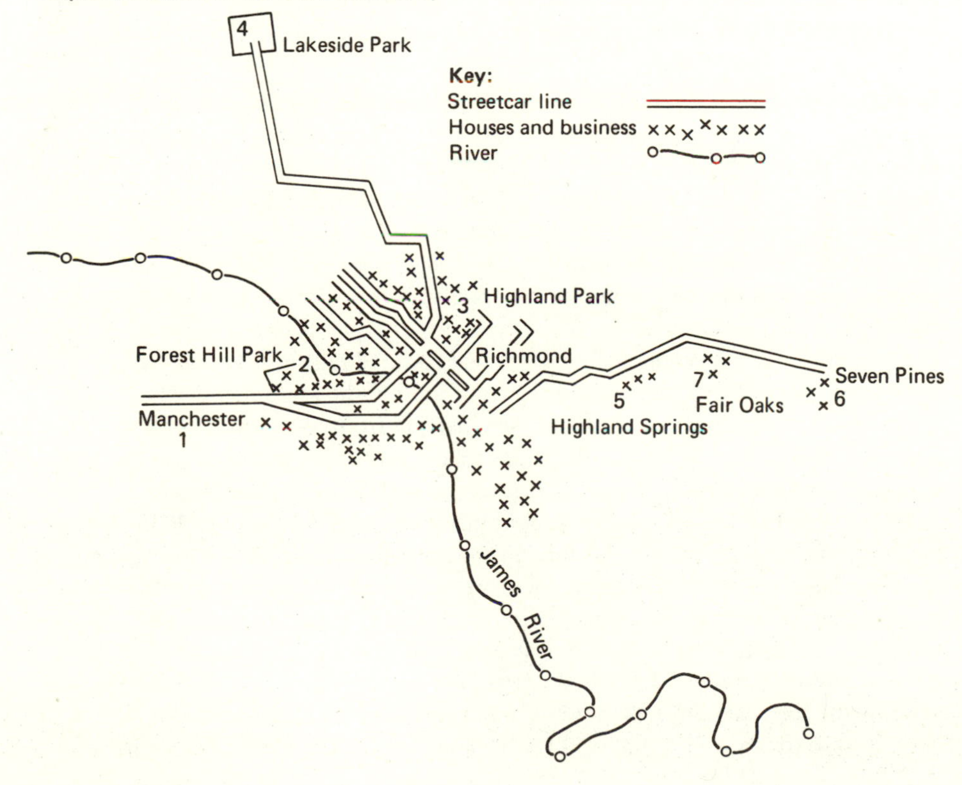

both cities. Shortly afterward, the lines were electrified and extended from Forest Hill Park (2), an amusement and picnic area, to Highland Park (3) over the Fifth Street Bridge. The bridge was erected jointly by the car companies and the real estate developers.

Other developments were Lakeside with a park and zoo (4), Highland Park (3), Highland Springs (5), Seven Pines (6), Fair Oaks (7), and others. Chartered trolley parties, with the summer cars decorated with colored lights, ranked next to the Sunday school picnics. Moonlight excursions down the James River were made available to the masses by the trolley extension. The excellent streetcar service made seaside resorts accessible.

Travel in New York in the late 1870's

Changes in transportation occurred within the central area of the city as well as between the central area and the suburbs. People used many forms of transportation within the downtown area. They traveled by foot, small carriages, hackney carriages, horsedrawn streetcars, elevated railways, and streetcar. In the following account, Walter G. Marshall, and English visitor in 1878–1879, describes the many forms of transportation in the downtown area of New York.

1. How did the new transportation affect the downtown area of the city?
2. How would the elevated railways affect journey-to-work patterns in the city?

New York built the first elevated railway. It now provides rapid movement through the city without interfering with the traffic because it is raised high above the streets. The elevated, 'el', as New Yorkers usually call it, has a height of thirty feet and is supported by iron pillars. On one side of the street the train moves one-way on the tracks and on the other side of the street the train moves the other way. Beneath the raised lines is the roadway for horses and carriages, and the lines of rail for the tramway cars, with the pavements beyond.

As might be expected, many people ride elevated railways. Trains run at frequent intervals on the several lines, from 5:30 in the morning till 12 o'clock at night. During the crowded hours, namely from 5:30 a.m. to 7:30 a.m., and from 5 p.m. to 7 p.m., the trains follow each other as fast as can be managed. One company runs daily 840 trains up and down its lines between 5:30 a.m. and 12 p.m. Seventy trains per hour are run during the crowded hours mornings and evenings. The fare during these busy hours is five cents, at other times, ten cents. Of course, there are no classes, but all ride together in a long car, or carriage, the seats ranged lengthwise at the sides, with a passage down the middle and a door at each end. Only trains of four car lengths are run on the "elevated." Everybody pays the same fare no matter how long or short the ride. The three elevated railway companies have carried their lines far into the upper portion of the city. You can, for the sum of five cents,

Courtesy Carnegie Library, Pittsburgh.

Courtesy Chicago Historical Society.

Do you think a return to streetcar transportation would help solve our traffic problems in our cities? Why, or why not?

take a ten or twelve mile ride without changing cars. The trains run at a good speed. There is little delay at the stations.

There are very few cross tracks, so that the chances of collision are reduced. However, the trains must approach the many sharp curves cautiously or they will never go around. Tickets are given up before the passengers enter the train. As a financial enterprise the elevated railway has turned out a success beyond even the expectations of its promoters. As a result of the introduction of the elevated railway, property next to the railways has depreciated in value. The constant rumbling of the passing trains, the blocking out of sufficient light, the close view passengers have into rooms on the second and third floors, the squirtings of oil from the engines, have unjustly ruined the comfort of the occupants of the houses next to the train lines.

There are other ways of getting about New York besides taking the "elevated." Railways for horse-streetcars are laid along nearly every avenue and many of the cross streets. A horse drawn streetcar is one without a conductor or man to collect the fares. Passengers instead drop their fares into a box inside the car. If he wants change he can obtain it from the driver. He can not change more than two dollars. The driver will hand back to the passenger a little sealed packet containing the whole amount returned in the form of small change. Thus, the proper fare of five cents can be dropped into the till. In a larger stagelike bus, however, there is no communication between the passenger and driver. You must have exact change. The fare-box is so placed that the driver can peep down from his seat and see if everyone inside has paid. If you don't pay immediately, the driver will rap away at you until you do. When you do pay he will turn a slide and pass the money out of sight. Stages are painted red, white, and blue, and have bright colored pictures on the sides. It is fashionable in the Empire City to travel by horse-car, or else take the elevated.

Of course there are hackney carriages to be obtained. These are very few and far between. They consist mostly of big family coaches-and-pairs, with room enough inside to comfortably seat six. There is another form of public conveyance called a "coupè," holding only two people. These coupès are invariably well cushioned. They are as comfortable a class of conveyance as one could desire. The pity is there is not more of them. But driving about in public carriages in New York is very expensive. The fare is one dollar an hour . . . .

The city and the nineteenth century suburb

Technology affects peoples' attitudes, but the change of attitudes affects technological developments as well. Some people wanted to escape the congested cities and therefore invested in streetcars and suburban development. The following reading examines the attitudes of the suburbanite, and the problem of the fate of the central city when the middle and upper classes flee to the suburbs.

1. What were the advantages and disadvantages of living in the city?
2. How did suburban growth affect the central city?
3. What conclusions can you make about how new transportation changed physical and social aspects of city life?

A generation ago debating societies threshed over the question of the relative advantages of city and of country life. There were then two distinct human types—the city man and the country man. A third type has been added in recent years—the suburbanite. He emerges into view at great world centers such as London and New York, and in a hundred lesser cities in Europe and America. He differs from both the city man and the country man. He is the product of new conditions. A complex set of influences operate upon him. What causes have produced him? How does he differ from other men, and is he good for anything?

The suburbanite is a recent growth because of cheap and rapid streetcar transportation. In other days the choice of residence lay between the purely country and the purely city environment.[29]

Truly, cities are still the goal of the average American heart. The question of suburban versus urban residence has its pros and cons. As the city man walks briskly to his office in the morning or strolls leisurely uptown in the afternoon or saunters over to his club after dinner, or drops into the theater, he is proudly conscious of the fact that his daily course is not hurried by timetables. He has easy access to the best that the rich, resourceful city offers in the way of music, theaters, lectures, preaching, and libraries. His soul is stirred by the mighty beat of the city, its wonderful varied life, and its tremendous forces for good and evil. A good city man loves his city. He strives to conserve its best traditions and make it more beautiful.

On the other hand, Mr. Suburbanite arises and puts in his claim to be heard. "It's all well enough for bachelors and elderly couples and people who like crowds, to reside in town, but if you want to bring up a family, to prolong your life, to cultivate the neighborly feeling, to get acquainted with nature, leave your city block and become like me. It may be a little more difficult for us to attend the opera, but we can listen to the birds."

Such a burst of enthusiasm, may signify that the suburbanite is still under the spell of first impressions. His enthusiasm will cool after he has experienced late trains and learned the inconvenience of no drugstores on every corner. But, after all, he is a rare man who ever permanently returns to the city after migrating to the suburbs.

For the wholesomeness of suburban life grows upon one. Suburbs, small colonies of people, will return us to the old, beautiful neighborhood life that characterized this nation before the rush to the cities began. The next house looks inviting, and people will loiter and chat. The women of

[29]Given your choice would you prefer to live in the city or its suburbs? Why?

the colony get to know each other because their children play together. The men become more talkative. Club life becomes more than just lounging, smoking and swapping gossip.

Suburbs give a feeling of community to the people. Suburbs will create a better social order. A generation or two of hard fighting will cleanse the big cities of their foulness. In the suburbs a peaceful life is already here. The smaller land area in suburbs reduces the problem of obtaining sanitary conditions, good highways, and first-class schools. There is no excuse for corrupt government. Already there are many such suburban communities with citizens filled with civic pride.

However the great danger is that the complacent suburbanite will ignore his obligations to the city in which he earns his daily bread.[30] He has an obligation to the city even if he no longer lives there. If he evades his responsibilities he contributes the "curse of suburbanity." In the city the suburbanite makes his money. The thousands of suburbanites must not forget the needs of the city. They cannot forget the thousands of men, women, and little children living night and day in alleys and tenements.

Churches and other agencies of good are weakened by the constant drift to the suburbs. These agencies are left with improvished foreign elements whose need of education, evangelization, and Americanization is great.

What attitude shall the suburbanite take to the city? Shall he look upon it simply as a good place to earn his daily bread—a place that he is well rid of at night? Shall he hurry by the slum section and never notice the bundles of rags and misery that disfigure the streets? Shall he not be concerned about corruption in city government? Shall he show no concern about whether the city's streets are clean and its parks large enough for the thousands of people who are crowded into the tenement districts? Because he has become a suburbanite shall he cast off responsibility for the city and center all his interests and all his activities on his fellow men in the suburbs?

Our ideal suburbanite is in the process of evolution. When he emerges he will blend the best traits of the pure city man and the pure country man. He will be like his grandfather, who kept a store in Ruralville in his simplicity, integrity, and industry. He will be like his father, the great city merchant, in his firm grasp of large undertakings. But he will be better than either his father or grandfather. The influences of both city and country will make him responsive to life on all sides and alive to all life's obligations.

For thought and discussion

Do you think the late nineteenth century suburbanite could know his city as well as Mr. Norcross knew Atlanta? Why or why not?

[30]What obligations, if any, does the suburbanite have toward his or her city? Why?

Individual and small group activities

1. Keep a record of your movement in you city for twenty-four hours. Draw a simple map of your city from your movements. Does your knowledge of your city depend on your transportation routes? How much do the activities you engage in depend on motor transportation? How much depends on walking? Report to class and compare your conclusions with your classmates' conclusions.
2. Keep a record for several days of the time you spend commuting to work, school, and other economic and social activities. What benefits do you gain for your commuting efforts? What does your commuting cost you in time and money? What else could you do with that time and money? Report to class.

The economy of the streetcar city

Assignment 18

Changes in technology transformed the entire economy of the city, and contributed to phenomenal urban growth between 1860 and 1910. In Assignment 13 you learned that the walking city functioned primarily as a trading center. Only a few cities such as Pittsburgh and Lowell had great factories. Streetcar cities remained commercial centers. Manufacturing and service-related industries, however, became an increasingly important part of the economy of the streetcar city.

The first three sections of this assignment examine how natural, human, and capital resources were used to produce and distribute goods and services in the streetcar city. The final section of Assignment 18 will help you to determine who received these goods and services. The case study of the Pullman strike of 1877, reveals the conflict between management and workers over working conditions, and the distribution of goods and services. This conflict resulted in considerable violence, and in the formation of labor unions in the twentieth century.

Measuring economic growth

The amount and value of goods produced grew rapidly between 1860 and 1910. The graph and table which follow provide information to help you measure the extent of this growth. The graph uses a tool economists call an index. This index compares manufacturing production in a number of years with production in a base year. The base year always receives the number 100. Thus, if more goods were produced in 1910 that were produced in the base year, the index for 1910 would be higher than 100. If less goods were produced, the number would be less than 100. The base year in this graph is 1899. Examine the graph and table, then answer the question below each.

The production of goods and services

The amount of goods produced depends on how much and what kind of natural, human, and capital resources are used. Economists say that the total production of

Table 18.1
The percentage of population engaged in manufacturing in ten U. S. cities

City	*1860*	*1890*
New York	9.0	19.0
Philadelphia	12.5	24.0
Chicago	4.8	19.1
St. Louis	6.8	20.8
Boston	10.8	20.2
Baltimore	8.0	19.3
Pittsburgh	18.0	23.7
San Francisco	2.6	16.2
Cleveland	8.0	19.4
Detroit	5.2	18.5

How important is manufacturing to employment in cities in 1860 and 1890?

Figure 18.1
Index of manufacturing production: 1860-1910

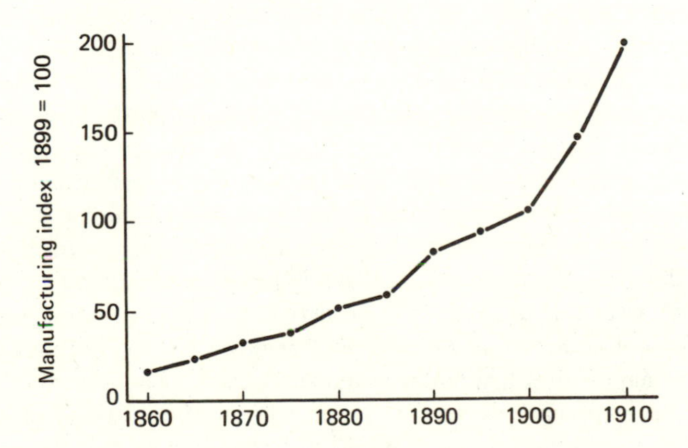

In what years did manufacturing begin to expand rapidly?

goods is equal to the specific amounts of natural, human, and capital resources combined to make a particular good. For example, suppose you wanted to produce 1 bar of steel. You might need 20 pounds of natural resources, 2 hours of labor resources, and $20.00 worth of capital resources. If you wanted to produce 2 bars of steel you would have to use 40 pounds of natural resources, 4 hours of labor resources, and $40.00 worth of capital resources. You must always use the resources in the same relationship (ratio). However, you can also increase the production output through a technological change. For example, you can invent a new machine which cuts the labor time in half. Now, in order to produce 1 bar of steel you need 20 pounds of natural resources, 1 hour of labor resources, and $20.00 worth of capital resources. You have changed the ratio of resources required.

In the following reading, Adam Smith, a major 18th century English economist, describes how you can increase the production of pins. As you read Smith's account answer these questions:

1. List three different kinds of technological changes that Smith describes?
2. Does the increased production of pins depend on a simple increase in the amount of natural, labor, and capital resources or on a technological change?

The advantages of specialization

The great improvement in the productive ability of labor comes from the division of labor. A particular manufacturing example will best illustrate the effects of the division of labor on the general business of society.

We will take as our example the pin industry. An untrained worker, working alone, could make about one pin a day. Today, however, men are trained and each worker has a part of the job of making one pin. One man draws out the wire; another straightens the wire. A third man cuts the wire; a fourth points the wire. A fifth man grinds the wire at the top for receiving the head. Moreover, to make the head of the pin requires two or three different operations. One man puts the head on; another whitens the pins. The last man puts the pins into the paper. Thus the business of making a pin is divided into about eight different jobs. In some factories a different man does each job. In other factories the same man will sometimes perform two or three of the jobs. In one mechanized factory eight men each had a separate job. They were able to produce about twelve pounds of pins in a day. There are about 48,000 pins in a pound. Each man was averaging about 72,000 pins a day. If they had not been trained, lacked machinery, and had not divided the labor, each would have produced only about twenty pins.

This increase in the amount of production results from three circumstances: first, the increased skill of each workman as a result of training; second, the saved time as a result of the division of labor; and third, the invention of a great number of machines as a result of human creativity . . . .

Distribution and transportation of goods and services

In Assignment 17 you examined ways in which the streetcar changed the distribution patterns of people within the late 19th century city. At the same time, the railroad changed the distribution of goods and services among cities. The following graphs offer evidence about the growth of available rail transportation and the amount of goods carried by rail, Graph 18.2 indicates the growth of the number of revenue tons (the number of tons of goods assessed a carrying charge) moved by rail between 1861 and 1890. Graph 18.3 indicates the growth in total number of railroad tracks available for the shipment of goods, services, and passengers between 1860 and 1910. As you examine the graphs answer the accompanying questions.

Figure 18.2
Total revenue tons freight service (in millions)

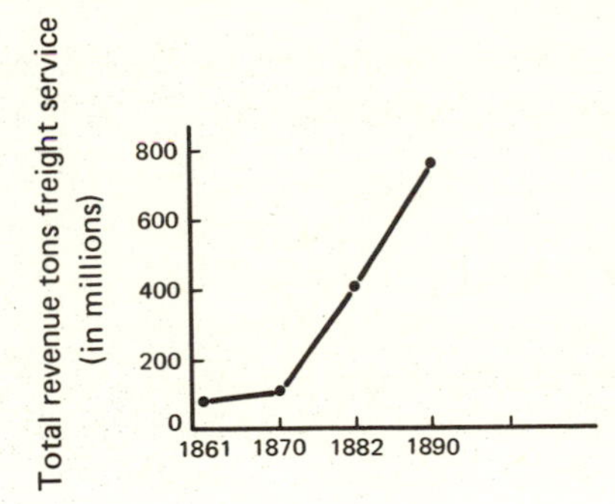

Figure 18.3
Track available (in miles)

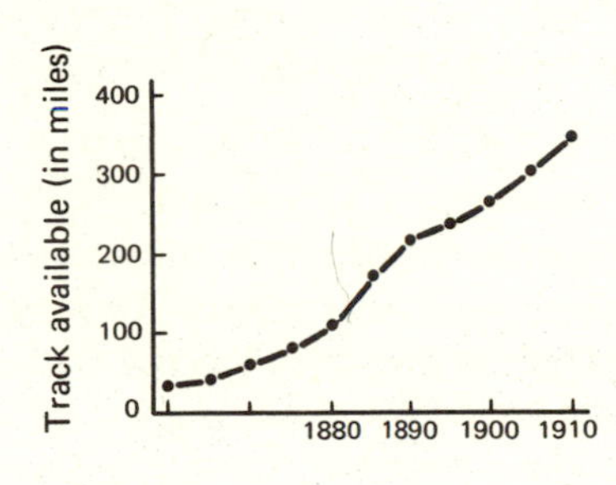

1. When does the biggest increase in freight carried and available miles of railroad track occur?
2. Do the years of the greatest increase in freight and railtrack available correspond to the years of greatest increase in manufacturing output indicated in the graph on page 215? Why or why not?

Distribution of goods and services in the streetcar city: Who gets what and how much?

The concept of distribution concerns the movement of goods and services between cities. This concept also refers to the amount and kinds of goods and services people received for their labors. In other words, who gets what and how much? For example, a group of workers in a company in 1880 may have produced $100,000 worth of goods but they may have been paid only $5,000 for their labor. The owners received a great profit. In this part of Assignment 18 you will examine the conflict between management and labor over the distribution of goods and services.

In Assignment 16 you hypothesized about the characteristics of the streetcar city. The menus of the rich and poor, Woolworth's skyscraper, and conditions in tenement housing illustrated both great wealth and great poverty. While the workingman worked fewer hours in 1890 than in 1840 and wages had risen, poor working and living conditions produced conflicts between owners and workers. Workers' unions attempted to bargain collectively with management. When bargaining failed strikes and violence often broke out.

Beginning in the summer of 1893, a severe economic depression spread across the United States. The Pullman Palace Car Company of Chicago, in an attempt to maintain its profits, reduced salaries and wages throughout its plant. Rental rates in homes owned by the Pullman Company, however, remained at the old 1893 level. Employees of Pullman called a strike in May, 1894, after futile attempts to negotiate with company officials. One month later, the American Railway Union, consisting of 150,000, members called a boycott against all trains pulling Pullman cars. The following documents illustrate the various positions and attitudes of labor and management.

1. What were the major grievances of the Pullman workers? Of George Pullman?
2. Do you think Pullman Town was an improvement over other urban residential areas of the 1890's? Why?

The Pullman Company describes the town of Pullman

Imagine a perfectly equipped town of 12,000 workers. Flowers and green lawns border this town. Trees and parks add to the lovely atmosphere. The modest homes are bright, wholesome, and filled with pure air and light. We have eliminated all that is ugly, discordant, and demoralizing for this town.

Mr. Pullman built this town on the business theory that the better the man, the more valuable he is to himself and his employer. We have attempted to bring out the best in our men. We assume that the Pullman men are the best type of American workmen. They stand solidly and firmly on their own feet. They work out valuable and well-rounded lives in proportion to their opportunities.

A resident of the model town provides a different picture of the community

The residents in the city, paid rent to the Pullman Company, they bought gas from the Pullman Company, they walked on streets owned by the Pullman Company, they paid water-tax to the Pullman Company. Indeed, even when they bought gingham for their wives or sugar for their tables at the store or the market-house, they dealt with the Pullman Company. They sent their children to Pullman's school and attended Pullman's church. They looked at but dared not enter Pullman's hotel with its private bar, for that was the limit. Pullman did not sell them their grog. They had to go to the settlement at the railroad crossing called, because of its long row of saloons, 'bumtown.' There the moral and spiritual disorder of Pullman Town was emptied, just as the physical sewage flowed out on the Pullman farm a few miles further south. The Pullman Company also owned the sewerage system, and turned the waste into a fluid, forced through pipes and conducted underground to enrich the soil of a large farm. The lives of the working men were surrounded on all sides by the Pullman Company.

Reverend Cawardine, the minister of the Methodist church defends the workers

I cannot keep still and smother my convictions. You need not fear that the company will retalitate upon this church. It dare not in the face of public opinion.

I will not praise Mr. Pullman.

In this age of rapidly increasing fortunes, when men become rich in a day by speculation and ruining others lives, I am willing to accord him all honour. However, when Mr. Pullman, as a public man, demands that we regard him as a benefactor to his race, as a true philanthropist, as one who respects his fellow men, who regards his employees with the love of a father for his children, I fail utterly to see the point. If he is all this, then let me ask him a question or two. Why does Mr. Pullman, in the midst of a hard winter, when the hours of work were few and the wages at their lowest ebb, when whole families were in want, why did he not answer our cry for help?

Why does not Mr. Pullman do something for the moral and educational development of this place?[31] Why does he charge such exorbitant rents from the churches of this community? Why does he not give us a much needed emergency hospital? And, last but not least, why, does he not bring himself into a little closer contact with the public life of our town, cheer his employees with his fatherly presence?

The great trouble with this whole Pullman system is that it is not what it pretends to be. To a casual visitor it is a paradise; but it is a hollow mockery, a sham, an institution girdled with red tape, and as a solution of the labor problem most unsatisfactory . . . .

Statement by the Pullman workers explaining their reasons for striking

In June of 1894, the American Railway Union held its national convention in Chicago. The striking Pullman workers presented the statement below outlining their position to the Union. The responses by Union President Eugene Debs and George Pullman, company president follow.

1. What does each side in the strike want?

Mr. President and Brothers of the American Railway Union—We struck at Pullman because we were without hope. We joined the American Railway Union because it gave us a glimmer of hope. Twenty thousand souls—men, women, little ones—have their eyes turned toward this convention today.

In stating our grievances, it is hard to begin. Five reductions in wages,

[31] Do you feel that George Pullman had any obligation to foster the moral and educational development of his workers? Why, or why not?

in work, and in conditions of employment, swept through the shops at Pullman between May and December in 1893. The last was the most severe, amounting to nearly 30 per cent. But our rents have not fallen. We owed Pullman $70,000 when we struck May 11. We owe him twice as much to-day. He does not evict us for two reasons. First, he fears public opinion. Second, he hopes to starve us out and break the union. Water which Pullman buys from the city at 8 cents a thousand gallons he sells to us at 40 cents per thousand gallons, and claims he is losing $400 a month on it. Gas sells for 75 cents per 1,000 feet in Hyde Park. He sells it to us for $2.25. When we went to tell him our grievances he said we were all his "children."

Pullman, both the man and the town, is an ulcer on the body politic. He owns the houses, the schoolhouses and churches. The wages he pays out with one hand, the Pullman Palace Car Company, he takes back with the other, the Pullman Land Association. He is able to underbid any railroad car shop in this country. His competitors in business, to meet this, must reduce the wages of their men. This gives Pullman the excuse to reduce our wages to conform to the market. His business rivals must in turn cut wages. And thus the merry war, the dance of skeletons bathed in human tears, goes on. And it will go on brothers, for ever, unless you, the American Railway Union, stop it, end it, crush it out . . . . [32]

Statement by Debs, president of the American Railway Union

We have won every fight, and we have had eleven. Pullman is our twelfth, and we shall win that. I am in favour of the American Railway Union extending its last dollar and its last man in a cause so righteous.

The crisis is approaching, and we must invite it and not evade it. We have declared war on Pullman, and it is a fight to a finish. The Knights of Labour and the American Railway Union are united in a holy strife. When we begin our battle we will never rest. The result is certain. (Cheering.)

George M. Pullman responds to the workers

At the beginning of the very serious depression last year we were employing at Pullman 5,816 men, and paying out in wages $305,000 a month. Some intended purchasers of railway equipment stopped negotiations, and we were obliged to lay off a large number of men. By November 1st, 1893, there were only about one-third of the normal number of workers. I realized the necessity of finding work immediately.

I knew that if there was any work to be done, bids for it would be made upon a much lower basis than ever before. In the absence of any information to the contrary, I thought this would be acceptable to the men under

[32] If you were a union member and your union voted to strike against your wishes do you think you should be prevented from working? Why, or why not?

the circumstances. There is absolutely no possibility, during this depression, of getting any more orders for work at prices measured by the wages of May, 1893. Under such a scale the works would necessarily close down and the great majority of the employees be put in idleness.

On the question of rents, they make a very small return upon the investment, . . . The renting of the dwellings and employment of workmen at Pullman are in no way tied together.

On 10th May, the day after the second conference, work went on at Pullman as usual. At a meeting of the local committee held during the night of May 10, a strike was decided upon, and accordingly the next day about 2,500 of the employees quit leaving about 600 unskilled workers. It was impractical to keep the shops in operation with a force thus diminished and disorganized, the next day those remaining were laid off, and no work has since been done in the shops.

Violence erupts

On June 30th, before the boycott was a week old, violence occurred. By August 2, the date the Pullman plant reopened, twelve people were fatally wounded, hundreds were injured. Over five hundred men were arrested in the Chicago area and millions of dollars were lost by fire, destruction, and loss of work time. As you read the following account of the violence answer these questions:

1. What kind of action would have prevented the violence?
2. What concessions could each side have been reasonably expected to grant?

When the railroads attempted to bring special detectives into Chicago there was a commotion.

A riot was imminent at ten o'clock this morning when Illinois Central train No. 23 came in, bearing forty-five special detectives. Each detective was armed with a policeman's club, a revolver, and a Winchester rifle. As soon as their presence on the train became known, the crowd set up a cry of indignation. When the detectives stepped out of the coach they were attacked by the stikers. Three of them were beaten and disarmed. The others remained in the car all day on advice of the railroad officials. All attempts to get food to them were frustrated by the strikers. At six o'clock in the afternoon they gladly consented to leave the city. They went on the only train sent out on the Illinois Central. All day long an enormous crowd surged about the car taunting the detectives. Several strikers uncoupled the car in which they were seated. One of the detectives who rushed out to interfere was quickly covered by four pistols and a double-barrel shot-gun.

There was, however, no flinching on the part of the railroad company. Their representative declared:

"We shall punish every man possible. The whole course of the mob has been a series of vicious outrages. Were these crimes condoned, society would suffer. We shall fight these men to the bitter end, if it takes all the Winchesters and Gatling guns in the State or country. The law is slow, but it will triumph in the end."

The struggle although brief, was fierce. When the train, crowded with armed representatives of the law, steamed down the line, the strikers and their sympathizers blocked the line by standing on the rails, two thousand strong. As the engine slowed up to avoid making a wholesale massacre of the crowd, the strikers saluted it with a volley of stones. On board the cars the deputies drew their revolvers and stood ready to fire at word of command. When the engine came to a standstill, knives were brandished. Amid volleys of oaths and stones, the mob made a desperate and successful attempt to capture the train. The deputies beat them off with the butt end of their revolvers, but finally they were overpowered. One of the detectives was stabbed, but not seriously. No shots were fired, and the train remained in the strikers' hands.

The boycott had not lasted a week, but it was evidently gravitating into civil war. Mr. Debs kept denouncing violence. But the rank and file paid no heed to their leader. They saw that the strike was utterly hopeless unless the railroads could be terrorized into surrender.[33]

When all other means failed, the strikers showered stones upon the train, adjusted the switches so as to throw the trains off the track. In fact they did everything that they could imagine to embarrass their enemies. All this was, of course, in direct violation of law, and it interfered with the free passage of the United States mails, an offense which came little short of treason to the Commonwealth. It was obvious that this could not last. Something must be done, and promptly . . . .

The night of July 6 will long be remembered in Chicago. Until midnight the mobs held full control of the entire southern suburbs of Chicago . . . .

The police estimate that 50,000 men, strikers, idlers and marauders, many of them foreigners, had for two days held undisputed control over the suburbs of Chicago. They burned cars, looted railway sheds, wrecked railway shops, tore up rails, and generally spread devastation through the city, entailing a loss estimated in hard cash at six million dollars . . . .

The authorities, now thoroughly aroused, agreed to work together. They establised an armed camp from which reinforcements could easily be sent in any direction. They made it known throughout the city that orders had been given to shoot, and if need be, to kill. General Miles with his regular Army undertook to protect the Government buildings and the railway stations. The Mayor with the State troops and the police guarded the railway yards and dispersed the mob. The deputy-marshals and the police protected the stock-yards and the railway stations on the south . . . Altogether there were 10,000 armed men at the disposal of the authorities. Rioting ceased, fires were stopped. The trains began to move . . . .

[33]Under what circumstances, if any, is terror ever a justifiable weapon?

For thought and discussion

What ways, if any, can you suggest to determine a fair distribution of capital between labor and management?

Individual and small group activities

1. Arrange an interview with the officers of a local union. Ask about the union's requirements for joining. Find out what the union provides for its members. Then interview a union member and ask him what services the union renders to him? Compare the union officer's report and its member's report. Report your conclusions to the class.
2. With one or two classmates investigate the chain of events leading to a recent major strike in your city. Why did the strike occur? How was the strike settled? One person may investigate newspaper reports. Another person may interview a member of the striking union. Another person may interview a member of the company the strike was called against. Report to the class.

Newcomers from abroad and rural areas

Assignment 19

Cities experienced great population growth during the latter part of the nineteenth century. Many immigrants from Europe and Asia and persons from rural America came to urban centers. They expected the cities to offer opportunities for wealth and social status. Immigrants also expected greater political freedom than they had in the "old country." Popular Horatio Alger stories and reports of successful newcomers aided the movement to cities. Large numbers of the unsuccessful moved from city to city in search of better fortunes.

In Assignments 12 and 14 you examined the social structure of the walking city. You analyzed the criteria for class, status, and social interaction patterns in cities during this early period. This assignment will focus more on the question of mobility patterns than on social interaction among various classes in the late nineteenth century city. Historians use the term mobility in two ways. Movement up or down the success ladder is known as vertical mobility. They call movement in and out of the city and changes of residences within the city horizontal mobility. Assignment 19 provides evidence to help you support or refute the common belief that chances for success were greater in the 19th century than today, and that people move around more today than they did around 1890. You should also use the evidence to determine the general characteristics of persons who succeeded and which ones tended to remain in the same city.

Two American success stories

The following two readings express the expectations of persons who moved to the city in the 19th century from abroad and from rural areas in the United States. As you read these accounts answer the questions listed below.

1. What opportunities did the city offer Ben Barclay and the Italian immigrant?
2. How did both Ben and the Italian immigrant achieve their goals?
3. What hypothesis about the opportunities for success (social mobility) can you form from these two accounts?

The store boy: or the fortunes of Ben Barclay, 1887

Ben lived in the small town of Pentonville and worked in the local grocery store. He helped support his widowed mother whose home was being threatened by a crooked lawyer, Squire Davenport. Coincidently Ben Barclay's arch-rival for the hand of the fair Rose Gardiner was Squire Davenport's no-good son, Tom. But Rose told Ben not to worry–she thought Tom Davenport was almost beneath contempt.

"Most of our rich men were once poor boys," said Rose. "I have a book of biographies at home, and I find that not only rich men, but men distinguished in other ways, generally commenced in poverty."

"I wish you'd lend me that book," said Ben. "Sometimes I get discouraged and that will give me courage."

"You shall have it whenever you call at the house. But you mustn't think too much of getting money," said Rose.

"I don't mean to; but I should like to make my mother comfortable. I don't see much chance of it while I remain a grocer's boy, as Tom Davenport calls me."

"Better a grocer's boy than to spend your time in idleness as Tom does. Tom thinks it beneath him to work."

Later Ben left Pentonville for New York, working for a rich woman named Mrs. Hamilton. He worked hard for Mrs. Hamilton and was able to escape a plot to discredit him by another jealous rival, Conrad Hill, and Conrad's evil mother. In the end, Ben received $4,000 for helping Mrs. Hamilton and returned to Pentonville just in the nick of time to stop the crooked lawyer, Squire Davenport, from fraudulently foreclosing on Ben's mother's home.

Several years have elapsed. Ben is in the office of a real estate lawyer in New York, as a junior partner. All Mrs. Hamilton's business is in his hands, and it is generally thought that he will eventually receive a handsome inheritance from her. Mrs. Barclay prefers to live in Pentonville, but Ben visits her often. Whenever he goes to Pentonville he never fails to call on Rose Gardiner, a beautiful young lady of marriageable age now.

Tom Davenport is now in the city, but his course is far from creditable. His father has more than once been compelled to pay his debts, and has angrily refused to do so again. In fact, he has lost a large part of his once handsome fortune, and now bids fair to close his life in poverty. Success has come to Ben because he deserved it, and well-merited retribution to Tom Davenport.

Mrs. Hamilton still lives, happy in the success of her protege, Ben. Conrad Hill and his mother have tried more than once to regain their positions with Mrs. Hamilton, but in vain. *None of my young readers will pity them. They are fully rewarded for their treachery.*

The story of a successful immigrant, as told by himself

When I was a very small boy, I lived in Italy, in a dark cellar. I did not like it at all. Now and then I heard things about America–that it was a far off country where everybody was rich and that Italians went there and made plenty of money, so that they could return to Italy and live in pleasure ever after. One day a young man pulled out a handful of gold and told me he had made that in America in a few days.

This young man took me and my friend Francisco to a big ship going to America. He got us work away down where the fires are on the ship. We had to carry coal to the place where it could be thrown on the fires. We were glad to get over without giving money, but I have heard since that we should have been paid for our work among the coal and that the young man who had sent us got money for it. We came to Brooklyn . . .

There was a bootblack on the corner and when I had time I helped him and learned the business. Francisco cooked the lunch in the saloon and he, too, worked for the bootblack, and we were soon able to make the best polish. Then we thought we would go into business ourselves and we got a basement near the ferry, and put four chairs into it.

We had said that when we saved $1,000 each we would go back to Italy and buy a farm, but now that the time is coming we are so busy and making so much money that we think we will stay. We have opened another parlor. I own 19 now and have $700 saved. We shall open some more parlors soon. I know an Italian who was a bootblack ten years ago and now bosses bootblacks all over the city, who has so much money that if it was turned into gold it would wiegh more than himself.

There are plenty of rich Italians here, men who a few years ago had nothing and now have so much money that they could not count all their dollars in a week. The richest ones go away from the other Italians and live with the Americans.

Testing a hypothesis: Mobility, myth, or reality

Ben and the Italian immigrant represent late 19th century success stories. Was the opportunity for such rapid success truth or myth? Historians today are examining this question of social mobility in the 19th century. City directories are one important type of data they use to answer this question. City directories from this period indicate the persons name, occupation, home address, and occasionally work address. Using these directories over a period of time, historians can find out who remained in the city, what kinds of jobs individuals held over a long period of time, and how often they changed homes.

The following sample pages come from the city directories of Cincinnati in 1860, 1865, and 1880. As you examine these sample pages try to find the same person on the 1865 and 1880 directory pages. (Some persons do not appear in the 1880 directory.) List on a sheet of paper his type of employment in 1860, 1865, and 1880. Indicate his home address for these three periods, then answer the following questions:

1. What percent of the 85 people present in 1860 continued to live in the city in 1865? In 1880?
2. How many of those remaining changed jobs? If they changed jobs did they obtain a better one?
3. What type of jobs did people who remained have?
4. How many that continued to live in the city appear to own property? (Type of jobs often indicates property ownership. Ex. If a man is a shoemaker or merchant he often owned his own place of business.)
5. Of the people remaining, how often did they change homes?
6. Did people move quickly up the success ladder or did they make small advances upward?
7. Do your findings support or refute your initial hypothesis about social mobility in the 19th century city?

WILLIAMS'

CINCINNATI DIRECTORY,

FOR 1860.

ABBREVIATIONS.

acct., stands for..accountant.
al.,..............alley *or* allopathic.
atty.,............attorney.
b.,...............between.
bds.,.............boards.
b. h.,............boarding house.
b. k.,............book keeper.
bk.,..............book *or* brick.
bar. k.,..........bar keeper.
bldg.,............building.
bldr.,............builder.
bo.,..............botanic.
c.,...............corner.
cab. mkr.,........cabinet maker.
carp.,............carpenter.
cig.,.............cigar.

clk., stands for....clerk.
com.,.............commission.
con.,.............continuation.
cof. h.,..........coffee house.
confec.,..........confectioner.
e.,...............east.
ec.,..............eclectic.
ex.,..............exchange.
eng.,.............engineer.
h.,...............house.
Ham. road.........Hamilton road.
ho.,..............homeopathic.
lab.,.............laborer.
manufac.,.........{manufactory *or* manufacturer.
mach.,............machinist.

mer., stands for...merchant.
M.,...............Miami.
mkr...............maker.
n.,...............north.
nr................near.
not...............notary public.
opp...............opposite.
ov.,..............over.
prov..............provision.
s.,...............south.
tp.,..............township.
u.,...............upper.
w.,...............west.
wh.,..............wholesale.
W. W.,............White Water.
wks.,.............works.

ABL — ACK — ADA

A

Aaron Clement, trimmer, 72 W. Pearl, h. 175 W. 3d
Abbay Jos., engineer, 486 E. Front, h. E. Front, nr. Parsons
Abbey Benton, moulder, h. 323 W. 9th w. of W. Row
Abbich P., cab. mkr., 72 Rittenhouse
Abbott Carver M., b. k., 95 Walnut, res. Covington
Abbott John C., clk., Ross, Pettibone & Co's, h. York nr. W. Row
Abbott Wm., cooper, 259 Cutter
Abel A., clothing store. 936 W. Row
Abel F., (F. A. & Co.) 458 W. 3d
ABEL F. & CO., (Frederick A. & Henry Hakman,) Coal Dealers, c. Park and W. W. Canal
Abel Frank, lab., 702 E. Front
Abel Henry, grocer, 6th b. Horn and Harriett
Abel J., barber, 68 Findlay
Abel Jas., 426 Broadway
Abel Theresa, seamstress, Broadway Hotel
Abel Wm. J., bk. finisher, 43 Main, h. 337 W. 6th
Abel Mrs. Wm. J., music teacher, 337 W. 6th
Abeling F., boots and shoes, s.e.c. Water and Walnut, h. 18 Commercial
ABER Jacob S., (Wm. H. Comstock & Co.) res. Lynn, Mass.
Aberlz Lucius, med. student, bds. 107 W. 5th
Abermeyer G. M., cooper, 641 Race
Aberner Jacob, carp., 158 Richmond
Abernethy R. P., machinist, 138 Clark
Abernethy Wm. carp., wks. e. s. Hammond b. 3d and 4th
Abernethy W. J., clk., s. w. c. 2d and Broadway. h. 431 W. 4th
Abler Henry, bar k., 400 Vine
Ablett Isaac, carp., Taylor b. Carr and Freeman

Abraham A., clk., County Audtior's Office
Abraham Abram, clk., 106 Park
Abraham Christian, stone cutter, 84 Bremen
Abraham David. peddler, 491 Vine
Abraham David, rag peddler, 326 Elm
ABRAHAM JOSEPH, Attorney, 19 Bank Buildings, 8 W. 3d, h. 145 Smith
Abraham Louis, b. k., 56 Main, bds. E. Mayer's
Abrams Mrs. Elizabeth, 71 W. 9th
Abrams Mark, tailor, 100 W. Front
Achenburg Henry, carp., c. 8th and Sycamore, bds. s.w.c. 9th and Walnut
Achew Henry, 214 Walnut
Achhorn Geo., cig. mkr., wks. 187 Walnut
Achhener Leopold, 210 W. 6th
Achtest Conrad, varnisher, 44 Gest
Acker ——, mach., wks. n. w. c. Front and M. Canal
Acker C. W., painter, wks. s. w. c. Sycamore and 6th
Acker Valentine, carpet weaver, 24 15th
ACKERLAND ABRAHAM, Clothier, 66 W. Pearl, h. 160 Sycamore
Ackerman Geo., clk., 34 W. Court, res. E. Walnut Hills
Ackerman Geo., pipesman, 158 Hamilton Road
Ackerman John, cig. mkr., 449 Sycamore
Ackerman Theo., pewter worker, 11 E. 7th, h. 33 Rittenhouse
Ackermann Caspar, bds. n. s. Hunt b. Main and Sycamore
Ackermann Gottlieb, lab., 524 Walnut
Ackerstaf John, carp. 11 Orchard
Acking Thos., brass finisher, 281 W. 7th
Ackles Henry, carp., 120 Plum
Ackley Abraham, s.e.c. Court and John
Ackley H. H. policeman, 62 W. 9th w. of W. Row
Ackley Jas., blk. smith, 261 W. 7th, bds. 310 W. 9th

Ackley M., blk. smith, 199 W. 7th, h 304 W. 9th
Ackley Wm., stone cutter, 156 Cutter
Acky Mrs. Mary, 46 E. 8th, e. of Canal
Acoff Henry, lab., 52 Laurel
ACTON Clement J., (A. & Woodnutt,) 345 W. 7th
ACTON & WOODNUTT, (Clement J. A. & Thomas W.) Dry Goods, 103 W. Pearl
Ackva Wm., cof. h., c. Liberty and Main
Adae Carl A. G., teller, s. w. c. 3d and Main, h. Adae's Woods, nr. Cumminsville
ADAE Charles F., (C. F. A. & Co.) h. Adae's Woods, nr. Cumminsville
ADAE C. F. & CO., (Charles F. A. & Adolphus Seinecke,) German Savings Institution, s.w.c. 3d & Main
Adam Ambrose, tailor, 61 Clay
Adam Andrew, shoemkr., 29 Abigail
Adam Carl, shoemkr., bds 92 W. Court
Adam Geo. moulder. 61 Oliver
Adam John. bds 514 Vine
Adam John A., shoemkr., 383 Main, h. 29 Abigail
Adam Joseph, printer, 59 Buckeye
Adam L., boots and shoes, 173 Freeman
Adam Wm., wks. 469 Walnut
Adams ——, distiller, bds 80 W. 7th
Adams Mrs. A., 5 Home
Adams A. T., tobacco manuf., 34 Water, res. Covington
Adams Albert, dray, 526 W. 3d
Adams Alex., trader, bds. New b. North and Broadway
Adams Alonzo, chair mkr., 92 Clinton
Adams C. Columbus, clk., 120 W. 2d
Adams Charles F., printer, 139 George
ADAMS Christopher T., (Lowell Gano & Co.) 254 Longworth
Adams D. J., printer, bds. Jones House
Adams D. T., oyster dealer, bds. Henrie House
ADAMS EXPRESS COMPANY, Gaither Alfred, Superintendent, 56 E. 3d
Adams David T., salesman, 125 Walnut

Total Persons – 85

WILLIAMS'

CINCINNATI DIRECTORY,

JUNE, 1865.

ABBREVIATIONS.

acct., stands for	accountant	clk. stands for	clerk	mkr. stands for	maker
agt	agent	cof. h	coffee house	M	Miami
al	alley or allopathic	com	commission	n	north
atty	attorney	con	continuation	not. pub	notary public
av	avenue	confec	confectioner	nr	near
b	between	dray	drayman	opp	opposite
bar k	bar keeper	e	east	prov	provision
bds	boards	ec	eclectic	R.R.	railroad
b h	boarding house	eng	engineer	prop'r	proprietor
bk	book or brick	ex	exchange	res	residence
b k	book keeper	h	house	s	south or side
bk layer	brick layer	Ham. Road	Hamilton Road	servt	servant
bldr	builder	ho	homoepathic	tp	township
bldg	building	lab	laborer	u	upper
c	corner	manufac	manufactory or manufacturer	U. S. A.	United States Army
cab. mkr	cabinet maker	mach	machinist	U. S. N.	United States Navy
car	carriage	mer	merchant	w	west
carp	carpenter	mess	messenger	wh	wholesale
cig	cigars			wks	works

(ABL) (ACH) (ADA)

Aaron Emile, salesman, h. 164 Elm
Aaron Henry, clk. bds. 164 Elm
Aation Lizzie, seamstress, h. n. e. c. Court and Baymiller
Abart Rev. Dyonisius, h. 229 Bremen
Albeng Bernard, shoe mkr. h. n. s. Front, b. Carr and Harriet
Ablett Carver M. salesman, 95 Walnut, h. Newport
Abbezahl Diederich, h. 522 Main
Abbiehl Jacob, watchman, Lytle House
Abbot Caroline, widow, h. 129 York
Abbott Jenny, servt. 141 George
Abbott John, carp. h. 477 W. 3d
Abbott Richard, painter, wks. 241 Vine
Abbott T. W. clk. Clifton House
Abel Christian, undertaker, h. e. s. Donnersberger, b. Budd and 8th
Abel Frank, lab. h. n.w.c. Lawrence and River
Abel Frederick, lab. h. 417 W. 3d
Abel George, dry goods, 930 Central Av
Abel Henry, grocer, 17 Mill
Abel John, painter, wks. s.s. Pearl, b. Elm and Plum, h. Harrison Pike
Abel John, surgeon, h. 67 W. Liberty
Abel Miss M. A. music teacher, h. 294 W. 6th
Abel Martin, shoemkr. h. 140 Bremen
Abel Peter, lab. h. s.s. Harrison Av. [illegible] Freeman
Abeling Frank H. boot and shoemkr. 6 Walnut
Abeling Henry, shoemkr. h. 25 Commerce
Aberhart Max, atty. h. 294 W. 6th
Abernethy W. J. clk. h. 448 W. 3d
Abernethy Wm. boxmkr. h. 78 Melancthon
Abert Joseph, saddler, h. 623 Elm
Abinwen Gottlieb, cooper, h. 449 Linn
Abke Mrs. E. seamstress, h. 165 Pleasant
Abke William, lab. h. 25 Mill
Able F. car. mkr. wks. s.w.c. 6th and Sycamore
Able Lizzie, servt. n.w.c. Arch and Ludlow
Ablet Isaac, carp. wks. 45½ E. 3d, h. n e.c. Baymiller and Barr

Insure with THE PHŒNIX.

Abling Henry, shoemkr. wks. 6 Walnut
Abraham A. (J. H. Hart & Co.) h. 106 [illegible]
Abraham David, rag dealer, h. 452 W. Liberty
Abraham John D. b.k. h. 145 Smith
ABRAHAM JOSEPH, Attorney at Law and Notary Public, 16 Masonic Temple, n.e.c. 3d and Walnut, h. 145 Smith
Abraham L. liquors, h. 136 Longworth
Abraham Mary, widow, h. 143 Charlotte
Abraham Thomas, lab. h. 526 Main
Abraham Victor, clk. h 145 Smith
Abram Lewis, b.k. h. 136 Longworth
Abram Solomon, (Seeman & A.) h. 282 Main
Abrams Jane, widow, h. 179 Broadway
Abrance August, carp. h. 270 W. Liberty
Abriss Kate, servt. 268 W. 8th
Absprung Hy. lab. h. 52 York
Abt Paul, lab. wks. 161 W. 3d
ACADEMY OF DESIGN, 30 W. 4th, Miss M. W. Richardson, Principal
Acher L. tailor, wks. 124½ Walnut, h. Covington
Achert Fred. lithographer, wks. 2 Carlisle Building
Acheson Anthony, painter, h. 150 Pleasant
Achew Henry, steamboatman, h. 311 John
Achterkerch Wm. hostler, h. 7 Donnersberger
Achtermayer Justus, mer. h. 452 Elm
Achtermeier Rudolf, printer, h. 426 Sycamore
Achtermeyer August, bakery and confec. 522 Race
Acker E. mach. wks. 222 E. Front
Acker Valentine, carpet weaver, h. 87 W. Liberty
ACKERLAND A. & CO., (A. A. & L. Wyler,) Clothing, Cloths, and Gents' Furnishing Goods, 109 W. Pearl
Ackerland Abraham, (A. A. & Co.) 109 W. Pearl
Ackerman Andrew, varnisher, h. s.w. c. 5th and Smith
Ackermann Christopher, (Krumm & A.) h. 51 Broadway
Ackermann F. billiard tender, h. 245 Vine
Ackermann George, pipeman, h. 142 Ham. Road
Ackermann Theo. britannia mkr. h. 33 [illegible]
Ackermeier Wm. butcher, h. 88 Logan
Ackerschlag John, carp. h. 11 Orchard
Ackerstaff Rosina, seamstress, wks. 115 Woodward
Ackley Abram, driver, h. 190 Hopkins
Ackley Anna, seamstress, h. 190 Hopkins
Ackva Wm. cof. h. s.w.c. Race and 2d
ACTON, CLARK & CO., (Clement J. A., James M. C. & J. N. Myers,) Importers and Jobbers of Dry Goods, 103 W. Pearl
Acton Clement J., (A., Clark & Co.) h. 342 W. 7th
ADAE C. F. & CO., (Carl F. A. & Adolphus Seinecke,) Proprietors German Savings Institution, s.w.c. 3d and Main
Adae Carl F., (C. F. A. & Co.) and Foreign Consul, s.w.c. 3d and Main, h. Colerain Pike, nr. Cumminsville
Adae Charles A. clk. German Savings Institution, h. Adae's Woods, nr. Cumminsville
Adae Michael, tailor, h. 243 Ham. Road
Adam Jacob, clk. h. 479 Main

1865

WILLIAMS' CINCINNATI DIRECTORY. 27

(ADD) (AHL) (ALB)

16 Adam Joseph, h. 119 Mound
Adam Michael, lab. wks. Cab. Makers' Union
Adam Nicholas, miller, h. 549 Race
Adam Valentine, molder, h. 3 Corwine
Adams Mrs. h. 34 Rittenhouse
Adams A. L. mach. hand, wks. Cameron's Mill
17 Adams Abraham T. (Queen City Varnish Co.) h. 315 W. 7th
Adams Alexander, bar k. h. 15 New
Adams Alfred (Jewett & A.) res. Cleveland, Ohio
Adams Alonzo, chair mkr. h. 56 David
Adams Ann, widow, h. 31 Cutter
Adams Mrs. B. h. 52 Milton
Adams Charles, hostler, h. 452 W. 2d
18 Adams Christopher T. (Howell, Gano & Co.) h. 562 W. 9th, w. of Central av
Adams E. carp. h. W. Walnut Hills
Adams E. J. clk. h. 32 Richmond
Adams Elizabeth, h. 135 E. 6th
Adams Mrs. Elizabeth, widow, h. 279 W. Court, w. of Central av
Adams Enos, artist, h. 15 Elizabeth
ADAM'S EXPRESS CO., Office 67 W. 4th; Alfred Gaither, Superintendent
Adams Federal C. (A., Peckover & Co.) h. Covington
ADAM'S FIRE AND MARINE INSURANCE COMPANY, n. e. c. Front and Walnut. J. C. C. Holenshade, President; John M. Newton, Secretary; B. Campbell, Surveyor
Adams George, watch mkr. h. n. s. E. Front, near Foster
Adams Harriet, widow, h. 121 W. 2d
Adams Harriet, servt. 106 Elm
Adams Harriet, servt. 237 W. 6th
Adams Henrietta, dress mkr. h. 147 W. Court, w. of Central av
Adams Henry, saloon, 168 Race
Adams J. M. carp. h. 149 George
Adams J. Q. salesman, h. 167 Plum
Adams Jacob, finisher, bds. n. s. Milk nr. Vine
Adams James, mach. wks 190 E. Pearl
Adams James, lab. h. 93 Freeman
Adams John, baker, h. 13 Race
Adams John, carp. s. s. Goodloe, nr. Willow
Adams John, cutler, h. Vine St. Hill
Adams John, driver, h. 131 Everett
Adams John, tailor, h. 107 Elder
Adams John, tailor, h. 681 Race
Adams John N. carp. h. 521 W. 3d
Adams Josephine, seamstress, h. Walnut Hill
Adams Josephine, bds. 121 W. 2d
Adams Mary, servt. 232 W. 3d
Adams Michael, cab. mkr. h. rear of 1 Budd
Adams Nicholas, miller, wks. 157 Clay
ADAMS, PECKOVER & CO., (F. C. A., Joseph P., J. H. Smith, W. T. Nicholls and E. W. Martin,) Stoves, Ranges and Castings, s.w.c. 5th and Elm, Foundry s.w.c. Central av. and Front
Adams Robt. F. clk. h. 14 Stone
Adams S. H. blksmith, h. 12 Charles
Adams Samuel, bds. Orlean Hotel
Adams Samuel, finisher, bds. Orlean Hotel
Adams T. J. salesman, 54 W. 4th
Adams W. A. atty. h. 117 Broadway
Adams William, clk. h. 168 Central av
Adams William, driver, h. 30 Bank
Adams William, tailor, h. n.s Milk nr. Vine
Adams Wm. A. eng. O. H. & D. R. R.
Adams Wm. Q. (Buchanan & A.) h. 405 W. 3d
Adamson Robert, teamster, h. 108 Water
Addemaier Andrew, bk. layer, h. 677 Race
ADDERLEY WM. H. Druggist and Apothecary, n.e.c. 6th and Mound
Addison Mrs. E. J. widow, h. 81 Baymiller
Adeler M. pawnbroker, 195 Elm
ADDY, HULL & RAY, (Mathew A., Leverett R. H. & Cornelius M. R.) Commission and Forwarding Merchants, 68 Vine

Addy Mathew (A., Hull & Ray), h. 366 W. 7th
Adelsdorfer Sigmund, b.k. h. 46 Mound
Adelsdorfer Theodore, b.k h. 46 Mound
Ader ——, carpet weaver, h 25 W. Mulbery
Ader Andy, fruits, 337 Walnut
Ader Frank, grocer, 120 Clay
Ader Joseph, lab. h. 128 Clay
Adie John ——, h. 90 Laurel
Adkins John, jr. clk. 67 W. 4th
Adkins Silas, supt. gunboat yard, h. 1722 E. Front
Adle Hy, confec. h. 54 Mound
Adleman Lewis, driver, h 146 Clinton
Adler Bernard (Karlsruher & A.) h. 86 W. 9th
Adler Leonard, turner, h. 529 Walnut
Adlers Christina, widow, h. 549 Race
Adletts Martin, saloon, h. 568 Central av
Adolphi August, bar k. 475 Walnut
Aecholstzer John, lab. h. 7 E. 3d, e. of Parsons
Aeher John, baker, h. 219 Everett
Aeke Kate, servt. 355 John
Aelet Chas. grocery, 344 Freeman
Aelken Ignis, tobacco packer, 12 Main
AERATED BREAD CO. 179 Race
AETNA INSURANCE CO. OF HARTFORD, CONN. Office 171 Vine, J. B. Bennett, General Agent
AETNA LIFE INSURANCE CO. M. Grosvenor, Manager, Office 34 W. 3d
Affhepper Henry, lab. h. 115 Carr
Afterhause Rudolph, lab. h. 549 Main
Agbers Geo. lab. h. 35 Baum
Agen Anna, h. 120 Cent. Av
Agen Terry, U. S. A. h. e. s. 8th, b. Accommodation and Deerer'k Road
Ager Geo. carp. h. 948 Cent. Av
Agg Harey, clk. h. 145 Longworth
Agitig Annie, widow, h. 401 W. 7th
Agle Jacob, porter, h. 30 E. 5th
Agnes Mary, servt. 122 Hopkins
Agnew Wm. hatter, h. 339 W. 9th
Agno James, carriage mkr. h. 1548 E. Front
Agnoss James, h. 1357 E. Front
Ahaus Joseph, grocer, h. s.e.c. Liberty and Dudley
Ahearn Owen, contractor, h. 31 W. 9th, w. of Cent. Av
Ahern John, (A. & Robinson) bds 119 E. 5th
Ahern Joseph, clk. 93 W. Pearl
AHERN & ROBINSON, (John A. & Geo. R.) Patent Medicines, 216 & 218 Main
Ahl Daniel, Jr. (R. M. Pomeroy & Co.) res. Clifton
Ahl J. B. phys. h. 528 John
Ahl Thos. basket mkr. h. 83 W. Mulberry
Ahlbers Henry, polisher, h. 407 Elm
Ahle Louis, h. 103 Elder
Ahlendorff Henry, brewer, bds 622 Vine
Ahlensdorf Herman, shoemkr. h. 8 13th
Ahlering John F. mer. tailor, 39 Broadway, h. 135 E. 3d
Ahlering Herman H. (J. B. Brummer & Co.) h. 130 E. 4th
Ahlers Adolph, not. pub. bds 69 W. Court
Ahlers Arnold, saddler, bds 404 Sycamore
Ahlers Chas. saloon 69 W. Court
Ahlers Conrad, grocery 629 Main
Ahlers Fred. porter, 70 Vine
Ahlers Fred. H. grocer, 771 Vine
Ahlers Fred. J. clk. bds 771 Vine
Ahlers Henry, grain dealer, 430 Main, h. 14 Grant
Ahlers John, grocer, n. w. c. Findlay and Ham. Road
Ahlers John, h. 672 Cent. Av
Ahlers John H. boots & shoes, 404 Sycamore
Ahlers Phillip, finisher, h. 78 W. Liberty
Ahlert W. A. cap mkr. wks. 142 Walnut
Ahlfeld Louis, tinner, h. 13 Wade
Ahlfeld Wm. F. h. 115 Clay
Ahlott Wm. cap mkr. h. 25 Moore
Ahn Louis, cigar mkr, h. 100 Bremen
Ahning Henry, salesman, h. 113 Clay
Ahous Henry, lab. h. 11 Hannibal
Ahr Charles, tailor, h. 27 Jefferson
Ahrendt Mrs. Phillip, grocery, s.w.c. Bank and Whiteman
Ahrens Caroline, seamstress, wks. 115 Woodward
Ahrens Christ, finisher, h. 86 Bremen
Ahrens Frank, painter, h. 65 Peete
Ahrens H. molder, wks. 137 W. 2d
Ahrens Herman grocer, s.e.c. Mound and Richmond
Ahrens John G. stone yard, 341 Broadway, h. 422 Sycamore
Ahrens Kate, seamstress, wks. 115 Woodward
Ahrens Wm. chair mkr. h. 24 W. Mulberry
Ahrens Wm. porter, h. 13 Peete
Ahuns Wm. pattern mkr. wks. 190 E. Pearl
Ailar Bernard, turner, wks. P. J. Marqua's
Aiken Chas. A. clk 70 Vine
Aikin John, sheet iron mkr. wks. 53 E. Front
Aikins Eleanor, widow, h. 43 Mill
Aikman James, dray, h. n.e.c. Lock and 3d
Ainsworth Joseph, driver, h. 68 Butler
Ainsworth Judah T. b. k. Central National Bank, res. Columbia
Air Capt. Chas. h. 11 Oliver
Aiting Henry, molder, bds 76 Spring
Akemaier Mrs. A. seamstress, h. 644 Elm
Akemaier Samuel, butcher, h. 644 Elm
Akers Geo. tailor, 128 Abigail
Akin James, lab. h. s.s. E. Front nr. Broad
Akin Thos. finisher, h. e.s. Observatory, b. Hill and Hatch
Alanson Barnard, h. 120 Spring
Albaker Philip, lab. h. 71 Oregon
Albars H. wks. Greenwood's Foundry
Albeng Bernard, shoemkr. h. n. s. W. Front, bet. Carr and Harriet
Alberger L. bedstead mkr. bds. Farmers' hotel
Albers A. J. clk. s. e. c. 5th and Race
Albers Clements, grocer, 57 12th
Albers Fred. lab. h. 113 Clay
Albers G. W. (Stewart & A.) h. Newport
Albers Geo. lab. h. 83 Buckeye
Albers Henry, shoe mkr. h. 31 Green
Albers Hy. h. 32 Jackson
Albers John F. foreman h. 113 Clay
Albers John H. (Kersting & A.) h. 9 12th
Albers William, clk. h. 32 Jackson
Albersmann Theodore, brewer h. 709 Race
Albert Bernard, carp. h. 558 Walnut
Albert Berne, bk. binder wks. 43 Main
Albert Catharine, h. 52 Orchard
Albert Chas. carp. wks. C., H. & D. R. R. shop.
Albert Edward, elk. h. 48 Pleasant.
Albert Hy. varnisher h. 48 Pleasant.
Albert J. C. yawl bldr. 704 E. Front, h. 149 E. 3d, e. of Parsons
Albert John, cooper, h. 290 Findlay
Albert Lewis, cof. h. 66 W. Liberty
Albert Michael, huckster, h. 535 Race
Albert William, teller, 23 W. 3d, h. 48 Pleasant
Alberts John, stone mason, h. 457 Broadway
Albertson J. R. salesman, 56 W. 4th, h. 169 Clinton
Albertsat J. H. blk. smith, h. 766 W. Front
Albersart Hy. wks. Wood & McCoy's
Albiger Cecilia, widow, h. 68 Lock
Albig John, sawyer wks. M. H. Cook & Co's
Albrecht August, lab. h. 864 Race

WILLIAMS'

CINCINNATI DIRECTORY,

FOR 1880-81.

ABBREVIATIONS:

agt	agent	com	commission	n.w.c.	northwest corner
al	alley	confec	confectioner	not. pub	notary public
atty	attorney	corp	corporation	nr	near
av	avenue	dray	drayman	opp	opposite
b	between	E	east	prop'r	proprietor
bar k	bar keeper	h	house	S	South
bds	boards	lab	laborer	s.e.c.	southeast corner
b h	boarding house	manuf	manufacturer	s.w.c.	southwest corner
b k	book keeper	mach	machinist	servt	servant
bklayer	bricklayer	mer	merchant	U. S. A.	United States Army
cab mkr	cabinet maker	mess	messenger	U. S. N.	United States Navy
car	carriage	mkr	maker	W	West
carp	carpenter	N	north	wh	wholesale
clk	clerk	n.e.c.	northeast corner	wks	works

ABB ABE

Aab Kunigunda, widow, h. 4th Av., Camp Washington
Aarnenk Arnold, driver, rooms 21 Green
Aarnenk Geo. teamster, h. 5 John
Aaron Chas. bds. 29 W. Court
Aaron Chas. waiter, h. 11 Noble Court
Aaron Louis, foreman cutter, 114 W. 5th, h. 11 Noble Court
Abath Mrs. Annie, h. 38 Dunlap
Abba Belser, caulker, h. 504 E. Front
Abba Rosina, widow, h. 504 E. Front
Abbett Benj. E. collar mkr. h. 104 Mill
Abbett Carver M. boots and shoes, 166 W. 5th, res. Covington
Abbett Emma, saleslady, 166 W. 5th, res. Covington
Abbey Frank, engineer, h. 528 E. Front
Abbihl David, printer, h. 108 Pleasant
Abbihl Henry, printer, h. 108 Pleasant
ABBIHL J. J., Saloon and Restaurant, 82 and 84 Walnut; Residence, 860 Vine
Abbing Bernard, boots and shoes, s.e.c. 7th and Carr
Abbing Geo. blksmith, h. 616 W. 5th
Abbot Miss C. E. h. 353 W. 4th
Abbott Miss A. E. teacher, rooms 54 Everett
Abbott Arthur, bell boy, h. s.e.c. 6th and Mound
Abbott Ashley, porter, h. 269 W. 3d
Abbott C. O. engineer, h. Railroad east of Main, Columbia
Abbott Miss E. O. teacher, bds. 16 Clark
Abbott Henry, expressman, h. 139 W. Pearl
Abbott J. H. steam fitter, h. 64 Mound
Abbott J. K. steam heating engineer, s.e.c. Pearl and Ludlow, h. 64 Mound
Abbott Jackson L. expressman, h. 258 Findlay
Abbott John, rooms 46 W. 9th
Abbott John, polisher, h. 13 Fuller
Abbott John, solicitor, Cincinnati Star
Abbott Jos. carp. h. Crawfish Road north of Delta Station
Abbott Jos. contractor, h. 44 E. 3d
Abbott Maggie, seamstress, h. 1133 Eastern Av
Abbott Mary, widow, h. 285 Linn

Abbott Monroe, sawyer, h. 187 Sycamore
Abbott Nathan W. phys. 332 Clark
Abbott Thos. teamster, h. 289 Park Av., Walnut Hills
Abbott Wm. bds. s.e.c. 9th and Walnut
Abbott Wm. lab. h. 1133 Eastern Av
Abbott Wm. lab. wks. Geo. S. Crawford's, 21st Ward
Abel Adolph, cigar mkr. h. 338 Main
Abel Amelia, tailoress, h. 34 Moore
Abel Annie, bunch breaker, wks. 150 W. 4th
Abel August, locksmith, h. 221 Poplar
Abel Augusta, tailoress, h. 34 Moore
Abel Chas. bunch breaker, wks. 150 W. 4th
Abel Fannie, h. 45 Boal
Abel Frank, bds. 16 Pike
Abel Fred. blksmith, h. 536 Race
Abel Geo. collar mkr. bds. 16 Pike
Abel Henry, watchman, h. 536 Main
Abel Hortense, dress mkr. rear 191 State Av
Abel Jacob, gardener, h. Chapel st., Walnut Hills
Abel Jas. A. janitor, h. 57½ Hopkins
Abel John, lab. h. rear 191 State Av
Abel John, musician, h. 34 Moore
Abel John, jr. safe mkr. h. 34 Moore
Abel Louisa, midwife, h. 536 Race
ABEL MARCELLUS, Merchant Tailor; also, Dealer in Hats and Caps, and Ready-Made Clothing of my own Manufacture, 969 Central Av
Abel Mary, dress mkr. h. 969 Central Av
Abel Mary, seamstress, h. 51 Freeman Av
Abel Mary, widow, h. 969 Central Av

1880 – 81

Abel Michael, clothing renovator. 338 Main
Abel Regina, tailor shop, 45 Moore, h. 34 Moore
Abel Mrs. Stephania, h. 45 Boal
Abel Wm. blksmith, rooms 985 Central Av
Abele J. D. cigar mkr. wks. 150 W. 4th
Abeling Bernard, shoe mkr. h. 6 Walnut
Abeling F. boots and shoes, 4 Walnut, h. 6 Walnut
Abeling Henry, clk. n.w.c. Central Av. and Hopkins, h. 6 Walnut
Abeling Henry, porter, h. 4 Walnut
Abeln Herman A. butcher, h. 163 Cutter
Abendschoen Fred. mach. hand, bds. 958 Central Av
Abendschoen Wm. harness mkr. bds. 958 Central Av
Abenbach Christ. cartman, bds. John Byrne's, Clifton Heights
Aber Abraham, carp. h. 1827 Eastern Av
Abermann Chas. clk. bds. 131 Pike
Abernathy John B. sec'y Citizens' Ins Co. of Cincinnati, office, 79 W. 3d, res. Covington
Abernethy Mrs. S. B. dress mkr. h. 118 John
Abernethy Thos. clk. 429 Central Av. h. 52 Everett
Abernethy Wm. box mkr. h. 52 Everett
Abernethy Wm. J. b. k. County Auditor's Office, res. Red Bank Station, L. M. R. R
Abey Jos. V. printer, h. 73 George
Abke Wm. lab. h. 97 Carr
Aborn Chas. painter, h. Madison st., Corryville
ABORN E. S., Physician; Office and Residence, 215 W. 4th
Aborn Lizzie, tailoress, res. Chas. Aborn's, Corryville
Abraham Abraham, b. k. for Jacob Seasongood, h. 284 Longworth
Abraham Albert, clk. 99 W. 3d, h. 441 W. Court
Abraham Annie, dress mkr. h. 297 W. 6th
Abraham Albert, peddler, h. 17 Melancthon
Abraham Chas. saloon, 64 Western Av
Abraham David, peddler, h. n.w.c. 14th and Vine
Abraham Edward J. clk. h. 284 Longworth
Abraham Eliza D. teacher, h. 284 Longworth
Abraham Eva, widow, h. 441 W. Court
Abraham Gustav A. barber, h. 64 Western Av
Abraham John D., Cincinnati Lead Pipe and Sheet Lead Works, 17 E. 9th, h. 359 Richmond
Abraham Jos. atty. h. 289 George
Abraham Samuel, artist, h. 289 George
ABRAHAM VICTOR, Attorney at Law, Notary Public and Commissioner of Deeds, Office, Room 16, Masonic Temple; Residence, 136 Smith
Abraham Victor M. b. k. 102 W. Pearl, h. 284 Longworth
Abrahams Abe, b. k. 209 Central Av. h. 138 Richmond
Abrahams Jacob, tailor, 114 George, h. 138 Richmond
Abrahams Samuel, barber, h. 159 Central Av
Abrams Isaac, peddler, h. 25 S. Providence
Abrams Marx, tailor, h. 25 S. Providence
Abrams Sol. trav. agt. 129 W. Front, bds. Queen City Hotel
Abrams W. F. (Daniel Stone & Co.) rooms n.w.c. 4th and Plum
Abt Bessie, widow, h. s.w.c. 8th and Central Av
Abt Jacob F. foreman, 230 Main, h. 40 Harrison
Abt Josephine, widow, h. 630 Main
Abt Theodore, painter, h. 100 13th
Abts August, teacher, h 183 Bremen
Accident Insurance Co. of Hartford, Conn. 64 W. 3d
Achepohl Fred. W. teamster, h. 17 Jones
ACHERT F., General Artistic Designer, Illustrator, Wood Engraver and Lithographer, 119 W. 5th; Residence, 19 Jones
Achew Esther, widow, h. 287 John
Achew Harry, driver, h. 287 John
Achew Wm. J. lab. h. n.e.c. 9th and Linn
Achey Margaret, notions, 838 Central Av
Achey Wm. U. car. painter, h. 11 E. 4th
Achor Lafayette, salesman, 179 Race, h. 145 E. Liberty
Achtemeier August, clk. s.w.c. Betts and Cutter
Achten Herman, lab. h. e. s. Drake south of Keck
Achten John, expressman, h. 896 Eastern Av
Achter Frank, tailor, h. 163 Cutter
Achterkamp Catharine, widow, h. 98 Buckeye
Achtermann Henry, huckster, h. 97 Logan
Achtermeier Barbara, widow, h. 1 Hay al. b. 13th and Mercer and Walnut and Vine
Achtermeier Clara, widow, res. August Mueller's, 21st Ward
Achtermeyer Justus, clk. bds. s.w.c. Betts and Cutter
Achtermeyer Rudolph, lithographer, h. n.e.c. Bellevue Av. and Donohue, Mt. Auburn
Achzehner Louis, porter, h. 31 Ludlow
Ackemeyer Herman, blksmith, h. 22 Anderson al. b. 2d and 3d and Park and Mill
Ackemyer Samuel, butcher, h. 99 Elder
Ackemyer Wm. slaughter house, 51 Logan, h. 50 Logan
Acker Caroline, dress mkr. h. 14 Peete
Acker E. Wm. mach. h. Harrison Av., Fairmount
Acker Harry, car. painter, bds. 12 E. 6th
Acker Philip, carpet weaver, 14 Peete
Ackerland Abraham (A., Wyler & Co.) h. 360 W. 4th
Ackerland Max, trav. agt. s.w.c. Race and Pearl, h. 360 W. 4th
Ackerland Wm. (Ackerland, Wyler & Co.) h. 360 W. 4th
ACKERLAND, WYLER & CO., (Abraham A., Louis W., Isaac A. Wyler & Wm. Ackerland) Manufacturers of Clothing and Importers and Jobbers of Woolens, 89 Race, s.w.c. Pearl
Ackerman Andrew K. trav. agt. 144 Walnut, h. 20 McFarland
Ackerman Augustus, cigar mkr. h. 349 McMicken Av
Ackerman & Busch, (John Th. A. & August B.) livery stable, n.w c. Clark and Linn
Ackerman John, tobacco sorter, wks. 150 W. 4th
Ackerman John A. clk. 186 Linn, h. 207 Clark
Ackerman John T. (A. & Busch) h. 207 Clark
Ackerman Jos. clk. 92 W. Pearl, h. 207 Clark
Ackerman Jos. lab. h. 95 W. Court
Ackerman Leo, engraver, h. 207 Clark
Ackerman Ralph, h. 23 College
Ackerman Wm driver, h. 207 Clark
Ackermann Adam, lab. h. 137 Loth
Ackermann Albert, mach. rooms 39 Calhoun
Ackermann Annie, h. 7 Whiteman
Ackermann Anton, bar k. h. 104 Bremen
Ackermann David, foreman, 46 Poplar, h. 199 Findlay
Ackermann Frank, bakery, n.w.c. Broadway and 6th
Ackermann Fred. lab. h. 565 Main
Ackermann Geo. bakery, 282 Linn and 202 Clark
Ackermann Geo. foreman, n.e.c. Canal and Walnut, h. 535 Sycamore
Ackermann Geo. saloon, 349 McMicken Av
Ackermann Geo. jr. cigar mkr. h. 349 McMicken Av
Ackermann Henry, cigar mkr. h. 349 McMicken Av
Ackermann Henry, lab. h. 571 Main
Ackermann Henry, lab. h. 207 Western Av
Ackermann John, lab. rooms Herman Greber's, Colerain Av
Ackermann John, lab. h. 137 Loth

1880 – 81

Ackermann John, maltster, h. 38 Findlay
Ackermann John, presser, h. 549 Race
Ackermahn Louisa, h. 7 Whiteman
Ackermann Louisa, milliner, wks. 131 W. 4th
Ackermann Mary, stripper, h. 527 Freeman Av
Ackermann Peter, janitor, h. 20 McFarland
13 Ackermann Theo. cigar mkr. bds. 95 Clay
Ackermann Wm. butcher, h. 20 McFarland
Ackerstaff Henry, cigar mkr. h. 1167 McMillan
Ackerstaff John H. molder, h. 1167 McMillan
Ackerstaff John L. carp. h. 1167 McMillan
Ackerstaff Mena, tailoress, h. 1167 McMillan
Ackles Herman, lab. h. 169 W. Front
Ackley A. A. trav. salesman, 90 W. 2d, h. 650 Fulton Av
Ackley Clara, seamstress, h. n.e.c. Fulton Av. and Hill
Ackley E. C. tel. op. L. M. R. R. Passenger Depot, bds. 41 Kilgour
Ackley Emma E. seamstress, h. n.e.c. Fulton Av and Hill
Ackley Frank M. mach. h. n.e.c. Fulton Av. and Hill
Ackley Horace A. mach. res. Riverside
Ackley I. A. hair store, 14 W. 4th, h. Kenton st., Walnut Hills
Ackley Isaac, engineer, h. 29 Worth, Pendleton
Ackley M. V. policeman, h. 117 Betts
Ackley Oscar E. clk. n.e.c. Pearl and Broadway, h. 650 Fulton Av
Ackley Samuel, drayman, wks. 20 W. Front
Ackley Thos. A. railroad fireman, h. 29 Worth, Pendleton
Acklin Albert, coppersmith, h. s.e.c. 12th and [Elm
Ackmann Henry, maltster, h. 10 Fuller
Ackva Wm. engraver, h. 164 E. Liberty
Ackva Wm. F. clk. h. 164 E. Liberty
Acme Steam Laundry, 7 Emery Arcade
Acomb Geo. W. basket manuf. 156 Walnut, bds. 105 W. 5th
Acomb John W. willow ware, 196 Vine, h. 361 George
Acomb Lizzie J. dress mkr. 361 George
Active Manuf. Co. carriage dashes, 11 Home
Acton Chas. h. 172 Plum
Acton Chas. rooms 7 E. 5th
Acton Henry, cigar mkr. h. 172 Plum
Acton May, h. 172 Plum
widow Acton Mrs. Mary, h. 172 Plum
15 Adae Mrs. C. F. h. 133 Dayton
Adae C. F. & Co., Augustus A. Bennett and Philip H. Hartmann, assignees, 76 W. 3d, 2d floor
Adae Carl A. G. gen'l agt. New York Life Insurance Co. office s.e.c 3d and Vine, h. 111 Broadway
Adae Frank R. clk. 76 W. 3d, h. 133 Dayton
Adae Fielding M. clk. h. 133 Dayton
Adae Howard M. atty. room 11, Masonic Temple, h. 133 Dayton
Adae Otto M. h. 111 Broadway
Adair Chas. lab. h. foot of Plum
Adair Fred. clk. 5 Masonic Temple, h. 36 Barr
Adam Adam, blksmith, rooms 373 Colerain Av
Adam Alexander, h. 123 Browne
Adam Christian, lab. rooms 373 Colerain Av
Adam Fred. carp. h. 33 Bremen
Adam Geo. rope mkr. h. 11 Charlotte
Adam Gustav, baker, h. rear 490 Walnut
Adam Henry, malt house and saloon, 77 Mc-Micken Av
Adam Jacob, butcher, h. 52 Browne
Adam Jacob, lab. h. 71 Woodward
ADAM JACOB, Locksmith and Bell Hanger; also, Blacksmith, 5 E. 8th; Residence, Milk st., Corryville
Adam James, baker, Burnet House
Adam John, cutter, 135 Race, h. Milk nr. Vine
Adam Lizzie, tailoress, h. n. s. Milk b. Vine and McMillan
Adam Wm. tailor, h. n. s. Milk b. Vine and McMillan
Adams ——, stock dealer, bds. s.e.c. 9th and Walnut
Adams A. chair mkr. wks. s.e.c. 2d and John
17 Adams Abraham T. (Cincinnati Varnish Co.) 31 Main, rooms 67 Pike

Adams Albert, watchman, h. 526 W. 3d
Adams Alexander, h. 15 New
Adams Alexander C. canvasser, h. 15 New
Adams Alfred, (Jewett & A.) res. Cleveland
Adams Alfred L. foreman, 60 New, h. Western Av., Fairmount
Adams Andrew, lab. h. 210 E. 6th
Adams Anna, h. 271 W. Court
Adams Anna, shoe stitcher, h. 51 E. 3d
Adams Barbara, seamstress, bds. 571 Race
Adams C. carver, wks. s.e.c. 2d and John
18 Adams C. T. (Howell Gano & Co.) h. 534 W. Court
Adams Carrie, tailoress, h. 571 Race
Adams Chas. cooper, bds. Jos. Pfitzer's, Riverside
Adams Chas. C. potter, h. w. s. McLean Av. b. Dayton and Bank
Adams Chas. F. plasterer, h. 265 Freeman Av., old no. 237
Adams Chas. F. clothes wringers, 31 Emery Arcade, res Chicago
Adams Chas. M. printer, bds. 127 W. 5th
Adams Chas. R. car. smith, h. Lane st., Walnut Hills
Adams Chas. W. trav. agt. 54 W. 2d, res Somerset, Ky
Adams Clinton R. salesman, 138 Walnut, h. 534 W. Court
Adams Daniel, policeman, h. 732 Eastern Av
Adams David, waiter, h. 10 W. Mulberry
Adams David G. painter, h. 15 New
Adams E. P. watchman, h. 72 Baum
Adams Emeline J. h. 330 W. 4th
Adams Emma, cloak mkr. wks. 131 Race
Adams Emma, dress mkr. h. 72 Baum
ADAMS EXPRESS CO., L. C. Weir, Agent, 67 W. 4th
Adams Fannie K. music teacher, h. 15 New
Adams Fitch, (Jewett & Adams) res. Cleveland
Adams Frank, bill poster, wks. 19 Longworth
Adams Frank, conductor, h. 2 Horne
Adams Frank A. salesman, 99 W. 4th, h. 524 Elm
Adams Fred. M. teamster, h. 177 Smith
Adams G. W. salesman, bds. Walnut Street House
Adams Gustav, baker, h. rear 490 Walnut
Adams H. C. clk. Galt House
Adams Henry, car. painter, h. 290 W. Liberty
Adams Henry, foreman, 178 Main, res. Newport
Adams Henry, lab. h. 146 W. Pearl
Adams Henry, mach. wks. 147 W. 2d
Adams Henry C. clk. h. 417 Plum
Adams Herman C. clk. bds. 62 E. 4th
ADAMS ILLUSTRATED MAP OF HISTORY, J. S. Card, Manager, Office, 220 Main
Adams Isabella, widow, h. 48 Mansfield
Adams J. A. salesman, bds. St. James Hotel
Adams J. H. brakeman, h. 72 Baum
Adams J. M. chair caner, h. 157 E. 8th
Adams J. M. trav. salesman, 129 W. 4th
Adams J. U. (Coburn & A.) h. 182 Everett
Adams Jas. brakeman, L. M. R. R. Yards
Adams Jas. saddler, bds. Henrie House
Adams Jas. W. porter, h. 483 W. Liberty
Adams John, driver, h. 276 Poplar
Adams John, driver, h. 963 Central Av
Adams John, joiner, h. 13 Goodloe
Adams John, tailor, h. 290 W. Liberty
Adams John B. driver, h. w. s. McLean Av. b. Dayton and Bank
Adams John E. cutter, h. 290 W. Liberty
Adams John F. clk. 73 W. 3d, res. Riverside
Adams John Q. carp. rooms 189 Oliver

An historian's analysis of 19th century mobility patterns

The following reading indicates how other historians have answered similar questions about social mobility in the streetcar city. Michael Weber, the co-author of this book, recently completed a study of social mobility in Warren, Pennsylvania between 1870-1910. Warren, Pennsylvania grew from a population in 1870 of 2,800 to a population of 11,080 in 1910. The principal economic activity in Warren was extracting oil. Earlier studies indicated that social mobility–upward change in jobs, income, status, and property–was quite limited in the 19th century and that the Horatio Alger stories were myths. Weber found that while persons did not become millionaires overnight, residents of Warren did move up the mobility ladder. In the following reading, adapted from his conclusion, Weber compares his study to other studies of large and small cities and makes some generalizations about mobility in the Streetcar City.

1. Do the conclusions in Weber's account support your hypothesis about verticle-mobility (upward movement) and horizontal-mobility (changes in residence) in Cincinnati?
2. How would you summarize mobility patterns in the streetcar city? From your summary what conclusions can you draw about status and social class in the late 19th century? What additional types of data do you need to draw a fuller picture of mobility patterns.

The analysis of social mobility in nineteenth century Warren illustrates that native-born laborers, immigrants, and children of immigrants had different mobility opportunities. Native-born workers often attained better occupations, purchased property, and accumulated small amounts of money . . . The moderate successes of the native-born worker enabled him to view America as a land of opportunity, although few men achieved great riches.

Immigrants had less mobility success. Mobility varied among different national backgrounds. German, French, or English immigrants obtained skilled or non-manual occupations in Warren. These immigrants usually kept the same jobs. However, if they stayed in the community over ten years, they often accumulated small amounts of property. Irish and Italian immigrants secured primarily unskilled jobs. They too remained in these jobs, but rarely accumulated any amount of property.

Sons of immigrants enjoyed greater mobility. They started at the same level as new immigrants, but they gained occupation advances. In fact, mobility rates of all native-born workers and American-born sons of immigrants were quite similar. Both were able to advance in late nineteenth century Warren . . . .

Finally, the longer an individual remained in the community the greater his chance for a better job and more property. More native-born persons and white collar workers remained in the city than did immigrants and unskilled workers. One can only guess at the success or failure of the many who left Warren.

Other recent studies of social mobility suggest that workers in Warren and workers in other nineteenth century cities had similar experiences. Many people moved out of both large and small cities. In Omaha, Nebraska approximately 70 per cent of the population moved out of the city between 1880 and 1920. People in Omaha also changed their homes quite often. In San Antonio, Texas over 50 per cent of the adult males left the city between 1870 and 1880. In San Antonio, as in Warren, more native-born workers than immigrants remained in the city. Similar studies in Birmingham, Alabama; Atlanta, Georgia; and Cairo, Illinois also indicate great movement of the nineteenth century labor force.

Other studies indicate that people who stayed in cities often owned property. In Warren, Pennsylvania; Newburyport, Massachusetts; Poughkeepsie, New York; and Birmingham, Alabama those without property left the city much more frequently than those with property.

Occupational mobility among manual workers in Warren was similar to mobility in other American cities of the same time period. In late nineteenth century Boston, 25 to 30 per cent of the blue-collar workers accomplished at least minor occupational success. In Birmingham, more than half of the unskilled white workingmen who remained in the city for ten years acquired better jobs. In Atlanta one-fourth of all native-white manual laborers experienced some upward mobility between 1870 and 1880. Of this same group, the ones remaining in 1896 accomplished even greater advances.

The occupational mobility of immigrants in Warren is similar to immigrant mobility in Newburyport, Boston, and Omaha. However, immigrants in Atlanta and San Antonio gained better jobs as fast as American-born workers. In both cases, the almost total lack of Black or Mexican American mobility suggests that race more than nationality influenced one's chances for occupational success. In the South the Blacks and Mexican Americans occupied the lowly position of northern immigrants.

Thus, the social moblility patterns which occurred in Warren from 1870 to 1910 are similar to mobility patterns in other cities. While few moved from rags to riches, moderate mobility in cities perpetuated the ideal of America as a land of opportunity.

For thought and discussion

Popular games, like literature, often tell us much about the attitudes of people during a particular period of time. The game of *Monoply*, for example, illustrates the concerns and hopes of Americans during the depression of the 1930's. The following game was popular in the 1880's and 1890's. Examine the rules then play the game with a friend. What do you perceive to be the purpose of this game? How do you account for its popularity?

The District messenger boy, or merit rewarded

Directions: The object of the game is to see who will first become the president of the telegraph company. Two, three, or four persons can play: each using one piece (token) and moving it according to his throw of the dice (one). Play and throw in turn. Each player must first throw a 1 which makes him an "applicant" for a position, and upon doing so he puts his token upon the applicant space. On a throw of 2 the "applicant" moves to the "training school." On a throw of 3 he leaves the "training school" and takes his place on the "messenger force," or entrance space. From this space, he moves around the board in the direction of the openings and arrows, moving the number of spaces shown by his throw. If he stops on a space bearing words of command as ADVANCE or GO BACK; in addition to the move for his throw, he also moves as directed. The first to reach the space of PRESIDENT by the exact move wins the game. (Courtesy Pittsburgh Landmarks Society.)

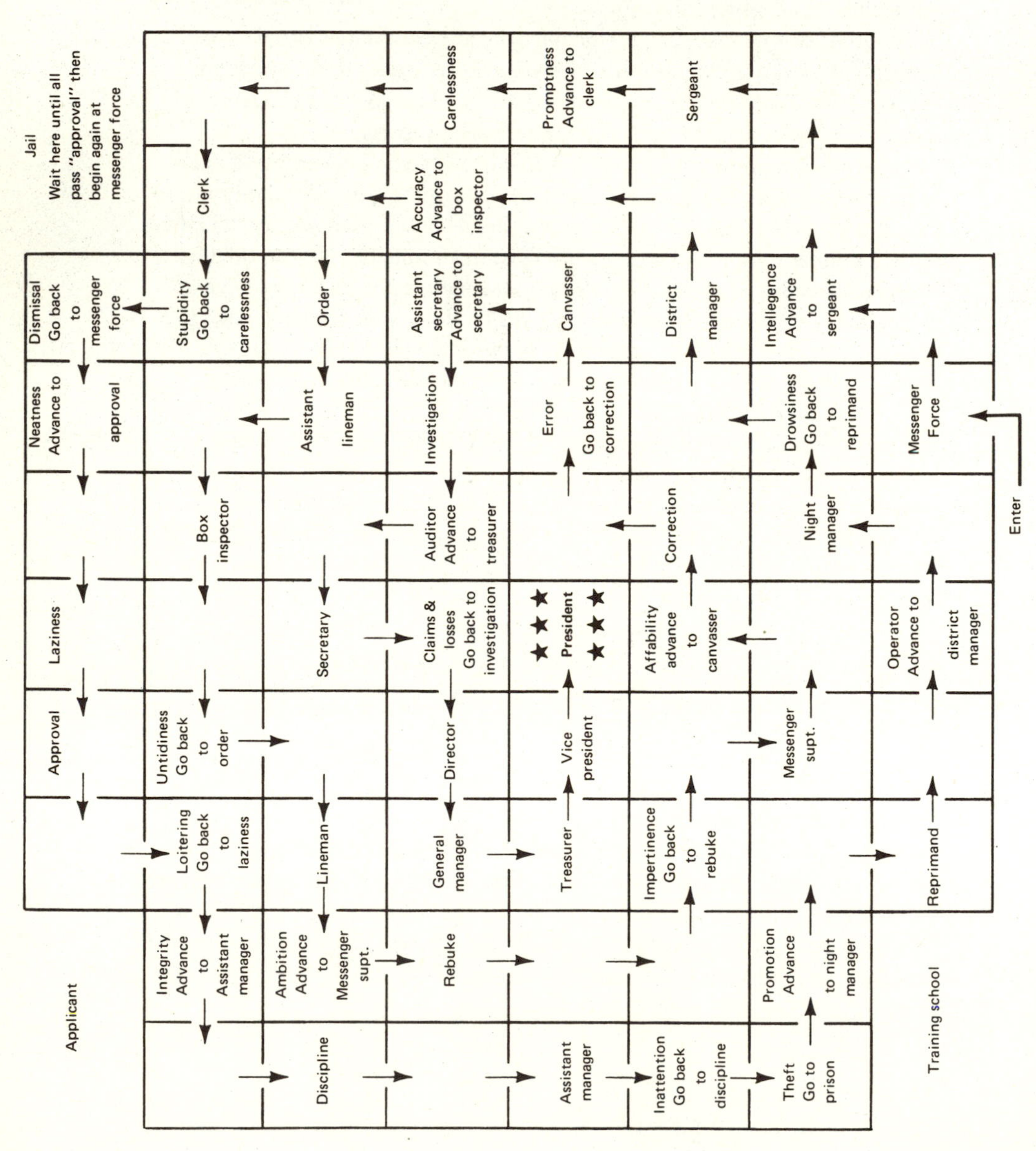

McLoughlin Brothers, New York circa 1880.

Individual and small group activities

1. Urban migration: Divide into five equal groups. Each group represents a just completed high school graduate living in Cleveland with one of the following personal characteristics: (1) a black, (2) a hippie, (3) a married man with one child, (4) a woman with a boyfriend in the service in Virginia, (5) a young swinger looking for rapid advancement.

   The following situation confronts each person:
   The Westinghouse Corporation has offered a job in their Philadelphia plant for $8,000 per year. The placement office tells the graduate that there is a similar job in the General Electric plant in Dallas, Texas paying $8,000 a year. Which job would your person accept? Why? What additional information would your person want?
2. How many times have you changed homes? Why did you or your family move? What factors were important in the decision to change homes? Report to the class what you perceive are the three most important reasons for changing homes?

The political machine and the streetcar city

Assignment 20

City governments in the late nineteenth century did not have sufficient power to solve the problems of rapid urban growth. City governmental structure often copied state and federal governments, with a mayor and a two-house council. The councilmen usually represented specific wards of the city. State and county government, on the other hand, held many of the city powers such as levying taxes. For example, when a city government wanted to grant a contract to a streetcar company the government had to go to the state legislature for permission.

Expanding cities needed services like transportation, water, gas, and electricity and needed them quickly. Growing numbers of poor immigrants also needed help from the city government. Out of this weak, disorganized government evolved the political machine and the political boss. The city boss of the late nineteenth century was shrewd, and an expert at running the business of a city. He stood at the center of a vast all-encompassing political web. He had connections with gambling and liquor, as well as with corporations and industry. A businessman or regular citizen could come to the boss or his assistants for a favor. At the top of this system was the boss, the key decision-maker, and his assistants. Below the boss and his assistants were the ward committeemen who selected minor candidates and gave out jobs. The ward workers at the bottom delivered the votes. The boss answered many needs of the city.

However, while people received help and projects were completed, the boss' organization was often corrupt. Reformers objected to this corruption and occasionally succeeded in defeating a political machine. The defeated machine usually returned to power with a different boss when other forms of city government were unable to deal with urban problems. This assignment will examine political leadership in the streetcar city.

A mayor and his people

The following short story describes how a mayor attempted to lead and govern his city. Examine the relationship of the citizens of the community with their mayor, noting the kinds of issues which win votes and those which fail to win support.

1. Why was the mayor at first successful? Why was he defeated later?
2. If you had been a citizen of the city would you have voted for or against the mayor in his final election? Why or why not?
3. What hypothesis can you form about the characteristics of a successful leader?

Here is the story of an individual whose political and social example, if such things are ever worth anything, should have been, . . . of the greatest importance to every citizen of the United States. Only it was not. Or was it? Who really knows? Anyway, he and his career are entirely forgotten by now.

He was the mayor of one of those dreary New England mill towns in northern Massachusetts—a bleak, pleasureless city of about forty thousand people in 1899. He was elected mayor primarily because the traditional parties failed to organize a campaign after the old mayor died. Few people turned out to vote and besides mayors were only elected for one year.[34]

No one knew, of course, who the new mayor was, or what he stood for. There were open assertions that the club behind him was anarchistic [opposed to law and order] (. . . that ever-ready charge against anything new in America) and that the courts should be called upon to prevent him from taking office. And this from people who were as poor commercially and socially as any might be. It was stated, . . . that he was, or had been, a mill worker! And, before that a grocery clerk—both at twelve dollars a week, or less!!

When introduced into his office in the small but pleasant city hall, he came into contact with a "ring," and a condition, which nobody imagined a lone young mayor could change. Old-time politicians sat there giving out contracts for street-cleaning, lighting, improvements and supplies of all kinds, and a bond of mutual profit bound them closely together.

"I don't think he can do much to hurt us," these individuals said one to another. "He don't amount to much."

"I think we ought to get together and have some sort of a conference about the letting of contracts," said the president of the city council to him one morning shortly after he had been installed. "You will find these gentlemen ready to meet you half-way in these matters."

"I'm very glad to hear that," he replied. "I've something to say in my message to the council, which I'll send over in the morning."

The next day his message was made public, and this was its key-note:

"All contract work for the city should be let with a provision, that the workmen employed receive not less than two dollars a day."

[34]Have you ever considered running for political office? What issues would you attempt to solve first?

The dissatisfied roar that followed was not long in making itself heard all over the city.

"Stuff and nonsense," yelled the office jobbers in a chorus. "Socialism!" "Anarchy!" "This thing must be put down!" "The city would be bankrupt in a year." "No contractor could afford to pay his ordinary day laborers two dollars a day. The city could not afford to pay any contractor enough to do it."

"The city cannot prosper unless all its individuals prosper," replied the mayor.

"We'll see about that," said the members of the opposition. "Why, the man's crazy. If he thinks he can run this town on a goody-good basis and make everybody rich and happy, he's going to get badly fooled, that's all there is to that."

Fortunately for him three of the eight council members were fellows of the mayor's own economic beliefs. These men could not pass a law, but they could stop one from being passed over the mayor's veto. Hence it was found that if the contracts could not be given at all, the mayor stood in a fair way to win.

"What the hell's the use of us sitting here day after day!" said the leader of the opposition when the fight became wearisome. "We can't pass the contracts over his veto. I say let 'em go."

So the proviso was tacked on, that two dollars a day was the minimum wage to be allowed, and the contracts passed.

The mayor's followers were exceedingly jubilant at this, more so than he, who was more cautious and less hopeful.

"Not out of the woods yet, gentlemen," he remarked to a group of his followers at the reform club. "We have to do a great many things sensibly if we expect to keep the people's confidence and win again."

Under the old system of letting contracts, whenever there was a wage rate stipulated, men were paid little or nothing, and the work was not done. There was no pretense of doing it. Garbage and ashes accumulated, and papers littered the streets. The old contractor who had pocketed the appropriated sum tried to do so again.

"I hear the citizens are complaining as much as ever," said the mayor to this individual one morning. "You will have to keep the streets clean."

The contractor, a robust, thick-necked, heavy-jawed Irishman, of just so much refinement as the sudden acquisition of a comfortable fortune would allow, looked him over quizzically, wondering whether he wanted a part of the money or whether he was really serious.

"We can fix that between us," he said.

"There's nothing to fix," replied the mayor. "All I want you to do is to clean the streets."

Repeatedly the mayor asked the contractors to clean the streets. The contractor failed to do his work arguing that he could not pay his men two dollars a day and make a profit. Finally the mayor fired the contractor from his work.[35]

The next day he appointed a new contractor, and with a schedule before him showed the contractor how many men should be employed and how much profit he might expect. The garbage was removed daily, and the streets carefully cleaned.

Similarly a new manual training school needed to be built. The mayor threw a bomb into the midst of the old-time jobbers at the city council. He decided that the city would hire its own architect and workers and build the school itself. To head off political trickery on the part of the enemy he secured bills for material as delivered, and publicly compared them with prices paid for similar amounts of the same material used in other buildings. So the public was kept aware of what was going on. It was the first public building erected by the city, and by all means the cheapest and best of all the city buildings.

Excellent as these services were in their way, the mayor realized later that a powerful opposition was being generated and that if he were to retain the interest of the voters he would have to do something which would endear him and his cause to the public.

"I may be honest," he told one of his friends, "but honesty will play a lone hand with these people. The public isn't interested in its own welfare very much. It can't be bothered or hasn't the time. What I need is something that will impress people and still be worth while. I can't be reelected on promises."

In the platform on which he had been elected was a plank to abolish local railroad grade crossings, the maintenance of which had been the cause of numerous accidents and much public complaint. With this plank he now proposed to deal.

In this, of course, he was hampered by the law which declared that no city could abolish its grade crossings without having first submitted the matter to the people during three successive years and obtained their approval each time. Behind this law was all the railroads which controlled New England, and to which brains and legislators, courts and juries, were mere servants. Furthermore, the question would have to be voted on at the same time as the vote for the mayor's re-election. This would have deterred many another more ambitious politician. The mayor was not to be deterred, however. He began his agitation, and the enemy began theirs.

A great fight was arranged for, in which every conceivable element of opposition was beautifully harmonized. Democrats, republicans, prohibitionists, saloon men, religious circles, and the railroads gathered into one harmonious body to defeat the mayor. Newspapers were subsidized; a large number of railroad-hands colonized.

As may be expected, this opposition did not lack daring in making false

[35]What, if anything, can we do to prevent corruption in government?

assertions. Charges were made that the mayor was in league with the railroad to foist upon the city a great burden of expense. Elevating the railroad tracks would saddle a debt of $250,000 upon the taxpayers.

Now came every conceivable sort of charge. If he were not defeated, all reputable merchants would surely leave the city. Capital was certainly being scared off. There would be idle factories and empty stomachs. Look out for hard times. No one but a fool would invest in a city thus hampered. In reply the mayor said city taxes would only be increased six cents to the individual. The mayor preached a fair return by corporations for benefits received. He called for the people to remember his past achievements.

The night preceding the election the enemy ended the campaign in a blaze of glory. A great parade was arranged by the anti-mayor forces, in which hundreds of men were brought in from nearby cities and palmed off as enthusiastic citizens. Money triumphed in the end. The opposing candidate won.[36]

The mayor attempted to get work in the town but was continuously hounded by various peoples. He finally left and took a managerial job in New York.

Several years later, I made a very careful study of his career for a current magazine. I went to see him and tried to get him to admit that he believed that his example might be fruitful for others in the future. I don't think he really agreed with me. "People do not remember; they forget. They remember so long as you are directly before them with something that interests. That may be clean streets, a lower gas-rate, or a band that plays good music. People like strong people, and only strong people, —good, bad, or indifferent— I've found that out. If a man or a corporation is stronger than I am, comes along and denounces me, or spends more money than I do (or can), buys more beers, makes larger promises, it is "too bad" for me. What has happened in my case is that I have come up against a strong corporation, stronger than I am. What I now need to do is to go out somewhere and get some more strength in some way, it doesn't matter much how. People are not so much interested in me or you, or my ideals in their behalf, as they are in strength or an interesting spectacle. And they are easily deceived. These big fighting corporations with their attorneys and politicians and newspapers make me look weak—puny. So the people forget me. If I could get out, raise one million or five hundred thousand dollars and give the corporations a good drubbing, they would adore me—for awhile. Then I would have to go out and get another five hundred thousand somewhere, or do something else."

Tom Johnson, mayor of Cleveland

Thomas L. Johnson, mayor of Cleveland from 1901 to 1909 represents both the boss and the reformer of the period. A wealthy self-made man, he read reform liter-

[36]Do you think the residents of the city fulfilled their obligations as citizens? Why, or why not?

Harper's Weekly, 1867.

In the 1860's political cartoonist Thomas Nast drew a series of cartoons in the periodical ***Harper's Weekly*** to illustrate the corruption of political boss Tweed of New York. What kinds of corruption do you see in this cartoon? Why do you think the people of New York tolerated the Tweed Ring?

ature and converted from an uncaring businessman to a political reformer. As mayor he attempted to eliminate monopolies and special privileges. Johnson desired greater self-governing power for cities, reform of city taxes, city ownership of utilities, and more efficient government. Once he decided upon his goals, he used few scruples and a lot of money to achieve his ends. He shrewdly fought for public utilities and for cheaper streetcar fares. The following three accounts examine the role of Tom Johnson as political leader in Cleveland. As you read the accounts answer the questions below:

1. Why was Tom Johnson a successful leader? Does his career support or refute your hypothesis about the characteristics of a successful leader?
2. What were Johnson's political beliefs?
3. Do you agree or disagree with Johnson's beliefs about leadership and government?

Tom Johnson

The following account by reformer Frederic Howe, describes Johnson's background, his political philosophy, and campaign techniques. In Assignment 16 you read Frederic Howe's thoughts on cities. Howe was a great friend and admirer of Johnson. He worked for Johnson in an effort to reform the Cleveland government.

Johnson had been a conscious monopolist. He knew all the practices of monopoly. Monopoly was an easy game for him. He had been cleverer than most of his associates. And he was far cleverer than the government could possibly be. Monopoly, he knew, could not be totally regulated. It was too powerful. Monopoly was on the job all the time. It employed the best attorneys. And it was in politics. Men like himself could always secure the appointment of commissioners or district attorneys or even judges favorable to their interests.

Later, he became a practical reformer. His program was economic, not moralistic. His program tried to take away special privileges and eliminate monopoly. Johnson believed that monopoly had a strangle-hold on natural resources. Monopoly was connected with transportation privilieges and kickbacks, with the protective tariff, with patents. Johnson's program rested on these four props.

Johnson believed that reform should begin in the cities. "Now you know," said Mr. Johnson, "why I am running for mayor. I have been in Congress, but there isn't much to be done there. The place to begin is the city. If one city should adopt the same taxes on all land, other cities would follow. If we are the first to take taxes off houses, factories, and machinery, we will have a tremendous advantage. Factories will be attracted to Cleveland. It will be a cheap city to do business and cheap to live in. Untaxing the things people use will cheapen them, it will encourage production. And if we tax the land heavily enough, we will discourage speculation. With cheap land, cheap houses, factories and goods, Cleveland will be the most attractive city in America.

Mr. Johnson's sincerity was convincing. But I had one more question to ask.

"Why don't you cut loose," Howe asked, "from the politicians whom the people distrust? [37] Then you could appeal to the educated classes and business interests."

"No," he replied, "they will never support me. There is nothing I could say or do that would make it possible for the "good people," as you term them, to support me. This fight cuts too deep. It touches too many interests, banks, business, preachers, doctors, lawyers, clubs, newspapers. They have to be on one side. And it isn't my side. They will be against me. They only people who will support me are the poor people and the politicians who will have to follow the poor people when they get started.

Mr. Johnson had to face and win the people to get elected. His methods of campaigning were spectacular. He purchased and equipped two big circus-tents, capable of seating several thousands. The tents were set up in vacant lots about the city, and the mayor with a group of supporters would motor from tent to tent, making three or four speeches an evening. Mr. Johnson drove his own car, known as the "Red Devil," with reckless speed.

[37] To what degree can you trust your political officials?

He had little respect for the law, and the police winked at his violations of the speeding ordinances.

Johnson's government

The following reading describes how Johnson ran his government.

There is no denying that Johnson had absolute control of his Council from the beginning to the end. During his first three terms his orders were unquestioned. Mayor Johnson never objected to being called a boss, though he was most of the time careful to hide his personality behind the Council when important issues were considered.

"It all depends," he used to say, "whether a boss is a good or a bad boss. A bad political organization is worse than a good political machine."

His City Hall machine worked to perfection, not only in a political way but also in the fulfilment of civic duties. The different departments organized and demanded a full day's work of their men. Of course, there were some instances of unfaithfulness and laziness on the part of employees. However such men would never last long, even if the culprit was backed by influential friends. . . . As an executive and organizer, Johnson had no superior.

It required only a short time for him to make the City of Cleveland one of the best and most honestly governed places in the country. He spent more money than any of the former mayors, and under his administration the city debt increased steadily.

The people of Cleveland rewarded his successful efforts in building up their city by re-electing him. Many streets had been paved since 1910, and many sewers built. The streets were clean and well lighted, the parks made accessible to the common people; the former "Keep off the Grass" signs had disappeared, and picnics could be held upon the lawns.

My story

In the following account Tom Johnson describes his approach to government.

But to give "good government" in the ordinarily accepted sense of the term, wasn't the thing I was in public life for. It was a part of our policy from the beginning but merely a side issue. We tried to give the people clean and well lighted streets, pure water, free access to their parks, public baths and comfort stations. We also established a good police department, careful market inspection, a rigid system of weights and measures, and made the charitable and correctional institutions aid rather than punish wrongdoers. We tried to do the hundred and one other things that a municipality ought to do for its inhabitants. While we tried to do all these things, we never lost sight of the fact they were not fundamental. However desirable good government, nothing worth while will be accomplished unless we have sufficient wisdom to search for the causes that really corrupt government. I agree with those who say that big business—the kind of big business that deals in and profits from public service grants and taxation injustices—is the real evil in our cities and the country today. This big business corrupts bosses regardless of political party. This big business stands against all movements that try to abolish its power.

For thought and discussion

In order to promote the best, most efficient government in your city would you support a political boss? Why or why not?

Individual and small group activities

1. With two other class members, choose a current political issue like mass transit in your city. One student should examine the newspapers to discover whether the mayor or council has more influence in the final decision of the issue. Another student should observe the city council and mayor in action at a council meeting to discover attitudes of the leaders and the decision-making process. The third student should interview several citizens to discover whether citizens think the mayor or the council has the most influence. Report your findings to class and conclude whether the mayor or council had the most influence in this particular decision.
2. Did your city have a political boss in the latter half of the nineteenth century? Go to your library or local historical association and find an account of the type of mayor your city had around 1900. Describe the leadership characteristics of your city's mayor to the class. Is your account similar to the accounts found by other class members? Why do you think these accounts are similar or different?

INTRODUCTION
to the unit on contemporary urban issues

In Parts I, II, and III of this book you examined the American city in three different time periods. The method of inquiry and the social science concepts you learned will help you to understand the structure of cities in any time and in any place. An understanding of city structure can help us to solve problems within our own city. Given a particular problem to solve, our understanding of the city enables us to determine the feasibility of various suggested solutions. For example, knowing the decision-making process within our own city may lead us to predict that a particular solution to the transportation problem will fail. Thus, we must search for other alternatives.

Part IV of *The American City* deals with eight contemporary urban issues. Some of these issues represent urban problems. Some do not. Each Issue contains two parts. In the first part you will examine data to determine the nature of the issue. The second part contains a number of suggested alternatives to the issue. You are to analyze each alternative to determine the best possible solution or most desirable position. The problem solving model listed below will aid you as you examine each of the contemporary urban issues.

1. Define the issue to be solved. This process includes understanding the issue thoroughly, deciding what goals should be reached, and recognizing the values implied in the decision.
2. State all possible ways to reach the goals.
3. Evaluate carefully the probable consequences that each alternate solution might have, discarding those that seem impractical or harmful in the process.
4. Choose the alternative that appears likely to achieve most of the goals aimed for. Remember that no alternative is perfect.

Courtesy of Charles A. Keffales.

Leisure time in the contemporary city: Stating the issue for Assignments 21 and 22

People living in cities today have a greater amount of leisure time than their parents or grandparents did. They also have more money to spend on leisure time activities. Many people now earn their living providing leisure time activities for others. Movies, sports, drive-in restaurants, television, plays, and opera all provide entertainment for urban dwellers. The media constantly bombard us with new ways to spend our money and time in leisure activities. These diverse choices, however, often result in confusion. We tend to spend our time and money participating in the same activities throughout our lives. Many of us remain unaware of all the possibilities for leisure in the city.

Few urban residents understand why they choose certain leisure time activities rather than others. Many sociologists suggest that one's leisure time choices reflect one's personal life style and attitudes toward the city and society in general. For example, you may enjoy sports and play tennis, golf, basketball, or football. These leisure time activities suggest that you value physical fitness and a chance to compete in situations where the "best person wins." The city offers you many challenging activities where you can prove your abilities. On the other hand, you may spend some of leisure time in voluntary activities. Some people lead boy or girl scout troops, collect funds for charities, or work as a volunteer in social service organizations. These people value helping others and working cooperatively in groups. People who spend their leisure watching movies or television have still other values.

Assignments 21 and 22 examine the relationships among leisure time activities, lifestyle, and values. Assignment 21 contains excerpts from a nineteenth century melodrama and a modern soap opera. Both plays imply sets of values. Assignment 22 consists largely of photographs which portray the range of leisure activities available in a large city. Both assignments give you an opportunity to think about your own leisure time activities and to relate them to your values and lifestyle.

Left: Photos by courtesy of Charles A. Kaffalles.

Leisure time in the contemporary city (1)

Assignment 21

In all its forms, the theatre has long cast a spell over urban dwellers. Until the twentieth century, however, only live audiences could enjoy the theatre. Movies and television now bring plays to people in their neighborhood theatres or seated in the comfort of their own living rooms.

Assignment 21 has two parts. The first part consists of an adaptation of a famous nineteenth century melodrama entitled *Rosina Meadows, The Village Maid, or Temptations Unveiled.* Night after night thousands of city dwellers saw this play and took part in the make-believe world which portrayed their dreams and fears. The poor sat in the balconys, the ladies and gentlemen sat in the boxes. For a few hours they escaped their day to day problems. Afterward they returned to the real world and disappeared down darkened, gas-lighted streets.

The second part of the assignment contains the script of one episode of a popular soap opera, *Love of Life*, which millions of people have watched. For a half hour Monday through Friday, people from all walks of life watch this drama about mating, marriage, and the family. As you read these two dramas, answer the following questions:

1. What attitudes about cities do these two plays imply? What do the plays say about the nature of city life?
2. What sorts of issues did the authors write about? Why were these issues popular with audiences?

The melodrama as a reflector of societal values

Melodramas reflect the concerns and beliefs of people who seldom left written records. The following melodrama, *Rosina Meadows, The Village Maid, or Temptations Unveiled*, won great popularity in many American cities after a successful first run in Boston in 1855.

Rosina Meadows, The Village Maid, or Temptations Unveiled

CHARACTERS

Rosina Meadows, a village maid who goes to the city to seek her fortune
Mr. Meadows, Rosina's father
George Milton, Rosina's village boyfriend
Harry Mendon, a city man and playboy

ACT I

SETTING

Rosina's Village. Harry Mendon has just arrived from Boston on a country drive. He meets Mr. Meadows and Rosina. He is obviously taken with Rosina's beauty. Harry Mendon has joined the Meadows family for breakfast.

Mr. Meadows: Tears come into my old eyes, when I think my dear daughter leaves us today.

Harry: Leaves you, for what?

Mr. Meadows: Why, sir, she goes to Boston, to seek what the girls call her fortune. Pray Heaven it may be a good one!

Harry: Has she any relatives or friends in Boston?

Mr. Meadows: Just an older aunt.

Harry: So young and innocent a girl will find many temptations in the city. I fear her course is over a wild sea, full of rocks and quicksands.

Mr. Meadows: (looking at Rosina) But while virtue and modesty are her guides, she has nothing to fear. She has learned both from the great book of Nature, written by the hand of God!

Rosina: Don't worry father, everything will be all right.

(Enters George Milton, Rosina's boyfriend)

George: Rosina, the stage will be here soon. Will you keep your promise and remain true to me?

Rosina: George, can you doubt me?

George: I do not doubt you, Rosina; but I know the temptations that beset a young female's path in a great city! O, beware the garb of friendship! Villany lurks unseen.

Rosina: I will remember your warnings. I remember that I am going to a gay and thoughtless city. Temptations will be thrown in my way–vice is there to deceive the young and innocent! The libertine (playboy) is there–he pollutes the air with his evil breath. Be assured, dear George, I will be true to you.

(The stage soon comes and Rosina leaves. Harry Mendon returns to the city at the end of the day.)

ACT II

SETTING

In the city of Boston, Harry Mendon is strolling down the street.

Harry: A whole week in town and no news yet of my rustic beauty! Devilish provoking that she should slip through my fingers thus! (He looks down the street) What do I see? As I live, the very figure and face, too! (He calls to Rosina) I am your servant, Rosina!
Rosina: Mr. Mendon!
Harry: The same. I trust you are not displeased at the meeting? My way lies the same as yours, Rosina—I beg pardon, Miss Meadows. May I know the place of your sojourn?
Rosina: I am living with my aunt at present, but am looking for employment.
Harry: I would be proud to render a service to you. Permit me to interest myself for you. You would prefer some light work; a milliner's employment might suit you. Rosina, do not think me rude, my heart will admit of no longer delay—Are your affections engaged?
Rosina: Sir, I fear you mock me, when the wealthy Harry Mendon declares his love for Rosina Meadows, a humble farmer's daughter. I have been taught to look with distrust upon everyone—even upon you!
Harry: (putting on an innocent look) Miss Meadows, you judge me too harshly. Your beauty might inspire some in this city to do wicked deeds, but I am a gentleman. In fact your parents asked me after you had left to look after you and help you. If you could read my heart, you would be assured that I am governed by the purest motives in offering my assistance!
Rosina: I believe you, Mr. Mendon, and will rely upon you.
Harry: Let me have your confidence, and you will attain all you desire. (An aside to the audience) And I'll get what I desire as well. Ha! Ha!

ACT III

(Harry achieves his desires. He takes Rosina to the house of a lady who makes lovely evening wear. Actually the dressmaking is only a front. Several girls reside at the house; they are the mistresses of wealthy young men around town. Rosina becomes the mistress of Harry. However, Harry loses all his money and becomes an embezzler. Rosina is turned out to beg and becomes a prostitute.)

SETTING

The scene opens with Mr. Meadows and George Milton wandering around Boston looking for Rosina. Someone had informed them of what had befallen her.

Mr. Meadows: A terrible retribution upon the seducer of my child! O, place me face to face with the despoiler, let me meet his eye, and if my gaze does not strike death to his coward heart, then shall my hands tear from him the guilty life.
George: Come, sir, be calm; let us go to our lodgings, and give up our search for this night. (They exit, enter Rosina)
Rosina: (Clad very poorly) Here I am wandering. Ten o'clock, and I have no home; poor, deserted, deceived, Rosina! O, false, deceitful man! Heaven will avenge my wrongs. My limbs grow weak. I faint—who'll give a cup of water to

the lost Rosina? (enter Harry and some friends)

(Rosina approaches them. Harry pretends not to know her. She asks him to step aside and talk to him.)

Harry: (steps aside and in a low voice) What do you want with me? Speak softly. I would not have my friends think that the wretched object before me was once my mistress.

Rosina: I am crushed and cannot sink any lower! I want money–I am famishing, houseless, and friendless–give me money!

Harry: You are disgraced now. I will give you some money so you will leave me alone. Never again notice me in the streets, or let me hear your voice. (He gives her money and pushes her aside. He strolls off with his friends.)

(Meanwhile, Harry and his friends attempt to rob a bank. The nightwatchman discovers them. The police catch everyone but Harry. Rosina hears that the police are looking for Harry. She knows where he is hiding and informs on him. The police and Rosina go to Harry's hiding place in a rundown bar. The father and George hear about Harry's hiding place and they rush there too.)

The Bettman Archive.

Sweet Liberty and the Abyss

In what ways, if any, does this cartoon illustrate your attitude toward urban life?

The police: Here's the embezzler and thief! Come let's pull him out in the open!

Rosina: Behold, Harry Mendon, this is my work! (Rosina falls to the floor)

Mr. Meadows: (rushing in with George) Where is he? Heaven, thou has heard my prayer! Villain! Thy days of wickedness are run! The time is come!–seducer! murderer of my child! (turning to Rosina) Look upon your father! I forgive you! Sweet, crushed flower, I forgive you! Bless you! Bless you!

Rosina: Then, I die happy! (She dies in the arms of George)

Mr. Meadows: She's gone. Now, villain, prepare!–the order hath gone forth which said blood for blood!

Harry: Officers, protect me from this madman!

(The officers, have their backs to the audience, and do not observe the movement of Meadows)

Mr. Meadows: Thou didst have no mercy, and canst expect none! Nay, do not shriek–she cannot hear thee–her spirit is even now hovering over thee, impatient to denounce thee at the judgement seat! Tis time for the sacrifice! (Seizes him.) Villain! Seducer!–Murderer! Die! Die!

(He strangles him. The police rush forward to rescue Harry from the grasp of Meadows–as they take him from Meadows, Harry falls dead. The watchmen stand at the side of Meadows who stand with one hand pointing to heaven, the other hand pointing to Rosina.)

The soap opera as a reflector of societal values

The following script comes from an episode in the well-known soap opera *Love of Life*. This series began in 1951, and still continues to attract a large audience each weekday between 11:30 and 12:00 on C.B.S. television stations.

Love of Life

by Robert Shaw

CHARACTERS

Ed
John
Bruce
Tess
Patrons & personnel at the Rosehill Inn

SETS

John's office;
Rosehill Inn;
Sterling patio.

TIME: day.

ACT I

(Fade in: Interior of John's office [10:00 A. M.] Ed stands waiting while John concludes a phone conversation.)

(To phone) I agree, Father, payment ought to be in Swiss francs. Exactly. I'll bring it up at the board meeting next week. Fine. How's the weather in Madrid? All right? Well, I'm glad to hear it. Yes, I will, Father. I'll tell her tonight. Good to talk to you. Yes, soon. Good-bye.

(He hangs up, and motions Ed to a chair)

John: Sorry to keep you waiting, Bridgeman. My father was calling from Madrid. Sit down.

Ed: Thank you. I'm afraid the May reports aren't quite ready, Mr. Randolph. I hope to finish them this afternoon.

John: No problem. If you do finish them, just leave them here on my desk.

Ed: I'll make sure of it.

John: Actually, I didn't call you in about the reports. I have good news for you.

Ed: Oh?

John: You're doing a good job, Bridgeman. In fact, you're doing more than a good job. You've taken on additional responsibilities and you're handling them very well indeed. I'm not unaware of that.

Ed: That's very nice of you to say, Mr. Randolph.

John: I've done more than just say it. You'll find a twenty per cent increase in you next salary check.

Ed: Why that's . . . that's handsome of you, sir. I am deeply grateful.

John: I'm grateful for your good work. And if I may be personal for just a moment, I was delighted to hear that things are going well for you at home.

Ed: Clare and I are trying, Mr. Randolph. At the moment, I'm content with just that. We *are* trying.

John: (puzzled) I'm sorry. I'm not sure I understand. I was talking about Sally.

Ed: Oh, I'm sorry. I thought you meant something else. You see, sir, Clare and I are trying to . . . how shall I say it? Put our house in order. Straighten out our lives, as it were, while we still can.

John: I'm glad to hear it. It's rather difficult to express, but I believe you have great potential. Not only here, but in other areas as well. As a family man, for example, and as a father. How is Sally? Getting along all right? (he sees Ed frown) I'm sorry. Is something wrong?

Ed: To tell you the truth, Mr. Randolph, it's too soon to tell. Sally's experience with drugs has had an effect. A very . . . disturbing effect. Whether it's permanent or not, we just don't know.

John: What kind of effect?

Ed: Apparently there's been some brain damage.

John: Oh, no!

Ed: Outwardly, she seems quite normal, except that she can't write. It's a

matter of correlation, apparently, between the brain and her hands.
John: Ed, I'm shocked. And deeply sorry. Can something be done?
Ed: Something has to be done. We're seeing about therapy for her now. I haven't told Clare, incidentally. I thought that could wait.
John: Of course. Well, again, I'm extremely sorry. And if there's anything I can do, anything at all, I want you to tell me.
Ed: You've done a great deal already. You can see now why I'm grateful for the raise.
John: Keep me advised, Ed. I mean that. For Sally's sake, and for yours, too.

(Fade out)

ACT II

(Fade in: Sterling Patio [5:00 P. M.] With what could be bloody marys or tomato juice.)
John: Bridgeman wasn't explicit, but apparently it's one form of brain damage.
Bruce: That's tragic. I hadn't heard.
John: Ed's keeping it quiet. In fact, he hasn't even told Clare.
Bruce: It's not uncommon, you know. Sally took an overdose of speed—a concentration of amphetamine.
John: Yes, I know.
Bruce: Damage to the central nervous system is often the result. What are they doing about it?
John: Ed mentioned therapy.
Bruce: That can be a long process. And not always successful.
John: You used the right word, I think. Tragic. The damage youngsters do to themselves. The sometimes irreparable damage.
Bruce: The worse part is, kids themselves won't believe it can happen.
John: I know. Incidentally, I hope you won't mention Sally's difficulty to Bill Prentiss. I'm not sure Ed wants it known.
Bruce: Oh, I wouldn't. Actually, Van and I see very little of Bill these days.
John: Isn't he living with you?
Bruce: Technically, yes. But he's out early in the morning and by the time he gets back from working for Tammy at the theater he's off to The End.
John: I'd heard he was working at the theater again this summer. This may sound strange, coming from me, but there's a lot to admire in Bill. His job at The End, his recording activity, working at the theater—one could hardly call him lazy.
Bruce: Far from it.
John: As long as we're talking about him, Bruce, tell me. Has he accepted the divorce pretty well?
Bruce: The young are resilient, John. They bounce back.
John: They can bounce, period. I'm an authority on the subject.
Bruce: Oh?

John: I imagine you've heard. Tess is moving back to Carrie's at the Potting Shed.
Bruce: Really?
John: Then you hadn't heard?
Bruce: No. I don't think Van has either.
John: She will, I'm sure. As I recall, the Potting Shed belongs to Van's mother.
Bruce: Yes, it does. Oh, Carrie has an interest in it, but the original money came from Sarah.
John: Well, the way things look Sarah's going to have a tenant, two tenants, really. Tess and the baby.
Bruce: Look, I . . . I don't want to get into something that's none of my business.
John: Nonsense, I brought it up.
Bruce: It's just that I thought . . . that is, I assumed . . . (he stops) Look. Maybe we'd better change the subject.
John: You assumed Tess and I would be married again.
Bruce: Frankly, yes.
John: So did I.
Bruce: Are you saying you won't?
John: Oh, no. Nothing like that. At least, I hope its nothing like that. And in a way, I can understand Tess's point of view.
Bruce: That isn't always easy.
John: What it comes down to, I think, is that Tess feels she's being manipulated. By my mother, and to a certain extent, by me. This decision to move back to Carrie's is really a blow for freedom, a desire to make up her own mind. As I say, I can understand it. Forgive me Bruce. I had no intention of pouring out my troubles.
Bruce: You really think Tess resents you?
John: I hope not. In fact, really to lay it on the line, there's only one thing I want Tess to understand. I'm in love with her, I want very much to marry her, and in time–in due time–I shall.

(Fade out)

ACT III

(Fade in: Interior of the Rosehill Inn [6:00 P. M.]. Tess and John are seated, with drinks.)
John: Father said the weather in Madrid has been perfect.
Tess: It always sounds so marvelous. Just to say, oh, by the way, I was talking to Spain this morning. Can I ask you something about your father?
John: Yes, of course.
Tess: Why doesn't he live with your mother? Because of business?
John: No it's not because of business. In order to remain friends *and* man and wife they find it best to live apart. Does that make any sense to you?
Tess: I guess so.

John: Tess, now to ask you a question. Are you concerned about expenses? The suite upstairs, Miss Blodgett's salary, all that?
Tess: I can't let your mother go on paying for all that, John.
John: Would you let me?
Tess: No. That would be the same thing. I can't let your mother or you pay for me, because then you'd never be sure. I'd never be sure myself.
John: I'm still a bit confused. Sure of what?
Tess: We'd never be sure why I married you again.
John: I see.
Tess: It's kind of hard to explain, but don't you see? If you or your mother are paying for me, then it might be that I'd marry you because I had to. Because I owed you so much. If I'm back living at Carrie's, and then we got married, it would be for just one reason.
John: What reason?
Tess: Because I wanted to. I didn't have to. I wanted to. Does that make any sense?
John: Yes. What you've just said, the way you've just explained yourself—is surely one of the nicest things you've ever said to me. Move back to Carrie's by all means. Provided, of course, you understand one thing.
Tess: What?
John: I love you. (he takes her hand) Remember that, Tess. Just that, and we'll be fine. I love you.

(Fade Out)

ACT IV

(Fade in: Interior of John's office [6:15]. The office is empty, and the door is open. We hear Ed's voice in John's office. Ed sits in John's chair, and begins to assume the posture of an executive, enjoying it. Ed pretends that John is speaking to him.)
John's voice: You're doing a good job, Bridgeman. In fact, you're doing more more than a good job. You've taken on additional responsibilities and you're handling them very well indeed.
Ed: (Expansive) Think nothing of it, John, old man.
John's voice: I believe you have great potential. Not only here, but in other areas as well.
Ed: (Nods) Other areas. Yes, that's quite true, sir.
John's voice: As a family man, for example, and as a father.
(Ed frowns, for this is not a completely pleasant area. He allows himself to sink into deep, and troubled, thought.)
Ed's voice: A family man. A father. Can that be true? After all these years, can that really come to be? Ed Bridgeman, a man of potential? A family man? A father? Not the Ed Bridgeman I know. Oh, never. Why, he's a . . . he's a . . . Well, go on, say it. What is he? A bum? A wanderer? A man born without one iota of responsibility? Isn't that the real Ed Bridgeman? Of course it is. He walked out on his wife and child, didn't he? You bet he did, and more than

once. Just disappeared into thin air. Gone for years at a time without a care in the world. That's a man of potential? Oh, now, come on! Ed Bridgeman? Never. (pause) Now wait a minute. That was before. That's all in the past. We're talking about the new Ed Bridgeman. Right? Right! The family man. The father. The father. Oh, Sally, Sally, how can I help you? If ever I wanted to make it up to you, if ever you needed me, it's now. Right now. But how? What do I do? How can I help you? Only God can do that now. Only God. Do I pray for you, my dearest? Is that now the only answer? Would God help me, do you suppose? Me, of all people? Would the dear Lord help me to help you? Would He help me?

(Ed pauses, and then comes out of his thoughts. He stands up, places the chair just as he found it, and turns out the desk light. He crosses to the door, and the light from the outer office illuminates him. He pauses and thinks.)

Ed: "Let each man think himself an act of God,
His mind a thought, his life a breath of God:
And let each try, by great thoughts and good deeds,
to show the most of Heaven he hath in him."

(He pauses, and then seems to fill with determination.)

Ed: And let each try.

(He turns off the lights, turns, and exits.)

(Fade Out)

For thought and discussion

Why did audiences find these two plays so appealing? What do you find appealing in your favorite plays, films, or television productions?

Individual and small group activities

1. Get together with a few other members of the class to go to a popular movie or view a television show. Prepare a report to the class about why the movie or show of your choice is popular among city dwellers. What values does it imply? To what emotions does it appeal? What characters play a vital role in the plot? What does it reveal about the nature of modern urban society?
2. Organize a group of students to do an informal survey of people who watch soap operas. Each member of the group should interview as many people as possible. The larger the number interviewed, the more reliable your results will be. The following information from each respondent will help you to organize your report. You will probably wish to add items to the list: age; sex; occupation; name of favorite soap opera; time when it is aired; setting (city, suburb, country; time); major characters by sex, age, and occupation; major features of the plot; major values to which the soap opera appeals; major reasons for preferring this soap opera to others. Compile the data from the interviews to make a report to the class. As a final part of your report, indicate what you would need to do in order to conduct scientifically reliable research on the subject of the audiences for soap operas. Your professor can help you with this part of your report.

Leisure time in the contemporary city (2)

Assignment 22

Sociologists and economists usually classify leisure time activities into four categories: recreation, relaxation, personal development, and work. In recreational leisure time the particular activity, such as playing or watching football, is most important and the center of attention. Relaxational leisure time provides the individual with a means of recuperation. For example, a person may go to a restaurant with friends more to relax and talk then to enjoy eating. In a personal development activity the individual acquires skill and/or knowledge. For example, people may take a night class in literature in order to improve their writing abilities. People who use leisure time for work choose to extend their work day to earn more money and/or success.

Some leisure time activities may serve several functions for a particular individual. Also, different individuals may take part in the same activity for quite different reasons. Hence, one activity may have different functions for different people. For example, a course at a community college might provide personal development and greater work success for one individual. The same course might provide relaxation and recreation for someone else.

This assignment contains two parts. In part one you will examine photographs illustrating many possible leisure time choices for urban dwellers. Consider your own attitudes and values toward these activities and classify each activity as relaxation, recreation, personal development, work, or a combination of the four. You should then rank the activities portrayed in the photographs in the order of your own personal preference.

In part two you will analyze your own values toward leisure time activity. Prepare a brief description of your favorite leisure time activity for class presentation. (You are not limited to the activities pictured). Indicate in your description whether your activity is relaxation, recreation, personal development, or work. Describe the activity briefly, tell why you enjoy it, and indicate how this activity reflects your lifestyle, your values, and your attitudes toward urban life.

1

2

3

4

5

6

7

8

9

10

11

12

13

14

15

16

17

18

19

21

20

22

23

24

25

26

27

For thought and discussion

What are your attitudes toward the relationship between your work time and your leisure time?

Individual and small group activities

1. A recent issue of the magazine *Popular Cuture* described the game of *Monopoly* as a simulation of the daily game of city life. The game's manufacturers claim that almost every person in our society has played *Monopoly* at least once. With three or four class members play the game of *Monopoly*. As you play analyze what elements of the game resemble urban activities and attitudes. Does the real life urban game depend mostly on chance or strategy? Why do you think this game enjoys such popularity? Report to the class.
2. Organize a group of students to do an informal survey of people's favorite leisure time activities. Each member of the group should interview as many people as possible. The following information from each respondent will help you to organize your report. You will probably wish to add items to the list: age; sez; occupation; favorite leisure time activity; reasons for preference; importance of the urban area to the enjoyment of the activity. Compile the data from the interviews to make a report to the class.

Diverse urban life styles: Stating the issue for Assignments 23 and 24

In Assignments 21 and 22 you examined a variety of leisure time activities. You classified these activities as relaxation, recreation, self development, or work related. The types of leisure time activities people choose to engage in tell us much about their personal life style. Leisure activities, however, are only one component of the pattern of living that sociologists call life style.

Many people judge a person's life style by examining his or her manner of dress, hair style, musical tastes, or political views. For example, some may classify a young person who wears mod clothing, prefers long hair, and hard rock music as being "far out" or a "hippie." On the other hand, one might judge a person with opposite tastes as "out of it." Most of us would agree that by these criteria hundreds of life styles exist in the large American city. One has only to walk the streets of any major city to find this diversity.

Sociologists examining life styles, however, find these characteristics often misleading and not very useful. They argue that people often appear to be something they are not. Sociologist Gideon Sjoberg, contends that life style includes much more than fashion, musical taste, or political views. Sjoberg defines life style as the nature and interrelations of three basic activities: leisure, work, and family-friend relationships. To understand one's lifestyle we need to examine the type of leisure, work, and friendship activities one engages in, the relationship of each of these activities to the other, and the setting in which these activities take place. These factors, according to Sjoberg, distinguish one life style from another.

Conventional, or typical middle-class life styles, tend to separate the various life activities. Work is performed "at the office." Leisure activities occur away from work. In addition, one has work friends, leisure friends, and relatives but seldom combines these groups. Unconventional, or alternative life styles unite these three basic elements of life. Thus work becomes leisure and leisure becomes work, all intertwined with family and friends. Work communes in which friends and family work together at something they enjoy provide one example of this unconventional life style.

In between these two life styles are several intermediate groups which combine certain elements of each of the above life styles. These groups include the playboy or "partying" group, week-end drop outs, and certain religious groups.

Assignments 23 and 24 provide information about a number of diverse urban life styles. Examine each alternative and determine whether the example follows a conventional, unconventional, or mixed life style. Then use the problem solving model, described on page 247, to evaluate and clarify your own values about each alternate life style.

Diverse urban life styles (1)

Assignment 23

The city provides a refuge for every imaginable life style. Playboys, business men and women, "swingers," and "flower children," all find acceptance, or at least tolerance, in the American city. One recent television series always began with the statement, "there are a million stories in the big city." Each of these stories represent a type of urban life style.

Assignment 23 contains accounts of three urban life styles. Examine each of the accounts then complete the exercise and answer the question listed below.

1. Draw a straight horizontal line on a piece of paper. At the right end of the line place the words "segmented" or "conventional" life style. At the left end of the line place the words "unified" or "unconventional life style. (Sociologists call this line a continuum.) Examine each of the accounts described in this assignment and place the group described at the appropriate spot on the line. For example, if you think the elements of a group's life style (work, leisure, family-friendship) are more unified than segmented, place the group somewhere near the left-hand side of the line.
2. Which life style is most like your own? Like that of your Parents?

The singles' complex

Some young people are experimenting with a new type of life style in "Singles Only" apartment complexes. The following account describes life in one such apartment in Houston, Texas.

No sports page ever said a word about it, but three years ago Houston, Texas, gave birth to a superman contest which, though officially ended, will probably be waged fiercely, if unofficially, for years. The object of the struggle was classically simple: to see which man could take the most girls to bed in a given year. In 1971 the winner was Charley Hazzard. (Like all the other names I'll give, this is a pseudonym.)

His winning score: 79.

A modestly built bachelor on the spare-tire side of 36, Charley discovered his sporting instincts when he moved into Woodway Square Apartments, a 48-acre complex of private hideaways and indoor and outdoor playpens dedicated to the greater glory of the Swinging Single. Recalling his first taste of the Woodway way of life, Charley says: "All of a sudden I realized—wow!—you can have just about anything you want around here. And you don't even have to say please."

Thousands of other Charleys, have recently been making the same discovery in singles apartment complexes all over America, and, since Houston's Woodway is one of the largest and most lavish of all such dormitories, it seemed to me a good place to find out what this lifestyle has done to the state of being single.

Last July and again in January I flew to Houston and drank Harvey Wallbangers and danced to Grand Funk and listened to the stories of a dozen Woodway lives. First there was Charley. Then some of the women who helped him reach his winning count of 79. I listened to fragile Texas wild flowers who thrive on one-night stands. And to sad 26-year-olds who've already had their day and now dream only of finding someone to take them away from it all.

It used to be, in the palmy Fifties, that boys and girls graduated from college, found a job in their hometown, and lived with their parents until marriage sprang them loose. Sexual freedom was limited to Saturday night and the back seat of the family DeSoto.

Then came the Sixties. Everybody started going straight from college dorm to big-city apartment to share the thrills and the rent with a gaggle of roommates. The era of mom's midnight curfews was over.

By 1965, singles in Southern California had discovered something called the Never-on-Sunday Club, a cluster of tiny apartments built around a swimming pool and party room. All the management asked was that tenants be single, fun-loving, and able to pay the rent. Soon half a dozen copies, called South Bay Clubs, sprang up in and around Los Angeles, and big developers began to take the new lifestyle eastward—first to Texas and Florida, then to suburbs around all the big cities.

The official population of Woodway's 1,800 apartments is 2,500. The real count, however, is rumored to be closer to 4,000, due to multiple roommates per apartment—a practice management smilingly denies knowing anything about. The architecture hasn't totally escaped the two-story Basic Training Camp look of most complexes, but it does have a certain style of its own, ranging from Swiss chalet to English Tudor and built of handsomely aged woods and dusty pink adobe brick. The grounds are faultlessly tweezered and manicured.

Nobody at Woodway seems to be saving for a rainy day. The men—most of whom are engineers, junior managers, or salesmen—earn between $10,000 and $20,000 a year, rarely more. The majority of the women are secretaries; the rest are apt to be either teachers or stewardesses. Their average income is probably no more than about $7,500, yet because they often live three or four in an apartment, they are likely to have plenty of spending money.

Management's primary concern is not the size of a tenant's income but that everybody be "the white-collar type." When I asked a rental agent if that included $5,000-a-year stenographers and high school-dropout bailing-wire salesmen, she sniffed that it certainly did—if they were the "right type." When you look around Woodway, you realize that the right type includes everyone but blacks and hippies.

Charley Hazzard was born in Minneapolis, sampled universities there and in California without graduating, and became a sign painter in San Diego. After a stint in the navy, he billed himself as a commercial artist. Now he earns $17,500 a year painting posters and advertising art. His friends call him Renoir—prounced rain-war.

Married at 21 and divorced nine years later, he sees his teen-age daughter twice a year. But his mind is made up. "All that bein' a one-woman man with kids to feed and a lawn to mow seems like it musta happened to somebody else, not old Charley," he says. "I'm into playin' and lovin' and not givin' a damn for the rest of my life.

Roughly half the men living in this singles complex have, like Charley, at least one broken marriage behind them. Unlike their younger, never-been-married counterparts, these men feel the need for a steady standby—someone ready to provide 4 A.M. consolation if the Gretchens of the world prove disappointing or simply wear out. Standbys are also expected to be genuinely in love with their Charleys. The amazing thing is, they often are.

At the cocktail party where Charley was animatedly replaying for me the highlights of 1971, his winning year in the Woodway Sexual Olympics, Charley's standby was no farther than five or six bodies away. Surely a few of his high notes were drifting into her pickup range. Yet, far from worrying about being overheard, Charley seemed to flirt with the possibility. When I looked nervously in her direction, he explained, "Oh, that's just Mindy. But she's beautiful people, she loves me." What about the love objects he spends six nights a week collecting? "Oh, she knows," Charley answered loudly. "I tell her and she tells me, and she's so damned honest it'd nearly make you upchuck." Tells him what? "Well, she loves me so much she doesn't play around—except with my best friends. So if she doesn't tell me, she knows they will."

Does he love her? Charley's nice gray eyes went almost dewy for a second and the broad patch of pink pate that his retreating hair was so carefully hot-combed to hide suddenly seemed as vulnerable as a new baby's. Hitching up his electric-blue embroidered bell bottoms, he drawled flintily. "Honey, old Charley don't love nobody. I went that route once, and the lady I promised to love, honor, and cherish, well, she woke up one morning and told me she never wanted to see my face again. From that day on, lovin's just been a lot of laughs for me."[38]

Two days later I was sipping peppermint tea in Mindy's apartment. No one I'd seen Charley give a second glance to at the wine-tasting was dressed nearly so conservatively: Peter Pan collar, knee-length plaid skirt, sensible shoes. Mindy has a trim figure, and her face is passively pretty—but unresponsive, as if all the electricity had been disconnected. For the last six years since she graduated from North Texas State she has been working an adding machine in the accounting department of a Houston tire company and living at Woodway.

I asked her if she found her job interesting; she answered with a lackluster mmmm. No elaboration. I inquired if her present job was the kind of work she would like to be doing ten years from now. Silence. She wasn't trying to be a difficult interviewee; it was simply that the possibility of being independent or intellectually satisfied was a totally new and alien thought. For the Woodway girl of today, there is only one possible tomorrow: marriage. And the odds are not in her favor. In this bastion of singleness, not one person I spoke to could remember more than one marriage that had taken place between two Woodway tenants in the past year. That couple is expecting their divorce to come through by June.

Of all the high-tension areas in a singles complex, by far the highest is the social center, or the club. Formally known as the wood hollow club, Woodway's social center is informally referred to as the meat rack, body works, or any number of other standard nicknames signifying a sexual market place. Besides accommodating all of Woodway's communal indoor social activities, the meat rack is the scene of a phenomenon called Ladies' Night. This takes place every Tuesday, rain or shine, and has nothing to do with baseball.

Cal, an attractive, 24-year-old Woodwayite who has participated in several Ladies' Nights, told me that most of the girls he approaches get right down to the basics fast. Their conversation on the dance floor goes something like: (1) "What do you do?" (2) "Does that pay pretty good?" (3) "Do you live upstairs or down?" (up is more expensive than down), and (4) "What kind of car do you drive?" Clearly their eye is on the checkbook, but they stay flexible. Cal's income is anemic, and he admits to driving an aging, dented Toyota, but his take-home rate of the girls he goes after at the club is, he says, at least 80 per cent.

As couples weave and bob in a self-conscious, almost chaste Sixties version of rock dancing, a revolving, multi-mirrored chandelier right out of the Avalon Ballroom era turns the meat rack's discotheque into a deep red fishbowl of undulating bodies and unblinking eyes tirelessly in search of bait.

By 1 A.M. most of the prettiest girls have disappeared, leaving a predominantly plain and thirtyish group for the remaining men to pick from. Youth is an *idée fixe* with Woodway men. Like Charley Hazzard, they are as likely

[38]Do you think Charley's life style makes him happy? Why, or why not?

to identify their girls by age as by name.

"I took Suellen home last night–she's 25," is a standard term used to impress people that she was worth having. Never mind what Suellen thinks or says or does. Her most valued accomplishment is not having turned 26.

Twenty-eight is the average age for women at Woodway. This means that for every coed fresh out of college and in no hurry to give up flirtin' and funnin' there is a single in her middle thirties still enduring weekends full of egg-throwing contests, beer busts, and $2 barbecues in the hope of finding someone who will give her a way out.

The false security of having a coterie of friends to join at the swimming pool or at the bar seduces a lot of girls who come to Woodway for a year or two into staying on past all hope of achieving either marriage or independence "It's like a group marriage," says one young observer. "After a couple of years here, they all know the same people, share the same jokes, trade the same gossip. It makes the older gals feel as if they belong even when they really don't."

Dr. Salomon Rettig, Chairman of the Department of Psychology of New York's Hunter College, specializes in the psychology of groups, and he cites some very immediate and tangible reasons why so many singles are turning to this kind of group living.

"One is simply the new affluence," he says. "Only recently have young people in their twenties been able to afford to live alone and in such luxurious surroundings. Another is the significant sexual changes that started way back with beatniks and flower children and continue to be popularized by hippies and the whole counterculture. The adults now living in these complexes were kids when all this began and they were inevitably influenced by it, even though they never dropped out of society themselves. The group creates for them a microsociety in which things are permitted that are permitted nowhere else and where the norms are the opposite of those in the world at large."

Dr. Rettig goes on to say, however, that by far the most significant factor is "the total meaninglessness and senselessness of their occupational existence. Generally speaking, these are people who find no meaning in what they do in life. Their work is routine, standardized. It does not permit genuine human participation in terms of planning, decision-making watching the results of their efforts. They are merely cogs in the enormous machinery of the office. So to combat this meaninglessness, they look for solutions in terms of affiliations and associations–even if only temporary ones."

Contrasting the complex with the kibbutz, where he has done ten years of socio-psychological research, Dr. Rettig says, "I see these singles complexes as simply a reaction to both the mass society and the lack of meaningful labor that people are caught in today."

In the communal life of a kibbutz, Dr. Rettig found, "the religion of labor was the most important criterion in making for a meaningful existence. Yet I'm not convinced that what you and I are doing is so much better than what these singles are doing. The apartment complex is only one of the total range of experiments in coexistence in America now, and I expect this kind of experiment to continue to a significant extent. The traditional family will not be the only way of existing, because in many ways the traditional family has failed us."[39]

A California life style

The Adamses live in Palos Verdes, California, a Los Angeles suburb. The following account describes their work, leisure, and family-friendship patterns.

They live in a modern ranch home in a fashionable suburb of Los Angeles. They drive two cars, one a Lincoln Continental. They belong to the Jack Kramer Tennis Club and the Republican Party. They have two robust, intelligent children. They own part of a $40,000 weekend home on Lake Arrowhead. And they often dress formally for dinner and eat by candlelight.

They are not at the top of the financial ladder as measured by the wealth of southern California. But they are members of that fast-moving society of successful, sun-tanned, self-assured families who in material terms are on their way up.

Clark Golden Adams is handsome, self-confident, and articulate. He and his attractive wife Barbara Jean, were not handed their affluence. They have earned it by hard work and determination. Perhaps they are living just a bit beyond their income but, young and vigorous, they see no impediments to their steady material progress.

"In a way it's a real success story and I ascribe lots of it to luck," Mr. Adams told me across his sleek walnut desk in the Los Angeles Division of North American Aviation, Inc., one of the largest aerospace corporations in the United States.

"I'm in the $30,000 bracket now as division director of contracts and pricing and I don't see any reason why with luck I won't continue to move ahead—hopefully next into a vice-presidency. I started with the company back in 1952 at $400 a month as a contract analyst and worked my way up through the company, and I've achieved what I have because of the amount of time I have put into the job. I usually work between 60 and 80 hours a week."

By training Clark Adams is a lawyer. He graduated from the University of Utah Law School and passed the bar exam in his home state of Utah.

"But I never really had an inclination to practice law," he explained. "I wanted to pursue my endeavors in a corporate life rather than in the combative atmosphere of other people's personal problems."

"I can't say honestly that I'm a self-made man. You see, I believe strongly in heredity, and the stock I came from is probably the finest you

[39]Do you agree with Dr. Rettig that, "in many ways the traditional family has failed us"? If so, can you name some of the ways?

can find. My mother and my father, a retired schoolteacher in Layton, Utah, were substantial people and basically industrious. I was given a heritage of pride, not money. But most important, my parents gave me a highly developed sense of responsibility."

"North American, and particularly the Los Angeles Division, has been good to me and my plans are to stay with the company as long as the job keeps its challenge," he commented as his office emptied momentarily. "But I feel that if at any point I've been plateaued out and still have greater capability, I'd move on, although the possibilities here are fertile and wide open."

The life which Clark and Barbara Jean Adams have fashioned for themselves on the arid bluffs of Palos Verdes Peninsula is in many ways typical of the fluid, shifting, dynamic society of southern California. Nothing is static in this sun-drenched, luxurious climate where changing houses is almost as common as changing clothes. The Adamses have had four homes since their arrival in this part of the country.

"BJ didn't want to live in Utah," related Mr. Adams one evening as the family and I were eating dinner on the outdoor deck of their home. The night was balmy. Below us, stretching into the distance, the lights of Los Angeles basin glittered like a carpet of gems.

"She felt as blanketed by all my relatives and Mormonism as I did by the sense of anonymity when I first came here. Salt Lake City is a very tight community, so we decided to go to California. First we moved into an apartment in Venice, a low-income area. Then, when BJ got pregnant with Clark II—and let me add that we were consciously planning our family—we moved into a duplex. When Vickey came along, we bought a place in Hawthorne for $14,500. It scared us, the financial responsibility! Later, in 1960, we moved up and bought this four-bedroom place. It cost us $34,500."

"And here we are in the process of selling again," added Mrs. Adams with a sigh. "This house is really fine, but we want a large rumpus room so that when the kids get a little older they'll be able to bring their friends here and entertain and not be away from home."

"I like the way California moves," went on Mr. Adams with enthusiasm, as his young daughter draped herself around his neck. "I like the way people buy houses they can't afford and grow into them on pure faith. I find great satisfaction in my job and the way I live. In fact, I consider myself one of the most fortunate people in the world—partly from the standpoint of a happy and full marriage and of having two healthy, happy children, but more important from the fact that I have within me the capacity to get enormous enjoyment from my family." [40]

However, with Clark working long hours and often away on business trips, Mrs. Adams has had to build a life for herself and her two children that does not rely solely on her husband's presence. But she obviously has no dif-

[40]If you led Mr. Adams' life style would you consider yourself "one of the most fortunate people in the world? Why, or why not?

ficulty keeping her days imaginatively busy and productive.

A smartly dressed, vivacious woman, her dark hair dramatically blond-streaked, Mrs. Adams runs her home with taste and distinction. And, as her husband proudly commented, "she's good at everything." An artist by avocation, she has invested her talents in decorating a home that shines with elegance and sophistication. Her own paintings, creative stitcheries, and artifacts grace every room.

As we were on our way early one morning to the Los Verdes Golf Course, where she was due for a lesson on her "forward press," I asked Mrs. Adams if she ever regretted not finishing college (she left to marry Clark) and pursuing her artistic talents professionally.

"Oh yes," the words came tumbling out, "I'm sorry I never finished—not sorry that I married of course. But some day I'll finish. I'm always taking art courses—interior decorating, oils, silk screening. A friend and I have formed a decorating partnership and have a resale license now to visit the wholesale houses. Recently I helped a friend decorate her home. I also assist in a course in crafts for the Peninsula Women's Club. Right now we're making papier-mache angels for a dance we're giving. The proceeds will go to charity."

Mrs. Adams is also a dressmaker. She sews all her own clothes, as well as those of 11-year-old Vicky, not merely because she likes to sew but because "I want something original."

Victoria Jean, a seventh grader who is all brown eyes and gangly legs, shares her mother's enthusiasm for making things. Her other interests run the gamut from rope climbing to guitar playing.

Vicky is among the gifted top of her class and, unlike her brother, Clark II, needs no urging to do her homework, pick up her clothes, and straighten out her room. Mr. and Mrs. Adams feel that Clark II is not pushing himself to his intellectual limit; while he may not be strong on homework, he's clearly no slouch in the things that interest him.

"I like electronics best," he said. "I've built two shortwave receiving sets. This one here has a special gismo so you can tune in real fine. I get reception from all over the world—Russia, Peru, the Netherlands. I know when they're speaking Russian 'cause it's kind of a weird sound. I've also built a stereo amplifier."

It is not surprising that in their well-ordered, active home the Adams children have posed no discipline problems for their parents, at least nothing more serious than youthful squabbles and occasional remonstrances when they do not get their way. But I asked Mr. and Mrs. Adams what they would do if their children ever got into trouble with the law.

"I really don't know," said Mrs. Adams thoughtfully. "Even here in Palos Verdes, where the children come from good homes, you hear of shoplifting—and those kids have money in their pockets. I once asked little Clark what he would do if one of his friends urged him to do something wrong. Was I surprised when he said, 'I don't know'! He didn't say he wouldn't! I guess we can only hope by our example that they turn out all right."

"Big" Clark's answer was a bit more precise.

"I'm a basic person," he said. "And I'd get pretty corporal with him. I don't know what I'd do with Vickey—but I'd be terribly disappointed if either did anything legally or morally wrong. I believe in ethical and moral standards—but not necessarily from a formal religious standpoint."

Religion, in fact, does not play a prominent role in the Adamses' life. The children attended Sunday school for a while and Mrs. Adams thinks they should know the Bible and "be good Christians." But no strong effort is made at churchgoing.

"I was brought up a Baptist," she related, "then started going to the Presbyterian Church. Clark's really a Mormon and always will be. Of course he's not a good one, since he married me and we weren't married in the temple. I don't push church any more."

"You hardly ever become not a Mormon," elaborated Mr. Adams. "I guess you'd say I'm sort of in limbo. I don't subscribe to all of the tenets of the church—like not smoking and drinking."

"Actually religion at this point in my life does not mean very much to me one way or the other. I suppose if I were to pursue it, I would find the beliefs of the Unitarian Church most easily acceptable to me at this stage of my development. You see, the way many people treat religion today . . . it's sort of like belonging to the Kiwanis Club, or the Rotary. People who find themselves unsatisfied in their avocation seek fulfillment elsewhere."

"I definitely don't agree," demurred Mrs. Adams emphatically.

If the Adamses do not quite see eye-to-eye on the subject of religion, however, they would seem to agree that they have established a desirable way of life, each pursuing activities that are "invigorating and stimulating." Their concern now is to give their children a good education. And in the years ahead they expect to improve their standard of living even more.

"What I want to do," stressed Mr. Adams "is to leave an estate for my family. I have a pure abhorrence of leaving my wife with nothing but social security. And I think it would be great to leave my children a big nest egg."

"Happiness, I feel, is a state of mind. Each person is born with a certain capacity to be happy. Essentially it matters little if he's in a prison or in a posh resort on the Riviera, he'll find his measure of happiness."[41]

"You know," he smiled, "I remember when we first went to work for NAA [North American Aviation] we used to have waffles on Thursday and Friday because we ran out of money by the end of the week. But we had great friends and we enjoyed ourselves. We were as happy then as we are now."

Today it's no longer waffles on Thursday and Friday. In fact, it's not even waffles for breakfast.

"Mom, can I make an avocado omelette?" shouted little Clark from the

[41]Do you agree with Mr. Adams that happiness is merely a state of mind? Why, or why not?

kitchen on Saturday morning.

"If you must. But don't use the beater. It'll blend too much. And don't forget to use a little sour cream to hold it together.

It seemed a long, epicurian way from waffles.

The good earth commune

In 1968, a middle-aged divorcee sold her interior decorating business and purchased one-hundred and fifty acres of farm land outside of Portland, Oregon. Angelina, and a young married couple started the Good Earth Commune that same year. Today thirty-eight adults and eight children live in the community. The final article of Assignment 23 describes how people work, play, and relate with each other on the commune. Compare this life style with the others you read about in this assignment.

I had arranged to first meet Angelina at a local coffee shop one afternoon. She was wearing a colorful dress, which, she explained, she had designed and sewn herself. She also explained that the couple with whom she had founded the commune had since left. And that among the thirty-eight members presently living in the commune there are five individuals with exceptional skills as plumbers, mechanics, electricians, and carpenters. A stonemason is also in residence. Financial support of the commune derives from a number of sources including member contributions, with Angelina—as owner of the property—playing a major role. We talked for about an hour over coffee, and then Angelina invited me to come to the commune for supper.

Located fifteen miles from town on a blacktop road, the commune is flanked by well-kept small farms. An elaborately carved and painted sign close to the road announces "The Good Earth Commune." Immediately behind the sign is an improvised parking field. It was filled with about two dozen cars and trucks and a bus, which obviously served as living quarters. Some of the cars had thick layers of dust and either were abandoned or had not been used for a long time. As we drove past, five boys and two girls, all deeply suntanned, were gathered around a pickup truck and were talking leisurely while watching two of their number work on the motor. They seemed like high school or college kids on a summer vacation.

Over a slight rise, hidden from the road and surrounded by old oak trees, stands the barn. This was the only building on the property when Angelina bought it and it now serves as the main gathering place of the commune. The interior of the barn has been rebuilt and there is a large kitchen with a long, well-scrubbed wooden table: this area also serves as the dining room. Next to this room is a communal quarter, with an improvised fireplace in the center of the dirt floor and barrels and pieces of logs on wooden blocks to sit on. Further construction is under way, but a well-stocked library can be reached by climbing a ladder. In the middle of the library's floor squats an old-fashioned woodburning iron stove. There are pillows scattered around to sit on and a few old easy chairs that show signs of having been repaired with care.

Hal, who is one of the four left from the original group of fifteen that started the commune with Angelina, volunteered to act as guide. He is a slender, blond-haired man in his middle or upper twenties; he was dressed in clean, faded bluejeans, sandals, and a multicolored shirt he had dyed himself. He was also wearing a medal suspended from a deceptively crude-looking, handmade brass chain around his neck. A dropout from a social science doctoral program at Yale, Hal has a habit of carefully forming his sentences. While dusk drew near, we walked together along paths through the wooded hillsides. More than a dozen single-room buildings have been so neatly fitted into the landscape that they are hard to distinguish from their surroundings. Each is different and has been constructed by the people who live in it from materials found on the land—old lumber and odds and ends. Some are built into the hillside and overlook the valley, and each structure is totally isolated, with no other neighbor visible. Only the sounds of birds could be heard; it was very peaceful.

Hal and I looked into several houses whose owners were away on trips. Most of these houses had one room dominated by a fireplace or an iron stove. There were mattresses on the floor, and chairs for the most part were improvised from lumber or were hand-hewn from logs. Navajo rugs and colorful madras cloth and prints from India provided decorative touches. Everything appeared neat and clean, and I was reminded of the outdoor shower and washing facilities near the barn, which we had investigated earlier and which had been shown with much pride.

On a different path back to the barn, we passed a tepee and a tent. A good-sized, intensively cultivated garden grows next to the barn; it furnishes the commune with most of the vegetables needed. Two nude girls with beautiful uniform tans were busy weeding. Hal explained that those who want to, go nude whenever they feel like it. As we passed the garden, we noticed Angelina walking along another path trying to join us. Although we slowed our pace so she could catch up with us, she had difficulty doing so, because out of nowhere would appear members who engaged her in intense conversations.

As we strolled on, I noticed several other people hovering in the background waiting. I asked Hal if Angelina functioned as guru or leader and if she were directing the course of the commune. He was emphatic—as were several others to whom I put the same question later—that Angelina is not in charge: "We all decide what we want to do."

Earlier, both Angelina and two of the other older members of the commune had made almost identical remarks: "We have lots of ideas and very little energy." Hal felt the reason was: "There is a lot of grass around and people drop acid." Although he did add, philosophically, "Everybody is into his own thing—each person is free to follow his own needs and interests. No one is forced to do anything. Everyone knows what needs to be done, and finally it gets done."

The commune has meetings once a week "to discuss everything that bothers us." There are seldom any major problems and in fact Hal felt that the commune's only significant problem was the lack of energy.[42] Other neighboring communes have factional disputes, hostile neighbors, suffer from lack of food and shelter or are unable to pay their taxes. The Good Earth Commune's relations with neighbors are friendly. As Angelina had put it at the coffee shop, "We live a very honest life." She had related a story of how one of the commune members had stolen a pump from a lumber company. This was discussed at one of the weekly meetings, and although the commune has definite strong feelings about lumber companies, the pump was returned.

During the weekly meetings, the group discusses what projects have priority; those members who want to then volunteer for a particular project. To feed the commune, there is a kitchen list. Two members are chosen daily to provide the food and help prepare it. Farmers bring fruits and vegetables, which they barter for home-baked bread.

Eventually, Angelina caught up with us and led the way to her house. The second largest building on the grounds, it is almost circular in shape; members of the commune built it for her of field stones, hand-hewn timber, and used lumber. The large bedroom in the two-room dwelling has a fireplace and a double bed; placed here and there are many healthy-looking green plants in pots and on stands. An antique desk, a chest of drawers, a candelabra, and antique paintings and prints add richness to the room. The combination kitchen-living room was filled with young people reading, talking quietly, or playing the guitar and singing. Here also is the only phone in the commune. A young blonde girl was talking to her father. I could overhear snatches of her conversation: "No, Dad, I don't need any money. Just send me the plane ticket to Santa Barbara and I'll see you there at the house." Later, Angelina casually mentioned that the seventeen-year-old daughter of a two-star general is at the commune with the consent of her father.

The clanging of an old school bell called us to the barn for supper. Everyone formed a huge circle around the dinner table on which candles and kerosene lamps flickered. The room slowly grew quiet as the children scampered to their places in the circle. We all held hands. There was a long moment of silent communion, with heads bowed and eyes closed. The only sound was a dog barking in the distance. With no word spoken, the circle was broken. Conversation resumed, and we served ourselves buffet-style. The vegetarian meal consisted of a pea soup spiced with garden herbs; a combination entree of brown rice with onions, green peppers, and squash; a mixed green salad; freshly baked bread; and, for dessert, bran muffins with nuts and dried fruit. Following supper, a fire was lighted in the large unfinished room next door and there was chanting, singing, and dancing.

As the evening progressed, Angelina told me that she would like to meet a warm, loving, sensitive type of man, maybe a minister—someone who knows

[42]Do you think you would enjoy living on a commune? Why, or why not?

how to counsel and work with young people. She said, "I haven't had a vacation for two years. I want to live in my house and get uninvolved. I want to travel. Older people point their finger at the commune instead of helping. I want some people with money to get involved. Where are the parents of these kids? Many of them come from well-to-do homes. Why am I so alone in this?"

As I prepared to leave, a phone call came from another commune asking for advice. Going out the door, I could hear Angelina's husky voice offering sympathy and suggestions. She was obviously very much involved and perhaps not really as alone as she thought.[43]

For thought and discussion

What do people find missing in the conventional life style that might cause them to seek an alternative?

Individual and small group activities

1. Young members of a certain religious sect are often seen distributing literature on the streets of cities throughout the nation. Interview one of these people to find out about their life style. You will need to ask questions about their work, leisure activities, family-friendship groups and the degree of integration of these elements. You might also find out why they chose this alternative life style. Report your findings to your class.
2. With one of your classmates visit a nearby commune, if possible. You will need permission from the commune's members to do this. Find out how these people have combined the work, leisure, and family-friendship aspects of their lives. Your instructor will inform you how to present your findings.

[43] Which of the three life styles discussed in this assignment appeals to you? Why? Can you do anything about it? Will you?

How well can you judge a person's life style from his or her manner of dress? The photographs below show four persons in leisure dress. Examine each photograph then try to match the person with the proper occupation from the list below. Your instructure can provide you with the correct answers.

1

2

3

4

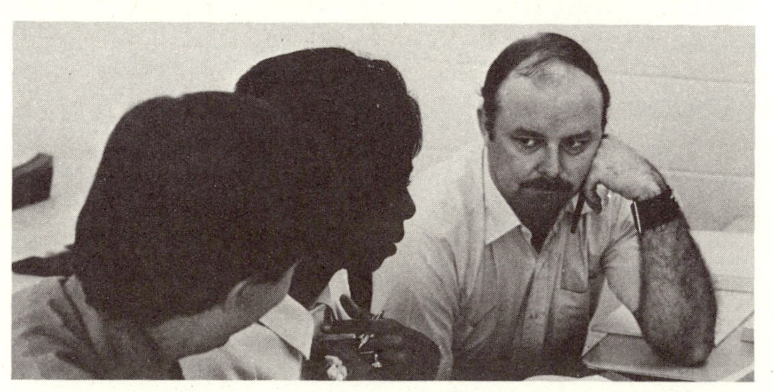

A. Athlete
B. Businessperson
C. Doctor
D. Religious Leader
E. Housewife

Diverse urban life styles (2)

Assignment 24

In Assignment 23 you examined three types of urban life styles. Other urban dwellers in addition to these groups, have developed alternative types of living. The aged, poor, religious, and ethnic groups often constitute unique types of urban life styles. Assignment 24 provides accounts of several additional urban groups to help you complete your analysis of urban life styles. Examine the style of living of each group and complete the classification of urban life styles you began for the previous assignment. Then answer the questions listed below.

1. Which of the alternate life styles discussed in Assignments 23 and 24 best integrates the elements of work, leisure, and family-friendship patterns.
2. Which of the alternate life styles discussed in each assignment most appeals to you? Why?
3. What are the consequences of each life style to its followers?

New life styles for the aged

Men and women over the age of 65 constitute nearly 10 per cent of the nation's population. For many of these people retirement presents special problems. No longer required to work, the aged often find themselves with unwanted time on their hands. To fill this time one man reported arising daily at seven in the morning and driving by his former office for years following his retirement. Other retired people try hobbies or pass the time at movies, watching television, or sitting in the park. Recently, however, many have established new life styles in retirement communities. The account on pages 287–291 describes the new living patterns of one group of retired persons.

Four years ago, when Donald Roszel retired from his job as vice-president of Olin Corp., exchanging his New York commuter's home in Darien, Conn., for a retirement home at Sun City Center, Fla., his son thought he was nuts.

"We didn't think he'd last six months," says Brantz Roszel, 28. "But six months later I went to visit him, and I knew he wasn't coming back. We had pictured our parents sitting around with shawls on, in rocking chairs, but I found they were busy all the time."

"We're happy as larks," says his 59-year-old father.

The senior Roszels are two of about 200,000 active, affluent retirees who live in the nation's 25 or so communities designed specifically for "mature adults." Once vaguely humorous fringe communities have become a $250-million business–one viewed with alarm by social scientists who deplore the growing age–stratification of U.S. life. The scholars say that older people who move away deprive their home towns of the wisdom life has taught them, and deprive youngsters of the models they need in order to mature in a healthy way. At the same time, they concede that many retirees lead richer lives among their peers.

Today the companies most involved in retirement communities–Webb, Leisure Technology of Lakewood, N.J., and Rossmoor Corp. of Laguna Beach, Calif.–feel that they have identified the fastest-growing sector of the housing market, and perhaps the most difficult to master. All three have suffered crippling setbacks in the past, in part because of the huge front-end investment required. Buyers who fear imminent physical decline will not move in unless the golf courses and swimming pools are ready for immediate use. A development of several thousand units requires an investment of $2.5 million to $5 million.

Now the developers feel that social and economic factors are working in their favor. They cite higher pensions, early retirements, better health, greater mobility, and also soaring property taxes in older communities, urban decay, fear of crime, and the homogenization of many communities. Industry leaders believe that the jump from a $50 million industry a decade ago to this year's $250 million is just the beginning.

Leisure Technology, whose five communities are concentrated in the Northeast, plans to open four more this year, including one near Chicago. It expects to sell 2,500 to 3,000 homes and garden apartments. Rossmoor's flagship community at Laguna Hills has 14,000 residents, mostly in three- and four-unit garden apartments. It hopes to double that number in five years and to develop a retirement community in Montgomery County, Md.

Retirement apartment buildings also are available, often sponsored by churches. Canterbury Court in Atlanta, sponsored by two Episcopal churches, has a yard-long waiting list for its 122 units. It charges $10,000 to $35,000 for a lifetime lease plus $200 to $560 for monthly maintenance, including meals.

All the projects ban sales to couples with growing children, and most require that one of the buying partners be above a certain age, usually 50 or 52.

The typical resident, says Webb, is "the guy who worked for the power company in Chicago. He has a $50,000 house all paid for. He gets a touch of rheumatism. His doctor tells him to go to Arizona. He's never quite had the country club life. He comes out here and God, he's got something he never thought he'd have before."

What he has at Sun City, Ariz.—among other benefits—is one hole of golf for every 200 residents and a special spot in his garage for his electric golf cart, with an electrical outlet for charging the batteries.

Schmertz of Leisure Technology adds another detail to the picture of the average resident: he's not strapped for cash. More than 90 per cent of the Lakewood Leisure Village residents bought their living units outright. And one California trust company with full-time trust officers at several retirement communities reports that they handle $100,000 and $200,000 portfolios.

Even brief contact with the residents reveals other common qualities: they tend to be Republican, and white. Most appear active and healthy. Sun City, Ariz., is a swarm with bicycles, golf carts, and late-model, air-conditioned cars. The city's motorcycle club boasts at least one member who whizzes about attired in crash helmet and white jumpsuit.

But if the residents seem happy with their lot, academicans who ponder the state of society are beginning to express doubts. They wonder what happens when the well-educated, well-off, active elderly uproot themselves to resettle in what detractors call geriatric ghettos.[44]

What happens, says George Rosenberg, professor of sociology at Case Western Reserve University in Cleveland, is that "you take away from the neighborhood the kind of person who can be a very valuable asset"—exactly the type who puts his experience to public use by serving on local government and community boards.

What happens, too, says Daniel M. Wilner, a social psychologist at the University of California at Los Angeles, is that young people lack models who can assist them in learning how to cope with age and the complexities of life. "If you don't have appropriate role models to pattern yourself after, there's going to be some antisocial outcome," according to Wilner.

Although it causes changes, the shift itself results from earlier changes in society. "This is the second revolution," says a retired hearing aid distributor who moved to Sun City, Ariz., from Grand Forks, N.D. "The first was the kids moving out to their own apartments." The growth of suburbs, peopled largely by families with young children, also served to push out older folk. Says retiree Roszel: "If we lived in a town where we were old and most of the people were young, we'd stick out like sore thumbs. They'd be working and we wouldn't have anyone to play golf with."

Along with oldster-retirement communities and child-oriented suburbs have come apartments for "young marrieds" and "swinging singles," apartments that admit infants but not teen-agers or vice versa, and nursing homes for the elderly infirm. Simultaneously, the country has experienced a growing concentration of the aged, the poor, and racial minorities within inner cities and rural villages. The result is a distinct change from the traditional

[44]What dangers, if any, do you see in these retirement communities? To the residents? To the society?

community in which all generations lived together, sometimes under one roof.

Much of the change was historically inevitable. "The kinship family is shot all to hell, and it had to be," says James A. Peterson, a gerontologist at the University of Southern California. "You can't have a mobile labor force if you have to take grandmother and grandfather along."

Most residents of retirement communities are as aware of the intellectual capital they represent as are the sociologists who deplore its withdrawal from the home community. "All the knowledge in the world is here," says Burt Freireich, editor of the weekly Sun City, Ariz., *News-Sun.* "There is no subject on which I can editorialize that someone isn't an expert on." Says Sun City (Fla.) resident Cecil C. Cross, a retired Air Force colonel: "We have people here from every field of endeavor. Everytime I go around the area. I meet people who are more interesting than the ones I met before."

Certainly the opportunity to meet new people and to keep busy draws customers. Last year, another Sun City, Fla., resident kept score of the cocktail parties he attended: 200. "That sounds like we're a bunch of drunks," he says. "But that's not so. We meet, we get invited to someone's home, and we go."

Most oldsters benefit from this the-more-the-merrier atmosphere, sociologists say. USC's Peterson, who has studied Leisure World at Laguna Hills, says that a retiree's "friendship network" doubles there. "Life satisfaction goes up for almost all older people who go in for congregate living," he says.[45]

In the sociologists' view, the arrangement that works best for both retiree and society is a community close to the city that was formerly the retirees' home, or a housing development that is part of a well-rounded community—for instance, the retirees' segment of San Diego's Rancho Bernardo, which is near young families.

In all the communities, an undercurrent of depression sometimes fissures the hurry-up-and-have-fun atmosphere. At Leisure World in Laguna, a woman tells of a neighbor who does not mix well, becomes depressed, and takes sedatives. Says another Laguna resident, Lillian F. Gaines, 64: "Sometimes in the evenings, it's depressing to look out and see only elderly people walking around. It's sad."

But Florence Clark, 68, says, "you just get used to having people come into the swimming pool with two canes. Soon it isn't depressing."

For others, the whole scene is depressing. Kenneth Gregory, a retired Ford Motor Co. employee who lived in Sun City, Fla., for a year, says he never got so sick of a place in his life. "There it was, out in the middle of nowhere," says Gregory. "There was nothing to do, and you had to drive 40 miles into Tampa to see a movie or buy a pair of socks. The shopping was practically nonexistent. It was just plain dull."

[45]What similarities, if any, do you see between the retirement community and the Good Earth Commune?

Deteriorating health and the effect of inflation on fixed incomes are predictable concerns among the retired. Still, romance blossoms, says the Reverand Water W. Witt, pastor of the Arizona Sun City's largest church, the United Church of Christ. In a typical year, he officiates at the same number of marriages as funerals—40 to 50.

Many of the newlyweds are widows and widowers of Sun City residents, but others marry old friends from their hometown. Many of the retirement communities have single clubs.

For most residents of Rossmoor and Leisure Technology developments, keeping in touch with children and grandchildren is easy because most live within two hours' drive of their former homes. Both Sun Cities draw most of their buyers from far away, but residents seem untroubled by the distance. They say children and grandchildren write and visit regularly and the retirees travel quite a bit themselves. As for other children, a retired Coast Guard commander at Sun City, Ariz., apparently speaks for many residents when he says he is "happy to get away from the uproar of youngsters. They trample your flowers."

One person's asset, of course, may be another's liability. Visiting a friend at Sun City, Ariz., Mrs. Anna Etzler of Arlington, Va., says with a shudder, "I wouldn't like it. I couldn't live in a community with no children around."

For most residents of retirement communities, however, the mix is just right. Says Mrs. Roszel: "We see the children. They come at Christmas, Easter, and the other holidays. But it's nice to see the backs of their necks when they leave."[46]

Searching for a new life through religion

During the last several years young people turned to religion in search of new meaning for their lives. These "Jesus Freaks," as they call themselves, usually scorn the pleasures and trials of the material world. Two sociologists studying the movement explained, "they do not concern themselves with improving our decaying cities, solving the problems of poverty, war, and disease—all can be left up to God." The following account describes the life style created by one Los Angeles religious group.

"It's the greatest rush I've ever had," commenced one hip young man describing his experience in turning on to Jesus. Similar drug culture metaphors are used by other former drug users who have joined the spreading movement of evangelical religion among the young—a movement that originated largely in Southern California. The ranks of the "Jesus people" or "Jesus freaks," as

[46]Would you want your parents, at age 65, to move to a retirement community? Why, or why not?

some call them, have grown considerably during 1970. Thousands have been baptized off the beaches of Southern California, and the movement has spread across the country trailing colorful publicity in its wake.

"We made *Time*!" exulted a young prophet of the movement recently. Bumper stickers substitute "Have a Nice Forever" for the familiar California expression, "Have a Nice Day." The Jesus-oriented *Free Paper* is sent to 50 states and 11 foreign countries, a biweekly, it claims a circulation of 260,000. In new recordings featuring "Jesus rock" the composers search for spiritual guidance and direction. Musical groups such as The J. C. Power Outlet and The Love Song proliferate. A new social system blends the hip style of dress, music and speech into the "Jesus culture"—something new, yet something old indeed! The Jesus trip is The Great Awakening revisited; it is American frontier religion revisited with Volkswagens and amplifiers supplanting the horses, wagons and saddlebacks of Cane Ridge, Kentucky, 1801.

The young whites of middle-class background turning toward revivalist religion come from two rather distinct groups. From observations of crowds at religious services, one of these groups consists largely of teenagers whom we call "Jesus-boppers." In them, rock groups turned on to Jesus have a ready-made audience from the large ranks of rock music fans. Free concerts followed by an invitation to accept Jesus Christ attract large youth audiences.

The other element in the Jesus movement is a smaller and more intense group of young adults (usually in their twenties) who have opted out of the drug culture. Many are former peace movement activists who have dropped out of society over the past four or five years. For them, the Jesus movement constitutes a ritual of re-entry into the system.

As an institution, Gethsemane Chapel is three years old. It is an independent, nondenominational congregation whose basically conservative Baptist theology is a blend of holiness and pentecostalism. Its ministry is anti-establishment in its rejection of the theology and social positions of the major Protestant denominations.

Sunday morning and evening as well as several week nights are Bible study sessions, attended mainly by older persons. Some week-night meetings find Gethsemane Chapel jammed with youth, but the big youth night is Wednesday, when a number of musical groups are featured. The church is packed two hours prior to the service—crowd estimates range from 1,300 to 1,400 persons; about one-third are outside listening on loudspeakers and participating visually through the chapel's glass walls. Approximately 80 per cent of the audience is female. The style of dress is informal—jeans and hip garb and long hair abounds. Over half the crowd consists of early teens and less than 15 per cent are over twenty.

A 22-year old lay minister—a former drug user, with flowing robe, long hair and beard—leads this service. Later, in an "afterglow" he leads a smaller group in receiving the baptism of the Holy Spirit—speaking in tongues. The interaction style in the worship and in the entire movement is intensely personal, a kind of "Gospel Anonymous," with pastors and members first-naming each other.

Following the singing, testimonies and music groups, Rennie (a young minister) reads from the Bible and gives a sermon. At the close, an invitation is given to accept Jesus. On an average Wednesday night, about 100 young persons come forward, affirm their faith in unison, and are then led to another part of the church to be presented with a Bible. When there were fewer converts, individual counseling was also conducted. Many of the converts are later baptized in the ocean, although apparently no set plan is announced for doing so immediately.

In the afterglow, another Bible study is conducted, after which Rennie invites those who want the baptism of the Spirit to come forward. A flute player provides an eerie background (he "plays by the Spirit") while Rennie assists those who wish to receive the Spirit, with such blandishments as, "you may kneel, if you wish," or "you may extend your arms toward heaven, if you wish."

Rennie moves in and out among those standing on the platform, touching and speaking to them. Eventually a cadence of people speaking in a babble and singing in tongues intertwines with the mystic tones of the flute. For this part of the service the church is full, but the aisles and the grounds are empty of people; some teenage girls attempt to sit in the aisle to get close to the platform where Rennie is leading the service. Following the afterglow, which is terminated at Rennie's command, certain individuals remain fixed in apparent hysterical stupor. "Counselors" help them to "give in" to the Spirit, some of whom are unable to pull out of their babbling and hysteria.

On Friday nights there are no music groups, although the service is supposedly for youth. Another young lay minister–more square than Rennie–leads this service. The attendance is about one-third of the Wednesday night assemblage, with fewer teenagers present. This difference is likely due to the drawing power of the professional gospel rock groups on Wednesday plus the charisma of Rennie.

The leaders of Gethsemane Chapel, being interested in reaching young people in the drug culture for Jesus, developed the idea of adopting the commune as a service-oriented institution. And the movement appears to be very successful. Scores of Jesus-oriented houses have sprung up along the entire West Coast under the sponsorship of Gethsemane Chapel.

Visits to these communes reveal a rigid separation of male and female living quarters, with a strict affirmation of asceticism. Many of the occupants have been members of drug-oriented communes, where sexual relations were available. The same individuals appear to move toward early marriage after being saved. Their frequently idealistic conception of marriage is exemplified by the response of one young man, who when asked if he thought sex could be misused in marriage, said, "Certainly not." (He believed that he had misused it out of marriage.)

The communes visited had approximately 20 to 30 permanent residents although their turnover appears high. When one commune becomes fairly large, another is established; when one is overpopulated, members move to another which has space. The commune also serves as a type of crash pad where anyone is welcome to eat and/or sleep.

Money earned by members is given to a central treasury, although one's worldly wealth is not demanded. Yard and gardening work is done for local residents to earn money to support the house as well as to learn to work and live together. Several deacons are in charge of finances plus the physical and spiritual nurture of the house. The leaders deny that there are rules, saying everyone is to follow God's will. Emphasis on cooperation rather than rules appears to be effective in accomplishing the day's tasks. There is a minimum of scheduling, although a list of those preparing breakfast is posted. The diet, which has a heavy starch content, is augmented by fruit and vegetable discards donated by local grocery stores. The direction of the Spirit is sought in all matters, including remodeling and obtaining materials for a new roof, for example.

Persons visiting a commune receive an open and friendly welcome. Such was the case at Mansion Messiah. A tour of the premises may reveal a young man speaking in tongues in the garden, a modest "prayer house" in the back yard, with another young man just leaving it to return to the main building. Just recently the "family" had added the eating room. There were no contractors hired to build the addition, and the plywood and materials for the roof were all donated. "The Lord just showed us where to lay the beams," and the members built the roof. The garage was converted into a bedroom by the members also and holes in the walls were left for the windows. "The Lord provided us with windows to fit the holes." In this bedroom at least nine men sleep, in three bunk-beds, three high, that the men had made themselves.

The girls (about ten in number) do all the cooking, mending, serving, washing and other housework and hold no outside jobs. The men do the yard work, gardening, repairs around the house, building of furniture and some hold outside jobs. It costs about $2,000 per month to run the house. Donations and contributions help to pay the expenses that are not covered by the men's pay.

Many individuals in the commune appear for the first time in their lives to be learning how to work and live with others. The leaders do not deny that conflicts arise in the house; such conflicts, they emphasize, are a creative opportunity for individuals to learn to live together. The nightly Bible study time is used to deal with such problems; leaders of the evening frequently pick a New Testament passage dealing with mutual sharing and responsibility.

The communes are the most impressive part of the Jesus movement. The contribution made by their members lies in the simplicity of their life style, their easy acceptance of themselves, their genuine attempts at learning to get along with others and participate in communal tasks. Although they have kicked the drug habit, their abstinence has been too brief to predict how successful they will be at giving up drugs permanently. We may wonder what will happen if and when they are no longer high on Jesus. The potential psychological difficulties could be enormous, for in large measure they have channeled their anxieties about the problems into displays of religious fervor rather than coming to terms with the realities of the identity crisis.

Life styles in the Puerto Rican ghetto

Since the Civil War residents of America's ethnic villages have provided the cities with a rich diversity in urban life styles. Generations of Americans grew up in these Italian, Irish, Polish, and Jewish communities. Second and third generation Americans, however, usually left these villages for homes in other urban zones or in the suburbs. Later arrivals often replaced the older immigrant groups in certain sections of the city. For example, the Germans, Irish, Jews, Italians, Blacks, and Puerto Ricans all followed each other in certain sections of New York City. The following essay describes the life style of one recent ethnic group, the Puerto Ricans.

The Puerto Ricans have brought an element of stability to New York. When the white middle class started its mass stampede to the suburbs, running like units of a defeated army across the frontier, the Puerto Ricans stayed on. They stayed on because they had to stay on. You simply do not have a choice if you can't ever imagine yourself having $2,000 for a down payment on a house. They stayed on, too, because they wanted to. More than the white-middle-class refugees, the Puerto Ricans understood early that this could be a mean and nasty and vicious town, but it was also a great one.

"I tried living in the country," my friend Jose Torres, the former light-heavy-weight champion of the world, once told me. "It was beautiful. There was grass and trees and clean air and birds. People were friendly. It was healthy. The schools were not crowded. The trouble was that I started going crazy. I needed noise." [47]

Noise. Not the noise of jackhammers and ripped sidewalks and coughing trucks. What Torres means is the noise of streets, to be able to walk along Smith Street in Brooklyn and hear people shouting back and forth at each other in greeting and guys coming out of saloons on Saturday afternoons to stop friends and whisper *piropos* to girls ("Ah, *mi vida*, it must have been a fine and splendid mother to have produced such a beauty as you"). The noise is at a party in my friend Cocolo's house on Dean Street, the bathtub packed with ice and beer, babies crying in the kitchen, the table groaning with pulpo, and arguments in English and Spanish over the Mets and Mario Procaccino and the cost of cigars and Fidel Castro and the best way to seduce a Swedish girl. Cocolo has hit the number for the third time this year, and all his friends are there, and his relatives. "Hey, you better eat all this stup, mon, because

[47] Do you sometimes feel the same as Torres? What do you do about it? Share your solution with a classmate.

you doan hit the number three times in a year every year." Cocolo is beaming, and on his wall he has a picture of Jack Kennedy and a poster from the O'Dwyer campaign and a smaller picture of Robert Kennedy, and later in the night, all of us slowed by beer and food, and the children asleep, and not much more to travel to daylight, Cocolo points up at the picture of Bob Kennedy and says, "Hey mon, you explain this country. What kine of a sum-of-a-bitch would shoot that guy? Huh? You explain that to me, mon." And the other three guys start to sing, because they've seen this happen before, and they don't want Cocolo, who is 38 years old and wieghs 240 pounds, to start crying all over again.

That kind of noise: and nights in Otero's on Smith Street, eating *pernil* in the back room, and talking boxing at the bar, and how one night we all came in late and the place was empty and Junior, the bartender, had a big bandage on his face. "What the hell happened?" someone said. "You get in a fight with your girl?" And Junior said, no, it wasn't a fight, it was a car accident. Pedro Ortiz, the meanest-looking man in Brooklyn, leers: "Hey, Junior, you don't have to lie to us." And Junior gets mad and goes into the back room and comes back with the door from his car, the whole door, smashed and crumpled, and everyone starts to laugh, and Pedro Ortiz falls off the stool, and we order another round.

That's what Jose Torres means by noise. Noise and life. Travel around a little and look at it: the Jefferson Theatre, with the children crying in the audience and guys selling ice cream right in the middle of the movie, and a great comic like Johnny El Men making jokes on the stage about being a Puerto Rican in New York. Move around: to the Broadway Casino, or Carlos Ortiz' place in the South Bronx, or the Club Caborrojeno, and make a Saturday night. Who's on? La Playa, or Tito Puente, or El Gran Combo, with the music thundering down, the musicians making bad jokes, and lights sly and romantic, the girl singers with impossibly narrow waists above implacable swelling hips. And on the dance floor, girls with soft fleshly faces doing hammering mambos with their shoes off. The guys weave baroque steps around them, the floor itself starting to groan from the pounding, the single guys lined against the walls, the people from the community clubs sitting in private parties at the tables, an occasional older woman chaperoning her daughter or niece. Ten years ago, Torres and I spent a lot of time in those places, and maybe he would have been a better fighter and I would have been a better writer if we had stayed home. I doubt it. We certainly wouldn't have had as much laughter.

For thought and discussion

What, if anything, can you do to make elements of your life style (work, leisure, family-friendship) more integrated?

Individual and small group activities

1. Get together with a group of your classmates and try to reach agreement on an ideal life style. Then make a list of the advantages of this life style. Make another list of the things you would have to give up if you lived this life style. If you are happy with your present life style analyze its advantages and disadvantages. Report your finding in a way which you and your instructor agree upon.
2. Write a poem, paint a picture, make a collage, or draw a cartoon that best illustrates your image of the ideal life style.

*

Poverty and welfare: Stating the issue for Assignments 25 and 26

The poor in America come from all walks of life. Most live in urban America, but others live in the rural hinterlands. They may be young, old, or middle aged; male, or female; black, white, red, or yellow. Poverty strikes both married persons with children and single Americans. The poor are America's forgotten people.

To be poor means not having enough money to live decently. But it is more than that. According to R. Sargent Shriver, the former director of the Office of Economic opportunity, "poverty is helplessness to cope with hostile or uncaring or exploitative institutions. It is lack of dignity. Poverty is personal, but it is also a terrifyingly impersonal and dehumanizing condition." In his testimony before the House of Representatives Subcommittee on Poverty, Shriver used the statement of a Colorado woman, Mrs. Janice Bradshaw, to describe the nature of poverty. Mrs. Bradshaw stated.

> Poverty is a personal thing! Poverty is taking your children to the hospital and spending the whole day waiting with no one even taking your name, and then coming back the next, and the next, until they finally get around to you.
>
> Poverty is having a landlady who is a public health nurse who turns off the heat when she leaves for work in the morning and turns it back on at six when she returns. It's being helpless to do anything about it because by the time the officials get around to it she has turned on the heat for the day and then it will be off the next.
>
> Poverty is having a child with glaucoma and watching that eye condition grow worse every day, while the welfare officials send you to the private agencies, and the private agencies send you back to the welfare . . .

In 1970 the U. S. Bureau of the Census reported that more than 25 million persons lived in poverty throughout the country. The Bureau defined poverty in 1973 as a family of four with a yearly income of less that $4275. Assignment 25 provides information to help you examine the causes and effects of poverty during several periods in American history. In Assignment 26 you will use the results of your analysis to evaluate several proposed solution to the problem of poverty. At the conclusion of these two assignments your instructor may ask you to suggest your own solutions to the problem of poverty in urban America.

Poverty and welfare (1)

Assignment 25

Perhaps you have been aware of the presence of poverty in American society for a long time. Since Colonial times Americans have tried to solve this problem in various ways. Some persons thought that God brought poverty to individuals as a test of their spirit. Poverty was considered uplifting to those who experienced it. Other people, also searching for religious causes, felt that poverty was a sign of one's weak or immoral character. Leading a better life could then supposedly improve an individuals position in life. By 1900 many reformers thought that a better organized society would eliminate the worst elements of poverty from American life. These reformers attempted to systematize the approach to poverty by collecting impressive and detailed information about the urban poor. Other solutions appeared in other times but essentially most Americans continued to feel that hard work and thrifty habits would enable one to rise from the depths of poverty.

However, in spite of all the solutions offered by clergy, industrialists, reformers, and government officials, poverty remains one of our most consistent and difficult problems. In Assignment 25 you will examine descriptions of urban poverty in several time periods. As you read these accounts answer the questions listed below.

1. What similarities or differences do you see in the conditions of the poor in each of the time periods?
2. Make a list of the social, economic, and psychological needs and characteristics of the poor. You will need this list for part II of Assignment 26.

Poverty in industrial America, 1885

In the 1880's a special Senate committee held a series of hearings to determine the nature of the existing relations between American entrepreneurs (businessmen) and workers. The committee interviewed hundreds of factory owners, social reformers, and workers. These interviews were published in five volumes. In the following account a semi-skilled mule-spinner (cotton worker) explains the causes of his impoverished condition to the Senate.

Question. Where do you live? *Answer.* At Fall River.

Q. How long have you lived in this country? *A.* Eleven years.

Q. Where were you born? *A.* In Ramsbotham, England.

Q. Have you been naturalized here? *A.* No, sir.

Q. What is your business? *A.* I am a mule-spinner by trade. I have worked at it since I have been in this country—eleven years.

Q. Are you a married man? *A.* Yes, sir; I am a married man; have a wife and two children. I am not very well educated. I went to work when I was was young, and have been working ever since in the cotton business; went to work when I was about eight or nine years old. I was going to state how I live. My children get along very well in summer time, on account of not having to buy fuel or shoes or one thing and another. I earn $1.50 a day and can't afford to pay a very big house rent. I pay $1.50 a week for rent, which comes to about $6 a month.

Q. That is, you pay this where you are at Fall River? *A.* Yes, sir.

Q. Do you have work right along? *A.* No, sir; since that strike we had down in Fall River about three years ago I have not worked much more than half the time, and that has brought my circumstances down very much.

Q. Why have you not worked more than half the time since then? *A.* Well, at Fall River if a man has not got a boy to act as "back-boy" it is very hard for him to get along. In a great many cases they discharge men in that work and put in men who have boys.

Q. Men who have boys of their own? *A.* Men who have boys of their own capable enough to work in a mill, to earn 30 or 40 cents a day.

Q. Is the object of that to enable the boy to earn something for himself? *A.* Well, no; the object is this: They are doing away with a great deal of mule-spinning there and putting in ring-spinning, and for that reason it takes a good deal of small help to run this ring work, and it throws the men out of work because they are doing away with the mules and putting these ring-frames in to take their places. For that reason they get all the small help they can to run these ring-frames. There are so many men in the city to work, and whoever has a boy can have work, and whoever has no boy stands no chance. Probably he may have a few months of work in the summer time, but will be discharged in the fall. That is what leaves me in poor circumstances. Our children, or course, are very often sickly from one cause or another, on account of not having sufficient clothes, or shoes, or food, or something. And also my woman; she never did work in a mill; she was a housekeeper, and for that reason she can't help me at present, as many women do help their husbands down there, by working like themselves. My wife never did work in a mill, and that leaves me to provide for the whole family. I have two children.

And another thing that helped to keep me down: A year ago this month month I buried the oldest boy we had, and that brings things very expensive on a poor man. For instance, it will cost there, to bury a body, about $100. Now, we could have that done in England for about £5; that would not amount to much more than about $20, or something in that neighborhood.

That makes a good deal of difference. Doctors' bills are very heavy—about $2 a visit; and if a doctor comes once a day for two or three weeks it is quite a pile for a poor man to pay.[48]

I have a brother who has four children, besides his wife and himself. All he earns is $1.50 a day. He works in the iron works at Fall River. He only works about nine months out of twelve. There is generally about three months of stoppage, taking the year right through, and his wife and his family all have to be supported for a year out of wages of nine months—$1.50 a day for nine months out of the twelve, to support six of them. It does not stand to reason that those children and he himself can have natural food or be naturally dressed. His children are often sick, and he has to call in doctors. That is always hanging over him, and is a great expense to him.

Q. How much money have you got? *A.* I have not got a cent in the house; didn't have when I came out this morning.

Q. How much money have you had within three months? *A.* I have had about $16 inside of three months.

Q. Is that all you have had within the last three months to live on? *A.* Yes; $16.

Q. How much have you had within a year? *A.* Since Thanksgiving I happened to get work in the Crescent Mill, and worked there exactly thirteen weeks. I got just $1.50 a day.

Q. Thirteen weeks would be seventy-eight days, and, at $1.50 a day, that would make $117, less whatever time you lost? *A.* Yes. I worked thirteen weeks there and ten days in another place, and then there was a dollar I got this week, Wednesday.

Q. Taking a full year back can you tell how much you have had? *A.* That would be about fifteen weeks' work. Last winter, as I told you, I got in, and I worked up to about somewhere around Fast Day, or may be New Year's day; anyway, Mr. Howard has it down on his record, if you wish to have an exact answer to that question; he can answer it better than I can, because we have a sort of union there to keep ourselves together.

Q. Do you think you have had $150 within a year? *A.* No sir.

Q. Have you had $125? *A.* Well, I could figure it up if I had time. The thirteen weeks is all I have had.

Q. The thirteen weeks and the $16 you have mentioned? *A.* Yes sir.

Q. That would be somewhere about $133, if you had not lost any time? *A.* Yes, sir.

Q. That is all you have had? *A.* Yes, sir.

Q. To support yourself and wife and two children? *A.* Yes sir.

Q. Have you had any help from outside? *A.* No sir.

Q. Do you mean that yourself and wife and two children have had

[48]Should all medical services be paid for by the government? Why, or why not?

nothing but that for all this time? *A.* That is all. I got a couple dollars' worth of coal last winter, and the wood I picked up myself. I goes around with with a shovel and picks up clams and wood.

Q. What do you do with the clams? *A.* We eat them. I don't get them to sell, but just to eat, for the family. That is the way my brother lives, too, mostly. He lives close by us.

Q. How many live in that way down there? *A.* I could not count them, they are so numerous. I suppose there are one thousand down there.

Q. A thousand that live on $150 a year? *A.* They live on less.

Q. Less than that? *A.* Yes; they live on less than I do.

Q. How long has that been so? *A.* Mostly so since I have been married.

Q. How long is that? *A.* Six years this month.

Q. Why do you not go West on a farm?[49] *A.* How could I go, walk?

Q. You say you think there are a thousand men or so with their families that live in that way in Fall River? *A.* Yes, sir; and I know many of them. They are around there by the shore. You can see them every day; and I am sure of it because men tell me.

Q. Are you a good workman? *A.* Yes, sir.

Q. Were you ever turned off because of misconduct or incapacity or unfitness for work? *A.* No, sir.

Q. Or because you did bad work? *A.* No, sir.

Q. Or because you made trouble among the help? *A.* No, sir.

Q. Did you ever have any personal trouble with an employer? *A.* No, sir.

Q. You have not anything now you say? *A.* No, sir.

Q. How old are you? *A.* About thirty.

Q. Is your health good? *A.* Yes, sir.

Q. What would you work for if you could get work right along; if you could be sure to have it for five years, staying right where you are? *A.* Well, if I was where my family could be with me, and I could have work every day I would take $1.50, and be glad to.

Q. One dollar and fifty cents a day, with three hundred days to the year, would make more than you make now in three or four years, would it not? *A.* Well, I would have no opportunity then to pick up clams. I have no coal except one dollar's worth since last Christmas.

Q. When do the clams give out? *A.* They give out in winter.

Q. You spoke of fuel–what do you have for fuel? *A.* Wood and coal.

Q. Where does the wood come from? *A.* I pick it up around the shore–any old pieces I see around that are not good for anything. There are

[49]Do you think unemployed workers should be forced to move to jobs in other areas? Why, or why not?

many more that do the same thing.

Q. Do you get meat to live on much? *A.* Very seldom.

Q. What kinds of meat do you get for your family? *A.* Well, once in a while we gets a piece of pork and some clams and make a clam chowder. That makes a very good meal. We sometimes get a piece of corn beef or something like that.

Q. Have you had any fresh beef within a month? *A.* Yes, we had a piece of pork steak for four of us yesterday.

Q. Have you had any beef within a month? *A.* No, sir. I was invited to a man's house on Sunday—he wanted me to go up to his house and we had a dinner of roast pork.

Q. That was an invitation out, but I mean have you had any beefsteak in your own family, of your own purchase, within a month? *A.* Yes; there was a half a pound, or a pound one Sunday—I think it was.

Q. Have you had only a pound or a half a pound on Sunday? *A.* That is all.

Q. Has there been any day in the year that you have had to go without anything to eat? *A.* Yes, sir, several days.

Q. More than one day at a time? *A.* No.

Q. What have the children got on in the way of clothing? *A.* They have got along very nicely all summer, but now they are beginning to feel quite sickly. One has one shoe on, a very poor one, and a slipper, that was picked up somewhere. The other has two odd shoes on, with the heel out. He has got cold and is sickly now.

Q. Have they any stockings? *A.* He had got stockings, but his feet comes through them, for there is a hole in the bottom of the shoe.

Q. What have they got on the rest of their person? *A.* Well, they have a little calico shirt—what should be a shirt; it is sewed up in some shape—and one little petticoat, and a kind of little dress.

Q. How many dresses has your wife got? *A.* She has got one since she was married, and she hasn't worn that more than half a dozen times; she has worn it just going to church and coming back. She is very good in going to church, but when she comes back she takes it off, and it is pretty near as good now as when she bought it.

Q. She keeps that dress to go to church in? *A.* Yes, sir.

Q. How many dresses aside from that has she? *A.* Well, she got one here three months ago.

Q. What did it cost? *A.* It cost $1 to make it and I guess about a dollar for the stuff, as near as I can tell.

Q. The dress cost $2? *A.* Yes.

Q. What else has she? *A.* Well, she has an undershirt that she got given to her, and she has an old wrapper, which is about a mile too big for her, somebody gave it to her.

Q. She did not buy it? *A.* No. That is all that I know that she has.

Q. Are you in debt? *A.* Yes, sir.

Q. How much? *A.* I am in debt for those funeral expenses now $15–since a year ago.

Q. Have you paid the rest? *A.* Yes, sir.

Q. You live in a hired tenement? *A.* Yes; but of course I can't pay a big rent. My rent is $6 a month. The man I am living under would come and put me right out and give me no notice either if I didn't pay my rent. He is a sheriff and auctioneer man. I don't know whether he has any authority to do it or not, but he does it with people.

Q. Is there anything else you wanted to say? *A.* Nothing further, except that I would like some remedy to be got to help us poor people down there in some way. Excepting the Government decides to do something with us we have a poor show. We are all, or mostly all, in good health; that is, as far as the men who are at work go.

The urban poor during the Great Depression—1934

The crash of the stock market on October 19, 1929 signaled the beginning of the most severe depression in the history of the United States. By mid-1932, nearly 12 million people, 25 per cent of the labor force, were without jobs. Soup kitchens and bread lines formed in every city throughout the country. Some persons tried to survive for another day by selling apples on street corners. The government, particularly under Franklin D. Roosevelt, instituted a series of relief measures. Yet the depression persisted. As late as January, 1937, four years after he became president, Roosevelt admitted that one third of the nation remained, "ill-housed, ill-clad, and ill-nourished." In the following article a middle-class college graduate, Ann Rivington, describes the frustrations, fear, and desperation of a family in poverty. As you read, continue your work on the list noted on page 300 of this assignment.

When I went to college I studied sociology. I was taught that hunger, squalor, dirt, and ignorance are the results of environment. Charity, therefore, is no solution. We must change the environment. In order to do this we have settlement houses, playgrounds, and social workers in the slums.

In the past year and a half I have again revised my opinion. I am no longer one of *us*. For all my education, my training in thrift and cleanliness, I am become one of *them*. My condition is shared by a large sector of the population. From my new place in society I regard the problems and misery of the poor with new eyes.

Two years ago I was living in comfort and apparent security. My husband had a good position in a well-known orchestra and I was teaching a large and promising class of piano pupils. When the orchestra was disbanded we started on a rapid down-hill path. My husband was unable to secure another position. My class gradually dwindled away. We were forced to live on our savings.

In the early summer of 1933 I was eight months pregnant and we had just spent our last twelve dollars on one month's rent for an apartment. We found that such apartments really exist. They lack the most elementary comforts such as steam heat, bathtubs, sunlight, and running hot water. They usually are infested with mice and bedbugs. Ours was. Quite often the ceilings leak.

What, then, did we do for food when our last money was spent on rent? In vain we tried to borrow more. So strong was the influence of our training that my husband kept looking feverishly for work when there was no work, and blaming himself because he was unable to find it. Another thing we did was to open a charge account at the corner grocery on the recommendation of our next-door neighbors. An application to the Emergency Home Relief Bureau was the last act of our desperation.

My husband took care of the actual application. I was then unable to walk the three miles to the public-school building that served as a relief station.

My husband came home some five hours later with an application blank in his pocket. All this time he had been waiting, he told me, with more than fifty other people.

We filled out the application with great care.

There were many questions to which we had no answer. "List property owned in full or in part." "Insurance. Give names of insurance companies." "How much money have you now? In the bank?" "Have any persons, friends or relatives, helped you in the past year?"

The next morning my husband started early for the bureau. He returned at about two o'clock, very hungry and weak from the heat. But he was encouraged.

"Well, I got to talk to somebody this time," he said. "She asked me over again all the questions on that paper and more besides. Then she said to go home and wait. An investigator should be around tomorrow or day after. On account of your condition she marked the paper urgent." The next day we waited, and all of two days more. The fourth day, which was Saturday, my husband went back to the bureau. It was closed until Monday.

On Sunday morning the Italian grocer reminded me of our bill. "It get too big," he said. We cut down to one meal a day, and toast.

Monday brought no investigator, Tuesday my husband was at the bureau again. This time he came home angry.

"They said the investigator was here Friday and we were out. I got sore and told them somebody was lying."

"But you shouldn't. Now they won't help us."

"Now they will help us. She'll be here tomorrow."

Late Wednesday afternoon the investigator arrived. She questioned us closely for more than half an hour on our previous and present situation, our personal lives, our relatives. This time we certainly expected the check. But we were told to wait.

"I'm a special investigator. The regular one will be around Friday with the check."

My husband was in a torment of anxiety. "But we can't wait till Friday. We owe ten dollars downstairs now, and they won't let us charge any more. We have to eat something. My wife——."

The investigator looked tired. "You'll just have to put them off. I must make my report. And there are other cases ahead of yours."

By Monday morning we had nothing for breakfast but oatmeal, without sugar or milk. We decided we must go together to the bureau and find out what was wrong. It seemed to us that my appearance at that time would lend emphasis to our plea. Therefore, as soon as we had finished breakfast, we borrowed carfare from our kind neighbors and started out.

We reached the relief station a good fifteen minutes before nine, but the sidewalk was crowded with people. My husband explained to me that they were waiting to waylay the investigators on their way to work, to pour complaints and problems in their ears. As we were approaching, a little man with a briefcase hurried past us. A voice called out from the crowd, "Oh, Mr. Parsons!" The man hurried on, but in a moment a middle-aged Jewish workman laid hold of his coat lapel.

"We ain't got no gas yet, and you promised a month ago!" Impatiently, Mr. Parsons shook himself free.

"I haven't any time now. We'll talk about it Thursday." He went on into the building. We were following, but a guard stopped us.

"Over to the right," he said. "You can't go in there now."

"My wife can't stand in line," my husband told him.

"I can't help it. I got my orders." We hesitated. A policeman was leaning at the other side of the door. We were pushed over to another stairway leading into a corridor filled with shabby men and women. There must have been a hundred. Others kept crowding in behind us.

By half-past nine we had made our way up to the door.

"Room two," the guard said, handing us each a slip of paper.

I was already worn out, and I began to feel very faint. We sat down at the end of the rear bench. Those in front would get up and speak with the women at the desks, then either go away or wait at the side for an answer. Gradually we were able to slide to the end of our bench, then back along the next bench.

I watched the people around us. There they sat waiting, my fellow indigents. Bodies were gaunt or flabby, faces—some stoical, some sullen—all care-worn like my husband's. What had they done, or left undone, to inherit hunger? What was this relief we were asking for? Certainly it was not *charity*. It was dispensed too grudgingly, too harshly, to be that.

When our turn came to talk to one of the women behind the desks we were told that the checks had been held up for lack of funds and that we should go home and wait for an investigator "some time this week." We were not going to be put off in this manner. My husband told her, "We have to have something more than promises. There's no food in the house, and my wife can't live on air."

"Well, that's all I can tell you," said the woman. I went to the back of the room and sat down again. My husband stood near the desk, and between other cases he went up and talked further.

"If that's all you can tell me, who knows more than you? We're not leaving without a better answer."

The woman's voice rose. "You can't talk to me like that!" A guard was hovering near, ready, as I thought, to eject us.[50]

"Then whom can I talk to? I want the supervisor." I came up and stood beside my husband. At last the supervisor was called.

"The checks will be out tomorrow night. You will get yours Thursday."

"And what are we to do till Thursday? Already, you made us a promise you didn't keep. We need food now, and we're not leaving till we know where it's coming from."

The supervisor did not seem enthusiastic about our staying longer. If I had not been so obviously pregnant, I think we would have been thrown into the street. As it was, he picked up the telephone and, with my husband's instruction, called Pete the grocer and asked him to honor our account for two days more.

"As I told you, you will have the check Thursday morning," he repeated as we left.

Sure enough, early Thursday afternoon the regular investigator arrived. He gave us a check for eight-fifty to cover two weeks' food. We had already spent two dollars at the grocer's since the supervisor's phone call, and this amount, of course, was counted off the check. But Pete was not satisfied.

"Gotta take off more. I poor too."

I shook my head. "Wait," I said. "We'll pay you, but not this time."

I looked around the little shop hungrily. A pregnant woman's taste for delicacies was accentuated by the days of semi-starvation. I was tortured by a great longing for fresh fruit.

"How much are the grapes?" I asked.

"No grapes," said Pete. "No grapes for you."

"But why not, Pete?"

"Grapes are luxury. You get beans, potatoes, onions. Poor people no eat grapes."

I was bewildered. But Pete meant what he said. He showed me a bulletin he had received from the Relief Bureau, listing the things allowed on the food checks of the jobless. I cannot remember all the regulations. The paper was too long and involved for that. But I do remember that only dried fruit was listed. The quantities of eggs, butter, milk, were strictly limited. No meat

[50]How do you account for the attitudes of the government relief workers? Are they justified? Why, or why not?

except salt pork, unsliced bacon, pig's liver and other entrails. Rice, beans, potatoes, bread, onions were the main items to be sold. I saw no mention of fresh vegetables. I was highly indignant.

"Listen, Pete, my stomach isn't leather even if I have no money." I picked up a nice juicy cantaloupe and two bunches of carrots.

"These are onions and potatoes," I said, and marched out the door trailing carrot tops.

My baby was born one week later in a public ward where I was taken as an emergency case. By the first of October we were down once more to one meal a day, supplemented by toast and coffee. We told our investigator about this, but to no purpose. He repeated to us that we were getting all that was possible, that he was forced to skip other cases entirely some weeks because he had not enough money at his disposal.

Gradually the more and more difficult diet began to tell on us. We did not lose much weight—the very poor usually eat plenty of starch—but we began to suffer from general debility, colds, minor infections. The baby, who had thrived at first, cried a great deal, especially during the night. Finally we had her weighed, and found that in the last month and a half she had not gained an ounce, in fact, had lost a trifle. After we made that discovery we curtailed our own diet even farther, in order to give her Grade A milk and orange juice.

We began to have other serious worries. Now the landlord was becoming a frequent and insistent visitor. At last he gave us one more week in which to pay up all we owed him. He called again the next day. He stood in the doorway, dressed in his well-tailored suit, and explained dolefully that the bank was going to foreclose—all on account of us.

We admitted that we were on relief, and promised to ask for a rent check. He explained that such a thing was impossible. The relief was not giving out rent checks except after eviction. It would cost him fifteen dollars to evict us, and the check would be for only twelve. He would lose three dollars.

"Try to borrow," he said as he left, "or do something. I'll be back in a few days." When he was well out of earshot my husband and I looked at each other and burst into hysterical laughter.

"Poor landlord!" my husband cried: "He's almost as badly off as we are, just because we can't pay the rent!"

The problem of insufficient food was becoming daily more serious. I still held my baby to dry breasts before giving her the milk mixture. She was developing digestive troubles. My husband decided to complain once more at the bureau. He was told in so many words, "You can't expect to eat well. All we're trying to do is to keep you alive."[51] This was the only satisfaction he received and there seemed nothing we could do to help ourselves. A few

[51] Should people on relief expect to eat and dress well? Why or why not?

days later, when the investigator came on his regular visit, we found that by complaining we had done the best thing possible. Our food check was for nine dollars and a half.

As the cold weather came on our apartment became more and more unbearable. The damp chill ate into our bones. The place had no heating facilities except a fireplace without a grate. The end of November we received a coal order from the relief, and by taking it to the nearest police station my husband could obtain coal, provided he carried it home, half a mile, on his back. We gathered up kindling wood in the streets and started a fire, only to find that the coal was of such poor quality that it would not burn. Our only heat, therefore, had to come from our little two-burner gas plate. With this we were able to take the chill off the room, but the air became dry and we suffered from constant headaches, while our little daughter coughed continually.

To make matters worse we were hounded by the gas company. Whenever the man came to read the meter we would refuse to open the door, calling out some excuse: "I'm taking a bath," or "I'm nursing the baby. Come back later."

The thermometer dropped below freezing. Day after day we hovered over that little, evil-smelling fire. It was then that I learned how little cleanliness has to do with training. The whole meaning of life, for us, had become an escape from hunger and cold. We no longer made an attempt to keep the place clean. Our bodies and clothing we neglected, as well. We still tried to bathe the baby, but often that was impossible, even beside the gas plate. We would wash out her diapers and clothes and hang them around the room, so they contributed an additional dampness to the atmosphere.

One morning we were awakened by the sound of rough voices in the hallway, then a thundering on the door.

"Gas man! We got orders to take your meter." We held our breath, and the blessed baby did not cry. We heard the sound of filing on steel. A strong smell of gas seeped into the room. When they were gone we found that the gas pipe in the hall had been cut and covered with a metal cap.

Three days of nightmare we spent in that icy place while my husband searched out a shelter for us. At last, a friend who had a small steam-heated apartment in a slum even poorer than our own told us that he was leaving town and we might move into the place if we liked.

Meanwhile we are still living on relief. While our position in the new apartment is less desperate, the neighborhood is infinitely worse, and the uncertainty as maddening as ever. We feel ourselves always on the edge of a cliff with nothing to save us. We keep wondering, questioning. What if our check does not come next week? What will happen when the relief bureau stops paying rents for the summer? Will we be evicted? Will our family be broken up, our little girl taken away from us? After a time these questions reach out beyond our burning personal needs. What is the cause of our suffering? Whither is it leading us, and the increasing millions like us? What is wrong with the system, the civilization that brings with it such wholesale misery? My own voice is one of many that are asking, more and more insistently.

All of the people pictured here share one problem: poverty! What should be done to aid each of the groups represented by these photographs? What can you personally do?

Contemporary urban poverty

The aged comprise nearly one-fifth of the nation's 25 million poor. Many of these people held jobs for thirty or forty years. Now, however, because of inadequate pensions, they must live out their declining years in poverty and degredation. Many feel isolated and lonely. The following account describes the plight of the urban aged.

Many of the old people who shop at the A. & P. at First Avenue and 90th Street stand in front of the meat cases for long periods of time, like children gazing through a toy store window.

Some of them shuffle through the plastic-wrapped steaks and chops, as though they could taste them with their fingertips.

Occasionally, an old man or woman will bring a small package of chopped meat close to his eyes, to read the smudged price label, and, more often than not, put it back.

At the checkout counter they put down their purchases—two cans of spaghetti perhaps, a stock of celery, a couple of potatoes, a package of tea bags. Their attention never wavers as the clerk rings up the total, and then arthritic fingers dig reluctantly into worn change purses, and wallets to pay the bill.

In his office a couple of days ago, Eamon Murphy, the store manager, shook his head. "There's not much they can buy, and that's the truth," he said.

"Old people sometimes steal food," he went on. "It's never very much—a small package of chicken maybe—and I don't think very many do it. A woman could have it in her shopping bag or a man could drop it in his shirt.

"What can you do?" he said. "When I catch them, I tell them that we can't run the store that way and if they won't stop, then please not to come back. Sometimes they get very emotional. They cry and say they're sorry."

Sitting on a bench there on Wednesday, watching a group of youngsters run through a water spray, William Uchal, 72, a retired electrical worker, said, "I was talking to a man who drives a bulldozer over there where they're fixing the street. He told me he got $9.70 an hour.

"With those kind of wages you can buy meat, you can buy steak, but how about people who aren't making anything? Old people can't go on strike."[52]

On another bench, four women sat together talking. "It's not the price of steak that bothers you," said Mrs. Eva Bochino, "We haven't been able to eat that for years. What you notice is when potatoes go to $1.09 for five pounds."

Like virtually all of the city's senior citizens, the residents of the Isaacs Houses are entirely dependent on their monthly Social Security checks. The

[52]What, if anything, can the aged do to make their problems know to others?

amounts they receive differ, but the nation-wide average, according to the Social Security Administration, is $159 for a single person and $273 for a couple.

"You can't buy shoes, you can't buy clothes, you can't buy *anything*," said Mrs. Ernestine Brown, one of the women on the bench.

"Old people around here hate welfare like poison," said Mrs. Mary Yankauer, the executive director of the Burden Center for the Aging, at York Avenue and 85th Street. "They won't even go to the welfare office to get food stamps or to renew their half-fare subway cards."

What stops most old people from applying for welfare, even in desperation, is the requirement that they can have no more than $500 in liquid assets. Lacking either the guile or the wish to conceal, say, the existence of a savings account of a couple of thousand dollars, they prefer to do without.

"It's inhuman that they have to be stripped that far down," said Mrs. Yankauer. "That money gives the elderly a sense of identity, of not being totally impoverished. It may be set aside for their funeral, to make sure they aren't buried in Potter's Field."

What strikes Mrs. Yankauer as bitterly ironic is the fact that while most old people struggle to retain a shred of pride and independence on an income far below the poverty level, they could bankrupt the country if they simply decided to lie down on the sidewalk and wait to be carted off to a municipal hospital, nursing home or welfare hotel, at 10 times the cost.

For thought and discussion

America has been called the wealthiest nation on earth. If this is true why have we been unable to eliminate poverty?

Individual and small group activities

1. With a group of your classmates offer your services to "meals on wheels" or any other agency in your city designed to assist the poor. Keep a diary of your activities, feelings, and attitudes during this period. Your instructor may wish you to report your experiences to the class.
2. Interview your parents, grandparents, or any other people you know who lived during the depression of the 1930's. In what ways are their attitudes toward this period similar to or different from that of Ann Rivington? How were their experiences similar or different?

Poverty and welfare (2)

Assignment 26

Until 1932 most Americans thought that private religious and social organizations could provide ample assistance to the poor. A few state or local agencies offered occasional aid but no federal program existed to help eliminate poverty. Beginning in 1933 President Franklin Roosevelt's "New Deal" established a number of relief programs, but most were temporary measures designed to eliminate the ills of the depression. Following World War II the problem of poverty in America went unnoticed by most people until President Johnson announced a "War on Poverty." This comprehensive program, according to the President would eliminate poverty in America within a generation. The "War on Poverty" included such programs as: The Job Corps, Project Head Start, Neighborhood Youth Corps, Community Action Programs, and Work Training. Some of these programs remain in effect. Others were dropped by Richard Nixon after he became President in 1968. Mr. Nixon claimed that many of the "War on Poverty" programs were wasteful and inefficient.

In part one of Assignment 26 you will examine a number of graphs to determine what groups constitute America's poor. When you have concluded part one you should develop a hypothesis which suggests a solution to alleviate the worst evils suffered by these people.

In part two of Assignment 26 you will test your hypothesis by examining three current anti-poverty programs. Use the list of economic, social, and psychological needs of the poor you constructed in Assignment 25 to help you evaluate each program. Then answer these questions:

1. Which anti-poverty program seems to alleviate the greatest number of poverty problems?
2. Which problems are left untreated by all of the programs? What can be done about these?

Who are the poor?

Before you begin to evaluate anti-poverty programs in contemporary America you need to determine just which people need the most help. The graphs on pages 315–317 provide information about poverty in America in the 1970's. Examine each graph and answer the question under it. When you have completed your examination of all of the graphs develop a hypothesis suggesting a solution to the problems of poverty in America. Your hypothesis should state something like: "The largest groups of poor in America are the ____ , ____ , and ____ . Therefore a sound anti-poverty program should provide ____ , ____ , or ____ to assist these people." Use your hypothesis to evaluate the three anti-poverty programs discussed in part two of this assignment.

Figure 26.1
All poor persons by group

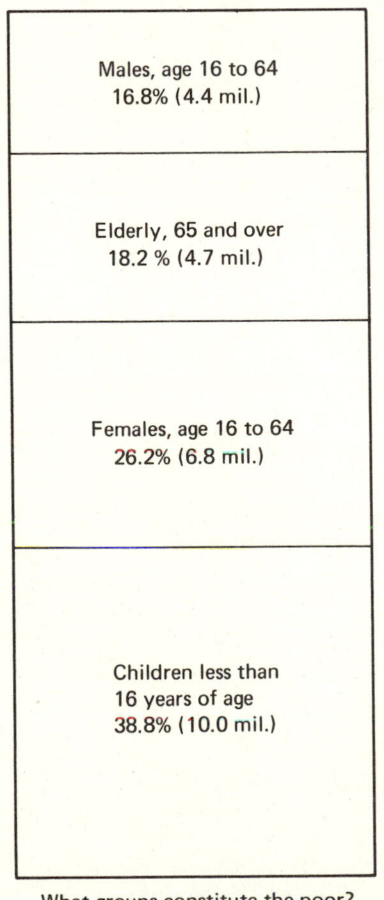

What groups constitute the poor?

Figure 26.2
All poor persons by location

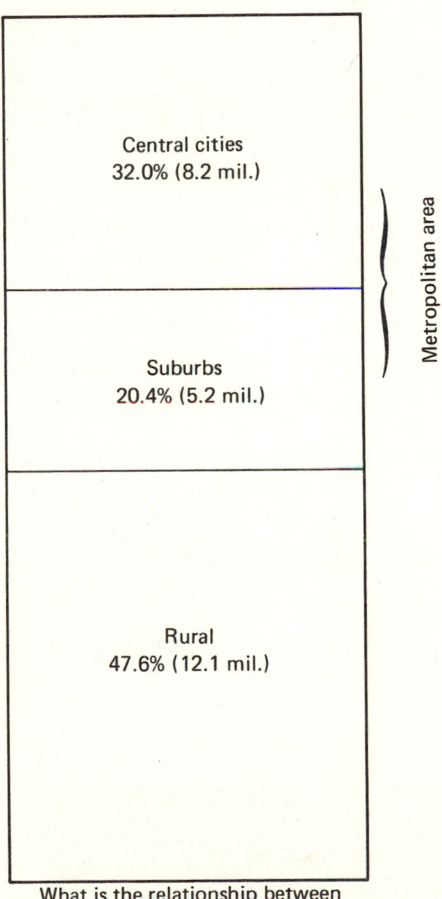

What is the relationship between place of residence and poverty?

Figure 26.3
The geographic location of the poor

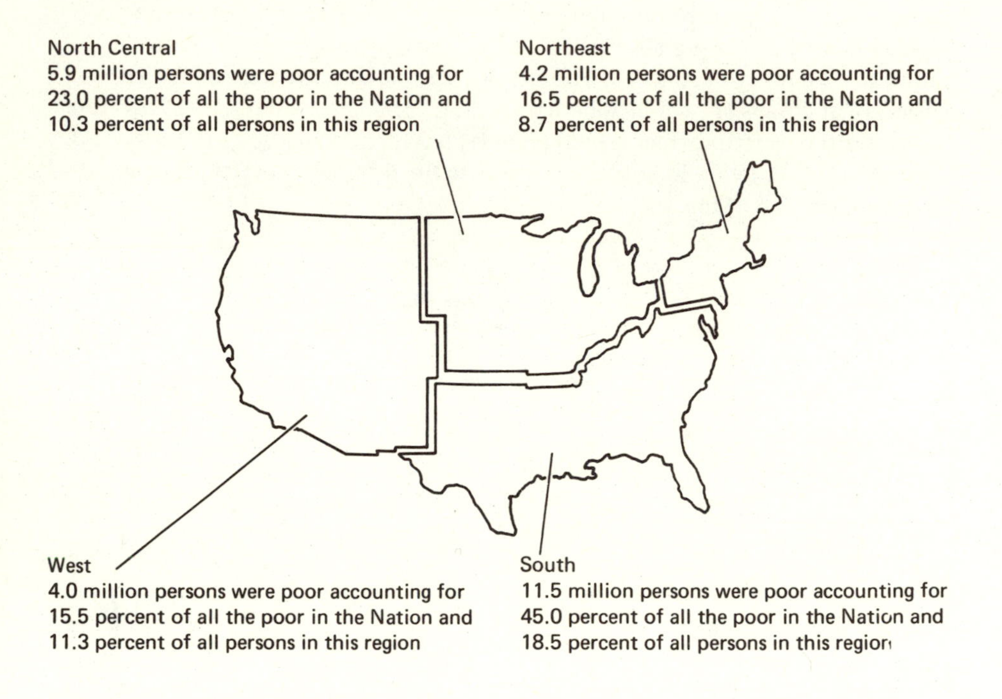

In which sections of the nation do the poor reside?

Figure 26.4
Years of school completed for the poor and the non-poor age 22 and over

	Poor age 22 and over
College, one year or more	10.3% (1.4 million)
12 years	18.9% (2.5 million)
9 to 11 years	18.8% (2.5 million)
8 years or less	52.0% (6.9 million)

Non-poor age 22 and over	
25.4% (26.8 million)	College, one year or more
37.5% (39.7 million)	12 years
16.3% (17.2 million)	9 to 11 years
20.8% (22.0 million)	8 years or less

What is the relationship between poverty and education?

Figure 26.5
The poor by race

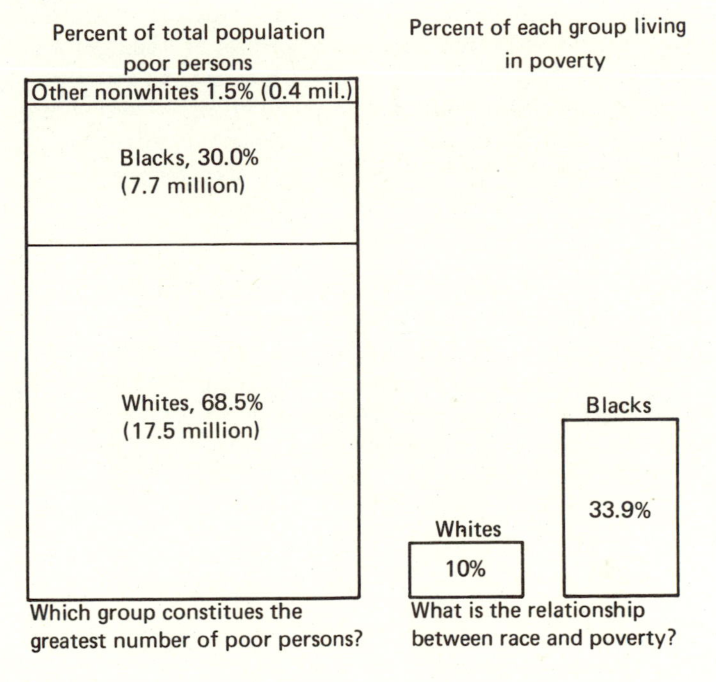

Figure 26.6
The incidence of poverty[53]

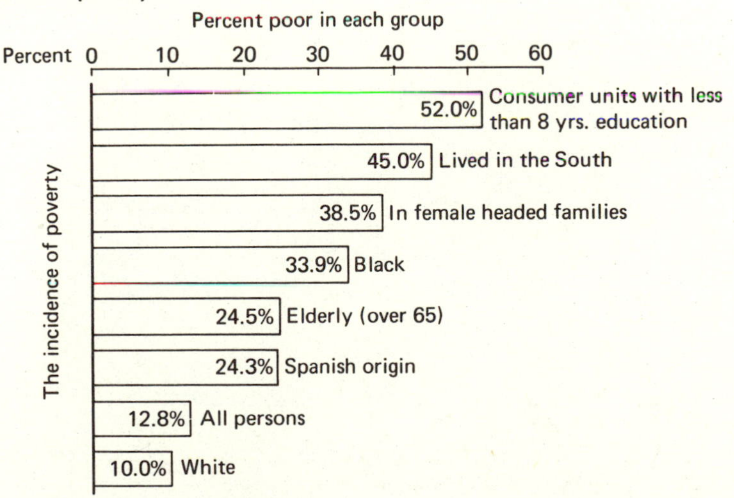

Who lives in poverty in the United States?

[53]The term, incidence of poverty, tells us how often poverty is likely to strike a particular group. You should read this table in the following manner: 52% of all persons in families headed by an individual with less than eight years of education were poor.

Three anti-poverty programs

In the final part of Assignment 26 you will examine a table and several readings to evaluate three current anti-poverty programs. The table provides information to help you analyze current poverty programs. In the first set of readings former President Nixon discusses his proposed anti-poverty program and his approach to poverty. The final reading presents one of the most controversial anti-poverty proposals, the negative income tax. Use your list of economic, social, and psychological needs of the poor and your hypothesis to evaluate each program.

Current welfare programs

In 1970 federal and state governments spent approximately 10 billion dollars, through five major programs, to provide aid to the poor. Each of these programs offer cash assistance, based upon need, to those who qualify. In addition, a number of programs, such as the food stamp program, provide goods and services to the poor. This section of Assignment 26 provides information on a number of these programs. Read each description and evaluate the total program.

Table 26.7
Current U. S. poverty programs, 1970
Cash Benefit Programs

Program	*Type of benefits*	*Average monthly payments*	*Number of people served*	*Total cost of program*
Old age assistance	Cash to elderly persons	$77.60	2,081,000	$1.9 billion
Aid to the blind	Cash payments	$104.00	81,000	$101 million
Aid to the disabled	Cash payments to totally or permanently disabled persons	$97.00	933,000	$1.04 billion
Aid to families with dependent children	Cash payments to mothers with dependent children	$45.50	9,657,000	$5.7 billion
General assistance (paid by state or local government)	Cash payments to poor who do not qualify under any other program	$58.00	1,062,000	$736 million
Goods and services programs				
Food stamp program	Stamps for food for needy families	N. A.	2,000,000	N. A.
Public housing	Public housing projects Rent based on ability to pay	N. A.	2,000,000	N. A.
Work training	Job training for unemployment men and women	N. A.	45,000	N. A.

N. A.–Data not available.

The Nixon family assistance plan

On August 8, 1969 former President Richard M. Nixon delivered a televised address to the people of the nation. In his speech Mr. Nixon proposed replacing the current welfare programs with his own six point program. Pages 319–321 of this assignment contain exerpts from that speech and several others by the ex-President. In the first excerpt Mr. Nixon outlines his own welfare program. The additional statements illustrate the Nixon philosophy toward welfare.

. . . I therefore propose that we abolish the present welfare system and that we adopt in its place a new family assistance system. Initially, this new system will cost more than welfare. But unlike welfare, it is designed to correct the condition it deals with and thus to lessen the long-range burden and cost.

1. Under this plan, the so-called "adult categories" of aid–aid to the aged, to the blind, the disabled–would be continued, and a national minimum standard for benefits would be set, with the Federal Government contributing to its cost and also sharing the cost of additional state payments above that amount . . . .

But the program now called "aid to families with dependent children"–the program we all normally think of when we think of "welfare"–would be done away with completely. The new family assistance system I propose in its place rests essentially on these three principles: equality of treatment across the nation, a work requirement and a work incentive.

Its benefits would go to the working poor, as well as the nonworking; to families with dependent children headed by a father, as well as to those headed by a mother; and a basic Federal minimum would be provided, the same in every state.

What I am proposing is that the Federal Government build a foundation under the income of every American family with dependent children that cannot care for itself–and wherever in America that family may live.

2. For a family of four now on welfare, with no outside income, the basic Federal payment would be $1,600 a year.

3. States could add to that amount and most states would add to it. In no case would anyone's present level of benefits be lowered.

4. At the same time, this foundation would be one on which the family itself could build. Outside earnings would be encouraged, not discouraged. The new worker could keep the first $60 a month of outside earnings with no reduction in his benefits, and beyond that this benefits would be reduced by only 50 cents for each dollar earned.

By the same token, a family head already employed at low wages could get a family assistance supplement; those who work would no longer be discriminated against. For example, a family of five in which the father earns $2,000 a year–which is the hard fact of life for many families in America today–would get family assistance payments of $1,260 so that they would have a total income of $3,260. A family of seven earning $3,000 a year would have its income raised to $4,360.

Thus, for the first time, the Government would recognize that it has no less an obligation to the working poor than to the nonworking poor; and for the first time, benefits would be scaled in such a way that it would always pay to work.

With such incentives, most recipients who can work will want to work. This is part of the American character.

But what of the others—those who can work but choose not to? Well, the answer is very simple.

5. Under this proposal, everyone who accepts benefits must also accept work or training provided suitable jobs are available either locally or at some distance if transportation is provided. The only exceptions would be those unable to work, and mothers of pre-school children.[54]

6. Even mothers of pre-school children, however, would have the opportunity to work—because I am also proposing along with this a major expansion of day-care centers to make it possible for mothers to take jobs by which they can support themselves and their children.

This national floor under incomes for working or dependent families is not a "guaranteed income." Under the guaranteed income proposal, everyone would be assured a minimum income, regardless of how much he was capable of earning, regardless of what his need was, regardless of whether or not he was willing to work.

No, during the Presidential campaign I opposed such a plan. I oppose it now, and I will continue to oppose it. And this is the reason. A guaranteed income would undermine the incentive to work; the family assistance plan that I propose increases the incentive to work. A guaranteed income establishes a responsibility. It provides help to those in need, and in turn requires that those who receive help work to the extent of their capabilities. There is no reason why one person should be taxed so that another can choose to live idly. (Delivered over National T. V., August 8, 1969.)

. . . In the last 10 years alone, the number of children on welfare has nearly tripled, to more than six million. Six million. Six million children caught up in an unfair and tragic system that rewards people for not working, instead of providing the incentives for self-support: and independence; that drives families apart, instead of holding them together; that brings welfare snoopers into their homes; that robs them of pride and destroys dignity. I want to change all that. The welfare system has become a consuming, monstrous, inhuman outrage against the community, against the family, against the individual . . . and, most of all, against the very children whom it was meant to help. We have taken long strides toward ending racial segregation;

[54]Do you agree with Mr. Nixon that everyone who is able to work should be required to do so or be cut off from all government assistance? Why or why not?

but welfare segregation can be almost as insidious. (At opening of White House Conference on Children, Washington, Dec. 13, 1970.)

. . . I advocate a (welfare) system that will encourage people to take work—and that means whatever work is available. It does not mean the attitude expressed not long ago . . . When a lady got up at a welfare hearing and screamed: "Don't talk to us about any of those menial jobs." I am not sure what she considers a menial job, but I probably have done quite a few in my lifetime. I never thought they were demeaning. If a job puts bread on the table, if it gives you the satisfaction of providing for your children and lets you look everyone else in the eye, I don't think that it is menial. But it is just this attitude than makes others, particularly low-income workers, feel somehow that certain kinds of work are demeaning—scrubbing floors, emptying bedpans. My mother used to do that. It is not enjoyable work, but a lot of people do it—and there is as much dignity in that as there is in any other work to be done in this country, including my own. (At Republican Governors Conference, Williamsburg, Va., April 19, 1971.)

. . . I believe that human welfare is too important to be left to the "welfare-staters." This is a nation with a conscience, and that conscience demands that we see to it the handicapped and the dependent are given what they need to lead lives of decency and self-respect. Because I believe in human dignity, I am fighting for a total overhaul of the demeaning welfare system—to provide a floor of income under every dependent family with children in the United States. And for that very same reason—because I believe in human dignity—I am against a guaranteed annual wage, and I am against any scheme that makes it more profitable for an able-bodied person to sit at home rather than to go to work.[55] When you make it possible for able-bodied men and women to get welfare, you make it impossible for those people to get ahead in life. If we were to underwrite everybody's income, we would be undermining everybody's income, we would be undermining everybody's character. (Before Chamber of Commerce of the United States, Washington, April 26, 1971.)

. . . I say that, instead of providing incentives for more millions to go on welfare, we need a program which will provide incentives for people to get off welfare and go to work. It is wrong for anyone on welfare to receive more than someone who works. Let us be generous to those who can't work without increasing the taxes of those who do work . . . Let us never destroy the principle that has made America the world's most prosperous nation—that a person should get what he works for and work for what he gets. (Accepting the Republican Presidential nomination, Miami Beach, August 23, 1972.)

[55]Do you think many able-bodied people prefer to sit at home rather than go to work? Why or why not?

A proposal for a negative income tax

Some economists and social reformers believe that a negative income tax provides the best method for eliminating poverty in America. Others, including President Ford are bitterly opposed to this proposal. Under this plan low income families would receive cash from the government just as others pay income taxes. In the following article Univeristy of Michigan economist Irwin Garfinkel discusses several versions of the controversial negative income tax plan.

. . . If we decided to eliminate poverty by guaranteeing families an annual income of $3335 (the 1966 poverty level), the government could simply give families with less than $3335 enough money to bring their income up to that level. If the family earned more than $3335, they would pay taxes. A family earning exactly $3335 would neither pay taxes nor receive a government grant. Let's call this Plan I.[56]

This seems very simple. But there is one probelm with Plan I which economists call the incentive problem. Suppose the family head was earning only $1500. When he files his income tax report, the government would give him $1835. This would make his total income $3335. Now suppose he was offered a better paying job—one that paid $2000. If he took the job, the government would then give him only $1335 to bring his income up to the poverty level. In other words, the family's total income (earned income plus government grant) would be the same in both cases. Hence there is no incentive for the man to take the better paying job. In fact, as long as the man cannot earn more than $3335, there is no incentive for him to work at all.

One way to solve the incentive problem is for the government to give poor families only part of the difference between the poverty line and their own income. Let's call this Plan II. For example, suppose we decide the government should give families 50 per cent of the difference between what they earn and the poverty line. Then, if the family head had a $1500 job, he would receive $918 from the government for a total income of $2418. If he took a job for $2000, he would only receive $668 from the government, but his total income would now be $2668.

Under Plan II, it pays for the man to take the better job. But Plan II does not give families enough money to bring them up to the poverty line.

There is another way, which we will call Plan III, to solve the incentive problem and at the same time bring all families up to or above the poverty line of $3335. A family with an income below $6670 would get a grant from the government equal to one-half of the difference between $6670 and the families own income. (Only families with income greater than $6670 would pay taxes.) Thus if the family earned nothing it would get $3335 from the government. No family would be permitted to fall below the poverty line.

[56]Adapted from Handout 6 of the Instructors' Guide for *The Incidence and Effects of Poverty in the United States* by Sociological Resources for the Social Studies, and agency of the American Sociological Association (Boston: Allyn and Bacon Inc., 1969). Reprinted by permission.

Yet it would still pay for family members to take jobs, or if they have jobs, to take better paying ones. For example, if the family head had a $1500 job, he would receive $2585 from the government, which added to the $1500 he earned, would give him a total income of $4085. If he took a job for $2000, he would then receive only $2325 from the government, but his total income would be $4325 instead of $4085.

Under Plan III, however, many nonpoor families (those with incomes between $3335 and $6670) also get money from the government. Moreover, these families would no longer pay taxes. (These nonpoor, however, are far from rich. They could be thought of as being near-poor.) For these reasons, Plan III is much more expensive than Plans I and II. While Plan I would cost about $11 billion and Plan II would cost only half of that, Plan III would cost over three times as much as Plan I.

The challenge to those who favor a negative income tax is to come up with a proposal that (1) eliminates or comes close to eliminating poverty, (2) provides adequate work incentives, and (3) costs no more than the American people are willing to spend. As we have seen, to do all three at once will not be easy.

Some of the arguments of those people who favor such a tax are presented below.

A country as rich as ours that allows poverty to continue to exist is not only unjust but also unwise. If we want to make our cities decent and safe places to live, work, and play in, we will first have to solve the poverty problem. Solving this problem, therefore, should be our country's most important goal. Eliminating poverty must take priority over developing new missiles, landing a man on the moon, or building new highways.

Our country is too rich to allow anyone to remain poor. Negative income tax programs that would eliminate poverty would cost from $11 billion to perhaps $40 billion. But in 1967, our country produced about $800 billion worth of goods and services. Moreover, the country's income grows every year by 4 or 5 per cent. Hence the annual cost of a negative income tax would only be about 1.6 to 3.8 per cent of our national income in 1967 and would be less than one year's increase in income.

A negative income tax would help the poor where they need help most. The poor lack money. About a third of the poor are in families where the family head works full time, and a third are over sixty-five. No one suggests that we put the elderly to work. What they need is more money. And the first group is already working full time. They also need more money.

While better education and other services might be helpful, these are long-term approaches. Moreover, they cannot be considered a substitute for income. Children with full stomachs learn better than hungry children.

Finally, contrary to what many opponents have suggested, a negative income tax might even encourage people to work harder and to seek out better jobs. Very few American families would be content with a $3335 income if they could earn more. It seems that the more money a family gets, the more it wants. There is no reason to believe the poor are any different from other

American families in this respect. In fact, it is quite likely that a taste of a better life will rekindle hope in our poor people and spur them on to renewed efforts to achieve the good life.

For thought and discussion

What additional programs can you suggest to help eliminate poverty in urban America?

Individual and small group activities

1. How much poverty exists in your city? Visit the social welfare agencies in your city to determine the extent of poverty. Find out what services your city provides to assist the poor. Do any long-range plans exist to help eliminate poverty? Report your findings to your class.
2. With a group of your classmates organize a drive to assist the poor in your city. You might collect canned goods, clothing, and blankets. Your local Salvation Army, Goodwill Agency, or other charitable organizations will help you distribute these goods to needy families.

Group conflict and accommodation: Stating the issue for Assignments 27 and 28

During the decade of the 1960's riots and racial disorders exploded in nearly 30 American cities. Property destruction ranged in the hundreds of millions of dollars and more than 100 persons were killed. Each night during the summers of 1966 and 1967 Americans sat glued to their television sets watching scenes of riots, looting, and burning in the black sections of our cities. Many of these people wondered what was happening to America. Some felt that this type of violence was an uncommon occurrence in our nation. Others felt these disorders were caused by a foreign conspiracy. A National Advisory Commission on Civil Disorders, however, warned that "our nation is moving toward two societies, one black, one white—separate and unequal." Discrimination and segregation," according to the Commission, "threatened the future of every American."

Racial disturbances have occurred quite frequently throughout our history. As early as 1712 black and white Americans clashed in New York City. Violent rioting also occurred in Cincinnati, Newark, Buffalo, and New York City during the Civil War. From 1900 through 1908 New York City, Springfield, Ohio; Greensburg, Indiana; and Springfield, Illinois all experienced anti-black riots. Other racial disturbances broke out in East St. Louis in 1917 (39 killed), Chicago in 1919 (38 killed), Detroit in 1943 (34 killed), and Harlem, New York in 1943 (6 killed). Urban America has had a long and violent racial history.

What caused these continuing outbreaks of violence? Does violence ever bring about meaningful change? How can it be prevented? In 1967 former President Lyndon Johnson attempted to answer these questions and warned the nation that:

The only genuine, long-range solution for what has happened lies in an attack—mounted at every level—upon the conditions that breed dispair and violence. All of us know what those conditions are: ignorance, discrimination, slums, poverty, disease, not enough jobs. We should attack these conditions—not because we are frightened by conflict, but because we are fired by conscience. We should attack them because there is simply no other way to achieve a decent and orderly society in America.

Assignments 27 and 28 examine the causes of racial conflict and provide solutions suggested by both black and white leaders. In Assignment 27 you will examine accounts of two serious racial conflicts: The Chicago riot of 1919 and the Watts riot of 1965. These accounts will help you determine the major causes of racial conflict. Assignment 28 discusses suggested methods of accommodating racial groups and preventing future violence. As you read Assignment 27 make a list of the major causes of racial unrest. Then use this list to evaluate the alternatives provided in Assignment 28.

Group conflict and accommodation (1)

Assignment 27

During the summers of 1919 and 1965 racial violence broke out in the cities of Chicago and Los Angeles. Each of these incidents began with a single isolated event. Yet they touched off days and nights of rioting, looting, burning, and killing. Both black and white residents died in the rioting but the majority of victims were black. At the conclusion of each of these riots independent commissions studied the causes and made recommendations, based on their findings, designed to accommodate both groups and prevent future violence. Assignment 27 provides three kinds of material about each event: Accounts illustrating the attitudes of blacks and whites prior to the incident, a description of the incident, and the recommendations of the study commissions. Examine each incident and make a list of the causes of urban racial violence. Then develop an hypothesis about the best solution to racial conflict. Your hypothesis should follow the model you used in the assignments on poverty and welfare, page 315. Finally, be prepared to answer the following question in your next class.

1. How do you account for the similarities in each of the commission reports?

The Chicago riot of 1919

Attitudes of black and white Americans

In 1919 race riots occurred in nearly forty cities throughout the United States. The worst of these took place in Chicago between July 27 and August 8. "These riots," said one newspaper editor, "are symptomatic of the attitudes of fear, hatred, and racism running amuck in our nation." The following accounts provide evidence to help you examine this statement. As you examine each of the statements by black and white Americans try to determine the causes of these outbreaks of racial violence.

Attitudes of black Americans: Claude McKay, black poet, (July 1919.)

If we must die–let it not be like hogs
Hunted and penned in an inglorious spot,
While round us bark the mad and hungry dogs,
Making their mock at our accursed lot.
If we must die–oh, let us nobly die,
So that our precious blood may not be shed
In vain; then even the monsters we defy
Shall be constrained to honor us though dead!

Oh, Kinsmen! We must meet the common foe;
Though far outnumbered, let us show us brave,
And for their thousand blows deal one death blow!
What though before us lies the open grave?
Like men we'll face the murderous, cowardly pack,
Pressed to the wall, dying but fighting back!

Letters from black migrants to the *Chicago Defender,* a black newspaper, 1917.

Lexington, Miss., May 12

My dear Mr. H____: I am writing to you for some information and assistance if you can give it. I am a young man and am disabled, in a very great degree, to do hard manual labor. I was educated at Alcorn College and have been teaching a few years: but ah: me, the Superintendent under whom we poor colored teachers have to teach cares less for a colored man than he does for the vilest beast. I am compelled to teach 150 children without any assistance and receives only $27.00 a month, the white with 30 get $100.

I am so sick I am so tired of such conditions that I sometime think that life for me is not worth while and most eminently believe with Patrick Henry "Give me liberty or give me death." If I was a strong able bodied man I would have gone from here long ago, but this handicaps me and, I must make inquiries before I Leap Do you think you can assist me to a position I am good at stenography, typewriting, and bookkeeping or any kind of work not to rough or heavy. I am 4 feet 6 in. high and weigh 105 pounds.

Houston, Texas, April 20, 1917

Dear Sir: Wanted to leave the South and Go and Place where a man will be anything except a Ker. (A dog) I thought would write you for advice as where would be a Good place for a comporedly young man that want to Better his Standing who has a very promising young family.

I am 30 years old and have Good experience in Freight Handler and can fill positions from Truck to Agent.

Would like Chicago or Philadelphia but I won't care where so long as I Go where a man is a man.

Statements of black Chicago residents, 1919.

A black businessman: There is no race problem; if the white people would only do as they would be done by we would not have need of commissions to better conditions. This won't be done, but an easier plan is to enforce the law. The laws are good enough but they are not enforced. Riots grow out of hate, jealousy, envy, and prejudice. When a man becomes a contented citizen there will be little chance of causing him to fight anymore. Give us those things that are due us–law, protection, and equal rights–then we will become contented citizens.

A black ex-soldier: I went to war, served eight months in France; I was married but I didn't claim exemption. I wanted to go, but I might as well have stayed here for all the good it has done me . . . . No, that ain't so, I'm glad I went. I done my part and I'm going to fight here till Uncle Sam does his. I can shoot as good as the next one and nobody better start anything. I ain't looking for trouble, but if it comes my way I ain't dodging.

A black lawyer: Agitation by the press, both white and colored, does nothing but create dissension. The religious and political leaders have gone from one extreme to the other. Formerly the Negroes were cringing and ingratiating when dealing with the whites. Now they are trying to be radical in order to gain notoriety. There is nothing to be gained in either being servile or radical. I have had indignities heaped upon me by the white man. Why, my mother was ill when a white man in Georgia took every bit of our furniture from us, pulling the bed from under her. She screamed with pain each time they moved the bed, but they left her on the floor. I swore that I would kill that man and for many years held hatred against him. Now I know it is wrong and only hope he has learned better.

A black shopkeeper: I am a radical. I despise and hate the white man. They will always be against the Ethiopian. I do not want to be called Negro, colored, or "nigger." Either term is an insult to me or to you. Our rightful name is Ethiopian. White men stole the black man from Africa and counseled with each other as to what to do with him and what to call him, for when the Negro learned that he was the first civilized human on earth he would rise up and rebel against the white man.

Attitudes of white Americans: Statements of white Chicago Residents, 1919.

A white elementary school principal: So far as books are concerned there are set types of learning which they take with great difficulty. Last Friday a colored boy came to me and said, "I want to go back to the first grade." We have gotten him in the third grade. He came to me and cried–a great big boy–because he said the work was much too hard for him, and he didn't want to study. His teacher was cross with him and insisted he must get to work. It is an exception to have a boy so frank. But I don't think the instance is far from the truth. I have never had a white child complain that he was graded too high and wanted to be put down. Sometimes when they come in, they say to me: "I went to school in the South, and I am in high fifth grade." "How long were you in school in the South?" "Three sessions." Two months, and they are in high fifth grade! I put them into the first or second grade. Sometimes I can't fit them into the smaller grades, and sometimes they resent it, but when they get into the actual school work and find they can't do it, they can't complain. I should say therefore that here is a certain amount of mental backwardness found in colored children not found in whites.

An article from White Americans, *a magazine circulated in Chicago:* In the United States Negroes not only vote and hold office, but the Negro vote is the deciding factor in the national elections, and also in many of the northern cities, and they trade their vote for jobs and offices and other privileges. The Negroes control the great city of Philadelphia, and the press said the Negro delegates at the Republican Convention in Chicago openly offered to sell their support to the presidential candidate who would pay the most money. Just think this thing over, you sovereign United States citizens: the Negroes control the elections, and thus your law-makers, judges, and officials; and the Negroes have so much pull and confidence, that they not only defend their political rights, but they start riots and race wars, and openly threaten that they are going to make the white folks stand around.

A white resident in the 6600 block on Langley Avenue: A colored family lives next door north of me, and you'll be surprised when I tell you that I haven't been able to open my bedroom window on that side to air that room for three years. I couldn't think of unlocking the windows because their window is so near somebody could easily step across into this house. It's awful to have to live in such fear of your life.

When asked if she considered her neighbors so dangerous as that, she said: Well, no, the woman seems pretty nice. I see her out in the back yard occasionally and bid her the time of day out of charity. You can't help but pity them, so I am charitable and speak. Where the danger really is, is that you never know who's in their house; they bring such trash to the neighborhood, even if they are good and decent. How do I know what kind of people this woman next door associates with? There's awful-looking people sit on the front porch sometimes. Why, I couldn't sit on my porch on the hottest day because I'd be afraid they would come out any minute. And what white person will sit on a porch next door to a porch with black ones on it? Not me, anyhow, nor you either I hope.

A white minister: All I want for the Negro is justice—then I think the economic laws will settle this problem.[57] Let the people interested try justice; they will find it will solve the race problem faster than any other course,

[57]Do you agree with the minister's argument that justice will solve the problems of racial discontent? Why, or why not? How would you define justice?

just as it will solve any other problem. Treat the bad Negro just as rough as you treat the bad white man, but acclaim the good Negro after the same manner of your acclamation of the good white man.

George Jean Nathan and H. L. Mencken in a 1918 volume, *The American Credo,* compiled a series of 435 commonly accepted beliefs covering a wide range. Among these 435 listed American beliefs there are some which involve and include the following popular notions about Negroes:

1. That a Negro's vote may always be readily bought for a dollar.
2. That every colored cook has a lover who never works and that she feeds him by stealing the best part of every dish she cooks.
3. That every Negro who went to France with the army has a liaison with a white woman and won't look at a colored woman any more.
4. That all male Negroes can sing.
5. That all Negroes born south of the Potomac can play the banjo and are excellent dancers.
6. That whenever a Negro is educated he refuses to work and becomes a criminal.
7. That all Negro prize fighters marry white women and then afterwards beat them.
8. That all Negroes who show any intelligence are two-thirds white and the sons of U. S. Senators.
9. That a Negro ball always ends up in a grand free-for-all fight in which several Negroes are mortally slashed with razors.
10. That Negroes are lazy; that they are indisposed to, though not incapable of, sustained physical exertion.
11. That they are happy-go-lucky. It is asserted that they do not purchase homes and do not save their money; that they spend lavishly for clothes to the neglect of home comforts and the demands even of their health; that they work by the day, and before the week is ended confuse bookkeeping by demanding their pay.
12. That they are overassertive; that constant harping on constitutional rights is a habit of Negroes, especially of the newer generation; that they resent imaginary insults and are generally supersensitive.
13. That they usually carry razors. Whenever a newspaper reporter is in doubt he gives a razor as the weapon used. Some time ago a woman was found murdered in a town near Chicago. She had been slashed with a razor, and the broken blade was left beside her body. The murder was particularly atrocious, and the murderer left no other clew. Several Negroes were arrested on suspicion but were released when a white youth confessed the crime.

The riot

Thirty-eight persons killed, 537 injured, and about 1,000 made homeless and destitute. The riot which broke out in Chicago on July 27, 1919 swept through parts of the city for four days. On August 2, the state militia restored order and withdrew the following day. Following the riot an independent commission investigated the event. Pages 332–333 of Assignment 27 contain the description of the riot.

Sunday afternoon, July 27, 1919, hundreds of white and Negro bathers crowded the lake-front beaches at Twenty-sixth and Twenty-ninth streets. This is the eastern boundary of the thickest Negro residence area. At Twenty-sixth Street Negroes were in great majority; at Twenty-ninth Street there were more whites. An imaginary line in the water separating the two beaches had been generally observed by the two races. Under the prevailing relations this line served virtually as a challenge to either side to cross it. Four Negroes who attempted to enter the water from the "white" side were driven away by the whites. They returned with more Negroes, and there followed a series of attacks with stones, first one side gaining the advantage, then the other.

Eugene Williams, a Negro boy of seventeen, entered the water from the side used by Negroes and drifted across the line supported by a railroad tie. He was observed by the crowd on the beach and promptly became a target for stones. He suddenly released the tie, went down and was drowned. Guilt was immediately placed on Stauber, a young white man, by Negro witnesses who declared that he threw the fatal stone.

White and Negro men dived for the boy without result. Negroes demanded that the policeman present arrest Stauber. He refused; and at this crucial moment arrested a Negro on a white man's complaint. Negroes then attacked the officer. These two facts, the drowning and the refusal of the policeman to arrest Stauber, together marked the beginning of the riot.

Two hours after the drowning, a Negro, James Crawford, fired into a group of officers summoned by the policeman at the beach and was killed by a Negro policeman. Reports and rumors circulated rapidly, and new crowds began to gather. Five white men were injured in clashes near the beach. As darkness came Negroes in white districts to the west suffered severly. Between 9:00 P.M. and 3:00 A.M. twenty-seven Negroes were beaten, seven stabbed, and four shot. Monday morning was quiet, and Negroes went to work as usual.

Returning from work in the afternoon many Negroes were attacked by white ruffians. Streetcar routes, especially at transfer points, were the centers of lawlessness. Trolleys were pulled from the wires, and Negro passengers were dragged into the street, beaten, stabbed, and shot. The police were powerless to cope with these numerous assaults. During Monday, four Negro men and one white assailant were killed, and thirty Negroes were severely beaten in street-car clashes. Four white men were killed, six stabbed, five shot, and nine severely beaten. It was rumored that the white occupants of the Angelus Building at Thirty-fifth Street and Wabash Avenue had shot a Negro. Negroes gathered about the building. The white tenants sought police protection, and one hundred policemen, mounted and on foot, responded. In a clash with the mob the police killed four Negroes and injured many.

Raids into the Negro residence area then began. Automobiles sped through the streets, the occupants shooting at random. Negroes retaliated by "sniping" from ambush.[58]

On Tuesday, July 29, Negro men en route to their jobs through hostile territory were killed. White soldiers and sailors in uniform, aided by civilians, raided the "Loop" business section, killing two Negroes and beating and robbing several others. Negroes living among white neighbors in Englewood, far to the south, were driven from their homes, their household goods were stolen, and their houses were burned or wrecked. On the West Side an Italian mob, excited by a false rumor that an Italian girl had been shot by a Negro, killed Joseph Lovings, a Negro.

On Saturday incendiary fires burned forty-nine houses in the immigrant neighborhood west of the Stock Yards. Nine hundred and forty-eight people, mostly Lithuanians, were made homeless, and the property loss was about $250,000. Responsibility for the fires was never fixed. The total casualties of this reign of terror were thirty-eight deaths—fifteen white, twenty-three Negro—and 537 people injured.

Recommendations of the Chicago Commission on Race Relations

Immediately after the Chicago riot the Governor of Illinois, Frank Lowden, appointed a commission to study its causes and provide recommendations to prevent future disturbances. The committees produced a 700 page report. Some of its recommendations are listed below.

1. We recommend that the police and militia work out a detailed plan for joint action in the control of race riots.
2. We recommend that, without regard to color, all persons arrested in connection with rioting be promptly tried and the guilty punished.
3. We recommend that the police, state's attorney, and other authorities promptly rid the Negro residence areas of vice resorts, whose prevalence is due to official laxity.
4. We recommend better co-operation between the city and park police in and near parks, bathing beaches, and other public recreation places.
5. We recommend that the authorities exercise their powers to condemn and raze all houses unfit for human habitation, many of which exist in the Negro residence areas on the South and West sides.
6. We recommend that the park and other authorities put an end to the present gross discrimination by white persons which practically bars Negroes out of certain recreation centers near their own congested residence areas.
7. We recommend that in the areas where the main part of the Negro population lives, and where elementary-school accommodations are deficient,

[58]In your opinion was the violence on the part of either side justified? Why, or why not? Is violence ever justified?

buildings, equipment, and teaching forces be provided which shall be equal to the average standard for the city.

8. We recommend that there must be more and better housing to accommodate the great increase in Negro population which was at the rate of 148 per cent from 1910 to 1920.
9. While we recognize the propriety and social values of race pride among Negroes, we warn them that thinking and talking too much in terms of race alone are calculated to promote separation of race interests and to interfere with racial adjustment.
10. We recommend that Negroes be employed, advanced, and promoted according to their capacities and proved merit.
11. We point out that Negroes are entitled by law to the same treatment as other persons in restaurants, theaters, stores, and other places of public accommodation, and we urge that owners and managers of such places govern their policies accordingly.

The Watts, Los Angeles riot of 1965

Attitudes of black and white Americans

In 1963, *Newsweek* magazine and Louis Harris Associates conducted a nationwide poll surveying more than 2,500 black and white Americans. The survey attempted to determine the attitudes of each race toward each other. These attitudes most likely contributed to the riots in Watts and other cities throughout the nation. The tables on pages 335–338 illustrate the results of the *Newsweek* survey. As you examine each table compare the attitudes displayed with those of black and white Chicagoans in 1919.

The riot

During the summer of 1965 one of the earliest and worst racial riots of the 1960's broke out in Watts, a black section of Los Angeles. Six days and nights of rioting produced 34 dead persons, 1,032 reported injuries, and more than 600 buildings damaged or destroyed. Following the riot the Governor of California, like the Illinois Governor in 1919, appointed a commission to study this violent event. Pages This Assignment contains the commission's description of the rioting. As you read this account continue your listings of the causes of racial violence.

On August 11, 1965, California Highway Patrolman Lee W. Minikus, a Caucasian, was riding his motorcycle along 122nd street, just south of the Los Angeles City boundary, when a passing Negro motorist told him he had just seen a car that was being driven recklessly. Minikus gave chase and pulled the car over at 116th and Avalon, in a predominantly Negro neighborhood, near

Attitudes of white Americans: Whites say *yes*

	Nationwide %	*South %*	*Whites who've had social contact with Negroes %*
Should the law guarantee Negroes rights equal to white people in:			
Job opportunities?	80	62	87
Voting?	95	92	96
Getting good housing?	85	81	90
Using buses and trains?	91	80	94
Giving their children integrated schooling?	75	43	90

Attitudes of white Americans: Whites say *no*

	Nationwide %	*South %*	*Whites who've had social contact with Negroes %*
Would you favor a quota system guaranteeing Negroes (10% of the nation) 10% of the jobs?	81	80	84
Do you agree Negroes should get preference in job openings to make up for discrimination?	97	97	97
Would you favor a Federal law forbidding discrimination in housing against Negroes?	56	80	35
If you were in the Negro's position, do you think you would be justified to:			
Sit-in at lunch counters?	67	84	49
Boycott products whose manufacturers don't hire enough Negroes?	55	66	43
Lie down in front of trucks at construction sites to protest hiring discrimination?	91	94	87
Go to jail to protest discrimination?	56	75	37
Should the Federal government have more power to make sure Negroes can register and vote?	43	69	34

Attitudes of white Americans: Where whites draw the line

	Nationwide %	*South %*	*Whites who've had social contact with Negroes %*
Percentage who would mind:			
Working next to a Negro on the job	18	7	33
Sitting next to a Negro at lunch counter	20	52	5
Sitting next to a Negro on a bus	20	48	6
Sitting next to a Negro at the movies	25	58	6
Own children going to school with Negroes	25	58	8
Using same rest room as Negroes	26	59	9
Having own child bring Negro home for supper	33	80	18
Having Negro family next door	58	77	30
Close friend or relative marrying Negro	87	95	75
Own daughter dating a Negro	93	98	83

Attitudes of white Americans: White stereotypes of the Negro

	Nationwide %	*South %*	*Whites who've had social contact with Negroes %*
Percentage of whites who believe that:			
Negroes laugh a lot	85	94	77
Negroes tend to have less ambition	75	88	56
Negroes smell different	71	88	56
Negroes have looser morals	69	89	49
Negroes keep untidy homes	61	72	38
Negroes have less native intelligence	50	73	27
Negroes want to live off the handout	49	71	29
Negroes breed crime	44	58	24
Negroes care less for the family	39	60	24
Negroes are inferior to whites	36	61	17

Attitudes of black Americans: Housing

	All blacks	*Non-south*	*South*
If you could find the housing you want and like, would you rather live in a neighborhood with Negroes, or in a neighborhood that had both whites and Negroes?			
Negro neighborhood	20	11	27
Mixed neighborhood	64	75	55
Not sure	16	14	18

Attitudes of black Americans: Boycotts

	All blacks	*Non-south*	*South*
Have you stopped buying in certain stores in town because they won't hire Negroes?			
YES	29	24	30
NO	71	76	70
Have you stopped buying certain companies' products because you have heard they discriminate against Negroes?			
YES	19	14	18
NO	81	86	82
If asked, would you do the following? (Percentage yes)			
Picket a store?	47	54	40
Stop buying at a store?	63	66	59

Where whites and Negroes agree

	% Yes
Negro jobs are not equal to whites	
Whites	64%
Negroes	63%
Negro education is inferior to whites	
Whites	54%
Negroes	57%
Job integration is acceptable now	
Whites	82%
Negroes	87%
Negroes should have access to public accommodations	
Whites	82%
Negroes	96%
Integrated education is acceptable	
Whites	76%
Negroes	89%
Negro jobs will be better 5 years from now	
Whites	77%
Negroes	77%

Where whites and Negroes disagree

	% Yes
Negroes are moving too fast	
Whites	74%
Negroes	3%
Revolt is suported by rank and file of Negroes	
Whites	34%
Negroes	91%
Integrated housing is desirable	
Whites	42%
Negroes	78%

but not in Watts. It was 7:00 P. M.

The driver was Marquette Frye, a 21-year-old Negro, and his older brother, Ronald, 22, was a passenger. Minikus asked Marquette to get out and take the standard Highway Patrol sobriety test. Frye failed the test, and at 7:05 P. M., Minikus told him he was under arrest. He radioed for his motorcycle partner, for a car to take Marquette to jail, and a tow truck to take the car away. . . .

Ronald Frye, having been told he could not take the car when Marquette was taken to jail, went to get their mother so that she could claim the car. They returned to the scene about 7:15 P. M. as the second motorcycle patrolman, the patrol car, and tow truck arrived. The original group of 25 to 50 curious spectators had grown to 250 to 300 persons.

The watching crowd became hostile and one of the patrolmen radioed for more help. Within minutes three more highway patrolmen arrived. Minikus and his partner were now struggling with both Frye brothers. Mrs. Frye, now belligerent, jumped on the back of one of the officers and ripped his shirt. In an attempt to subdue Marquette, one officer swung at his shoulder with a night stick, missed, and struck him on the forehead, inflicting a minor cut. By 7:23 P. M., all three of the Fryes were under arrest, and other California Highway Patrolmen and, for the first time, Los Angeles police officers had arrived in response to the call for help.

Officers on the scene said there were now more than 1,000 persons in the crowd. About 7:25 P. M., the patrol car with the prisoners, and the tow truck pulling the Frye car, left the scene. At 7:31 P. M., the Fryes arrived at a nearby sheriff's substation . . . .

As the officers were leaving the scene, someone in the crowd spat on one of them. They stopped withdrawing and two highway patrolmen went into the crowd and arrested a young Negro woman and a man who was said to have been inciting the crowd to violence when the officers were arresting her.

Following these arrests, all officers withdrew at 7:40 P. M. As the last police car left the scene, it was stoned by the now irate mob.

The crowd did not disperse, but ranged in small groups up and down the street, although never more than a few blocks from the arrest scene. Between 8:15 P. M. and midnight, the mob stoned automobiles, pulled Caucasian motorists out of their cars and beat them, and menaced a police field command post which had been set up in the area. By 1:00 A. M., the outbreak seemed to be under control but, until early morning hours, there were sporadic reports of unruly mobs, vandalism, and rock throwing. Twenty-nine persons were arrested . . . Between 6:45 and 7:15 P. M., on August 12, crowds at the scene of the trouble of the night before had grown to more than 1,000. The first fire in a commercial establishment was set only one block from the location of the Frye arrests, and police had to hold back rioters as firemen fought the blaze.

Shortly before midnight rock-throwing and looting crowds for the first time ranged outside the perimeter. Five hundred police officers, deputy sheriffs and highway patrolmen used various techniques, including fender-to-fender sweeps by police cars, in seeking to disperse the mob. By 4:00 A. M. Friday, the police department felt that the situation was at least for the moment under control. At 5:09 A. M., officers were withdrawn from emergency perimeter control . . . .

Friday afternoon, rioters jammed the streets, and began systematically to burn two blocks of 103rd Street in Watts, and drove off firemen by sniper fire and by throwing missiles. By late afternoon, gang activity began to spread the disturbance as far as fifty and sixty blocks to the north.

Lieutenant Governor Anderson arrived at the Van Nuys Air National Guard Base at 3:35 P. M. After talking with Hale Champion who urged him to call the Guard, Anderson ordered General Hill to commit the troops. At 4:00 P. M., he announced this decision to the press. At 5:00 P. M., in the Governor's office downtown, he signed the proclamation officially calling the Guard.

Friday was the worst night. The riot moved out of the Watts area and burning and looting spread over wide areas of Southeast Los Angeles several miles apart. At 1:00 A. M. Saturday, there were 100 engine companies fighting fires in the area. Snipers shot at firemen as they fought new fires. That night, a fireman was crushed and killed on the fire line by a falling wall, and a deputy sheriff was killed when another sheriff's shotgun was discharged in a struggle with rioters.

Despite new tactics and 15,000 armed troops, the area was not under control at any time on Friday night, as major calls of looting, burning, and shooting were reported every two to three minutes. On throughout the morning hours of Saturday and during the long day, the crowds of looters and patterns of burning spread out and increased still further until it became necessary to impose a curfew on the 46.5 square-mile area on Saturday. Lieutenant Governnor Anderson appeared on television early Saturday evening to explain the curfew, which made it a crime for any unauthorized persons to be on the streets in the curfew area after 8:00 P. M.

Much of the Saturday burning had been along Central Avenue. Again using sweep tactics, the guardsmen and police were able to clear this area by 3:30 P. M. Guardsmen rode "shotgun" on the fire engines and effectively stopped the sniping and rock throwing at firemen. Saturday evening, road blocks were set up in anticipation of the curfew. The massive show of force was having some effect although there was still riot activity and rumors spread regarding proposed activity in the south central area.

When the curfew started at 8:00 P. M., police and guardsmen were able to deal with the riot area as a whole. Compared with the holocaust of Friday evening, the streets were relatively quiet. The only major exception was the burning of a block of stores on Broadway between 46th and 48th Streets. Snipers again prevented firemen from entering the area, and while the buildings burned, a gun battle ensued between law enforcement officers, the Guard, and the snipers.

During the day Sunday, the curfew area was relatively quiet. Because many markets had been destroyed, food distribution was started by churches, community groups, and government agencies. Governor Brown, who had returned Saturday night, personally toured the area, talking to residents. Major fires were under control but there were new fires and some rekindling of old ones. By Tuesday, Governor Brown was able to lift the curfew and by the following Sunday, only 252 guardsmen remained.

The recommendations of the Commission

The commission studying the Watts riot conducted an intensive investigation and like the Chicago Commission of 1919 produced a lengthy report. Examine the major findings of the McCone Commission and compare them with those of the Chicago Commission. Then write your hypotheses about the best solution to the problems of racial conflict.

Our recommendations concern many areas where improvement can be made but three we consider to be of highest priority and greatest importance.

1. Because idleness brings a harvest of distressing problems, employment for those in the Negro community who are unemployed and able to work is a first priority. Our metropolitan area employs upwards of three millions of men and women in industry and in the service trades, and we face a shortage of skilled and semiskilled workers as our economy expands. We recommend that our robust community take immediate steps to relieve the lack of job opportunity for Negroes by cooperative programs for employment and training, participated in by the Negro community, by governmental agencies, by employers and by organized labor.

2. In education, we recommend a new and costly approach to educating the Negro child who has been deprived of the early training that customarily starts at infancy and who because of early deficiencies advances through school on a basis of age rather than scholastic attainment. What is clearly needed and what we recommend is an emergency program designed

to raise the level of scholastic attainment of those who would otherwise fall behind. This requires pre-school education, intensive instruction in small classes, remedial courses and other special treatment. The cost will be great but until the level of scholastic achievement of the disadvantaged child is raised, we cannot expect to overcome the existing spiral of failure.

3. We recommend that law enforcement agencies place greater emphasis on their responsibilities for crime prevention as an essential element of the law enforcement task, and that they institute improved means for handling citizen complaints and community relationships.

The road to the improvement of the condition of the disadvantaged Negro which lies through education and employment is hard and long, but there is no shorter route. The avenue of violence and lawlessness leads to a dead end. To travel the long and difficult road will require courageous leadership and determined participation by all parts of our community, but no task in our times is more important. Of what shall it avail our nation if we can place a man on the moon but cannot cure the sickness in our cities?

For thought and discussion

Do you think the attitudes of black and white Americans have changed from those of 1963? If so, in what ways?

Individual and small group activities

1. With a group of your classmates conduct your own poll of white and black attitudes. Use the questions listed in the Newsweek poll in this assignment and interview a number of black and white Americans to determine how attitudes have changed since 1963. The more people you survey the more valid your results will be. Prepare a set of tables to compare the attitudes you find with those of 1963. Report your findings to the class in a way that you and your instructor agree upon.
2. In 1968 a Presidential Commission of distinguished Americans investigated a number of the race riots of the 1960's. The report was published as *The National Advisory Commission on Civil Disorders.* Compare the findings and recommendations of this commission with those of the Chicago and Los Angeles' Commission. How are they similar? Different? How do you account for this? Prepare an oral report for your class on one of the following topics: 1) The futility of investigatory commissions; 2) The value of investigatory commissions.

Group conflict and accommodation (2)

Assignment 28

In Assignment 27 you examined one alternative to the problem of racial conflict in urban America. Many people feel, however, that violence seldom leads to improved race relations. During the last decade both black and white Americans have suggested other alternative solutions. Assignment 28 contains a number of these alternatives. Use the list of racial problems and the hypothesis you developed for Assignment 27 to help you evaluate each alternative. When you have concluded your examination of all of the alternatives write a short paper defending one of the solutions. Your paper should begin with a statement something like: "I feel that _____ provides the most reasonable solution to urban racial conflict for the following reasons": You should also be prepared to argue against any solution you rejected in your next class.

The dream of Martin Luther King, Jr.

Until his death at the hand of an assassin in 1968 the Reverend Martin Luther King, Jr. led the struggle for black civil rights throughout the nation. As head of the Southern Christian Leadership Conference Dr. King's tactics of civil disobedience and his oratory inspired millions of black and white Americans. In the following account, taken from his most famous speech, delivered on the occasion of the March on Washington, August 28, 1963 Reverend King expresses his hopes for the future of America.

. . . Five score years ago, a great American, in whose symbolic shadow we stand today, signed the Emancipation Proclamation. This momentous decree came as the great beacon light of hope for millions of Negro slaves who had been seared in the flames of withering injustice. It came as the joyous daybreak to end the long night of their captivity.

But one hundred years later the Negro still is not free. One hundred years later, the life of the Negro is still badly crippled by the manacles of segregation and the chains of discrimination. One hundred years later, the Negro lives on a lonely island of poverty in the midst of a vast ocean of material prosperity. One hundred years later, the Negro is still languished in the corners of American society and finds himself an exile in his own land. So we have come here today to dramatize the shameful condition.

In a sense we've come to our Nation's Capital to cash a check. When the architects of our republic wrote the magnificent words of the Constitution and the Declaration of Independence, they were signing a promissory note to which every American was to fall heir. This note was a promise that all men, yes, black men as well as white men, should be guaranteed the unalienable rights of life, liberty and the pursuit of happiness.

It is obvious today that America has defaulted on this promissory note insofar as her citizens of color are concerned. Instead of honoring this sacred obligation, America has given the Negro people a bad check, a check which has come back marked "Insufficient Funds." But we refuse to believe the bank of justice is bankrupt. We refuse to believe that there are insufficient funds in the great vaults of opportunity of this nation. So we have come to cash this check, a check that will give us upon demand, the riches of freedom and the security of justice. We have also come to this hallowed spot to remind America of the fierce urgency of now . . . .

It would be fatal for the nation to overlook the urgency of the moment. This sweltering summer of the Negro's legitimate discontent will not pass until there is an invigorating autumn of freedom and equality. Nineteen sixty-three is not an end but a beginning. Those who hoped that the Negro needed to blow off steam and will now be content will have a rude awakening if the nation returns to business as usual. There will be neither rest nor tranquility in America until the Negro is guaranteed his citizenship rights. The whirlwinds of revolt will continue to shake the foundations of our nation until the bright day of justice emerges.

But there is something I must say to my people who stand on the warm threshold which leads them to the palace of justice. In the process of gaining our rightful place we must not be guilty of wrongful deeds. Let us not seek to satisfy our thirst for freedom by drinking from the cup of bitterness and hatred. We must forever conduct our struggle on the high plane of dignity and discipline. We must not allow our creative protest to degenerate into physical violence. Again and again we must rise to the majestic heights of meeting physical force with soul force . . . .

I have dream that one day every valley shall be exalted, every hill and mountain shall be made low, the rough places will be made plain and the crooked places will be made straight, and the glory of the Lord shall be revealed, and all flesh shall see it together.

This is our hope. This is the faith that I go back to the South with. With this faith we will be able to hew out of the mountain of despair a stone of hope. With this faith we will be able to transform the jangling discords of our nation into a beautiful symphony of brotherhood. With this faith we will be able to work together, to pray together, to struggle together, to go to jail together, to stand up for freedom together, knowing that we will be free one day.

This will be the day when all of God's children will be able to sing with new meaning:

My country 'tis of thee,
Sweet land of liberty,
Of thee I sing:
Land where my fathers died,
Land of the pilgrims' pride,
From every mountain-side
Let Freedom ring.

And if America is to be a great nation, this must become true. So, let freedom ring from the prodigious hill tops of New Hampshire. Let freedom ring from the mighty mountains of New York. Let freedom ring from the heightening Alleghenies of Pennsylvania. Let freedom ring from the snow-capped Rockies of Colorado. Let freedom ring from the curvacous slopes of California. But not only that, let freedom ring from Stone Mountain of Georgia.

Let freedom ring from Lookout Mountain of Tennessee.

Let freedom ring from every hill and molehill of Mississippi. From every mountainside, let freedom ring. And when we allow freedom to ring, when we let it ring from every village, from every hamlet, from every state and every city, we will be able to speed up that day when all of God's children, black men and white men, Jews and Gentiles, Protestants and Catholics, will be able to join hands and sing in the words of the old Negro spiritual: "Free at last! free at last! thank God almighty, we are free at last!

Elijah Muhammad speaks out

Since 1960 the Nation of Islam, usually known as the Black Muslims, has attracted thousands of black followers. Muhammed Ali (Cassius Clay), Kareem Abdul Jabbar (Lew Alcinder), and Malcom X (Malcom Little) became converts to the Black Muslim faith. In the article on page 345, the late Elijah Muhammad, former spiritual leader of the Black Muslims, presents one alternative to America's racial problems.

"Freedom is not enough."
Lyndon B. Johnson

During his years as Senate Majority Leader, and later as President of the United States, Lyndon Johnson presided over several pieces of historic civil rights legislation. The Civil Rights Acts of 1957 and 1960 attempted to protect the voting rights of minority groups. The Civil Rights Act of 1964 prohibited discrimination in public

Dedicated to Freedom, Justice and Equality for the so - called Negro. The Earth Belongs to Allah.

Vol. 13 No. 24 2-Sections 32 pages FEBRUARY 22, 1974 20¢—OUTSIDE ILLINOIS—25¢

What the Muslims Want

This is the question asked most frequently by both the whites and the blacks. The answers to this question I shall state as simply as possible.

1. We want freedom. We want a full and complete freedom.

2. We want justice. Equal justice under the law. We want justice applied equally to all, regardless of creed or class or color.

3. We want equality of opportunity. We want equal membership in society with the best in civilized society.

4. We want our people in America whose parents or grandparents were descendants from slaves, to be allowed to establish a separate state or territory of their own—either on this continent or elsewhere. We believe that our former slave masters are obligated to provide such land and that the area must be fertile and minerally rich. We believe that our former slave masters are obligated to maintain and supply our needs in this separate territory for the next 20 to 25 years—until we are able to produce and supply our own needs. [59]

Since we cannot get along with them in peace and equality, after giving them 400 years of our sweat and blood and receiving in return some of the worst treatment human beings have ever experienced, we believe our contributions to this land and the suffering forced upon us by white America justifies our demand for complete separation in a state or territory of our own.

5. We want freedom for all Believers of Islam now held in federal prisons. We want freedom for all black men and women now under death sentence in innumerable prisons in the North as well as the South.

We want every black man and woman to have the freedom to accept or reject being separated from the slave master's children and establish a land of their own.

We know that the above plan for the solution of the black and white conflict is the best and only answer to the problem between two people.

6. We want an immediate end to the police brutality and mob attacks against the so-called Negro throughout the United States.

We believe that the Federal government should intercede to see that black men and women tried in white courts receive justice in accordance with the laws of the land—or allow us to build a new nation for ourselves, dedicated to justice, freedom and liberty.

7. As long as we are not allowed to establish a state or territory of our own, we demand not only equal justice under the laws of the United States, but equal employment opportunities—**NOW!**

We do not believe that after 400 years of free or nearly free labor, sweat and blood, which has helped America become rich and powerful, that so many thousands of black people should have to subsist on relief, charity or live in poor houses.

8. We want the government of the United States to exempt our people from ALL taxation as long as we are deprived of equal justice under the laws of the land.

9. We want equal education—but separate schools up to 16 for boys and 18 for girls on the condition that the girls be sent to women's colleges and universities. We want all black children educated, taught and trained by their own teachers.

Under such schooling system we believe we will make a better nation of people. The United States government should provide, free, all necessary text books and equipment, schools and college buildings. The Muslim teachers shall be left free to teach and train their people in the way of righteousness, decency and self respect.

10. We believe that intermarriage or race mixing should be prohibited. We want the religion of Islam taught without hinderance or suppression.

These are some of the things that we, the Muslims, want for our people in North America. [60]

accommodations and by employers and unions. It also set up the Equal Employment Opportunity Commission to prevent discriminatory hiring practices. In 1965, at Howard University in Washington, D. C. President Johnson discussed the rights of black Americans and outlined his proposal for future action. Pages 345–347 contain excerpts from that speech. As you read Johnson's position continue your evaluation of each alternative.

In our time change has come to this Nation. The American Negro, acting with impressive restraint, has peacefully protested and marched, entered the courtrooms and the seats of government, demanding a justice that has long been denied. The voice of the Negro was the call to action. But it is a tribute to America that, once aroused, the courts and the Congress, the President and most of the people, have been the allies of progress . . . .

The voting rights bill will be the latest, and among the most important, in a long series of victories. But this victory—as Winston Churchill said of another triumph for freedom—"is not the end. It is not even the beginning of the end. But it is perhaps, the end of the beginning."

That beginning is freedom. And the barriers to that freedom are tumb-

[59] Do you feel that establishing separate states for descendants of slaves will help solve the problem of racial conflict in America? Why, or why not?

[60] Do you think the demands of Elijah Muhammad are justified? Why, or why not?

ling down. Freedom is the right to share fully and equally in American society—to vote, to hold a job, to enter a public place, to go to school. It is the right to be treated in every part of our national life as a person equal in dignity and promise to all others.

But freedom is not enough. You do not wipe away the scars of centuries by saying: Now you are free to go where you want, do as you desire, and choose the leaders you please.

You do not take a person who, for years, has been hobbled by chains and liberate him, bring him up to the starting line of a race and then say, "You are free to compete with all the others," and still justly believe that you have been completely fair.

Thus it is not enough just to open the gates of opportunity. All of our citizens must have the ability to walk through those gates.

This is the next and more profound stage of the battle for civil rights. We seek not just freedom but opportunity—not just legal equity but human ability—not just equality as a right and a theory, but equality as a fact and as a result.

For the task is to give 20 million Negroes the same chance as every other American to learn and grow, to work and share in society, to develop their abilities—physical, mental, and spiritual, and to pursue their individual happiness.

To this end equal opportunity is essential, but not enough. Men and women of all races are born with the same range of abilities. But ability is not just the product of birth. Ability is stretched or stunted by the family you live with, and the neighborhood you live in, by the school you go to and the poverty or the richness of your surroundings. It is the product of a hundred unseen forces playing upon the infant, the child, and the man . . . .

But for the great majority of Negro Americans—the poor, the unemployed, the uprooted and the dispossessed—there is a much grimmer story. They still are another nation. Despite the court orders and the laws, despite the legislative victories and the speeches, for them the walls are rising and the gulf is widening.

Here are some of the facts of this American failure.

Thirty-five years ago the rate of unemployment for Negroes and whites was about the same. Today the Negro rate is twice as high.

In 1948 the 8 per cent unemployment rate for Negro teenage boys was actually less than that of whites. By last year that rate had grown to 23 per cent, as against 13 per cent for whites.

Between 1949 and 1959, the income of Negro men relative to white men declined in every section of this country. From 1952 to 1963 the median income of Negro families compared to white actually dropped from 57 per cent to 53 per cent.

In the years 1955 through 1957, 22 per cent of experienced Negro workers were out of work at some time during the year. In 1961 through 1963 that proportion had soared to 29 per cent.

Since 1947 the number of white families living in poverty has decreased 27 per cent, while the number of poor nonwhite families decreased only 3 per cent.

The infant mortality of nonwhites in 1940 was 70 per cent greater than whites. Twenty-two years later it was 90 per cent greater.[61]

Moreover, the isolation of Negroes from white communities is increasing, rather than decreasing, as Negroes crowd into the central cities and become a city within a city.

Of course Negro Americans as well as white Americans have shared in our rising national abundance. But the harsh fact of the matter is that in the battle for true equality too many are losing ground every day.

We are not completely sure why this is. The causes are complex and subtle. But we do know the two broad basic reasons. And we do know that we have to act.

First, Negroes are trapped—as many whites are trapped—in inherited, gateless poverty. They lack training and skills. They are shut in slums, without decent medical care. Private and public poverty combine to cripple their capacities.

We are trying to attack these evils through our poverty program, through our education program, through our medical care and our other health programs and a dozen more of the Great Society programs that are aimed at the root causes of this poverty.

We will increase, and accelerate, and broaden this attack in years to come until this most enduring of foes finally yields to our unyielding will. But there is a second cause—much more difficult to explain, more deeply grounded, more desperate in its force. It is the devastating heritage of long years of slavery; and a century of oppression, hatred and injustice . . . .

There is no single easy answer to all of these problems.

Jobs are part of the answer. They bring the income which permits a man to provide for his family.

Decent homes in decent surroundings, and a chance to learn—an equal chance to learn—are part of the answer.

Welfare and social programs better designed to hold families together are part of the answer.

Care of the sick is part of the answer.

An understanding heart by all Americans is also a large part of the answer . . . .

Operation Breadbasket

Many black leaders feel that the struggle for equal rights must now be won on the economic rather than on the political front. They argue that one cannot expect further civil rights legislation from a dominant white majority. Since 1966 the Rever-

[61]What, if anything, account for this increasing gap between white and black Americans?

end Jesse Jackson has successfully led one such economic fight in Chicago's South Side. "Operation Breadbasket's" success has now spread to eight other northern cities. The following article describes the program of "Operation Breadbasket."

. . . As the Chicago-based national director of the Southern Christian Leadership Conference's economic arm, Operation Breadbasket, the Rev. Jesse Jackson has effectively coerced some 15 companies in Chicago's heavily black South Side into opening up 5,000 new jobs for blacks in the past four years. At 28, he effectively bridges the widening gulf between the young activists and the old-style moralistic preachers. His strength is his use of evangelistic fervor to achieve practical ends. "You can be an orator or an organizer," he insists. "I am an organizer." Actually, he is a blend of both, and sometimes describes his occupation as that of a "moral engineer . . . ."

Some of Chicago's tough-minded businessmen have learned the hard way that Jesse Jackson is no country preacher. They have felt the black-pocketbook power of his Operation Breadbasket . . . Estimating the blacks constitute a consumer market that spends about $36 billion per year, Jackson says, "We are the margin of profit of every major item produced in America from General Motors cars down to Kellogg's Corn Flakes," he contends. "If we've got his margin of profit, we've got his genitals." Theoretically, if all blacks were to act together, that statement might be credible; practically, it is of course a vast exaggeration.

Appointed by Martin Luther King in 1966 to establish a Breadbasket office in Chicago, Jackson works out of a dingy building in the South Side ghetto. He began by gaining the support of many of the community's ministers. Their strategy was simple: they first demanded to see the employment records of a target company in their neighborhood. They then told the company how many more jobs it must offer to blacks and at what levels. It told them which black products must be displayed on their shelves. If the company would not sign a statement of agreement, the ministers spread the word: Do not buy there. [62]

The first firm that Breadbasket approached was a dairy, Country Delight Inc., which refused to disclose any of its records. On the following Sunday, the call for a boycott was heard in 100 black churches. Within three days, Country Delight agreed to offer 44 new or upgraded jobs to blacks—a full 20 per cent of its employment. It took ten days for Breadbasket to crack High-Low Foods, Inc., a Chicago grocery chain with 54 stores. It agreed to hire 183 blacks in jobs ranging from department managers to delivery boys. One badly managed grocery chain, Red Rooster, Inc., was boycotted by blacks who objected to its inferior meat. It could not take the pressure and went out of business. Its bitter president called Jackson "a liar and a phony,"

[62]Would you boycott a store that discriminates against minority groups in its hiring practices? Why, or why not?

while other white executives complained that they were being victimized by an extortionist. Obviously, however, blacks had long been more severely victimized by high prices, surly service and shoddy products, as well as job discrimination, in many ghetto stores.

Breadbasket's most spectacular success was its 16-week drive against A. & P., which operates more than 40 markets in Chicago's black neighborhoods. The chain finally surrendered. It not only signed a compact to hire 268 more blacks, including twelve as store managers and six as warehouse supervisors, but it agreed to stock some 25 black products, including Grove Fresh orange juice, Mumbo Barbecue Sauce, Staff of Life bread, Joe Louis milk and King Solomon spray deodorant, and to give them prominent display. A. & P. also agreed to use black-owned companies for its janitor services, garbage removal, and rodent extermination ("We have a monopoly on rats in the ghetto—and we're going to have a monopoly on killing them").

After that victory, Jackson's troops moved on to persuade neighborhood companies to do their banking in black banks and savings and loan associations. The combined assets of two such banks rose quickly from $5,000,000 to $22 million. Grocery chains were pressed into using black contractors to build their new stores in the ghetto. Many stores have given in to Breadbasket without any direct pressure at all because, as Jackson puts it, "they heard our footsteps coming."

With less success, but considerable potential, Jackson has set up other Breadbasket operations in Los Angeles, Milwaukee, Indianapolis, Brooklyn, Houston and Cleveland.

These efforts serve to strengthen blacks' conviction that they can eventually compete with whites, but in a sense these steps can offer only distant hopes for real interracial progress. Proud as he is of his pact with A. & P., Jesse Jackson concedes that it accomplished little toward eliminating racism in the Chicago area. "We didn't change, the hearts of the executives," he says. "We simply changed the behavior of the corporation. You don't strive for love between institutions; you strive for love between individuals and justice between institutions. And sometimes justice has its own way of creating, if not love, at least respect."

Respect will also come, as Jackson and many of his peers among the new black leaders see it, when the slowly expanding middle class in black communities commits itself more completely to racial progress rather than self-service. "The black doctor should study medicine in order to improve public health and not just to secure personal wealth," warns Jackson. "The black lawyer should study law to distribute justice, not just to secure a judgeship. The black teacher should teach to spread information and not want to tear the school down for a $10 raise."

Such a change would not erase racism overnight, but today's restive blacks insist that racism is a white, not a black problem. "When blacks are unemployed, they are considered lazy and apathetic," observes Jackson. "When whites are unemployed, it's considered a depression. That's racism . . ." But, in Jesse Jackson's apt summation: "There is still reason for optimism. But it is not based upon what the white man is going to do. It is based upon what we are going to do—and upon what we are going to make the Man do."[63]

Three other alternatives

Julian Bond, Whitney Young Jr., and Bobby Seale have all gained national reputations as black leaders. Each represents a different approach toward change.

In 1965 Julian Bond won election to the Georgia House of Representatives at the age of 25. Three years later he became the first black man to be nominated for vice-president at the Democratic National Convention.

In 1969 and 1970 Bobby Seale gained national prominence as the founder of the militant Black Panther Party and one of the original defendents in the Chicago conspiracy trial.

.Whitney Young Jr. heads the National Urban League and writes a nationally syndicated newspaper column, "To Be Equal." He frequently works with white businessmen to advance black causes.

In 1970 *Time* Correspondent Wallace Terry interviewed the three men. As you examine their answers to Terry's questions continue your evaluation of each alternative.

Where does the black American go from here in his drive for a racially equal society? What should he do?

Bond: We should develop greater unity in the black community. There ought be at least a community-wide consensus of what ought to be done, politically, socially, economically and educationally. In Atlanta, we're going to have two black candidates running in the same congressional district. Two black candidates can only hurt the prospect of one's being elected.

Young: Any further riots will be met with swift massive law enforcement, so riots as a possible tool quickly outlived their usefulness. There are three or four viable techniques. There is economic power, which can be mobilized to reward one's friends and punish one's enemies. There is brain power, where one can, through sheer competence, move into strategic places in the Establishment and from that vantage point have an influence on policy. And there is political power. Economic and brain power are both the best long-range instruments. The political can be mobilized immediately, and therein lies the hope for rapid change.

Seale: Black people, brothers and sisters in this country, have to move to a level of revolutionary struggle in terms of what we understand to be the true enemy, the enemy who perpetuates tyranny and oppression, poverty and

[63]Considering that white Americans outnumber blacks by 9 to 1 do you think Jesse Jackson's plan is realistic? Why? Why not?

the wretched conditions that we're subjected to in the black community. This enemy, as Eldrigde [Cleaver] always puts it, is at three levels of oppression: the big-time, tycooning, avaricious businessmen, the lying, demagogic, tricky politicians, and the fascist pig cops, militia, and pig agents who work for the avaricious, demogogic ruling class. Black people's direction should be to wage a relentless revolutionary struggle against the three levels of oppression. But it can't be handled alone by blacks. We need alliances with those whose own self-interest is to seek communities free of disorders.[64]

What are your recommendations for achieving black goals in the next ten years?

Bond: . . . Congress has to make good on its promises of almost 30 years years ago that every American will live in a decent home. You must guarantee full employment. You have to provide income maintenance for those who cannot earn an income. You need make-work programs. We should break the control of the unions over the skilled trades. It's ridiculous that in a city like New York you have so much difficulty getting a plumber. Why couldn't the plumbers' union let some blacks in? Fourth, we must improve the quality of primary and secondary schools, particularly among minority people. In some schools, a kid goes to school twelve years and comes out on the fifth-grade level.

Young: We must modify attitudes. This must start at the elementary-school level. This is why I pushed so hard for integration and desegregation. It can't wait until people get into high school. It's like that song in *South Pacific*, "You've got to be taught before you are six, or seven, or eight."

Seale: When we speak of what is to be accomplished, we have to deal with an understanding that the political, economic and social injustices that exist have to be solved with some practical program. The Panther party's free-breakfast program for children and its attack on hunger are related to where we're going. There are 15 million people in this country who are hungry, and 50 per cent of them are black, and when you move in this fashion, you start taking care of the children, because they will have to sustain the struggle.

What it's going to entail, though, is black people institutionalizing such programs in the community, where they have control over them. Even the poor white people have to oppose the system with these kinds of programs. It's a need for co-operative housing, cooperative marketing, more unity with the workers. The workers are going to have to start demanding a 30-hour work week with the same 40-hour pay. The poor oppressed are predominantly white unemployed. The courts have to be controlled more by the people, and the constitutional rights of the people are going to have to be secured.

What is your prescription for ending white racism in America?

[64]Do you think Seale's position would lead to more or less racial violence in America? Why, or why not?

Bond: It is part of the human condition, but it can be controlled. Government is the force to control it. If Government doesn't sanction it, its manifestations will be less severe. Some predicted that when lunch counters were integrated, blood would flow in the streets. But the Government said the counters would integrate. As resentful as white people were, and as much as white people dislike black people, blood didn't flow. There was no official Government sanction for it. Unfortunately, the Federal Government is sanctioning more racism today than five or ten years ago . . . You see Nixon trying to kill the Voting Rights Act of 1965 and trying to reverse the very slow process of desegregation. You see Congress trying to curb the work foundations have done among poor people. This is giving rise to overt acts of racism, like attacking school buses.

Young: We need to unleash all of the great researchers who have been spending all their time studying black people—and making money—onto the subject of white people to find out what in the world is wrong with that Man that makes him so obsessed with feeling superior. Why does he have to have somebody to feel superior to? I'd like to study why he wants to bring up his children in those bland, sterile, antiseptic, gilded ghettos, giving sameness to each other producing stagnation and uncreative people in a world that's become a neighborhood. Why does he want to teach his child to disrespect people because of their occupation or their race? I think there's a sickness here, and it ought to be studied by those same people who've been making their living revealing the pathologies of black people.[65]

Work must be done in the next few years to project the strengths of black people. We are seen always as a problem and a burden, never as an asset. I don't know of any other group of people who could have survived and grown, if they hadn't had some hidden assets like resilience and patience and soul, or whatever it is. We need to let white Americans know that we're talking not about cultural absorption but about cultural exchange. We don't know how to make napalm. They're smarter than we are on that. We don't know how to do price fixing. We don't know how to manipulate the stock market. But that apparently has not led to a very happy America, even at the very highest levels. When they begin to see that we bring something to the New Order, then this old condescending feeling of always giving and never taking will change.

Seale: What you have to do to end white racism is civilize white America. You have to educate the masses of white America to the trick bag that the power structure's putting them into.

[65]Do you agree with Whitney Young Jr. that researchers should begin to study the attitudes of white Americans? Why, or why not?

Busing as an alternative

In 1968 George Wallace, Governor of Alabama, ran as an independent for the office of President of the United States. In 1972 he campaigned for the Democratic nomination for President until an attempted assassination cut short his primary campaign. Wallace surprised many political experts with his primary victories in Florida, Tennessee, Michigan, and Maryland. In his primary speeches Wallace particularly emphasized his stand against busing of school children to achieve racial balance. In the final account of Assignment 28 writer Theodore White captures the Wallace position on busing from a number of the Governor's speeches.

He, George Wallace, was for the average man. The average man was being gutted by government. Taxes were important in George Wallace's message. "The greatest thing that exists in the air today is the unfair tax structure and you had better give tax relief to the average man in this country and put it on the filthy rich in Wall Street, or you . . . might wind up short at the next election period in the Unites States."

But, above all: busing. Busing was what really got to the average man. "This senseless business of trifling with the health and safety of your child, regardless of his color, by busing him across state lines, and city lines and . . . into kingdom come–has got to go." (Cheers.) This was "social scheming" imposed by "anthropologists, zoologists and sociologists." "The common people" should come together and say, "Our children are precious to us, and we want a stop to this busing." Or, in another speech, ". . . in China, the President asked Mousey Tongue [sic] for advice on busing and Mousey Tongue said, "I can't advise you on busing 'cause when I take a notion to bus 'em and they don't like it, I just bus 'em anyhow.' And that's just about the way they're doing it here." And, "Busin' . . . it's the most atrocious, callous, cruel, asinine thing you can do for little children . . . these hypocrites who live over in Maryland or Virginia and they've got their children in a private school . . . tomorrow the chickens are coming home to roost. They gonna be sorry they bused your little children and had somethin' to do with it. So, my friends, you give 'em a good jolt tomorrow. You give 'em the St. Vitus Dance."[66]

For thought and discussion

What other alternatives can you think of to solve the problem of racial conflict in America?

[66]Do you think busing to achieve racial balance would increase or decrease racial conflict? Why?

Individual and small group activities

1. What has been the history of race relations in your city? Examine old newspapers and other historical data to determine the recent (1960's) history of race relations in your own city. If your city experienced violence in the 1960's find out what has been done to improve conditions since then. If your city remained peaceful in the 1960's interview black and white citizens and government officials to determine how your city managed to escape violence. Report your findings to your class.
2. In 1963 Martin Luther King Jr. wrote a letter to a group of black ministers defending his tactics of civil disobedience. In his letter Reverend King argues that, "there are two types of laws: There are just *laws* and there are *unjust* laws." He states that, "One has a legal responsibility to obey just laws but, one also has a moral responsibility to disobey unjust laws." Ask your librarian for a copy of Reverend King's letter and examine his reasoning for this statement. Do you agree or disagree with him? Prepare a statement defending your position for your next class.

Protecting public order: Stating the issue for Assignments 29 and 30

In Assignment 27 you examined the history of violence as a response to racial inequities in America. Acts of violence against private citizens have also occurred quite frequently throughout American History. Since 1900, nearly 800,000 Americans have been killed by privately owned guns. During the last decade we witnessed the assassination of a president, a senator, and a civil rights leader. In 1966 Richard Speck killed eight nurses in Chicago and Charles Whitman shot 46 persons from a clock tower at the University of Texas in Austin. People became so concerned with crime and violence that Richard Nixon successfully campaigned for president in 1968 on a law and order platform.

During the first three years of the 1970's spectacular murders claimed lives in Texas, California, and New Mexico. The Federal Bureau of Investigation reported more than 15,000 murders each year since 1970. In addition, another five million persons are victims of robbery, rape, burglary, and other serious crimes. All of these facts support the conclusion of the President's Commission on the Causes and Prevention of Violence that "Americans are a bloody-minded people both in action and reaction."

Most violence, of course, occurs in or near large cities. Many people now express fear when traveling the streets of some cities at mid-afternoon. Others have fled the city in hopes of escaping violence. Yet many experts insist that abandoning the city will not solve the problem of urban crime. In fact, recent trends indicate that crime is now following the wealthier Americans to the suburbs. The experts, however, argue that better law enforcement procedures and cooperation between police and private citizens can curb violence in the American city.

Assignments 29 and 30 deal with the issue of protecting public order. In Assignment 29 you will examine some graphs, police reports, and several written accounts to determine the nature of urban violence. Assignment 30 provides a number of suggested alternatives to solve the problem of crime in the cities. You should evaluate each alternative and decide which ones will make our cities safer.

Protecting public order (1)

Assignment 29

During the last decade urban Americans have expressed a growing concern with rising crime rates. In a recent *Life* magazine poll nearly 80 per cent of all respondents said that they sometimes feel unsafe in their own homes. Another 80 per cent, living in large cities, expressed fear walking in the streets at night. One respondent commented: "the old idea that America is the home of the free and the brave is the biggest paradox of all time. America is actually the home of the imprisoned and the scared." Many Americans wonder what can be done to prevent the spread of crime and make our cities safe places in which to live. However, before we begin to speculate upon solutions to the problem of crime in the streets we must understand the nature of the problem. Assignment 29 provides you with information about crime in urban America. Examine this evidence and make a list of the factors which you think help explain the problem of urban crime. You should include factors you learned in earlier Assignments as well as those contained within this Assignment. When you have completed Assignment 29 answer the following questions.

1. What types of crimes seem to be the greatest threat to urban Americans?
2. What solutions can you suggest to make our cities safer?

Living with crime

Some critics suggest that the situation does not justify our fear. They contend that the news media, particularly television, over-dramatizes violent crime creating unwarranted fears. Others admit the problem exists but point to undertrained, overworked police as the major cause. Assignment 29 contains a variety of data about crime and police in urban United States. As you examine these data attempt to form your own conclusions about the nature of crime in the cities.

National crime statistics

The tables on pages 357–361 will help you to determine recent trends in urban crime. Examine each table and begin to list the factors which you think contribute to urban crime.

Figure 29.1
The increase in violent crime in the last decade, 1963–73

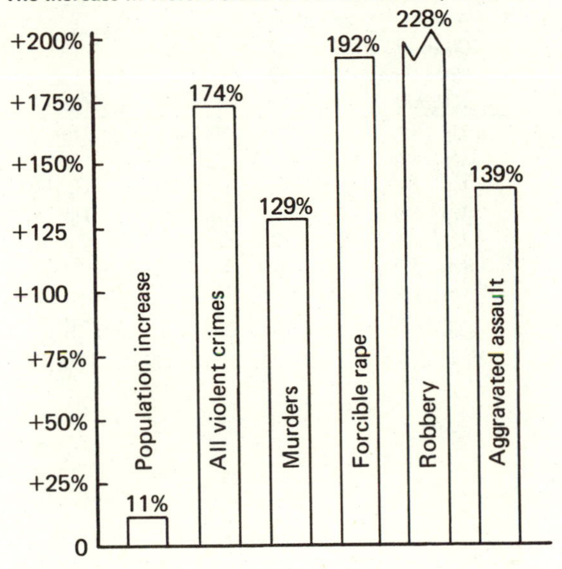

Table 29.1
Rise in crime in selected areas—Serious crimes in 1971 compared with 1970

Suburban areas	Up 11%
Rural areas	Up 10%
Cities under 25,000	Up 12%
Cities 25,000 to 100,000	Up 10%
Cities 100,000 to 500,000	Up 6%
Cities 500,000 to 1 million	Down 3%
Cities over 1 million	Up 3%

Note: Crimes reported include murder, forcible rape, robbery, aggravated assault, burglary larceny over $50 and auto theft.

Source: Federal Bureau of Investigation

Table 29.2
National trends in crime 1971 compared with 1970
(Reprinted from *U. S. News & World Report*)

Types of crime	*Cities of More than 250,000*	*Cities of 100,000-250,000*	*Suburbs*	*Rural*	*Over all*
Murder	Up 10%	Up 13%	Up 6%	Up 2%	Up 11%
Rape	Up 8%	Up 16%	Up 10%	Up 7%	Up 11%
Robbery	Up 8%	Up 16%	Up 17%	Up 11%	Up 11%
Assault	Up 6%	Up 11%	Up 12%	Up 5%	Up 10%
Burglary	Up 4%	Up 9%	Up 11%	Up 6%	Up 9%
Larceny	Down 3%	Up 4%	Up 13%	Up 9%	Up 7%
Auto theft	Down 1%	Up 2%	Up 6%	Down 1%	Up 2%
All serious crimes	Up 2%	Up 7%	Up 11%	Up 6%	Up 7%

Figure 29.2

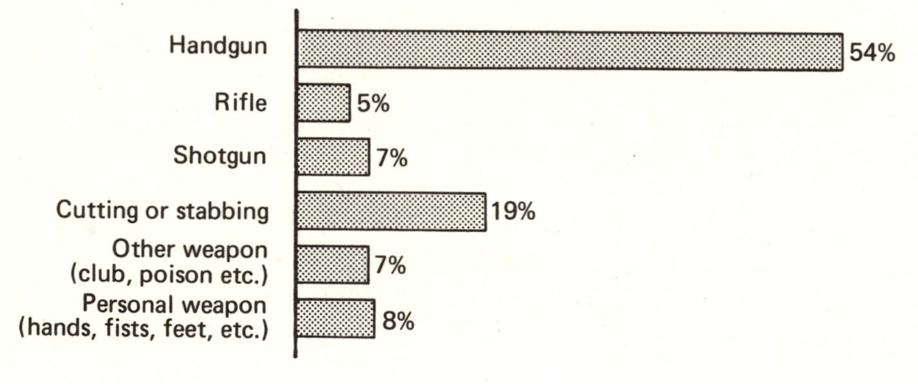

Table 29.3
Big city crime, 1971
In the nation's 50 largest cities, FBI figures for 1971 on serious crimes revealed that:

22 cities showed drop		*28 cities showed rise*	
Cities	*Decrease in 1971, compared with 1970*	*Cities*	*Increase in 1971, compared with 1970*
Seattle, Wash.	14%	El Paso, Tex.	40%
Washington, D. C.	13%	Philadelphia, Pa.	34%
Baltimore, Md.	12%	Cincinnati, Ohio	26%
Fort Worth, Tex.	11%	San Jose, Calif.	23%
Oakland, Calif.	11%	Nashville, Tenn.	17%
Indianapolis, Ind.	10%	Portland, Oreg.	14%
Louisville, Ky.	10%	Oklahoma City, Okla.	14%
Rochester, N. Y.	10%	Boston, Mass.	11%
Dallas, Tex.	8%	Buffalo, N. Y.	11%
Pittsburgh, Pa.	7%	San Diego, Calif.	10%
Omaha, Nebr.	5%	Memphis, Tenn.	10%
Jacksonville, Fla.	4%	Atlanta, Ga.	10%
Kansas City, Mo.	4%	Milwaukee, Wis.	9%
St. Paul, Minn.	4%	Newark, N. J.	9%
St. Louis, Mo.	3%	Long Beach, Calif.	9%
Houston, Tex.	2%	Birmingham, Ala.	6%
San Antonio, Tex.	2%	Los Angeles, Calif.	5%
Tulsa, Okla.	2%	Cleveland, Ohio	4%
Tampa, Fla.	1%	Phoenix, Ariz.	4%
Chicago, Ill., Denver, Colo. and Detroit, Mich.	under 1%	Miami, Fla.	4%
		Norfolk, Va.	4%
		Columbus, Ohio	3%
		Toledo, Ohio	3%
		New York, N. Y.	2%
		Minneapolis, Minn.	2%
		Honolulu, Hawaii	2%
		San Francisco, Calif.	1%
		New Orleans, La.	under 1%

Note: Serious crime is defined as murder, forcible rape, robbery, aggravated assault, burglary, auto theft or larceny of $50 or more. Changes from 1970 may be influenced by increased surveillance and reporting of crimes. Source: Federal Bureau of Investigation.

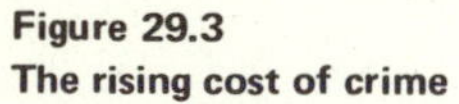

Figure 29.3
The rising cost of crime

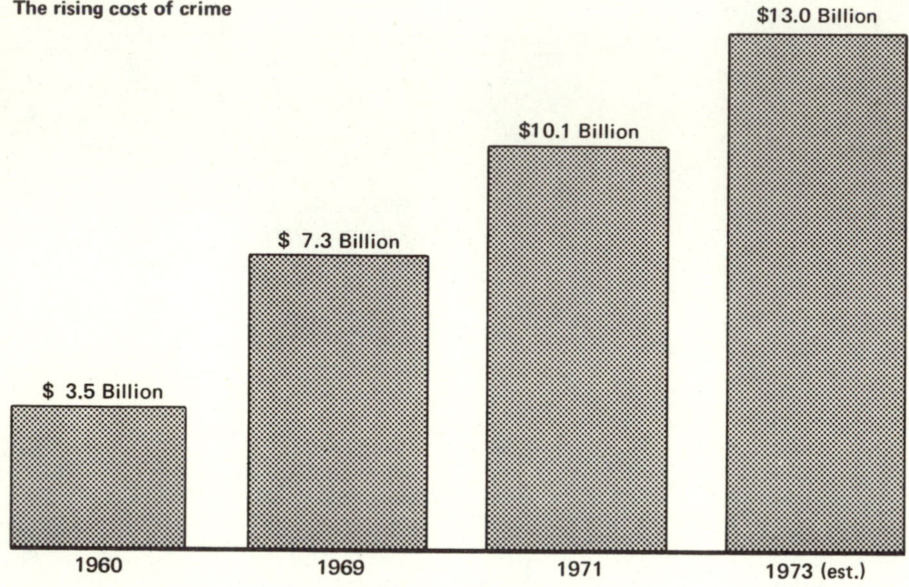

Years ended June 30

Figure 29.4
Who pays for law enforcement?

Estimate for year ended June 30, 1971–

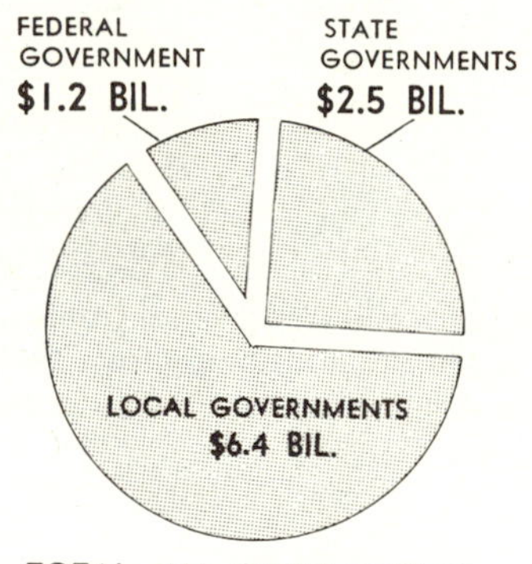

TOTAL, ALL GOVERNMENTS
$10.1 BILLION

Figure 29.5

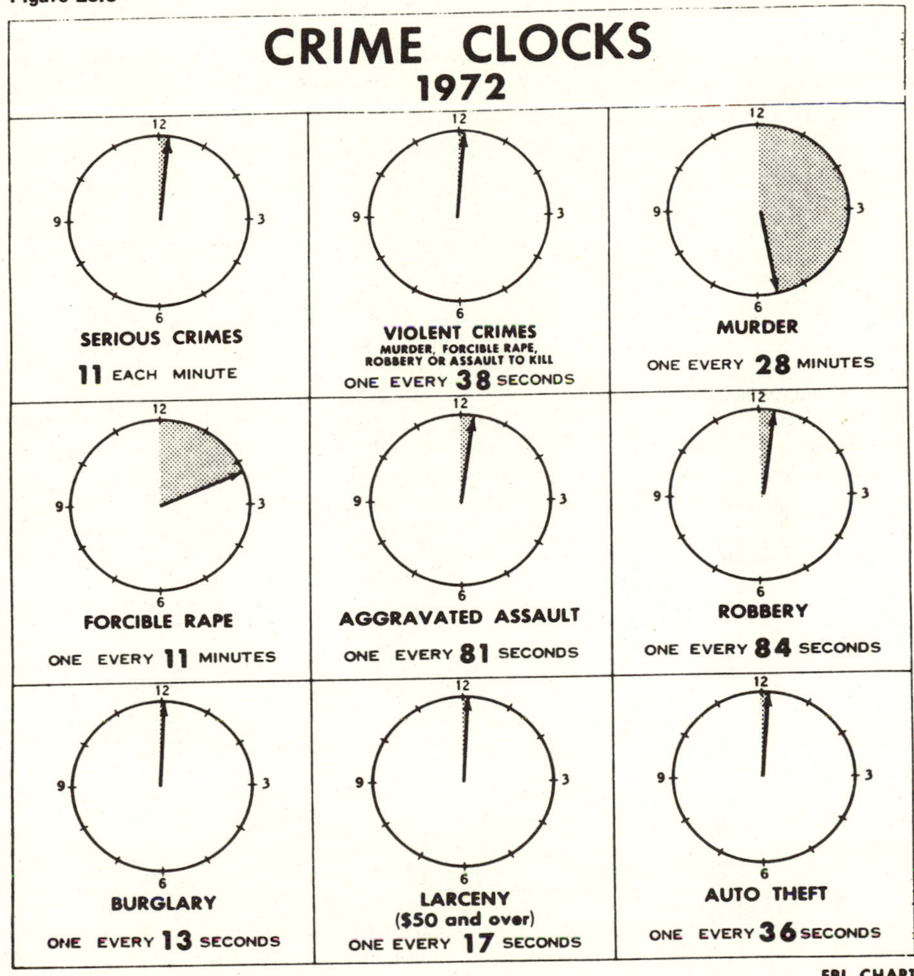

FBI CHART

Crime in one American city, 1972

Pages 362–363 of Assignment 29 provide statistics about crime in one American city. This city contains approximately one-half of one million people and has a police force of 1,800 persons. During 1972 this city spent more than $23 million on law enforcement. These statistics, however, could come from any city of its size in the nation. As you analyze these statistics try to determine which incidents might occupy the greatest amount of a police force's time.

Table 29.4
Major crimes—1972

	All offenses		*All offenses*
Murder and nonnegligent manslaughter	51	Assaults, other (non-aggravated)	2499
Manslaughter by negligence	45	Arson	224
Rape by force	191	Forgery and counterfeiting	98
Assault to rape and attempts	129	Fraud	330
Robbery, armed	1461	Embezzlement	24
Robbery, strong-arm	1219	Stolen Property	71
Assault, gun	318	Vandalism	4287
Assault, knife or cutting instr.	501	Weapons, carrying, possession, etc.	508
Assault, other weapon	764	Prostitution and commercialized vice	49
Assault, other aggravated	254	Sex offenses (except 2 and 16)	407
Burglary, forcible entry	5002	Narcotic drug laws	1184
Burglary, unlawful entry	2158	Gambling	391
Burglary, attempted	751	Family and children	57
Larceny, $50 and over	4795	D. U. I. L.	639
Larceny, under $50	4677	Liquor laws	102
Auto theft	6145	Drunkenness	9077
		Disorderly conduct	1084
		Vagrancy	194
		All others (except traffic)	1285
		Totals	50,971

Table 29.5
Calls for aid and services—1972 summary
(One American city)

Complaint Classification	*Amount*	*Percentage of total*
Abandoned cars	3632	1.41
Assault and battery reports	4176	1.61
Accident reports (traffic)	18940	7.34
Aided-injury reports	31551	12.22
Animal (bites)	4338	1.67
Animal (concerning)	436	.17
Bank robbery	56	.02
Box call	9932	3.85
Burglary reports	13759	5.33
Burglar alarms	11133	4.31
Burning rubbish	366	.14
Cars (recovered-stolen) reports	15527	6.01
Complainant, see	18434	7.14
Demonstration-riots	75	.03
Details	5314	2.06
Detours	16	.00
Disorderly man (woman)	7872	3.05
Domestic disturbance	10811	4.19
Explosions	543	.21
Fallen trees, wires, etc.	1328	.51
Fight on street	3515	1.36
Fires	5368	2.06
Fireworks	458	.17
Gambling	158	.06
Gas (water) leaks	483	.18
Intoxication	3921	1.51
Juveniles	14455	5.60
Larceny reports	7723	3.03
Loitering	180	.07
Malicious mischief-vandalism	6322	2.45
Man with gun-knife	2388	.92
Mental case	1045	.40
Murder-manslaughter	49	.02
Notifications	1016	.39
Noisy gang-party	7849	3.04
Officer in trouble	200	.08
Playing in street	765	.29
Parked car (suspicious)	1599	.62
Persons missing	1642	.64
Prowler	2847	1.10
Purse snatch report	1130	.44
River incidents	12	.00
Roadblocks	104	.04
Robbery reports	2233	.88
Sex offenses	870	.34
Shooting-stabbing	901	.35
Traffic tie-ups	975	.38
Traffic violations	14409	5.58
Unlocked doors	729	.28
Miscellaneous	16665	6.45
Total	258250	100.00

Activities of two urban policemen

The typical urban policeman graduated from high school, has six years experience on the police force, and receives between $9,000 and $13,000 per year. Training usually consists of 12 to 16 weeks at a police academy and on-the-job experience. The following account, taken from an actual tour of duty of two patrol car police officers, will help you to determine responsibilities of these men.

5:30 P. M.–We check locks on several businesses on Perrysville, drive past several schools that often are teenage hangouts, then check two homes being built on Cherryland Street.

6:05–We're called back to No. 9 Station to deliver the day's arrest reports to the Public Safety Building, Downtown. There we quickly tour the radio dispatch center where civilians man the emergency phones–a police job until a few years ago. "I'm in favor of letting civilians handle these jobs, provided they're well trained," officer Bahur said. But he indicated some apprehension. "You don't want to get a call the 'see the complaintant' and walk in on a guy with a gun," officer Oggier said.

6:30–Back in our district, Oggier and I stop at a donut shop on East Ohio Street. Bahur stays in the car, listening to the police radio. The job doesn't include a lunch hour. You eat when you can, knowing you might have to leave it on the counter.

6:40–Report of a disorderly gang at Perrysville and Wilson. The corner is deserted when we arrive five minutes later. "You can always tell a neighborhood by the amount of glass on the street," Bahur said pointing to a beer bottle on the sidewalk. "I lived in Manchester for 17 years. We weren't rich but everyone took pride in keeping the place clean," he said.

7:15–Oggier stops to ticket two cars beside a fire hydrant on Federal Street.

7:20–We see perhaps a dozen teenagers beside McNaugher School on Maple Avenue. The kids flee at the sight of the police car, leaving three quarts of beer which Oggier pours in the gutter.

7:35–Report of a purse snatching in West Park sends us speeding to the scene. Two squad cars, two wagons, one unmarked car and a park police jeep are already there. Two juveniles are apprehended quickly. "A slap on the fingers and a 'Don't do it again boys,' " Oggier says as we hear of the arrests on the radio. "They'll be out on the street tomorrow," Bahur adds.

7:42–Fire truck with red lights flashing and siren blaring roars up Monterly Street and we follow. Firemen put out a car engine fire and we take the report, checking the license number via radio through a computer to see if the car was stolen. We learn in three minutes that it wasn't.

8 P. M.–"Burglary in progress" at Cowley School. We rush over to find lights on and doors broken open. Inside the place is a mess. Vandals have broken windows, ripped doors off hinges, spilled paint on the floors and dumped contents of filing cabinets everywhere. The school had been closed for months.

8:45–A broken window at 205 Jackson St., several blocks away. Kids in the back of a passing pickup truck threw a rock through the living room window.

9:55–Six teenagers on the corner of Meadville and Cemetery Streets. Two of the boys are hiding beer cans under their shirts. "Is that getting cold on your side there?" Oggier asks.

"Yeah, it sure is," one of the boys answers with a laugh. He agrees to pour the contents into the gutter.

10:10–Report of a man stripping a car in Northview Heights. It turns out he is merely changing his tires.

10:55–On the way to a domestic in Northview Heights, we are rerouted to an "accident with injuries" in the 3200 Block of Perrysville. There were no injuries. A speeding car had smashed into an unoccupied parked car, then drove away. "He's gone, you'll never find him now," a neighbor said after returning from a futile chase in his car.

But Oggier points to a small wet spot on the pavement near the crumpled compact car, noting that the fleeing car apparently has a damaged radiator. "We'll get him for you," he tells the upset woman owner. We move out on Perrysville following the water marks like footprints. "I figure as far as he could go is Penford and Mt. Pleasant without burning up his car," Oggier said. "Probably a kid." . . . .

"I think we got him," Oggier shouted pulling up behind a parked car and dashing out to check its smashed front end–steam still rising from a broken radiator. A young man in his mid 20's sauntered over, admitted he had been driving his father's car, then asked: "What's the problem here?"

He got a ticket for leaving the scene of an accident which both Oggier and Bahur said probably would be thrown out in traffic court because they didn't actually see him driving the car. "He could barely stand up but we couldn't give him a drunken driving ticket," Bahur said, "You can't prove he was driving." "At least the woman will know who to collect damages from," Oggier said.

They returned to the station at 11:45 P. M. after 69 miles on rough city streets. It was someone else's turn at the wheel.

Crime: A growing threat

Many urban Americans live in constant fear of being mugged or raped. Some refuse to go out of doors at night. Others carry mace, clubs, or handguns to protect themselves in the streets. These fears, says one psychologist, are creating a fortress mentality in America. Yet crimes of violence, particularly rape, continue to increase. Pages 365–367 of this assignment illustrate the extent of the problem of crime in urban America.

Billions of dollars have been spent in recent years to improve law enforcement–yet crime has continued to rise, and many Americans are worried about whether it can ever be brought under control.

All sorts of new crime-fighting techniques have been tried. Police forces have been enlarged in almost every city. Local spending on law enforcement has multiplied more than 7 times—up from less than 1 billion dollars in 1964 to more than 7 billion in 1973. The U. S. Government, through its Law Enforcement Assistance Administration, has poured in an additional 3.5 billion dollars in the last five years to help state and local crime-fighting agencies.

For one brief period, it appeared that real progress was being made. In 1972 came the first decline in 17 years in the number of major crimes. That was hailed by the Nixon Administration as an indication that the corner had at last been turned. But the hope proved short-lived. In 1973, crime increased again—up 5 per cent over 1972. Then came a study by the Law Enforcement Assistance Administration indicating that the crime is really far worse than shown in official reports.

Less than half the crimes actually committed are even reported to the police, according to that study, released in April. In some cities it appeared, the number of crimes committed was as high as five times the number reported.

A nationwide poll taken by Phillips-Sindlinger in March, showed 40 per cent of all people interviewed were afraid to walk the streets at night. In major metropolitan areas, the number was even higher—67 per cent.

A result of all this, the poll showed, is a decline in public confidence in the police. In large metropolitan areas, 32 per cent of those polled said they had less confidence in their local police than they did five years ago. Only 17 per cent had more confidence.

It is not only the citizen—the victim of all this crime—who has become disillusioned. There is a great feeling of frustration among police and law-enforcement officials as well. "Look at all the things we've tried," they say, in effect, "and still crime continues to rise."

To find out what things have been tried—and how they worked—members of the staff of *U. S. News & World Report* made a survey of major cities throughout the country.

Operating on the seemingly logical theory that more police might be the answer, authorities in some cities have increased their law enforcement forces substantially during the last decade. Results were mixed, inconclusive.

In Chicago, the police force was expanded by nearly one third—from 10,269 in 1964 to 13,125 in 1972. Yet the number of reported crimes rose by 4,435 in that period. Then, in 1973, violent crimes went up 5 per cent and property crimes 11 per cent.

Los Angeles enlarged its police force by 37 per cent—from 5,181 in 1964 to 7,083 in 1972. In that eight-year period, the number of crimes jumped by 70,767. Finally, in 1973, there came an improvement; violent crimes went down 5 per cent and property crimes went down 7 per cent.

Washington D. C. is commonly cited as one city where increasing the number of police paid off. The nations capital after gaining a reputation as being the crime capital, increased its police force by 55 per cent in a three-year period beginning in late 1968. A dramatic drop in crime followed, down 38 per cent between 1969 and 1973.

Most cities, traditionally short of money have been unable to extend their law enforcement services very much. During the eight years from 1964 to 1972, the nation's total of municipal officers grew less than 12 per cent, from 360,000 in 1964 to 400,000 in 1972. Since the population of the country grew at roughly the same percentage rate, the ratio of police to civilians changed very little.

Safe cities

Crime does not occur in all cities at the same rate. In fact, some cities have relatively little crime. Recently David Franke, co-author of *Safe Places* examined the crime statistics of 396 major American cities. He found a number of safe cities. The following accounts contain descriptions of four of these cities. As you read these accounts try to determine the reasons for the absence of crime in these areas. What, if anything, does this suggest about preventing crime in your own city?

Lakewood, Ohio

America's safest city is right next door to Cleveland, America's three hundred fifty-first safest city (and *that's* not very safe). The oldest suburb in the metropolitan area, Lakewood has three miles of Lake Erie shore front lined by high rises and middle-class-to-plush homes in a bewildering variety of architectural designs.

The crime rate is kept down in Lakewood by bright mercury-vapor streetlights, a seventy-five-man police force, and criminal files that the Lakewood Police Department claims are the best in the area. In addition, local business is zoned to keep it apart from the residential areas.

Lakewood's civic pride extends beyond crime prevention. Its community-owned and operated hospital has been extensively modernized and two ambulances are on duty at all times. Project Pride is the city's program of inspecting homes for electrical, plumbing, heating, and structural defects. Lakewood has earned thirteen national awards as the "fire-safest" city in the 50,000-to-100,000 population bracket.

Explaining how he and his wife came to live in Lakewood, Ray Biesmeyer, Cleveland manager for *House & Garden*, recalls that "we started out by disappointing a couple of real-estate men in Shaker Heights. The first time we drove through, we were impressed by the way Lakewood homes and yards were maintained. Yet, at the same time, we felt a lack of pretension. It didn't look as if there were two cars in every garage and a second mortgage on every house."

Nashua, New Hampshire

Nashua is a boom town. Its population has increased 42.8 per cent in the last decade, and now stands at 55,820. Located on the Massachusetts border, it has easy access to Boston, the White Mountains, and the Maine coast.

Half of Nahua's work force is employed by manufacturers, and half is unionized. The town's major industries are electronic equipment, shoes, paper goods, plastics, and machinery. Like most New England industrial towns, Nashua has a population divided between many ethnic groups.

Police Chief Craig D. Sandler feels that Nashua owes its low crime rate in large measure to the fact that "the Nashua police are free from local politics with regard to enforcement policy." He notes that since 1913 "the department has been governed by a three-man Police Commission appointed by the Governor of the state. The Commission has power to set compensation, hire and dismiss as the situation may dictate, and establish rules and regulations as necessary."

Provo, Utah

Among America's ten safest cities, Provo is unique in a number of respects. It is the only Western city on the list. It has a high unemployment rate, and its average annual family income ($7,167) ranks tenth of ten, but there are no slums in Provo. Finally, Provo is a university town. While Berkeley and Cambridge are among the most dangerous cities in the country, Provo is home to an equally large but vastly different academic population–Mormon-run Brigham Young University, whose 25,000 students make it one of the largest private universities in the U. S.

Police Chief Jesse Evans emphasizes the role of Provo's many programs to combat juvenile delinquency in controlling crime. During the Nineteen Forties and early Fifties, he says, "we had a tremendous problem of malicious destruction, and many burglaries. We learned that the majority of the crimes were being committed by juveniles and teen-agers." Police, courts, civic groups, churches, service clubs, schools, and the parks department put together an ambitious youth program that is still in effect and has, apparently paid off.

Greenwich, Connecticut

Affluence usually attracts criminals, but not in Greenwich. U. S. Census statisticians have apparently given up trying to estimate the median value of Greenwich homes; it is listed merely as "$50,000." There are 10,635 houses worth more than $25,000, only 526 worth less.

Greenwich is the sort of town where many of the rambling estates may be seen only by following a network of bridle trails; where there are several hundred *private* fire hydrants; where the police, in addition to the usual police services, maintain a scuba team.

Delinquency and drug usage among the spoiled children of the executives class are reputedly rampant on Connecticut's Gold Coast–everywhere but Greenwich. The town stands alone, an emerald island of calm against a troubled sea of life's commoner annoyances. As the Chamber of Commerce puts it, "There is no heavy industry and therefore no noise or odors."

For thought and discussion

What, if anything, accounts for the rise of violent crime in America during the last decade?

Individual and small group activities

1. With a group of your classmates list all the things an individual could do to prevent harm to himself or herself on the streets at night. Your list should include suggestions about what to do if one is stopped by a would-be thief. Ditto enough copies of your completed list of suggestions to hand out in class.
2. Make an appointment to interview the Superintendent of Police in your own city. Find out which types of crimes are increasing in your city. What recommendations do the police have to deal with these crimes?

Protecting public order (2)

Assignment 30

Many Americans are seeking new ways to prevent the spread of violent crime. In some cities law enforcement officers, judges, criminologists, and private citizens joined together to examine alternative solutions. In other cities citizen action groups established private police forces or hired guards to protect themselves and their communities. Assignment 30 contains descriptions of a number of these alternative solutions. Examine each alternative and determine which ones provide the best solutions to the problem of urban crime. Use the list of factors contributing to urban crime, which you compiled for Assignment 29 to help you complete your analysis. Remember to consider the consequences of each alternative.

Reforming the police

In 1968 President Lyndon Johnson appointed a commission to study the problem of crime in America. The President's Commission on Law Enforcement and the Administration of justice recommended the reorganization of police departments throughout the country. The following three accounts suggest some ways to increase the effectiveness of law enforcement agencies.

Many cities are seeking alternatives to larger police forces as ways of getting more officers on the street.

One alternative: civilians are being hired to replace policemen in non-law enforcement functions, such a clerical, maintenance and motor-pool jobs. This leaves uniformed officers formerly doing those jobs free to concentrate on law enforcement. The civilians do not require as much specialized training and generally receive less pay than police officers. A recent survey of 41 medium-sized cities revealed that, on the average 17 per cent of their police-department personnel were civilians.

Other police departments across the country are experimenting with different ways of patrolling the streets.

Kansas City, MO. with the assistance of the privately financed Police Foundation, engaged in a program of trying to find out which kind of patrol is most effective in deterring crime. During the year ending last September 30, three types of patrols were tried. In some areas, a single car roamed the streets, as had been done for years. In other areas, four or five vehicles were assigned to provide highly intensive patrols. In still other areas, no cars were assigned to regular patrols, but police were dispatched to answer specific calls for assistance.

Results: officials were startled to find that the total cars on patrol seemed to have little effect on the amount of crime in an area. Said a police spokesman, "We wanted to find out whether a conspicuous police patrol acts as a deterrent, and we found that it did not."

Almost every large city and many smaller ones have established "tactical" police units, small highly mobile groups of officers which can be used against many types of crime problems in the city. One tactic is to put both male and female officers on the street in plain clothes as "stake-outs," or decoys, to catch criminals in the act.

This tactic, sometimes called "zero visibility patrol", is meeting with some success. In New York City, the nation's largest decoy patrol is credited with making 23 per cent of all felony arrests. In Atlanta a similar program accounts for 45 per cent of all arrests at the scene of the crime. Says Major D.M. Edwards, head of the Atlanta Police planning and research division, "It is better than anything else we have tried. I think it will work in any city."

Another special unit being tried by many cities is the anti-terrorist team. Such teams are trained by the FBI in the use of military weapons and tactics to combat the growing number of snipers and bands of self-styled guerrillas. It was such a police unit in Los Angeles, called "SWAT" for "Special Weapons and Tactics," that recently raided a house occupied by six members of the Symbionese Liberation Army which kidnaped Patricia Hearst. All six of the SLA members died in the raid.

Still another technique being tried in some cities is something called "team policing." This is an effort to get away from the citywide patrols and back to neighborhood beats. The idea is that police officers work best when they know the area and the people they are protecting and the people know and trust the police. Cities which use team policing, in various forms, include New York, Los Angeles, Detroit, Dayton, and Syracuse. However, the technique is regarded with suspicion by a number of police officials who are afraid that it reduces discipline and encourages police corruption.

Millions of dollars are being spent on new kinds of equipment for police. Helicopters, tested in the Vietnam war, are being used for aerial patrols or to swoop down on criminals. They are found effective in speeding police response to a crime call, and the aircraft can hover at low speeds to observe suspicious activity on the ground.

In Atlanta, residential burglaries declined in an area patrolled by helicopters. But the choppers irritate some residents by the noise they make.

One city after another has installed computers to handle many police duties. Used most effectively, computers and speed identification of suspects, determine the most efficient deployment of police manpower, analyze crime trends and evaluate methods of crime control. The spread of computers is stirring fears, however. Civil libertarians warn that computer banks already contain potentially damaging information about millions of Americans. They say safeguards must be placed on the use of that information to prevent unwarranted invasions of citizens' privacy. (Copyright, 1974, *U.S. News & World Report.*)

The women in blue

Family quarrels are a recurring nightmare for policemen, who frequently end up on the receiving end of a warring couple's wrath. In an effort to be more effective at peacemaking, an increasing number of police departments are now trying a new strategy. They are sending police-women to do what was once strictly a male cop's job. The reason: women seem to calm these disputes far better than men. "Some of these families will call you back two or three times a night," observed a battle-tested Indianapolis patrolman, "but I've noticed that when the women go, that's the last time we hear from that family."

Women are also being assigned to other police duties traditionally reserved for men. In at least seven cities, lady cops are driving squad cars, responding to radio calls and investigating crimes. Their experience to date indicates that their sex does not handicap them on the job. Indeed, for the service calls that account for 80 per cent to 90 per cent of police activity, it may be an asset.

In the family quarrel, for example, male officers "feed the fire through their own aggressive, provocative behavior," says Lewis J. Sherman, a University of Missouri-St. Louis psychologist who studied the activities of security guards in eight St. Louis housing projects last summer. Women, on the other hand stepped in "with greater tact and sublety. They tended to stay longer and seemed much more concerned about getting to the root causes of the conflict." The women had another advantage: a built-in "calming effect," discovered during psychodramas that were part of the guards' training. Enraged men, Sherman found, "simply could not respond as angrily or violently to the women as to the men."

This feminine capacity to dispel male anger (also observed in studies of aides in mental wards) may be due to the value system of male criminals: assaults on male authority figures are ranked high. Policemen are often attacked "because it is heroic," says Ronald G. Talney of the Multinomah County, Ore., sheriff's department. But policewomen might avoid such assaults simply because "it is cowardly to attack a woman, even though she is a police officer." Actual incidents seem to support Talney's view: a child-beating suspect who had twice resisted arrest surrendered peacefully when Private Mary Ellen Abrecht and two Washington patrolmen came to his door.

Such experiences suggest that more women on the beat could mean less use of force by police, contends Catherine H. Milton, assistant director of the Police Foundation, an organization that promotes new methods of law enforcement. Her prodding is apparently winning some converts among police chiefs. About 45 women are currently pounding police beats across the U.S., and the first large-scale experiment in the use of patrolwomen is under way in Washington, D.C., where the metropolitan police force is hiring 100 women for regular patrol duty.[67] Still, resistance to the trend–mostly from officials who think being a patrolman is too dangerous for the "weaker sex"–must be overcome before many more of the nation's 6,000 policewomen (out of 400,000 police) are assigned to the streets.

Those who are there already have provided a devastating new weapon to the police crime-fighting arsenal, one that has helped women to get their men for centuries. It worked well for diminutive Patrolwoman Ina Sheperd after she collared a muscular shoplifter in Miami last December and discovered that there were no other cops–or even a telephone–around. Unable to summon to help, she burst into tears. "If I don't bring you in. I'll lose my job" she sobbed to her prisoner, who chivalrously accompanied her until a squad car could be found.

Views of a career policeman

Inspector William Moore is not a typical policeman. During his 22 years as a member of one of America's largest city police forces he has seen violent crime, race riots, and police corruption. Yet, he maintains a sense of humor and a sincere concern for the well-being of the city's citizens. He began his career as a patrolman walking a beat in 1951. He rose steadily through the ranks and became one of America's higher ranking black policemen.

"Police work has changed a great deal since I joined the force," says Inspector Moore. "Police in the 1950's received little training, most of it dealing with defining arrests and traffic violations. The riots of the 1960's changed all that. We're more concerned with human and community relations now. New recruits to the force now receive 12 weeks of training in things such as child psychology, mental health, juvenile work, and community relations. Positive attitudes, not marksmanship make a good police officer. In addition, all new recruits undergo extensive psychological testing to determine if they are mentally fit to be policemen. "The trouble," according to Inspector Moore, "is that most police officers want to be specialists. Everyone wants the glamour jobs: narcotics, vice and undercover work. We really need more general police officers just as society needs more general medical doctors."

Inspector Moore contends that urban police forces could increase their effectiveness by hiring civilians to handle some of the administrative and clerical work. "We need our trained men and women out with the people, not

[67]Do you think women police should be assigned less dangerous duty than male police? Why, or why not?

sitting behind a desk filling out forms. We also need more women and minority group members on the force." Of the 1800 uniformed police persons in inspector Moore's city only 83, less than 5 per cent, are black. "Women," says Inspector Moore, "generally handle domestic problems better than men. In fact, nearly 90 per cent of our work could be handled by women as well as by men."

When asked how urban police could increase their effectiveness the Inspector provided several specific suggestions. "Perhaps most importantly, we need more manpower on the streets, more visibility.[68] I'm more interested in preventing crime than apprehending criminals. Suppose, for example, a guy is planning to rob a 'ma and pa' grocery store or mug someone. If he sees a cop he might decide to forget it. That's important. You have to remember that most people who get into trouble aren't criminals. They usually have a reason. Many who get involved with the law are poor and need help. Another thing we need is more effective police-community relations. People need to understand our job, but more importantly we must understand people."

Inspector Moore scoffs at the suggestion that punishment and prisons deter crime. "Most sociologists," he explains, "will tell you that prisons generally teach people to become more skilled criminals. Capital punishment, for example, never prevented a murder. Most homocides are crimes of passion and couldn't be prevented by capital punishment. That's where greater police visibility comes in. Also I can't buy the argument that the supreme court or soft judges have tied the policeman's hands. We just have to do a better job of law enforcement and preparing our cases. Besides, it's not the police officer's concern if a person gets a light sentence or no sentence at all. We are not the judge, jury, and executioners. We're here to protect citizens not put people in prison."

Laws and the courts

Some individuals feel that reforming the police will reduce urban crime. Others, however, argue that gun controls or more certain punishment will deter would-be criminals. In the following two accounts a number of criminal experts present arguments for swift and sure punishment and for gun control.

Gun control

"Policemen do not have the manpower or the time to guard businesses and homes," writes Jack Hampton, a former Dallas assistant district attorney. "Consequently self-defense is a matter for the individual and his only effective defense is the gun." "The Constitution states specifically that the people, all

[68] Would you be willing to pay higher taxes to support an increase in the size of your city's police force? Why, or why not?

of us, have the right to keep and bear arms," says Police Chief Hale of Lexington, Ky. "In spite of this, legislation like New York's insidious Sullivan Law makes it illegal for a law abiding citizen to defend himself, and he is a sitting duck."

Attorney Randolph Slocum of Roseburg, Oregon, thinks that kind of reasoning is wrong. "An honest man with a firearm has about as much chance against a criminal as a jack rabbit would have at a coyote convention." "A six gun under the pillow is no solution to the crime problem," says Mortimer Braus of the San Fernando Valley Legal Aid Association. "Nor is turning the U.S. into an armed camp a solution.

Fort Lee, N.J.'s Police Chief Theodore warns: "The instant there is a gun in your hands the chance of your being hurt or killed by an intruder becomes hundreds of times greater. Remember, only when an intruder comes at you with a weapon, to do you great bodily harm, will the law of self-defense protect you if you happen to shoot him."

Congressman Abner Mikva of Illinois concluded: "Handguns have but one purpose—to kill, wound, or intimidate human beings. We already have had enough of both the killing and the guns. We do not need more."

Crime and the Courts, **Patrick J. Murphy, New York Police Commissioner**
There is more crime today than ever before. There are more criminals today than ever before. There are more victims today than ever before. But too many criminals are not going to jail, and their victims scream that the criminal-justice system has broken down—and they are right. The victims scream that the police are at fault, but this is not right and it is not fair.

We, the police, are far from perfect, but we have shouldered the entire blame long enough. We, the police, are more efficient today than ever. We pour arrested criminals into the wide end of the criminal-justice funnel, and they choke it up until they spill over the top. And when I say spill over—they spill over into the street and commit more crime.

So we arrest them again, pour them into the funnel as far as the court system again, and they spill out again. And the cycle repeats itself day after day after day . . . .

In today's courts, everything is aimed at disposition of cases. Our courts have become totally committed to clearing the calendar. Partly this is due to the fact that there are no jail cells to put criminals into. I admit this. Corrections is still another sad story . . . .

But the court system is what I am talking about tonight. The surest deterrent to crime is the knowledge by potential criminals that they are likely to get caught, and the certainty—the certainty, I said—that once caught they will be promptly prosecuted, convicted if guilty, and jailed.[69] There is no

[69]Do you agree with police commissioner Murphy that the certainty of punishment will prevent crime? Why, or why not?

such certainty today. This idea has become a farce.

Professional stick-up men, narcotics pushers, gamblers laugh at it. Not only are we not jailing them, but each arrest that they walk away from leads to an increased disrespect of the law, not only by the persons arrested but also by young criminals, amateur criminals, would-be criminals who would emulate them.

In 1960, the New York City police department made 35,629 felony arrests. Last year we made 94,042 felony arrests, an increase of 165 per cent over a 10-year period. You ask what happened to last year's 94,000 felony arrests? Exactly 552 of them went to trial–552 out of 94,000. The rest of them were "disposed of." Disposed of means dismissed outright, reduced to misdemeanors via plea bargaining, reduced to much lesser felonies via plea bargaining.

No doubt certain of the honest, dedicated policemen who made these 94,000 arrests last year came to the belief that conscientious police work is a waste of time, a waste of effort and a waste of devotion . . . .

All we can do is take criminals out of circulation as far as the court system, and we do this. We are arresting criminals, often the same ones, over and over again.

Does this effectively remove them from circulation? It does not . . . . The court system is not dealing with these criminals. They get out on bail, and in the months and sometimes years before the case comes to trial some of them have committed 20 to 50 more crimes and have been apprehended 5 or 10 or 20 additional times.

Or the courts, in their desperate struggle to dispose of cases, send vicious criminals out on the street again on probation or after very brief sentences on much reduced charges, and another 10 or 100 citizens get mugged as a result . . . .

I will state emphatically that the court system must accept the giant share of the blame for the continual rise in crime.

We in the criminal-justice system realize that the courts have problems, that money and time are needed, that the system wasn't designed to cope with modern violence and modern crime nor with the criminal subculture in drugs. Some improvements to the system have been made already. Yet they have been too few and too slow. We can't wait much longer. Society can't wait much longer.

The citizens take action

During the last few years citizen outrage at crime in the streets has replaced public apathy. Residence of some communities, angered by lootings, rape, and mugging in their cities organized to provide their own protection. The final part of Assignment

30 contains accounts of several citizen action plans. Each account illustrates an alternative solution to the problem of urban crime. As you examine each account continue your analysis of these alternatives.

Citizen police

"When I first spotted them out there in those orange Batman capes I thought it was the most awful paranoid dumb thing I'd ever heard of," said my friend who consistently overreacts. "It's a waste of time and negative and fortress mentality." That was *her* opinion of the Parents League Child Safety Campaign, But I love it. I bloom with affection for those flapping orange figures that march up and down Madison Avenue just when my little ones strike out along streets rich in hazard.

One would think that being for any organized effort that helps guarantee childrens' safety would be like standing up for Motherhood—these days, in fact, even less controversial. Yet there are those who see the ghost of white vigilantism in any citizens' patrol. Visions are immediately conjured of white sheets, rifles across knees, and car brakes shrieking in the night. But at the Parents League program there are no rifles, just a pad, a pencil, and an extremely shrill whistle. There are no cars; it is all on foot, and the 400 police-trained volunteers are black, white, male, female, bachelors, spinsters, and parents of children in public, parochial and private schools and temples.

Sue Stachelberg, a tall, pleasant woman who is one of the coordinators of the program, says: "It has been a very healthy thing to bring our 'walking safety guidelines' to the schools' and children's attention. Too many people just weren't facing the problem. Too many children were having street encounters they were too frightened to report. When we face it, and discuss what to do, it becomes less frightening."

According to Webster's Third, a vigilance committee is "organized to suppress and punish crime summarily." The men and women, however, who walk the nine routes the Parents League thus far has been able to man on the East and West Sides, are no crime busters. "We don't ask them to be policemen. All we ask is that they become an extension of our eyes and ears," said Officer Cecil T. Bryant of the 23rd Precinct who helped set up the program in 1971. The patrols, walking in pairs and wearing orange ponchos donated by Gimbel's East for ready identification, not only keep a lookout for trouble but check to see that police call boxes, public telephones, and traffic lights are all in working order. In their daily reports left off at a cooperating or "key" store to be gathered up later by the police, volunteers have even reported such unattended eyesores as rubble left by Con Edison or road defects or poorly organized traffic patterns requiring attention. What the volunteers do *not* do is jump into threatening situations either verbally or physically. Instead, one patrol partner blows his whistle and dials 911 (a certain amount of good judgment, naturally, is warranted), while the other writes a precise description of the incident. Police scooters assigned to stay in touch appear in seconds. Everybody involved in the effort agrees the routes have become refreshingly monotonous.

The police are delighted by this kind of help. "We can't be everywhere," said Sergeant John St. Jeanos, citywide coordinator of Civil Patrols in Deputy Commissioner Roosevelt Dunning's office. "This program is a terrific success. It really works." He said that while the department has not carried out an expensive "in-depth analysis" iced with statistics, it is satisfied that there has been a marked improvement in the reduction of street crimes during those crucial hours, 7:45 to 8:45 a.m. and 2:45 to 4 p.m., when the patrols are out. "It's the hue-and-cry method, really," summed up Officer Bryant. "The last thing a person doing something wrong wants is to be center stage."

The safety campaign began with the area between East 86th Street and 96th Streets in the 23rd Precinct, which has the heaviest flow of children and schools. After soliciting volunteers, community support, and the cooperation of the 23rd, it took to the streets in April, 1972. Now the campaign has been extended to the 19th, 20th, and 34th precincts. Admittedly, training sessions occassionally unearth a potential hothead eager to wield his mace and discharge fantasies of surrogate policemanship, but such people are quickly weeded out.

Contrary to what some may think, the programmers declare they have not geared the effort to those fashionable schools with the greatest clout. "We set up routes with great care," said Mrs. Stachelberg firmly. "They are put along the most traveled paths. But people call up and say they need a patrol at their school—as if we were some sort of service with 9,000 volunteers with nothing else to do." She sighed, "But it's hard, I guess, to get people to give up the notion of *my* church, *my* block, *my* school . . . . "

Fortress California

Sir Edward Coke, the keenest legal mind of the 16th century, first laid down the principle that a man's home is "his castle and fortress, his defense against injury and violence." Sir Edward was speaking figuratively, of course, but now it appears that many Americans are taking him literally. The National Commission on the Causes and Prevention of Violence, taking note of the rapid rise in urban crime, not long ago made a grim prediction: "high-rise apartment buildings and residential compounds protected by private guards and security devices will be fortified cells for upper-middle and high-income populations." The fortifications are already appearing across the land, most notably in California (where burglaries have increased by 149 per cent in the past decade) and particularly in the southern part of the state, where Los Angeles County suffers the nation's highest suburban crime rate.

By the latest count, there are at least three dozen walled "total security" communities in the desert, beach and woodland areas of Southern California, and more are on the drawing boards. [70] "Until about five years ago," says Los

[70]Would you like to live in a walled total security community? Why, or why not?

Angeles County Deputy Planning Director Frederick Barlow, "most subdividers wanted the county to maintain their streets. Now a majority of the subdivisions we are approving have private streets" (which entitles the communities to block off the streets with gates and guards).

Typical of the walled communities is a 200-house complex called The Shores in Laguna Niguel, north of San Diego, where many of the armed guards at the gatehouses are ex-Marine combat veterans of the Viet Nam War. "More than likely, the presence of a guard cuts out a lot of crime," understates John Rogers, a burly guard. Nearby Rossmoor Leisure World, in Laguna Hills, is a retirement community surrounded by six-foot-high pink walls and guarded by a security force of 170 un-armed resident patrolmen led by four armed professionals. They man the community's eight carefully guarded gates and patrol its streets round the clock in radio cars.

Some of the newer walled communities are installing remarkably sophisticated security systems. The Mission Hills condominium in the desert near Palm Springs is being rigged with electronic Westinghouse units that monitor for fires, burglaries or equipment failures. Signals are fed to a local computer center that alerts firemen, police or maintenance men and, in addition activates a net of ultra-sensitive microphones installed inside each house allowing a dispatcher to listen in while help is on the way. Residents are enthusiastic. "I feel so good when I know that I'm entering a house that is untouched," says a Mission Hills housewife.

Another guarded community, 125-home Westlake Island, north of Los Angeles, is reachable only by bridge. A guard inspects visitors at the entrance to the bridge, checks with the resident to be sure that company is expected, and only then allows the guest to drive across the moat. As a result, the island is crime-free. "The biggest problem we have" says one guard, "is keeping sightseers off the island and breaking up teen-age parties that get out of hand." Each homeowner on the island pays an annual $220 assessment (nondeductible) covering the cost of the guards and general upkeep, but Islander Walter Smith, robbed twice in his previous flat, thinks the price is a bargain. "I always used to keep a loaded gun by the bed in our Beverly Hills apartment," he says, "But now I don't give it a thought." Rumors about the surrounding waters may contribute to the islanders' sense of security. "Some people claim there are crocodiles in there," jokes Airline Pilot Richard Neet. "The water is better than a wall," says his wife, Ellie, "I don't feel claustrophobic here."

Water does not always guarantee security. Even Westlake Island could learn something from an exclusive, 21-home development in Florida's Hobe Sound, which uses the Westinghouse system with an added touch: because the community is built along a network of canals, a closed-circuit television system monitors the waterways to keep amphibious thieves away.

Humans against rape and molestation

Boulder, Colorado, is a beautiful sprawling college town of 67,000 located at the base of the Rocky Mountains. In the spring and summer, residents

Coming: a citizens crime alarm

Police departments in several American cities are currently testing a wrist radio that will let a crime victim send out a coded signal. The alarm would be relayed through a regular police call box to a central monitoring station. The monitor identifies the victim by name and tells where he or she is. Police are dispatched directly to the scene of the crime.

frolic in the nearby foothills; in the fall and winter they cheer the University of Colorado's fine football team. But in recent months, this idyllic state of affairs has been shaken badly by a wave of rapes. In the last year alone there have been 68 reported sexual assaults (30 of them rapes) and police estimate that hundreds more go unreported. The vast majority of Boulder's rape victims are hitchhiking women students. [71]

Hitchhiking is a way of life to many students in Boulder. Most can't afford cars and those who can are often unable to start them on cold winter mornings. Public transportation is limited and taxis are terribly expensive. And because the distance between residential, business and recreational areas is so great, most students are left with no alternative but to take a chance and hitchhike.

Recently, however, Boulder's residents have created some alternatives. A number of concerned citizens have banded together in a group called HARM (Humans Against Rape and Molestation). Besides informing women about the dangers of riding with strangers, HARM also offers free counseling services for women who have been assaulted. On the Colorado campus, students have created their own service. Called "People Walker," the organization provides male escorts for unaccompanied women walking across campus.

[71]Would you favor the passage of laws to prohibit women from hitchhiking? Why, or why not?

It is still too early to judge the effectiveness of the new anti-rape programs, but local authorities endorse them wholeheartedly. Since "People Walker" was started last month, there seems to be a common bond between police and the college community. "I never thought I'd see the day a student would help reinforce the law," beams one officer. "I think it's great."

Operation Identification[72]

Spreading rapidly across this country is a simple, inexpensive program which enables an ordinary citizen to help fight crime—and to protect his own home and property.

Already in action in more than 200 cities and towns, this antiburglary effort is known most widely as "Operation Identification." It is also, in some places, called by such names as "Crime Trap" and "Project Theft-Guard."

The program operates this way:

A house or apartment dweller engraves his driver's-license number or other designated figures on all his possessions which would interest a burglar.

The number, if not already easily available, is filed with the local police department.

The dweller then puts a sticker on his door which reads: "All items of value on these premises have been marked for ready identification by law-enforcement agencies."

The aim is to deter burglars, and—failing that—to help police recover and identify stolen property.

The project is highly successful, according to reports from many of the communities where it is operating.

In Monterey Park, Calif., where the idea originated in 1963, half the 11,000 home-owners have joined the plan—and, since its start, only 23 participants have reported burglaries while some 2,000 break-ins have been reported by those not taking part.

In Saginaw Township, Mich., there were 206 breakings and enterings during 1971, but not one of those occurred in a home involved in the operation.

Some cities, such as Pasadena, Calif., and Columbus, Ga., report a significant decrease in burglaries. Others such as New Orleans, say that stolen goods, with their telltale numbers, are being more easily recovered and returned to their rightful owners.

The plan is supported by police departments, business firms, the National Exchange Club, the National Association of Insurance Agents and other groups.

In Washington, D.C., where the program is just getting under way, a police official reports that there have been "hundreds of calls" from interested citizens and that "organizations are begging to underwrite the project."

[72]Reprinted from *U.S. News & World Report.*

Said the police chief of Hickory Hills, a Chicago suburb: "It's one of the best things ever to happen to police officers–it's making our job easier."

Similar enthusiasm has been evident all across the country. Police and other officials make the following points:

The program is cheap, costing the home-owner little or nothing. The etching pencils used to mark property sell as low as $5, and hundreds of home stickers can be printed for a few dollars. Businesses, clubs, and police departments usually pay for the items.

In a typical operation, a citizen goes to a central location–such as a police or fire department–and borrows an etching pencil, free or for a small fee. After numbering his possessions, he returns the tool and gets a door decal announcing his participation.

Though most things–TV sets, guitars, bicycles, car batteries, appliances–can be engraved, there are limitations. For instance, one would have difficulty labeling every piece of silver or china even if he wanted to do so.

In states where driver's license numbers are permanent, the home-owner does not necessarily have to leave his number with police. A computer already has all licenses recorded and will quickly tell police who owns recovered stolen goods which are engraved. Social security numbers have been used in some places, but generally are not used for identification purposes.

Two main deterrents to crime are credited to the program.

First, burglars often will not enter a participants home once they see the sticker on a door or window because the thieves don't want to be caught with identifiable goods.

The project also makes catching thieves easier. A suspect with a TV set in the back of his car would be hard put to explain its presence if it had the number of stolen property . . . . (Copyright © 1972, *U.S. News & World Report Inc.)*

For thought and discussion

Should police spend less time dealing with "victimless crimes"?

Individual and small group activities

1. Make arrangements with your city's police department to spend a day or evening riding with a squad car policeman. Keep a diary of all activities performed by the police officer. How many of these activities involve dealing with lawbreakers? How many involve providing assistance to persons in need of aid. Report your findings to your class.
2. Interview the director of your college security force. Find out how they maintain security on the campus. Do they work with the city police or independently? What can student's do to increase the effectiveness of the security force. Your instructor will inform you how to report your findings.

Protecting the urban environment: Stating the issue for Assignments 31 and 32

The issue of the destruction of our environment confronts all members of our society. A group of scientists recently stated that either civilization or growth must end, and soon. Supporters of this statement argue that since our land, air, and water resources are limited, we must conserve them by regulating the growth of population and industrial development. Those who disagree argue that technology and new inventions will develop ways to reuse resources and control pollution. Either way, metropolitan areas continue to experience the greatest population and industrial growth and consequently have the severest environmental problems.

Urban residents are increasingly concerned about the metropolitan environment. The mass media bombard citizens with news of high air pollution levels, diminishing energy and water supplies, inadequate waste disposal facilities, and the general physical decay of the city. Citizens often bemoan the environmental problems but have either failed to consider alternative solutions or are unwilling to make the necessary sacrifices to correct these problems.

Many ecological problems result from the fact that urban residents have not analyzed their attitudes concerning the urban environment. For example, should citizens rely on private individuals and companies or upon government and laws to solve pollution problems? Citizens must realize that societal attitudes and values are a combination of individual attitudes and values. Until many individual attitudes and values have been clarified, and perhaps altered, environmental problems will continue to plague our cities.

Assignment 31 asks you to define the problem and goals of one urban environmental issue. Examine the alternative solutions to this problem, and state the roles you think private citizens, industry, and local and federal governments should play in solving this problem. Assignment 32 examines the inner city's environmental problems and suggests some ways to solve problems of the urban environment.

Protecting the urban environment (1)

Assignment 31

Some environmental issues such as clean air and water, and conservation of fuel receive continued publicity and much government attention and money. Other issues such as garbage disposal do not receive such attention. However, methods of garbage and waste disposal affect air, water, and energy resources of our cities. In this assignment you will examine the environmental issue of garbage disposal in the cities and define the problem and goals. Once you have determined the nature of the problem you should examine each alternative solution and determine the consequences of each solution. Finally choose the solution you think best in the light of your analysis. The questions below should guide your search for the best solution.

1. What are the alternative solutions to the problem of garbage disposal?
2. If lawmakers or citizens enact alternative 1 what will happen to urban residents? To the urban environment? Will this alternative solve the problem of garbage disposal? (You should ask these questions for each of the four alternative discussed in this assignment.)

Garbage smothered cities

The statistical data and the reading on pages 384–386 offer information about the issue of garbage disposal in the city. Use this information to define the problem or problems of garbage disposal in the urban community.

America's cities are smothering in garbage. Almost half of the cities will run out of places to dump their trash within five years. Action is urgently needed to avoid strangulation of cities on their own wastes.

Cities are annually accumulating a trash heap of 250 million tons: 28 billion bottles, 48 billion cans, 4 million tons of plastic, 30 million tons of paper, 100 million tires and over 3 million junk cars.

Cities are concerned because the wastefulness of Americans is reaching crisis proportions in this area. While the amount of solid waste discarded by the popula-

What Americans throw out each day

3.5 Pounds per person	
Paper	50%
Metals, Ceramics, Glass, Rubber, Cloth, Leather, Wood, and Plastics	29%
Garbage	12%
Garden Waste	9%

Urban trash

Average accumulation 250 million tons a year including:

Tires	100,000,000
Cans	48,000,000
Paper (tons)	38,000,000
Bottles	28,000,000
Plastic (tons)	4,000,000
Junk cars	3,000,000

Disposal Costs $6-billion a year

tion has doubled in the last fifty years, it has doubled in the cities in the last twenty years.

The future looks even bleaker because of the fascination with packaging. Packaging will increase 63 per cent between 1958 and 1976. Ninety per cent of all packaging is tossed on the trash heap.

While mayors and city managers insist they do not oppose environmental protection laws, they believe that these very laws have intensified the problem of disposal.

"Federal policies and regulations aimed at protection of the air and water," the mayors said, "have produced immense waste disposal problems for the cities. Cities must find larger and larger land areas in which to dump the waste since they can not dump it into the water or burn it."

Also Federal policies do not favor the recycling of waste products. "The markets for recycled materials," said the mayors, "are severely limited due to federal policies favoring use of virgin materials."

"It is not the choice of cities that only one per cent of municipal wastes are recycled," city officials say. "It is an aggregated choice compelled by Federal policies, limited markets and consumer preferences."

Examining alternative solutions to the problem

The following four accounts describe alternative solutions to the problem of garbage disposal in urban areas. The questions provided on page 384 of this assignment will help you determine the best solution.

Alternative one: The Huttons' recycling program

In 1968 a New Hope, Pennsylvania couple, the Huttons, began a drive to recycle garbage and solve their city's growing garbage disposal problem. The essay below describes their efforts. As you read this account decide whether the Hutton's approach could help your city.

Americans, for the most part, have a perpetual fantasy that the world's resources are infinite. Thus, even when concerned researchers pointed out in the late 1960's that we were running out of essential resources, we inevitably continued on our wasteful ways. In part, of course, this was because America as a nation still retains much of the "exploit-exploit-exploit" philosophy of the 19th century robber barons (businessmen). In part, however we were still rather muddleheaded about "convenience." We had to have convenience foods, utensils, bottles, plates, everything.

Today, however, some people are beginning to recognize and look for solutions to these very serious problems. Two of these people are the Huttons of New Hope, Pennsylvania.

Unlike many others who choose to remain part of the super-plasticnonreturnable-overpackaged-throwaway society that America has become, the Huttons are actively involved in recycling.[73]

In 1968 the Huttons and the Bucks County Audubon Society began to implement an action plan that included recycling. After that, things happened fast. Newspapers covered their efforts and the Huttons were swamped with requests from more than 7,000 people.

Meanwhile, the Huttons were busy organizing a recycling drive and finding markets for the materials collected. In the beginning, a mere handful of collection points operated on a once per month basis, but now there are 23 sites throughout the county.

"Better yet," say the Huttons, "the venture is making a profit. Six collection points have taken in about $12,000 in profits. The money was used to send school teachers to Audubon camps.

By contrast, New Hope's 1,200 residents pay out $8,000 yearly for garbage collection.

However the recycling program was not always overwhelmingly successful: Local officials were not cooperative, and many people did not participate. "What's really ususual," muse the Huttons, "is that we've found it very hard to elicit cooperation from what we choose to call the 'cocktail lounge group.' These people are well-educated; they know what's happening, but they seem to have a 'we pay the trash hauler' syndrome. Most of the help has come from the 25 to 30 set. They're young *and* concerned."

The Huttons continue, "Industry also has been helpful. There are only two plants here, but we've had trucks donated once each month."

What can you do after you've fostered a successful recycling program?

If you're like the Huttons, you don't stop there. After all, recycling is only an interim solution to the solid waste problem. The real answers lie in cutting down on the amount of individual waste and encouraging returnables. We must reject all the plastic wrapping and throw-away cans. "We have to go back to returnables, and we have to put a deposit on them that will really encourage people to take them back—and that's where the eco-green bottle comes in," said Mr. Huttons.

The ecology green bottle would, the Huttons believe, help in two ways. It would make it easier to recycle glass because bottles would not have to be separated by color. That would enable trash haulers to spend less time, and make more money, hauling glass to recycling points. The bottle would also establish a trend back toward returnables, especially if it were adopted by one of the major soft drink companies.

"The public should try to convince the soft drink industry to use such a bottle. If they would buy the idea, the glass industry would gladly follow. But there has to be a *demand* for 'ecology green' or else there is no practical reason why we should make it."

People can help to create that demand by writing to the various soft

[73]Do you have any responsibilities to recycle garbage? If so, what are they?

drink companies and asking them to support the eco-green bottle. Let's see if the "Real Thing" *really* cares about the environment, or if the Pepsi generation is going strong on ecology—or if it's true that the Uncola is *un*concerned.[74]

"It will work," say the Huttons, "You just have to keep pounding away, but it will work."

Alternative two: Alcoa aids the recycling effort

The following advertisement from a popular magazine shows Alcoa's concern and effort to solve the garbage disposal problem confronting urban areas. Alcoa calls for the recycling of all aluminum cans.[75]

Courtesy of Aluminum Company of America

[74] Would you help form a volunteer group to lobby for returnable eco-green bottles? Why, or why not?

[75] Would you be willing to go without disposable bottles, and products packaged in plastic, or aluminum as a protest against solid wastes? Why, or why not?

Alternative three: Garbage recycling helps out a town

The following newspaper report describes how one town in New York tried to solve its garbage disposal problems. Residents and town officials joined in a concerted effort to collect, sell, and recycle garbage.

Briarcliff Manor, New York, March 14,1972. The skeptics said it could not be done, but this attractive little town, in the garbage business for less than a year, is breaking even on recycling. By the end of the year, it may even be turning a profit.

The town sells newspapers to a contractor in New York City, its cans to a chemical plant in Elizabeth, New Jersey, and its bottles in Orangeburg, New York. The town has reduced by 15 per cent the amount of solid waste sent to the country landfill each year—less 3,000 tons last year at a dumping fee of $3.50 a ton.

The income from the recycled material, plus the savings from less use of the county dump, are now running about equal to the added cost of the project to the village. If the campaign continues, Briarcliff Manor may even make a profit.

Michael Markl, the town administrator, credits Briarcliff's success to the fact that "recycling was not something generated by the town and sold to the people; it was generated by the people and sold to us." The idea came from a group of high school students who approached the town board in November, 1970.

The question of economic feasibility of recycling as proved by this community of 6,500 people has added fuel to the debate about how other towns and cities should handle their garbage problems in years to come.

Officials from different parts of the country maintain that although philosophically they favor recycling, neither the technology nor the market for recycled material is developed enough to make the process a feasible alternative to landfill.

Most community recycling efforts around the country have been small scale projects manned by volunteers. But it is difficult to generate enough volume to make the effort pay.

One of Briarcliff's leading recycling advocates, says, "It's a question of *attitude*."

From its modest volunteer beginnings, the Briarcliff recycling project soon became an official town effort. The project coincided with the town government's decision to drop its private garbage contractor and begin municipal garbage collection for the first time.

Beginning last June, the new Briarcliff sanitationmen began a monthly, house-to-house pickup of newspapers in addition to regular garbage collection. Saving newspapers is voluntary. The first month, residents saved 9,000 pounds. By December, the public works department was picking up 40,000 pounds a month.

Residents bring their own cans and bottles to four huge bins alongside the post office. The bins are 7 feet high and 16 feet long, and weigh about 10 tons when they are full of broken glass. They fill up in three to five weeks. The village pays a contractor to take the bins to recycling center. "It's become the *in* thing," said the superintendent of public works. "People really take out their aggressions trying to break the bottles."

Since June, the town has taken in $4,462 and saved $620 in dumping fees. It receives $20 a ton for glass and tin, $10 for other metal, and from $8 to $15 for paper. The main expenses now are $235 a month for leasing the bins, and $12.50 an hour for the contractor to haul the bins away.

Other town and city officials have visited Briarcliff. Town officials welcome the interest, but doubt whether large towns could duplicate Briarcliff's success as long as recycling generally remains voluntary.

Even here there are still numerous newspapers, bottles, and cans thrown out in the household garbage and sent on to the dump. But there is little support for following the example of North Hempstead, Long Island, which last year passed a law requiring residents to separate newspapers from other trash.[76]

"It would seem kind of self-defeating to force the residents to do something that was their idea in the first place," said a town official.

Alternative four: City turns garbage into electricity

The following newspaper article indicates how one city converted its garbage into electricity. The city is optimistic about the applicability of its process to garbage problems in cities throughout the country.

Industry treated early recycling efforts with a knowing smile, but where industry and government have rolled up their sleeves, some interesting events are taking place.

They're turning garbage into electric power in St. Louis, making garbage power, no less.

It's an experimental program, about to be improved measureably, but so far it appears feasible to mix shredded garbage with crushed coal to produce electricity.

Obviously, this method gets rid of the garbage, a mounting urban problem. And every ounce of energy produced by burning garbage serves to ease the energy crisis.

While there is some science to the St. Louis effort, it really is quite simple:

Garbage trucks deliver to the Union Electric Company. The garbage is shredded and a magnetic conveyor pulls out the iron and steel, mostly tin cans.

[76]Do you think laws should be made to force people to recycle products and use returnable bottles? Why, or why not?

Through large pipes, the garbage is blended with crushed coal and blown into the furnaces . . . to make the steam . . . which turns the turbines . . . which turn the generators . . . which generate the electricity. In addition, secondary shredding facilities are being added so the steel recovered can be sold.

The original effort was funded by the U. S. Environmental Protection Agency ($1.8 million), St. Louis ($450,000) and Union Electric ($550,000).

The Environmental Agency, St. Louis, and the American Iron and Steel Institute are providing funds to upgrade the project.

During the first year's operation the experiment did away with 300,000 pounds of garbage daily–about one-sixth of St. Louis' output or what some 73,000 people pile up each day.

Power generated by garbage alone serves the needs of some 1,500 people.

The steel recovered amounts to between 15 and 20 tons.

Indirect savings include shipping coal to the power plant, and ore to the steel mill, but the largest savings, of course, are at the St. Louis landfill, where all the garbage does not need to be buried.

Estimates are the new equipment will boost the efficiency of the system by 20 per cent, and once the system is perfected, it could be applied to any city generating garbage and steam power–virtually every city in the United States.

Choosing a solution

After individuals and governments consider all alternatives to a solution to a problem they must choose the solution that best corresponds to their goals. Reconsider the four alternative solutions to urban garbage disposal and choose the solution you prefer. Answer the following questions:

1. Why did you choose your particular alternative?
2. How does your solution correspond to your initial definition of the problem and goals for the solution of the problem?
3. How does your choice reflect your attitudes and values about private and public actions to protect the urban environment?

For thought and discussion

Should we rely on individuals' consciences or public governmental programs and laws to solve environmental problems?

Individual and small group activities

1. Find out how your city disposes of its garbage. Is your city's disposal method adequate to meet present and future needs? What future plans does your Sanitation Department have for the disposal and recycling of garbage? Report to

your class. In your report assess the future situation of garbage disposal in your city.

2. With another student visit a meeting of a local environmental action group. (If such a group does not exist on your campus, call the newspaper and ask them for the names of citizens active in ecological problems. Many cities have a department of city government concerned with environmental issues and they may put you in contact with a group.) What plan of action does the particular environmental action group advocate? How much individual responsibility and/or governmental action is required to meet the aims of the group? Assess the group's effectiveness and consider alternative actions that group might take in order to become more effective. Report your findings to the class.

Protecting the urban environment (2)

Assignment 32

The environmental issue of garbage disposal concerns only one ecological problem of the urban area. The city faces a number of interrelated and complex problems. Most of these problems require combined public and private action. For example, the problem of air pollution may require laws to prevent companies and citizens from polluting the air. On the other hand, private citizens and companies must be willing to pay for anti-pollution devices on cars and in industries to improve air quality.

Assignment 32 provides information and alternative solutions about a number of environmental problems confronting the inner city. You should use this information to evaluate the suggested solutions. When you have concluded your evaluation write a short statement defending the approach that you consider best answers the needs of the inner city environment. As you read this assignment you should answer these questions:

1. What are the environmental problems faced by the residents of the inner city?
2. What are the alternative solutions to these problems? What are the implications and consequences of each alternative?

The quality of the environment in the inner city

Environmental problems surround us every day, yet many of us fail to recognize their presence. The nine photographs on pages 394–397 were all taken in a small section of one major American city. You might see these same sights on a stroll through your city. Examine each photograph carefully, then make a list of all the environmental problems you see.

1

2

3

4

5

6

7

8

9

The following essay provides additional information about a number of environmental problems confronting the inner city. Use this information to complete your list of urban environmental problems.

The inner city, whatever its precise boundaries, is recognized by its inferior environment. Air pollution, a problem for nearly all of the Nation, lays its pall most heavily over the inner city in many metropolitan areas. Open space, parks, and recreational opportunity are high priorities for a better environment. Yet in the inner city they are lacking to a higher degree than in other parts of the urban complex. Problems of noise, sanitation, and congestion affect nearly all sectors of the larger cities. But overcrowding, rats, flaking leaded paint, deteriorating housing, and everpresent litter and garbage are afflictions more typical of the inner city.

The environmental decay of the inner city, of course, affects more than the poor. Middle and upper income families residing within inner city sanctuaries are not spared the health and economic toll of air pollution, noise, and traffic congestion. Yet they can insulate themselves from some of the environmental burdens of life in the city: Air conditioners screen the air and shut out street noise, housing is kept in repair against the assaults of weather and rodents, much more living space is available, and mobility and higher income make it possible to escape periodically to more pleasant environments. For the inner city poor, however, there is little relief and limited opportunity for escape.

The traditional environmental objectives of clean air and water and preservation of national parks and wilderness are not the central concerns of most inner city poor. They focus instead on more immediate economic and social problems. Some spokesmen for inner city areas fear that the environmental movement may divert public attention and funds from these issues to more traditional environmental issues. For many inner city residents, the overwhelming concern is poverty and its accompanying ills–inadequate housing, high crime rates, poor health, unsanitary conditions, inadequate education and recreation, and drug addiction–all of which are worsened by racial discrimination. These factors may not be environmental when looked at individually. But their net effect is to lower the quality of life.

Nevertheless, there is growing evidence that among the urban poor–those with the most to gain from environmental improvements–are some who have decided to embrace environmentalism in their own distinct way. Their use of the term environment is broader than the traditional definition. The concept embraces not only more parks, but better housing; not only cleaner air and water, but rat extermination.

Air pollution generally hangs more heavily over the inner city than the rest of the urban area, and far more heavily than over most suburban and rural areas. In some cities the central business district absorbs the most severe air pollution; in other cities close-in industrial areas bear the heaviest pollution loads. The largest concentrations of the urban poor often live near these two areas.

Inner city residents are delivered the same water as any other urban residents. But they frequently face added problems. Water pipes in inner city housing are sometimes old and ill-kept and often contain pipe or joint cementing compound made of lead (no longer used in construction). Under such conditions, water containing as much as 920 micrograms of lead per liter has been found in inner city areas, compared to an average of 20 micrograms per liter elsewhere.

Inner city residents have limited access to water recreation. Conclusive data are lacking on how often the urban poor use nearby water bodies. Rivers and harbors located within and next to large cities often contain dangerously high levels of bacteria and other pollutants. Yet they often constitute the only source of water recreation easily accessible to the urban poor. The cleaner waters are for many inner city dwellers more distant than a convenient one-day round trip will allow, and thus out of reach for those not able to afford overnight accommodations.

Junk and litter accumulated in streets, on sidewalks, and in vacant lots and doorways are a familiar sight in poverty areas and cannot help having a psychological effect on those who live there. The resident often despairs of keeping his small living space clean when all around him are litter and garbage.

He may conclude that since refuse collection is a public service, the abundance of uncollected litter indicates that his neighborhood is being discriminated against. Yet, solving the problem involves more than merely upgrading municipal services. Some New York City poverty areas have garbage pickups six times a week, compared to three times a week elsewhere in the city. In Chicago, inner city poor are served by three collections a week, compared to one collection in the rest of the city. Yet inner city littering and unsanitary conditions continue, and there is widespread disenchantment at the failure of cleanup campaigns to have any lasting effect.

The reasons for this failure to maintain sanitary conditions in the inner city are complex and interrelated. Frustration over limited opportunities for housing, employment, and education can lead residents of the inner city to withdraw from active efforts to improve conditions around them. This psychological impact is worsened by physical conditions which work against sanitation. Buildings designed in earlier days have been subdivided into numerous crowded living units, with little provision for storage areas, common spaces, or refuse collection systems. Receptacles are often nonexistent, makeshift, or in poor condition—all leading to a situation in which wind, animals, and vandals spread litter throughout houses and neighborhoods. The abundance of vacant lots and abandoned structures, already strewn with refuse encourage further junk, garbage, and other debris. Together these forces work to frustrate even the most willing city sanitation department in working with residents toward a cleaner neighborhood.

Strewn garbage, besides being unattractive and odorous, also invites rodents. Rats feed on easily accessible garbage and present a health problem to inner city residents. Greater than the danger of the diseases they carry is the insecurity and fear they inspire, especially in parents with small children.

Landlord abandonment of buildings, widespread dilapidation, and health effects of lead paint chips on children are all problems characteristic of many inner city neighborhoods. Some inner city areas show their scars openly with vacant stores, burned-out buildings, and boarded-up windows. Deteriorating on the inside, litter-strewn on the outside, block after block of decay provides a depressing setting for life.

It is estimated that there are more than 100,000 abandoned dwelling units in New York City, between 20,000 and 30,000 in Philadelphia, more than 10,000 in St. Louis, 4,000 or more in Baltimore, and 5,000 or more in Chicago. Abandonment often occurs even in cities with relatively limited supplies of available housing. The percentage of dwelling units for rent or sale in New York City is only 1.7, in Philadelphia, only 2.8. These low vacancy rates, coupled with a heavy rate of abandonment, indicate that buildings are being abandoned even when people need homes. Moreover, the problem is not confined to the biggest cities. Erie, Pa., for instance, has a vacancy rate of 2.3 per cent and 5,000 abandoned units.

Automobile ownership often makes the difference between access to outdoor recreation areas and confinement to the limited parklands of many inner city areas. On the other hand, new highways which serve the car owner further diminish urban open space. Highway construction can also cost the city dweller his home, increase the pollution of his air, and add to the noise from which he suffers. In some cases, resistance to proposed new highway construction has knitted inner city groups and environmental organizations into new coalitions.

If a new highway cuts through a neighborhood, it decreases casual, social interaction between the two severed sides. It creates a psychological or visual barrier and often a physical obstacle. More than liberal vehicular access and an occasional pedestrian crossing are necessary to overcome the highway barrier. Even when continuous across-highway access is provided—as in the case of elevated structure construction—the highway's uninhabited strip remains a psychological and social barricade.

The presence of a highway near a neighborhood may have other impacts beyond the border or barrier effect. Noise, increased dirt, and fumes tend to make outdoor activities less pleasant and thus, to some degree, diminish the contacts needed to produce neighborhood cohesion.

Heightened surface traffic can also develop from changes in traffic patterns after a new highway is built. Feeder streets in the vicinity of an interchange often suffer enormously increased loads. The effects of this increased traffic may turn the street into a greater barrier to social interaction.

Examining alternative solutions to the problems in the inner city environment

The following essays describe some federal, state, and local private and public attempts to solve the environmental problems of the inner city. Read each alternative and determine the implications and consequences of each solution. Select the solution you think best in the light of your analysis.

Local private and public efforts

In 1965 members of the black ghetto community of Watts in Los Angeles, California rioted and destroyed much of their urban area. Following the riot, black leaders commented on the causes of the hatred and frustration that resulted in riots. One observer stated, "The people don't feel bad about what happened. They had nothing to lose. They don't have decent homes. What else could they do?" "Another black leader called for better jobs, better schooling, decent homes and black control of businesses in Watts. Still another leader called for preferential treatment for blacks. "The black, after years of denial and deprivation, finds himself in a highly technical society unable to compete even *with* opportunity. He's up against invisible barriers that can only be overcome through massive programs. Not just equal. Admittedly better."

In the wake of the riots, business, industry, and government joined concerned black citizens in an effort to make Watts a better place to live. They formed The Watts Labor Community Action Committee (WLCAC) with the aim of improving the environment of the Watts inner city area. Ted Watkins, a black labor leader, lead the WLCAC's drive to rebuild Watts. He cajoled government, business and Watts' residents into cooperating on a host of projects: running gasoline stations, growing vegetables on 236 acres of unused land, sending ghetto kids to summer camp, building nearly a dozen vest-pocket parks, and planting some 3,000 trees. In addition, WLCAC successfully organized an educational center to help 250 school dropouts learn skills ranging from horticulture to auto repair.

The WLCAC used contributions from Federal and state agencies, labor unions, the Ford and Rockefeller Foundations and other local sources, to purchase four Shop Rite supermarkets in 1970. This $9 million-a-year business is now owned and operated by black residents of Watts.[77] WLCAC plans to use the stores as an outlet for the farm produce and to upgrade food quality. Prices, always a sore spot in the ghetto, will come under control, too—but, says one WLCAC official, "only as far as good profit practices dictate." Although whites initially helped to manage the stores gradually blacks moved into all levels of the operation and management.

Watkins views the stores as forerunners of a whole new line of black-owned businesses—janitorial services, maintenance companies, security firms, and other small businesses in Watts. According to Watkins, local control of businesses should help to foster community concern, offer more job opportunities to black residents, and eliminate some of the resentment over white controlled businesses. An example of black entrepreneurship is Watkins' deal with the state to move 900 condemned houses near Los Angeles International Airport to Watts; the houses had been slated to be razed for airport expansion. "This move will upgrade the whole community, and provide middle-class housing for low-income people," Watkins stated.

The WLCAC maintains that in order to improve the community environment in Watts they must improve the economic base of its citizens. Residents must have jobs and a strong economic position in the community before they can concern themselves with improving the environment. Several members of the WLCAC believe that many urban renewal efforts failed because they only cleaned up the environment and did not provide residents with the economic means to maintain the environmental improvements.

[77]Do you think businesses located in a community should be owned by local residents? Why, or why not?

Governmental and business efforts

What does a new sports arena in Oklahoma City have in common with a triangle of new office and apartment towers in Indianapolis or with a three-block pedestrian mall, garnished with fountains, here in Denver?

They are all centerpieces in the attempt by American cities to resurrect their dying or deceased inner areas.

It has been said of these cities that after dark, when office workers and daytime shoppers have gone, a person could roll a bowling ball the length of the main street and never hit anybody.

An increasing number of unhappy city residents have fled to the suburbs in search of safer streets, better schools and environments. Downtown department stores, theaters, and movie houses have been transplanted to outlying shopping centers. Many downtown hotels, once locally famous as the focus of city dining and entertainment, are now old and half empty.

Each year there have been fewer reasons for anyone either to live in the largely deserted wastelands or to come back to them after dark.

But now, some of the afflicted cities have begun to fight back with carefully planned inner city developments that they hope will bring some families downtown to live, and bring others back after dark to play. With the feeling of safety that mere numbers can engender, they hope to recreate the lively atmosphere that once drew people downtown in the first place.

Most of this is being financed through combinations of urban renewal money from Washington and municipal bond issues (private investment guaranteed by local tax money) and generous offerings of private development funds.

For models, these cities have studied projects like Philadelphia's Society Hill and Independence Mall developments; Pittsburgh's Market Square and Gateway Center; Altanta's conversion of airspace over its railways to shopping and entertainment arcades; and the graceful pedestrian mall and apartment towers that replaced Skid Row in downtown Minneapolis.

Denver's Skyline Project, now more than a third completed, utilizes almost all of these approaches.

The Skyline area, on the northern edge of Denver's center, was once the heart of the city in the late 19th century. At that time Denver was already the commercial and cultural capital of a rip-roaring cattle and mining empire.

The city's outward growth since the early nineteen-fifties has been as breathless as any other city's. Denver proper is past 500,000 in population, but the metropolitan-suburban area is over 1.2 million and the city is skirted with "regional type" shopping center where a Denverite can purchase anything he needs to wear, eat or be entertained by.

After World War II, the city's commercial core moved southeastward and the cultural attractions scattered in many directions. This left a spreading section of tacky two-story buildings, many of them vacant and the others housing cheap bars, flophouses or girlie shows.

With a $40-million Federal grant, the Denver Urban Renewal Authority bought up a 27-block rectangle surrounding the Clocktower of the old D. & F. department store, a Denver landmark.

Today a luxury apartment tower, two middle and low income housing developments and an apartment complex for the elderly have been completed and are being occupied. The 25-story Prudential Plaza Building is partly occupied and the $33-million Park Central Bank and office building has just been completed. Underground parking garages beneath a three-block-long pedestrian mall are finished, and so is one of the three enormous fountains planned for the tree-lined mall.

At Skyline's northwest corner, Larimer Square, a block of old mining day buildings has already been converted into shops, restaurants and a movie house. A block to the southeast has been deeded to the Sheraton Hotel Corporation for a new hotel and luxury apartment tower.

Denver's convention center and adjoining arena now touch the southwest corner of the Skyline area. Denver taxpayers have approved an $80-million bond issue for a new performing arts center on Skyline's western edge, next to the area in which the University of Colorado's Denver branch is expanding . . . .[78]

Actions from the Department of Health, Education, and Welfare

In 1971, a division of hte Department of Health, Education, and Welfare, known as NEEDS (Neighborhood Environmental Evaluation and Decision System), began a comprehensive investigation of the environmental problems of the inner city. Instead of tackling one environmental problem at a time, NEEDS tried to determine the relationships among the many environmental problems and then develop a plan to remedy them. When local communities ask for help, NEEDS assists them in identifying their problems establish priorities for solving them. NEEDS emphasized that poor air, poor water, noise, crowding, bad housing, and neighborhood instability all affect both the individual's physical and mental health.

NEEDS conducts physical surveys and household interviews to determine the particular problems of a community. Interviewers live in the local area. They contact the families, conduct interviews, and seek community participation. Government experts use the results of these surveys and computers to analyze the problems and propose solutions. NEEDS acts as a consultant to local communities. Once the communities have developed a plan they must then seek money from another department of HEW or the Department of Housing and Urban Affairs.

For example, NEEDS helped Philadelphia to analyze some of its environmental problems. They allocated money to provide health or social work-

[78] What happens to the low-income inner city residents with these urban renewal projects?

ers, aides, who went from door to door to determine the problems of families of the inner city.[79] If the family desperately needed better housing, the social worker contacted the local public housing agency or some other assistance source. Social workers would show people how to contact agencies, go to clinics for health care, prepare garbage for collection or improve their sanitation. The health aide would bring in housing inspectors to do what was necessary about rat control. Many of the social workers recognized that in order to really alter the environment inner city residents had to alter their attitudes toward their environment.

For thought and discussion

What is another alternative solution to the environmental problems of the inner city?

Individual and small group activities

1. Between 40 and 60 per cent of the total number of pollutants found in our air come from the automobile. In many American cities, motor vehicles contribute as much as 75 per cent of the noise and 80 per cent of the air pollution. The typical automobile releases for each mile driven: 23 grams of carbon monoxide, 4 grams of nitrogen oxide, .4 grams of particles, and 2.2 grams of hydrocarbons. Automobiles dump about 86 millions tons of pollutants into the atmosphere each year. With Detroit producing 22,000 cars per day, even pollution control devices will have little effect on our air pollution problems.

   Make a record of the number of automobile trips and the mileage you travel each day. How much does your car pollute each day? How can you cut the number and length of your automobile trips? List a number of different ways you can get where you want to go. Would you support legislation to limit the number of miles an individual could drive daily? Report to class.
2. Identify the inner area of your city. Write a description of the physical conditions and activities of this area. What are the particular reasons for the present environmental conditions of your inner city? Has your city initiated efforts to change the environment of the inner areas? What would you change first in your inner city? Report to class.

[79] If you were an inner city resident would you cooperate with social welfare workers seeking information about your needs? Why or why not?

City planning: Stating the issue for Assignments 33 and 34

From the founding of this country, people have designed plans for better cities. In the eighteenth century, William Penn established a grid street plan for Philadelphia. Other cities quickly adopted Penn's plan. The small and narrow streets of the grid, however, proved inadequate for growing cities. In the late nineteenth century concerned citizens advocated zoning to answer the growing urban problems. Unfortunately, zoning usually served only to maintain existing city patterns and did not provide progressive strategies for city growth.

During the depression of the 1930's some planners devised "Green-belt" cities as escapes from over-crowded urban areas. Green belt cities were built in Radburn, New Jersey, Greenbelt, Maryland, and Greendale, Wisconsin. Each Greenbelt was built in the form of a horseshoe and surrounded by a "green belt" of forest. They contained only 25,000 people. These new towns failed to attract industry and only the middle and upper middle-classes could afford to live in them. In the 1950's and 1960's federal, state, and local governments pumped billions of dollars into rebuilding urban areas. Few plans for urban renewal, however, included city residents in the process. Thus citizen concern and expertise for urban renewal did not develop.

City planners in the 1970's are concerned with involving urban residents in the planning process. Both planners of new and existing cities wish to plan for a sense of community identification and participation of residents. These planners feel the forms of future cities will result from the attitudes of residents as well as from the existing technology available for growth.

In Assignments 33 and 34 you will examine alternative approaches to city planning. Assignment 33 includes an example of planning a new town. Assignment 34 describes two strategies to planning for existing cities. Examine each alternative and determine the one that best solves the complex problems of urban living.

City planning (1)

Assignment 33

City planners encounter many problems when they design strategies for future urban growth or redevelopment. Planners must consider transportation, architecture, environment, and sources and amounts of funds. They must also include citizen, business, and government positions and expectations in their designs. The following two articles raise questions about the conflicting strategies of urban planning in the United States. The first article, "Tomorrow's Cities," describes several growth patterns for cities and examines the conflicting opinions among city planners today. The second article, "A Dubious Dogma of Urban Planning," describes the problem of the role of the individual in urban planning. As you read the first article answer the following:

1. What are three patterns for city growth?

As you read the second article answer the following:

1. What is the problem of defining the role of the individual in urban planning?

After you have defined the problems of urban planning you will examine a new town alternative to these problems. In Assignment 34 you will examine other alternatives to these problems.

Tomorrow's cities

The following article describes the future growth patterns of urban development and outlines the varying attitudes among several planners and residents toward city planning.

All over the world, people are moving into cities. In the past decade while our own country was growing 11.4 per cent, its one-hundred largest metropolitan areas grew 13.2 per cent. Already 57 per cent of us live in these largest metropolitan areas. Every month we add to our population a city the size of Toledo, Ohio. Every year we add a new Philadelphia. In twenty years we will double the size of Los Angeles and the San Francisco Bay area. In twenty years we will add 6,000,000 to the New York region. Where in the world are all these people to live?

Well, we will have to build. In what is left of this century, we must build as much as has been built in the whole nation since the white man came. By the year 2000 nearly half of our people will live in houses or apartments not yet started and on land not yet broken. And most of this building will have to be in cities.

Every daily newspaper tells of cities rotting from the inside out and of deadly polarities deepening all the time between affluent and poor, powerful and powerless, white and nonwhite, privileged and deprived, urb and suburb. Growth begins to sound like a dread disease. However, not everybody takes a gloomy view. Some businessmen and planners see this growth as an opportunity for business, for jobs, for developing new and better institutions. How? Not by patching and propping up the old cities but by building entirely new cities, cities that are free of the mistakes that are destroying the old ones.

We are better able to build than the city builders of a century ago. They had to find advantageous natural settings, such as mountain passes and navigable rivers; we don't even need to depend on the manmade nets of rails and roads. Our technological know-how enables us to build anywhere—in space, on the moon, in Wyoming, anywhere we have a mind to. As urban problems become uglier, the easier it becomes to dream of leaving the old city behind for a shimmering new city built upon the fruited plain.

This dream has such appeal, in fact, that for a while every new run-of-the-mill subdivision was promoted as a "new city," even though it was nothing more than a commuters' bedroom community with semi-detached shopping center. The new city label got so blurred from misuse that it is now difficult to know precisely what a new city is . . . .

Then the question becomes, *How* shall our cities grow, higher or wider?

In some places, greater density seems to be the choice. That is, more and more people living closer and closer together. High-rise apartments and townhouses both help to densify a city, and architectural dreamers often have envisioned tower cities. Chicago's 100-story John Hancock Center includes dwellings as well as commercial and recreation areas and office floors. With a population of 12,000 persons, it is something of a vertical city, all by itself. Projects of relatively comparable scale are being talked of for other cities, so we may be about to enter a new epoch of tower building.

As Manhattan is the typical high-density city, Los Angeles represents the opposite alternative—loose-jointed, low-density sprawl. Merely mentioning its name is enough to evoke the specter of megalopolis, the super-metropolis that engulfs and consumes all community life in its path . . . .

Even so, Los Angeles has its friends, including some who make the city its own justification: "If L.A.'s so bad, how come so many people live there?" A geographer noted how typically "downtown" facilities—major department stores, theaters, financial institutions, fashionable shops—are appearing in outlying centers of the Los Angeles region and has concluded that Los Angeles is not really being flung apart by some insane force at all. What's happening is that the city is developing a brand-new form of urbanism made possible by the automobile. One day the new West Coast urbanism may outmode and replace the traditional urbanism.

So where do we go from here? What manner of city do we plan for the future?

A dubious dogma of urban planning

The following article describes the conflict between the city planner and the urban resident. The author, Philip Arctander, is the Director of the Danish Building Institute.

. . . *Planning dogma: that we know what is good for people* . . . This most conceited dogma belongs in a dictatorship rather than in a democracy. Although rarely stated openly, it is certainly implied in most of our planning . . . . We know very little about the environmental needs and desires of the people of today. And we know even less about their children and great-grandchildren who are destined to be the victims of our planning decisions.

Are fresh air and isolation good—or the nearness of neighbours? Is high interaction good-or personal segregation? Is the nuclear family good—or group families, or interacting individuals? Is it good for a mother to work 40 hours a week outside the home—or bad for the child? Are supermarkets good because they are cheap—or shops because they are in the neighborhood? Or on a different level: Is growth good? Private transport? Speed?

Of course a single plan cannot solve such questions . . . . Is planning impossible, then? No. The conclusion from all the uncertainties is that to most planning problems there is not one answer but numerous different answers during the lifetime of the plan. Planning is not a plan, planning is a process. The planner does not . . . "form the canals in which life shall flow." He makes a modest contribution to a process. What he might aim at is to avoid building more obstacles to future unknown kinds of life.

That planning should be a process is even more true for the city's residents than for the planner. It is doubtful which is worse, for a democratic citizen to be forced to live under a bad plan, or to have a supposedly good plan forced upon you without being asked. The only possible way to include all the different future answers to each problem in one plan is to include the citizens in a continuous active role—and in the chairman's seat. [80]

Happiness is making up your own mind . . . .

The purpose of planning is not to produce a desirable state, for that would immediately vanish in thin air anyway. The purpose must be a dynamic

[80] Do you agree with Arctander that the citizens of a city should have a voice in urban planning decisions? Why, or why not?

one: to open the way for a planning and decision process, with the residents in charge . . . . The process is the purpose. This statement is dynamic and democratic: It places the city resident in a position to control his own environment . . . .

This does not mean less planning or fewer planners. Planning with the people will inevitably use more planners and ask more from them. But the demand on the planned will be even greater. If direct involvement in planning is to function at all, and I see no other way, the people whose experience in democracy is a silly vote every four years must undergo some sort of a revolution . . . .

To plan properly we must change the concept of planning, its purpose, its tools, and the planner-resident relation . . . .

New town community planning

The new town of Columbia, Maryland, illustrates one alternative toward community planning. By building a new town, planners may escape many of the problems and constraints of community development in old cities. Examine the photographs of Columbia, and read the essay and the comments by the residents of this city. Then decide whether you would prefer living in a new town or an older city.

1. To what extent does Columbia provide a sense of community identification for its residents?
2. What are the major strengths and weaknesses of new towns such as Columbia?

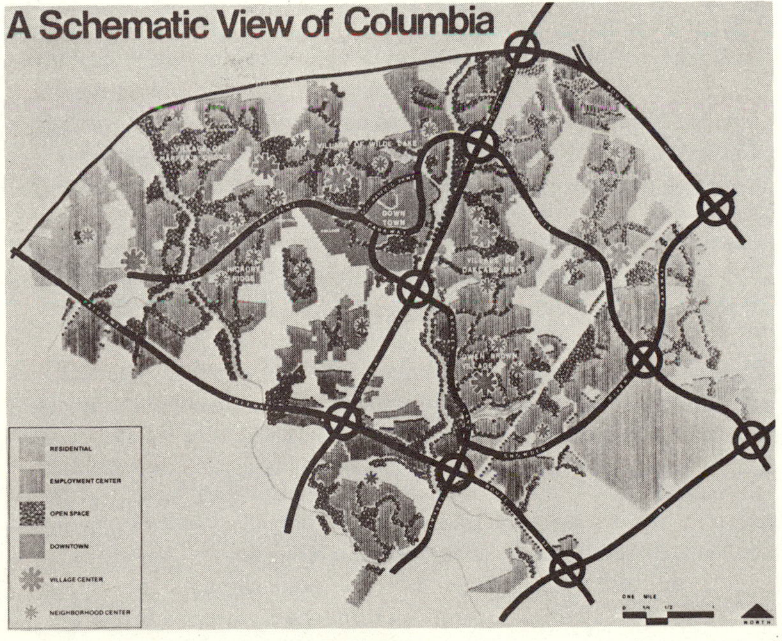

1

All photographs of Columbia supplied by the Howard Research and Development Corporation.

Columbia, Maryland

The new town of Columbia, located midway between Washington, D.C. and Baltimore, Maryland, began in 1963 as a joint venture of James W. Rouse and the Connecticut General Life Insurance Company. In October of 1963, Rouse announced that his corporation had purchased 14,000 acres of land in Howard County, Maryland. On this land they proposed to build a new city for 100,000 people. This new city would become an ideal setting for urban man.

Unlike many suburban developments Rouse announced that trees would be removed only when necessary. Moreover, he planned to build new lakes, golf courses, parks, and walking trails to compliment the trees, streams, and open spaces of Columbia.

Five years after the initial announcement by Rouse, Columbia accepted its first permanent residents. Today it contains more than 25,000 people and is growing rapidly. Town officials expect the population to reach 105,000 by 1981. Visitors and residents alike agree that Columbia provides a unique urban environment.

At first glance one is struck by the fact that everything in Columbia is new and modern. However, other geographical features quickly become apparent. The familiar checkerboard street pattern of most cities is absent in Columbia. All streets curve gently. Residential streets end in oval cul-de-sacs. Overhead one encounters no wires, utility poles, or TV aerials blotting out the sky. All wires, even in the downtown section remain hidden underground.

As you drive through Cblumbia and talk with its people other interesting features appear.

Housing: Columbia's first three villages Wilde Lake, Harper's Choice, and Oakland Mills, contain a diversity of housing unknown in the typical residential area. Single family dwellings, townhouses, apartments, condominium units, and federally subsidized housing blend harmoniously into residential clusters. Columbia provides housing at rents ranging from $99 to $450 per month and at sale prices from $15,000 to more than $100,000.

Shopping: Designers of Columbia planned its commerical areas for easy accessability and comfortable, pleasant surroundings. Each village contains its own small shopping plaza within walking or cycling distance from most residences. The lakefront downtown area contains an enclosed mall which will eventually hold more than two million square feet of store space. The mall will house more than 300 business establishments. Other stores and businesses in the downtown area are located on broad streets dotted with benches, sparkling pools and water fountains, and a wide variety of trees.

Industry: Since 1968 more than 60 industries agreed to locate in Columbia. General Electric recently completed a $350 million Appliance Park East, adjacent to the city of Columbia. This plant alone provides more than 10,000 jobs. Two additional industrial centers are currently under development.

2

3

4

5

What are the advantages
of living in a new town?
What are the disadvantages?

6

Downtown Columbia contains over 300,000 square feet of office space. Two new office buildings will add another 103,000 square feet of office space. When the city nears completion, 1980, planners expect to have 5 million square feet of office space.

Activities: The Columbia Association was formed in 1968 to provide a high level of amenities and services for an active urban-oriented community. When the city is fully developed, the Association will own more than 3,000 acres of parks and open space and at least $27.5 million worth of improvements.

Properties operated by the non-profit Columbia Park and Recreation Association include a year-round indoor swimming pool, the Columbia Tennis Club, thirteen tennis and four basketball courts, the Columbia Athletic Club, two 18-hole golf courses, the Columbia Ice Rink, twenty play areas for small children, three village community centers and nearly 900 acres of parks and open spaces. The Association also operates Columbia's two lakes. Eight neighborhood centers each with a swimming pool and community meeting room, are currently in operation.

In addition to recreational facilities operated by the Columbia Association, the city offers a number of other recreational opportunities. The Columbia Tennis Barn offers indoor tennis on a membership basis. Two 18-hole miniature golf courses opened in 1972. Stables, horses and riding are provided at the Columbia Horse center, and the River Hill game preserve provides opportunities for pheasant and quail hunting. The Merriweather Post Pavillion of Music, with seats under cover for 5,000 has completed its eighth season. Other attractions include the Garland Dinner Theatre and a number of fine restaurants.

Columbia, Maryland, has received both praise and criticism. Former Secretary of Housing and Urban Development, George Romney claimed, "The establishment of Columbia shows the entire nation and the world an important, viable step toward solving the crushing problems of our wildly expanding and exploding cities." One planner, however, stated that, "ten years from now Columbia will be like the first little Vanguard satellite. Already, we can see we did many things too conservatively. For example, we could have clustered houses much better with a big common open space for every three or four houses instead of the quarter-acre lot . . ."

For James Rouse the building of even better new towns is too tame. He is now busy trying to apply what he has learned in constructing Columbia to the problems of the old cities. "Now that's the real job," he says.

Residents' comment on life in Columbia

In November, 1973, the authors questioned about thirty residents of Columbia about their perception of life in the city. These residents indicated that housing, cleanliness of the environment, public schools, population size and density, and integration were the most important qualities of life in Columbia. Residents repeatedly criticized the lack of adequate transportation and recreation facilities in Columbia. Several of the teenagers indicated that life in Columbia was dull. Some of the comments of residents follow:

A government analyst, 50 years old, with a family of five, living in Columbia for three years commented: "Columbia, unlike other cities, is integrated; but like other cities has transportation problems." "I like the beauty of a planned city, the convenience to shopping and medical facilities, the proximity to Washington and Baltimore, and the variety of housing."

A black government worker, 37 years old, with a family of four, living in Columbia for two years commented: "Columbia offers a clean environment for my family and social life for blacks. It's great if you have transportation and don't mind going to Baltimore or D.C. for down to earth Soul."

A secretary, 48 years old, with a family of three, living in Columbia for a year commented: "I like living with others who believe in integration and the rights of people to choose their residence as they please. The moderate rules and laws make it impossible for Columbia to look like a slum. However, cultural events are almost non-existent. If you come from a cosmopolitan city, Columbia could be considered dull and boring. Also, most of the population is under 35."

A single teacher, 23 years, living in Columbia for four months commented: "I appreciate the convenience–everything is here, most of its within walking distance. Columbia offers the advantages of the big city without the bad points. Yet it is still close to the cultural and recreational facilities of Baltimore and Washington. But Columbia is much more than a bedroom suburban area–it is a self-contained, planned environment. It's a great alternative to random growth and the prospect of the future metro-slum."

A single teacher, 22 years old, living in Columbia for two months commented: "I moved to Columbia for a job. This city is much more sterile. It would be difficult to become part of this city. It seems to be cheaply constructed. Like other cities the people are hard to become acquainted with. The cost of living is ridiculously high! It's dull. There are very few young, single professionals."

A teenager, 16 years old, living in Columbia for a year commented: "In other cities, if you don't have your own transportation, you can catch the bus. Life as a teenager is mostly a drag. They don't have enough things for you to do."

A teenager, 16 years old, living in Columbia for three years commented: "The planning of Columbia provides for generally more attractive appearance. Columbia provides numerous opportunities for recreation and community involvement. The religious opportunities here are great. Columbia is still subject to bureaucratic inefficiency and has transportation problems like other cities.

7

8

Living here is extremely 'good.'"

A teenager, 17 years old, living in Columbia for one year commented: "It is very slowpaced and unexciting. It is a very beautiful city to live in but beauty is only skin deep. If you are having fun where you live then stay there and don't move to Columbia."

For thought and discussion

What role will new towns play in future urban planning?

Individual and small group activities

1. Go to your library and gather information about other new towns in the United States. Have these towns fulfilled the needs of urban residents? How do these cities differ from Columbia? Report to class. (You may also wish to report on other new cities in England and Europe and compare them with American new cities.)
2. Go to your library and gather information about one of the greenbelt cities of the 1930's such as Radburn, New Jersey, Greenbelt, Maryland, or Greendale, Wisconsin. How was the plan of this city alike or unlike the plan of Columbia? What other similarities or differences can you determine? Report to class.

City planning (2)

Assignment 34

Planning redevelopment of existing cities is more difficult than planning for new towns. Cities such as New York, Boston, Miami, and Los Angeles are much larger than Columbia. They already possess defined living and work spaces, social patterns and attitudes, a greater mix of residents, and vast government bureaucracies. Planners must change old physical and attitude patterns as well as design new ones. The data in Assignment 34 describe two alternatives for improvement of existing urban areas. As you read each alternative consider which alternative you would most support.

1. To what degree does each alternative provide for the needs of the community?
2. What is the role of the citizen in each alternative?

San Francisco's urban design plan

San Francisco has long been known for its exciting physical qualities such as the unsurpassed setting on the peninsula and its brightly, textured panorama of buildings on the rolling hills. In the 1960's, however, San Franciscans becamed alarmed with the deterioration of the physical qualities of the city. Huge skyscrapers threatened to break-up the harmonious lines of buildings on the hills. New development obscured and destroyed historical landmarks. The sprawling city growth pattern threatened to destroy city life. Neighborhoods were breaking up and residents were losing a sense of identity with their neighborhood and city. Concerned officials and residents met and commissioned a group of planners to draw up a design for the physical maintenance and development of San Francisco. The plan grew out of extensive interviews with residents of San Francisco who related their ideas about the needs of the city. The following excerpts and pictures from the design plan indicate some guidelines for the preservation and development of the city. This alternative illustrates the technological and physical considerations of urban planning.

The San Francisco Urban Design Plan proposes different plans for conserving and developing the physical character and environment of the city and its neighborhoods. This plan is only one part of a larger master plan for San Francisco which includes designs for rapid transit, industrial growth, city services and government. The plan has four major objectives: the development of an overall city street and building pattern, the conservation of buildings and environment, the control of major new developments, and the upkeep of neighborhood character and environment.

The planners emphasize the development of a comprehensive city building and street pattern because they feel it will meet certain human needs. A city pattern will provide the individual with an organized city, a sense of belonging and purpose, and reduce the stress of urban life. This pattern of streets and buildings will help people to identify neighborhood districts and increase pride in the individual's city and neighborhood. Such a unified pattern will also aid residents on foot, in automobiles, and on public transportation.

The conservation of buildings and the environment will meet other human needs. Parks would provide recreation areas for urban residents. The preservation of old buildings provides a sense of tradition and historical perspective. Maintenance of neighborhoods will prevent the growth of slums.

The control of new developments is crucial to the preservation of city unity and the identity of neighborhoods. Controlled new development provides harmony for the urban residents. For example, when an individual views his city his view is not broken by a high ugly building. Uncontrolled new developments on the other hand, might breakup old living areas.

Finally, the maintenance of neighborhoods and its environment increases the personal safety, comfort, pride, and opportunities for neighborhood residents. Neighborhood residents may help to keep up their neighborhood if they feel proud and safe within their neighborhoods. Opportunities for recreation within a neighborhood stimulate interaction among the neighborhood residents. If urban residents feel safe and satisfied within their neighborhood they will not need to move to the suburbs for safety and a better environment.

The San Francisco plan illustrated

The following four pages of pictures illustrate the types of strategies developed to meet the objectives of the planners. The pictures are labeled before and after. Many of the strategies do not involve major changes but small changes that you may never have been aware would affect the physical character and environment of the city. Of course these strategies must link with other strategies in order to be effective. As you look at each "before and after" set of pictures notice what has been added, taken away, or changed in the "after" picture. What affect would this change have on your physical or psychological image of the city? What other physical changes might you recommend?

1 BEFORE

1 AFTER

2 BEFORE

2 AFTER

3 BEFORE

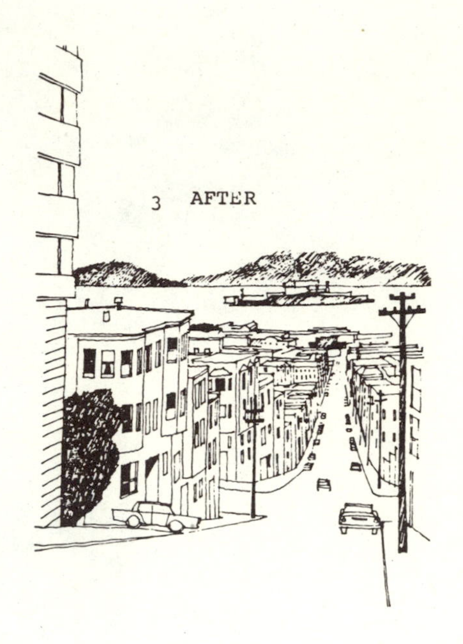
3 AFTER

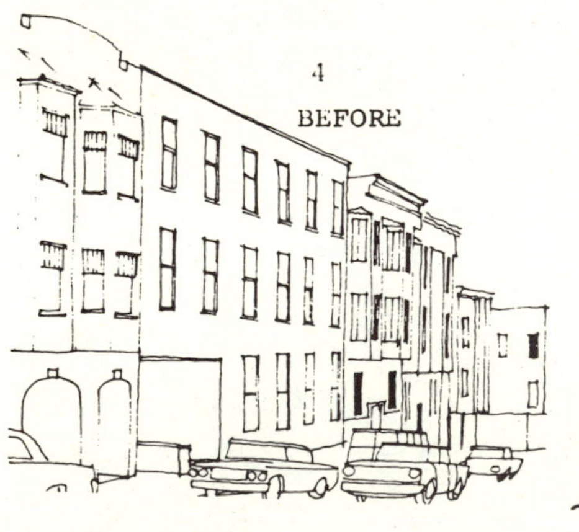
4
BEFORE

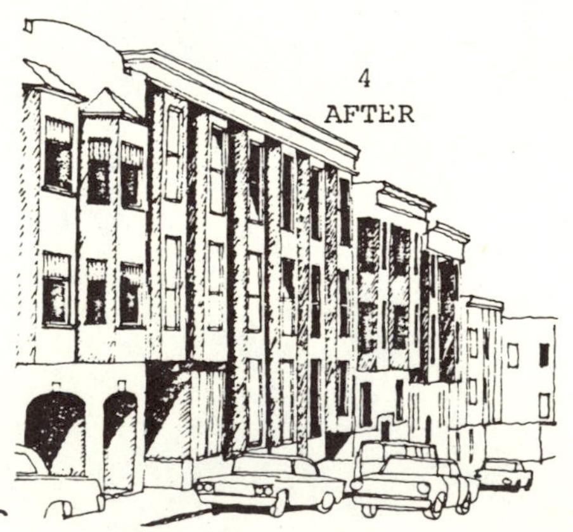
4
AFTER

5 BEFORE

5
AFTER

6
BEFORE

6
AFTER
PEILS
PEILS

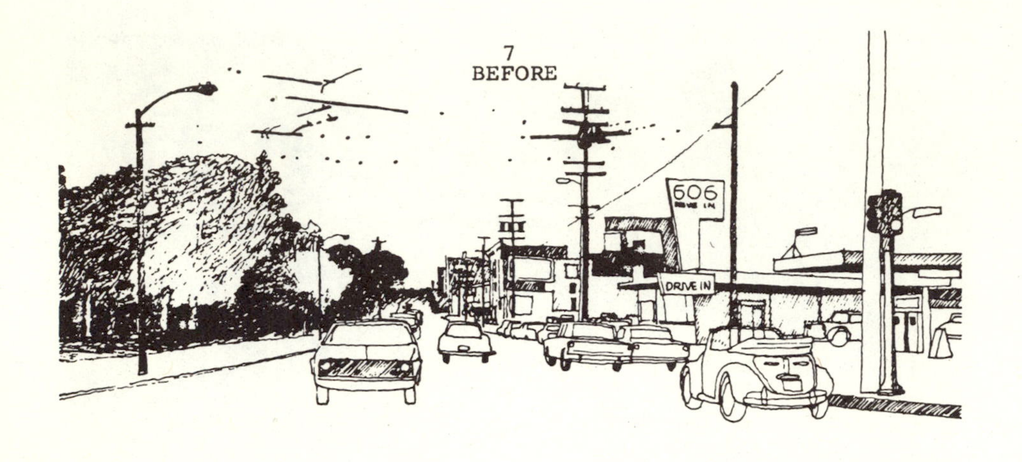
7
BEFORE
606
DRIVE IN

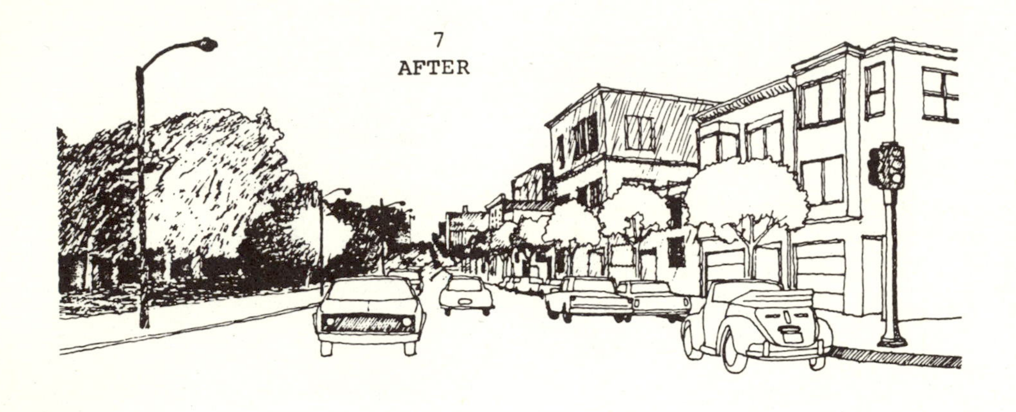
7
AFTER

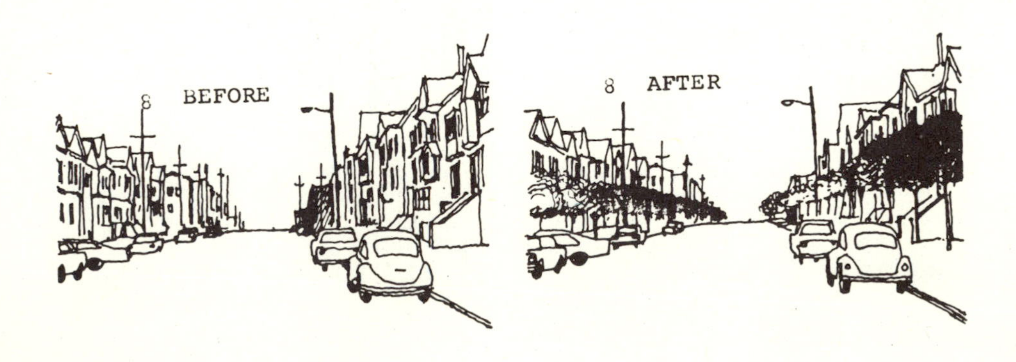
8 BEFORE
8 AFTER

Urban redevelopment in Hartford, Connecticut

In the 1960's Hartford, Connecticut, experienced a loss of population to the suburbs and growing physical decay of the inner city. Businessmen became concerned about declining land values and trade in the central city. At the same time, James Rouse, the builder of Columbia, Maryland, decided to develop strategies for the maintenance and development of already established cities. Hartford's businessmen retained the Rouse corporation to help develop a massive plan for the rebirth and development of Hartford and the surrounding region. The following article describes the plans for the redevelopment of Hartford.

The current planning program in Hartford, Connecticut is the most ambitious privately sponsored urban development effort ever undertaken. The sponsors and planners describe their program as an entirely new process of community life and growth for Hartford and its region.

The sponsors are thirty Hartford area businesses called The Greater Hartford Corporation. These businesses contributed more than $7.8 million for the planning phase and pledged to raise additional capital for the ensuing development. This development will include the creation of an entirely new community and new neighborhoods, the expansion of an existing suburb, and the rebirth of the North End ghetto.

The planners objective is to make the city work. Planners should not patch up non-working cities. They believe that the wealth and business expertise of American society can produce a working urban environment.

In 1969, the planners interviewed hundreds of people in the Hartford area. They then delivered a design for "the Hartford process." This process is a continuing examination over a decade of what makes the Hartford region tick (or what keeps it from ticking). The planners would examine education, law and justice, health, transportation, housing, and development and other potential Hartford problem areas. They would examine these systems individually and in relation to one another. (A "system" means a combination of things or parts forming a complex or unitary whole.) Through a comprehensive examination the planners would avoid the piecemeal strategies of past planners. The planners and businessmen believe that they must design an urban model of how each system relates to the other systems. For example, how does the school system affect the health system and welfare system?

The Hartford planners admit that the in-town development will be their most difficult job. They have no luxury of starting from scratch. They have no relief from the immense urban problems.

Acceptance of the planners' investigations and their ultimate design will depend on the involvement of the community people. The planners are attempting to work cooperatively with the residents of two neighborhoods in North Hartford. The planners realize that urban redevelopment programs often fail from lack of community involvement.

The planners and businessmen found a well-organized community group in Hartford's North End. These primarily black and Puerto Rican citizens, with the help of an architect, had already devised their own urban renewal plan. The community group had begun to implement an "Everywhere School" concept. This school, located in a community warehouse, trains students who have rejected the traditional school system.

The planners decided to work in a joint venture with this community organization. One planner commented, "They're a well-established and respected group and are certainly more representative of the people of the North Hartford area than we are."

The earliest joint effort is a housing relocation proposal. This proposal aims to keep as much of the original North Hartford population in the community as possible. A housing management company would manage units for temporary use until the new development is complete. An overall management proposal for the whole renewal project is also in the planning stage.

In general, the community organization is optimistic about their collarboration with the planners and businessmen. However, some community residents have doubts about the real aims of the other group: "They (the planners and businessmen) are not specific enough. They say they have some goals, but don't say how they're going to reach them. They do not state the reasons behind their goals. You won't get any answers out of them. But maybe it's not bad not to know."

Other community members feel they know the aims of the businessmen and planners: "It's not the business community saying we're going to do you a favor, it's in *their* interest. The business community is buying insurance, that's what it boils down to. By rebuilding the North End they will improve their own investment in the city."

In answer to these questions one planner stated that they were aiming at a new style of planning. This new style would be somewhere between 1) where citizens are told to go out and plan, and they can't "because they don't know how," and 2) where technicians show a full blown plan to the people "usually to be defeated in the political arena." Somewhere in between is a creative dialogue between the people and the planners. The people should identify the plan as theirs, i.e. "it's the kind of place I'd like to be; I can see myself there."

This planner was questioned about the chances that he and his colleagues would try to push something that went against the ideas of the community. He replied they might be foolish enough to try, but they wouldn't get very far. In response to the question of community support of the redevelopment, he replied that he believed that people will opt for what's in their best interest. "You don't need everybody, just enough brave leaders to bring the community along . . . . We hope to give enough details to get people to believe that it's possible to manage growth and change. We hope to have consulted enough people to have their enthusiasm—to have them say, 'Even if we planners are a bunch of carpetbaggers, there's something there that we need.' "

Community development in action: A progress report

By June, 1974, the planners and community organization produced a comprehensive renovation plan for the northern half of Hartford. The following progress report, by the Greater Hartford Process illustrates the scope of this innovative, massive planning project.

I. *Community Development in the City–The New Hartford*

A. *Neighborhood Planning and Development*

1. *South Arsenal Neighborhood Development (SAND)*
There is visible action taking place in the 58-acre urban renewal site south of Canton Street under the strong leadership of the South Arsenal Neighborhood Development Corporation.

Housing:
The first 274 units of low- and moderate-income housing are under construction and should be open for occupancy in late fall. This housing will consist of a series of 3-story, low-rise garden apartments; a high-rise tower building of 10 stories is scheduled for completion next year. Housing for the elderly is being incorporated into the high-rise unit.
Simultaneously, work has begun on thinning out 200 units of public housing in Bellevue Square, part of the SAND plan to reduce densities within the area. In the remaining units, rehabilitation of kitchens and bathrooms is taking place.

Education:
Paralleling the development of SAND housing, the Everywhere School, Hartford's first example of a true community school, has been approved, and, under a fast-track system, construction work should begin within a month. Planned as a series of separate multi-instructional areas (MIAS), the Everywhere School will form an educational spine running through the SAND project, replacing the obsolete Arsenal School. The Everywhere School is being constructed by the City with a $4 million bond issue already approved and, when completed, it will serve approximately 1,000 children.

2. *Northwest Hartford–Upper Albany, Asylum Hill*
At the invitation of the City, Process, Inc. began survey and planning work in the Upper Albany area in late 1972. A $93,700 HUD grant supported the planning work, and Asylum Hill Inc. agreed to prepare a community development plan for its neighborhood in tandem with the Upper Albany effort. The progress to date on the overall planning includes:
   a. The organization of a joint planning effort, including representatives of the City, the Upper Albany Community Association (UACO), Asylum Hill Inc., Blue Hills Civic Association, Urban Edge, Process, Inc., and several business, political and resident leaders in the neighborhoods.
   b. The publication of a report: *Northwest Hartford: An Action Program,* which summarizes the problems, needs and solutions necessary to re-

store these neighborhoods to social and economic health.

Upper Albany

Community Organization:
UACO, (Upper Albany Community Organization), a major new community association, is now active and viable, with a paid membership of over 500 people. This organization will play a key role in the overall execution of the neighborhood program. Presently under contract with Process, Inc., it is carrying out community organization and public information work.

Jobs, Social Services:
A neighborhood life center—the second in the City—has been opened at 1229 Albany Avenue and is offering Upper Albany residents self-support and social services programs.

Housing:
Rehabilitation of homes and home ownership will be the emphasis for the renewal of Upper Albany. Meetings have been held with HUD Hartford Area office, the State Department of Community Affairs and the State Housing Finance Agency; all have expressed a desire to participate in the proposed rehabilitation program.

Commercial Development:
To make the neighborhood more attractive and economically viable, a new 69,000 square foot shopping center is projected on Albany Avenue between Woodland and Milford Streets. Active negotiations are now taking place with the City for site acquisition and for construction of the shopping center with a combination of City funds and private capital. This kind of development at the western edge of Albany Avenue is critical to the well-being of the entire area, which is now an underserved market of some 24,000 people with a consumer potential of $30 million annually.

Asylum Hill Inc.
From its inception in 1971, Asylum Hill Inc. has focused on a series of priorities for the improvement and rehabilitation of its neighborhood. Emphasis of the first phase of its program was on the implementation of projects to strengthen public safety in the area, stem the exodus of residents who no longer found the neighborhood desirable, create a sense of community and develop the cohesiveness and heightened morale necessary to support physical redevelopment and renewal. Supported by four major financial institutions with particular interest in the neighborhood: Aetna Life, The Hartford, Connecticut Mutual and Society for Savings, Asylum Hill Inc. has carried out a series of programs designed to achieve these objectives:

Asylum Hill Inc. is also conducting feasibility studies which would permit large-scale intervention to reverse the deterioration of the neighborhood. This contemplates the extensive remodeling, rehabilitation and repair of 2,600 housing units in the neighborhood and the development of two "super blocks" in the general area of Asylum Avenue, with some streets closed to traffic, in which there will be almost 2,000 dwelling units intended to attract middle-income residents and provide upgraded housing for families already in the neighborhood. The new "super blocks" would be transformed into a landscaped area providing all amenities such as substantially improved parking, outdoor recreation, clubhouse facilities and a secure environment.

3. *Downtown*
A $70 million Hartford Civic Center complex with a coliseum seating 12,000 people, 112,000 sqaure feet of exhibition space, shopping mall and 400 room hotel will soon open in downtown Hartford.

For thought and discussion

Do you think most citizens wish to be included in the planning process and government of their community?

Individual and small group activities

1. Go to your local department of city planning and interview one of the city planners. Ask him to explain generally the building and design plans for your city in the next ten years. Compare your city's plans with the alternatives you considered in Assignments 33 and 34. Do your city's plans offer a better alternative than the ones you have considered? Report to class.
2. Working with several of your classmembers design a plan for a small city. Your plan will of course be very general, however, you should include on your design map:
   1. business area
   2. industry area
   3. shopping areas
   4. living areas by income levels
   5. recreation areas
   6. major streets and street patterns
   7. any other urban activities

   You should prepare your map on a ditto so that every class member will be able to follow your presentation of your plan. In your presentation you should state the reasons for the location of activities.

*

The future city: Stating the issue for Assignments 35 and 36

The future has always fascinated and concerned people. Some dream of greater technological advances. Others wish for an improved quality of life and a better world. In the late nineteenth century many futuristic writers predicted that technological development would provide the good life for all. One of these writers, Edward Bellamy, wrote a futuristic novel, *Looking Backward,* which sold a million copies. In his novel Bellamy described the experiences of a young Bostonian who, in 1887, went into a sleep and awakened in the year 2000. He found a new social order based on collective ownership of property. Technology made a new social order possible. In this new society want, politics, and evil were unknown. People were incredibly happy.

In the twentieth century writers increasingly refuted these utopian dreams. For example, in 1932, Aldous Huxley published his novel, *The Brave New World.* In this novel future society became increasingly mechanized and social relationships diminished. Machines controlled man instead of man controlling machines. Man lost his soul. Babies came from test tubes and grew up to behave like laboratory animals. Technology did not provide for man's salvation.

In contemporary times writers repeatedly voice pessimism about the future. Man's inability to adapt and control his life provides a major source of concern. For example, in his best-selling book, *Future Shock,* Alvin Toffler argues that technology and society change too quickly for the individual. The individual becomes confused and unable to cope with a fast-changing world. If man cannot cope with the present, continues Toffler, how can he plan for the future? Theodore Rozak, the author of *The Making of the Counter Culture* and *Where The Wasteland Ends*, foresees cities as "air conditioned nightmares." People will live in their little air-conditioned boxes while the world disintegrates around them. Reports from public and private sources forecast overpopulation, decay of cities, and destruction of our natural resources. Some criticize these reports and believe that technology will solve our future problems. Others reply that our very technology will destroy us unless people's attitudes change. For example, they argue that technology is not enough to build better cities. We must have a national commitment.

In Assignments 35 and 36 you will examine plans and conceptions for future cities. Several of the plans focus on the physical structure of future cities. The designers of these communities display great optimism about the future quality of life in their cities. The other two alternatives are more pessimistic. Evaluate each plan and decide which of the alternatives you would prefer to live under.

The future city (1)

Assignment 35

By the year 2000, five-sixths of our population will live in urban regions. An urban region is not a single super city but a regional group of urban centers. These regions will occupy one-sixth of the land area of the continental United States. The darkened areas on the following map indicate the location and area of urban regions in the year 2000.

Urban regions: Year 2000

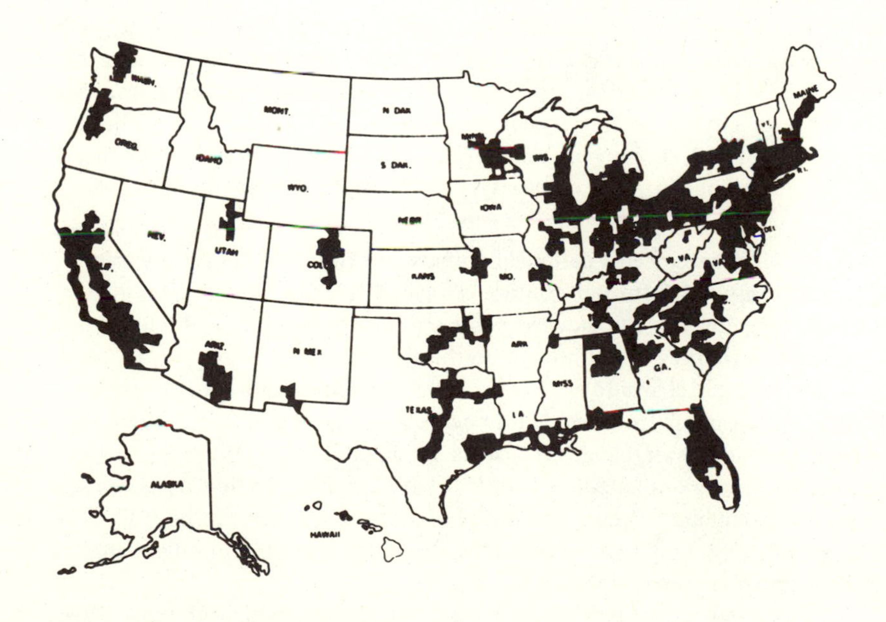

Based on a 2 child per family projection
Source: Commission on Population Growth and the American Future, Population and the American Future (Washington, D.C.: Government Printing Office, 1972).

This expansion of urban regions will bring new problems of physical design and social attitudes. However, many architects, planners, and philosophers remain optimistic about the future of our cities. They believe we have the technology available to create cities with a high quality of life for all. Their concern is that people's attitudes may not change to meet new conditions. People may not understand where they are and where they are going. In other words, our vision will not expand as our technology expands. Society must decide how to use our technology to create cities that will meet the needs of people in the next century. We need a comprehensive and systematic approach to building our future cities. Planners of future cities call for a systems approach to our future urban structures. For example planners can no longer deal with work, residence, recreation, and transportation as separate problems. They must consider the relationships between work, residence, and recreation areas and the transportation between each area.

In these final two assignments you will consider several alternatives for future cities. Answer the following questions for each alternative.

1. How will society use its technology in the future?
2. How does each alternative meet the needs of future people?

We can build space age cities now

James Hudson, an engineer and building consultant envisions a future city where nature plays a vital role in the city design. If planners of future cities encorporate trees and wildlife in the urban area, he argues, residents will no longer want to escape from the city to the countryside. Hudson believes the cities have a bright future if residents will support urban redevelopment. Hudson describes his future city in the essay and photographs on pages 432–457 of Assignment 35.

. . . In the 1970's we need a national commitment to transform American's dying cities into healthful and exciting living and working centers. This goal is no idle pipe dream. Any knowledgeable scientist or engineer will tell you we have the technology right now to do this job . . . .

What a colossal absurdity that we allow our central cities, the centers of modern American life, to crumble into depressing places where it is no fun to live and work. Dirty air, congested streets, cramped living quarters, and urban ugliness are driving out long-time residents who can afford to live in more pleasant surroundings. They leave behind only those who are too poor to cope with the grinding urban decay. Thus our cities are deteriorating at an alarming and increasing rate.

This tragedy is not inevitable. We can rescue and rebuild our cities. This rebuilding is just as practical as putting men on the moon. All it takes is a national commitment. Let's see how a comprehensive systematic approach can make cities more people-oriented.

One key part of our plan is the covering of existing streets with a roof, with a green carpet of grass and trees on top, about thirty feet above the

1

2

streets. This green roof opens the way to transforming the city's harsh concrete and smelly gasoline alleys into restful areas planted with lawns, trees, and flowers.

The space above the streets and between the buildings becomes an oasis in the cement jungle, a people-oriented environment with grassy playground, flowering shrubs, and chattering squirrels. There will be sidewalks for people in a hurry and meandering paths for others. These spaces will provide places to talk, to read, and to relax. Soft conversation and the songs of birds will replace the nerve-shattering construction and traffic.

Nature, using sunlight, chlorophyll, water, and soil, can go to work manufacturing clean, fresh air. Every tree leaf, every blade of grass is a miniature anti-pollution factory, absorbing gases from our polluted air and miraculously return pure oxygen.

Some highrise office and apartment buildings will be terraced with some floors set back for sunlight, and planted with lawns, flowers, shrubs, and small trees. Roof gardens will have pools for ducks and fish. Most of these terraces will be open to people for a host of activities including fishing, picnicking, and nature study.

Small animals will raise their families on some terraces which will be off limits to people. Coffee breaks can turn into nature breaks as office workers watch the life cycles of birds, rabbits, squirrels, and fish outside their windows.

The automobile . . . is responsible for 60 per cent of all air pollution. Urban people suffer most, trapped as they are in densely populated areas with many high-rise buildings. With filters and the addition of manufactured

3

4

oxygen, our city streets can become a closed system of vehicular tunnels.

Other advantages of the closed street system are just as exciting:

1. Fast, efficient monorail transportation can be suspended under the pedestrian level. This will greatly improve mass transportation with a minimum of cost.
2. Car and truck traffic will flow more easily. No longer need pedestrians compete with traffic. Sidewalks and islands now set aside as "people space" can be converted to additional traffic lanes.
3. Ground floors of buildings can become delivery areas, and the confused maze of double-parked trucks would disappear from traffic lanes. These lower floors will also contain parking lots, service stations, car washes, drive-in banks, restaurants, and newsstands.
4. The covered street will bottle up the noise from traffic, trash removal and road repair. No longer can a big storm paralyze the city.
5. Digging up streets to install and repair cables will become a thing of the past. Telephone wires and power cables will be accessible in overhead troughs.

What happens to the people displaced from the first two floors of the buildings? They can have first chance at moving into new buildings which will be built over some of the old intersections.

A flight over such a city will reveal beautiful patterns of shape and color. Foliage softens the hard, straight lines of streets and buildings. Rain falls on absorbent green belts instead of hitting miles of asphalt and concrete only to run off into sewers . . . .

In high-rise residential areas the first step is to draft an overall plan to provide for the remodeling or rebuilding of entire sections of the city at the same time so no new construction will be needed for twenty years or more.

This will give city dwellers a reprieve from constant construction, blocked traffic and swirling dust.

As in the downtown area we cover the streets and reserve the old street level for cars and trucks so people can move up to fresh air and quiet. Also, like the downtown area, lawns, trees, flowers, and shrubs are planted everywhere.

In planning recreations we must consider people of different ages and interests. So 80th Street might become 80th Belt, a five-mile-long kindergarten, nursery, and fairyland. A block away is 81st Belt for grammar school children. Here the swings and basketball goals are higher and the swimming pool deeper. And so the plan goes throughout the residential areas with green recreation belts instead of streets for sub-teens, teens, young adults, adults, and the aged.

As a systems engineer I have traveled coast to coast to meet with enthusiastic groups in more than a hundred cities . . . . But, politicians ask, will these plans be too expensive? My answer: Is health damage resulting from polluted air *inexpensive*? Is urban decay *inexpensive*? Is breakdown in city life *inexpensive*? Is an increasingly depressing life for the majority of Americans going to be tolerated?

. . . If we can spend nearly $100 billion a year for past, present, and future wars, then I'd say we can afford to take this approach of rebuilding our cities. Rebuilding our cities will help solve or lessen dozens of problems which cause endless misery and heavy tax burdens. Using modern technology we can reverse the centuries-old trend of moving people to big cities only to bury them in ugliness and filth.

And let's face it. When we ask people to pay higher taxes for conservation and wilderness, inner-city folks who choke on foul air daily, fight rats nightly, and watch their city decay about them are likely to ask: "Why don't you start here?"

Parts of this new concept are already in use. For example, the concept of covering the streets with a grassy roof for pedestrians has been used in Cuyahoga Community College in Cleveland, Ohio; Edmunds Community College in Lynwood, Washington; and the Health and Welfare Complex in Nassau County on Long Island. The American International Development Corporation is using some facets of this concept in the design of the 30-story One North High Building in Columbus, Ohio.

But Uncle Sam isn't going to wave a magic wand and rebuild your cities. Local planning and participation have to be the first step. Communities must evaluate their problems, consider solutions, and draw up tentative plans before the Federal government can help with money. But money should not be the limiting factor on programs like this one . . . . We have the technology. We know the depths of the problem. All we need is the commitment. Let's make one.

Hudson's future city

A. Platform: Besides rescuing pedestrians from traffic, it isolates auto exhaust so it can be purified and recirculated.

B. People level: Above, and isolated from the noisy, pollution-spewing traffic, is the people level with grass, trees, ponds, birds, and small animals

C. Recreation belt: Located on platform above the streets, these areas provide fun for every age group.

D. Traffic level: Below the grassy roof is the old street level, now given over exclusively to traffic which moves smoothly on wider streets with no pedestrian interferences.

E. Mass transportation: Speedy, efficient monorail trains are suspended from overhead platform.

F. Circular stations: Provide access to monorail from people level.

G. Utility service: Overhead troughs carry telephone and power cables for easy access. No street digging.

H. Service area: Lower floors of building at traffic level would be remodeled and used for deliveries, parking and service stations. Also drive-in banks and restaurants.

Buckminister Fuller's future cities

R. Buckminister Fuller, one of the foremost thinkers of contemporary times, works in many diverse fields such as architecture, engineering mathematics, science, philosophy, and literature. Fuller designs structures for future housing and cities. Like other planners he believes that we have the technology available to completely revolutionize our city structures but we must have the vision and commitment in order to affect such change. The following photographs and descriptions illustrate some of Fuller's plans for future cities.

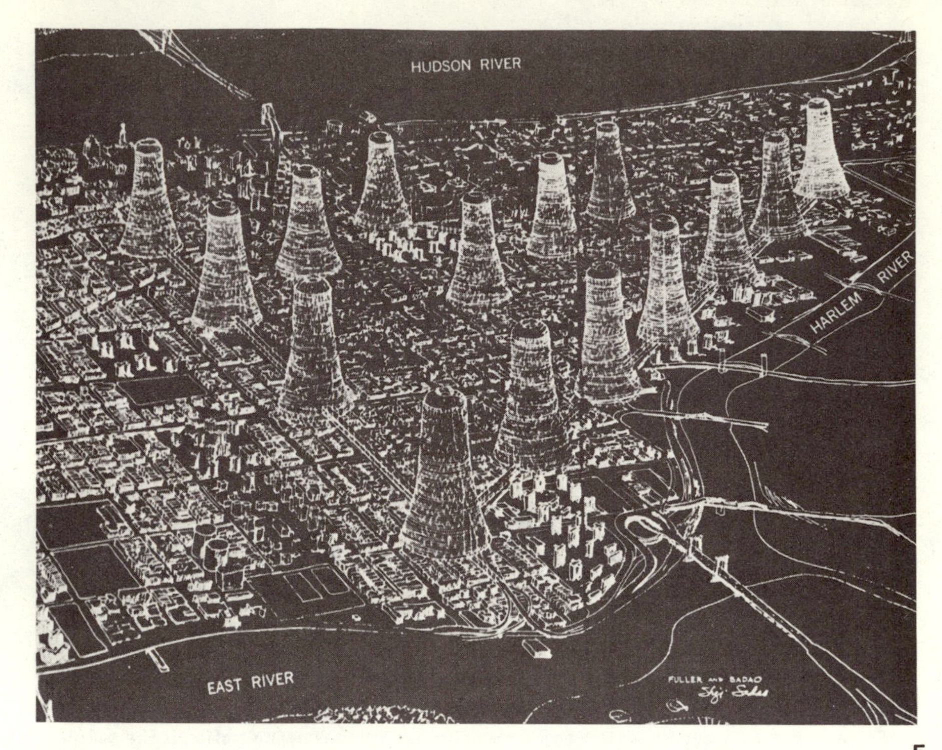

Clearance project 5

Above is Fuller's Instant Slum Clearance Project conceived in the mid-60's. His solution was to clear as little as possible. Instead, he proposed 15 widely spaced "skyrise" towers, each consisting of 100 circular living decks. Fuller suggested planting the tree-like towers in the back alleys of Harlem. Planned to house 110,000 families, these towers were intended to help relieve congestion on the ground, thus enabling the community to recycle itself as parks and rehabilitated neighborhoods.

Domed cities
In 1970, Fuller conceived a dome-covered moon crater of a city for 9,000 families. Beneath the 1,000-ft. high half-mile diameter dome, garden apartments for a broad housing mix will be deployed over the sloping outer surfaces of the crater. A compressed complex of civic, cultural, educational, commercial, and light industrial facilities is to be contained inside. The transparent dome will hover 30 feet above ground, allowing access from all directions. [81]

Floating cities
A "triangular structure floating on the ocean" Fuller's tetrahedral city, is a 200-story structure housing a million people. Roughly 300,000 families would live in 2,000 sq. ft. terrace apartments. These apartments were conceived as tray-like receptacles where owners could "plug in" their trailers, houseboats or other "mobile environment controls." For example, a family

[81] Would you want to live under a dome? Why, or why not?

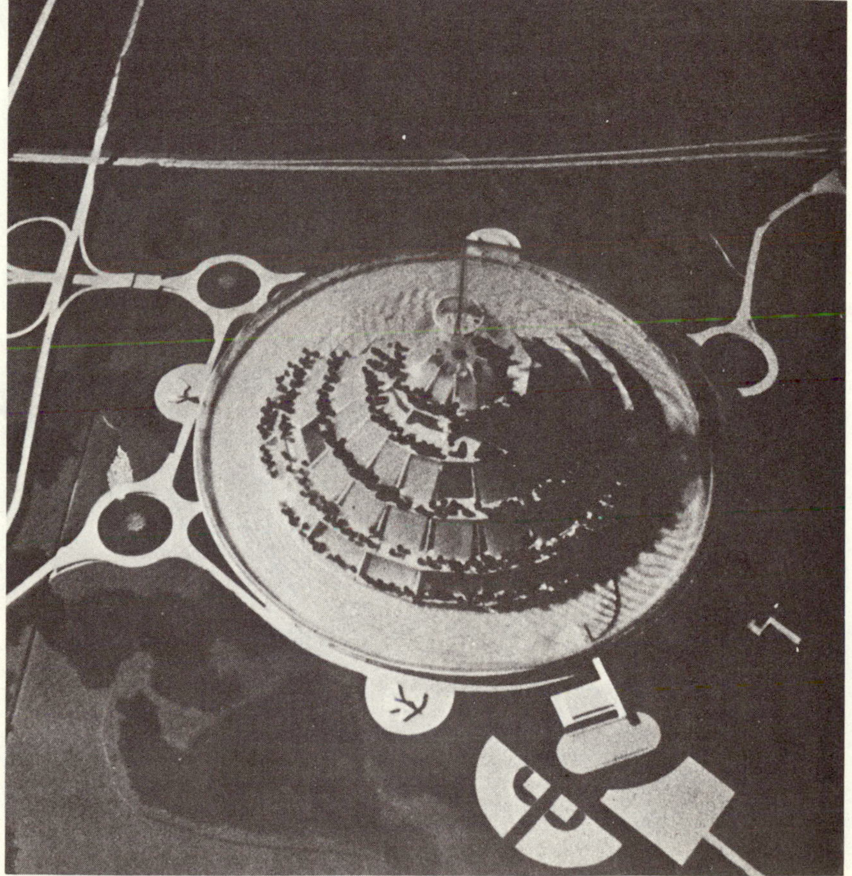

Domed cities

Tetrahedral city
7

8
Floating neighborhoods

could "plug in" their mobile houseboat into one city for six months and then "unplug" their houseboat and sail to another floating city. About half the apartment space could be used for gardening or recreation. Moreover, families could "peel off" with ease, taking their house along but leaving the terrace behind. The built-in transit system interconnects commercial, cultural, and community centers, each with its hanging gardens and cool lagoons. On land, the interior of the city would contain a vast park sunlit through broad openings every 50th floor. At sea, the interior would shelter a great harbor for the largest vessels. The city's foundations–hollow sections of reinforced concrete, 200 feet deep–would go below the ocean providing stability during earthquakes and storms. The foundations should enable the city to navigate the seas or rest at anchor.

Whenever the city might be at any given time, it would be accessible by jet plane because the outer edges of its triangular base, two miles to a side, would provide aircraft carrier style landing strips. Fuller envisions such cities will enable man to live in large numbers over the Earth's surface without further ruining our land resources. The heat of the city's atomic reactors would desalinate ocean water, waste would be recycled. Whole communities as well as individuals could circumnavigate the planet as casually as making a phone call.

Two kinds of floating neighborhoods were designed to lie at anchor in the waters off America's larger metropolitan areas. One is a series of four to six "rafts," each holding 1,000 people. The other, platform for 3,400 to 6,500, would support an elementary school, supermarket, stores, and services. Three to six of these "neighborhoods" would make a new town, and another platform would be added to accommodate a high school, and commercial, recreational, and civic functions. Three to seven of these new towns would make a new city of 90,000 to 125,000 people who would then presumably join still other platforms containing a community college or a government center. The single framework of each neighbrohood would make it a complete building. Modules for apartments, classrooms, stores, and offices would be prefabricated and plugged in or replaced without disturbing the overall city framework. Fuller states that floating structures of 20 stories can be engineered in water only 25 or 30 feet deep.

For thought and discussion

What are the most important needs of the individual in the future city?

Individual and small group activities

1. Go to your library and locate designs for future transportation systems. What are the major aspects of the designs? Who benefits most from these designs? Do these designs help social interaction or do they isolate the individual? Report

your research to class and if possible show some of the designs through drawings or photographs.

2. Read one of the following books about future society:
   Edward Bellamy, *Looking Backward*
   Aldous Huxley, *Brave New World, Brave New World Revisited*
   B. F. Skinner, *Walden Two*
   Kurt Vonnegut, *Player Piano*
   Theodore Rozak, *The Making of a Counter Culture, Where the Wasteland Ends*
   Alvin Toffler, *Future Shock*
   Charles Reich, *The Greening of America*
   Daniel Bell (ed.), *Toward the Year 2000*

   Report to class about the author's attitude toward technological advances. What is the impact of technology on man? What changes in society does the author advocate? Do you agree or disagree with the author's views about the future of society? Why, or why not?

The future city (2)

Assignment 36

Assignment 36 offers additional alternatives for future urban life. The first alternative illustrates an architect's plan for a compressed, integrated, future city. However, some writers fear these future verticle, highly compressed cities. In the last two alternatives a science fiction artist and writer describe life in these future cities. The quality of life changes drastically and they question if people enjoy life more in the future city. These fictional alternatives consider social attitudes rather than physical form of the city. For each alternative continue to answer the following questions:

1. How will society use its technology in the future?
2. How does each alternative meet the needs of future people?
3. Under which alternative would you prefer to live? Why?

Paolo Soleri's city of the future

Paolo Soleri, an architect, designs comprehensive and innovative future cities. He and his colleagues are presently building one of his experimental cities in a remote mesa in Arizona. Soleri believes this city, Arcosanti, is the prototype of future cities and an "alternative to urban disaster." The following essay and drawings illustrate Soleri's designs for future cities."

For Soleri the problem of urbanization is not that more and more people will live in cramped and overcrowded cities. He feels that we suffer from the opposite problem: our cities are not compressed enough. Cities have become incapable of concentrating urban activities. Thus parts of the urban environment are flung out onto the surrounding countryside.

Yet cities once contained fairly adquately all the people and activities they brought together. In the past cities had definite boundaries and the uncontaminated countryside lay within easy reach of city dwellers. Soleri believes that modern technology can make cities compressed again with the countryside accessible to urban-dwellers again.

In Soleri's visionary cities populations are enormously concentrated within small areas by a variety of technical means. Soleri's urban structures tightly coordinate and interweave areas of the city. For example, living areas serve as parts of a transportation network. Soleri's cities are three-dimensional environments, multi-leveled structures.

What makes this drastic compression possible is that each city is designed as a single, unified, and continuous structure. These buildings function like metropolises; metropolises in the form of buildings.

When we use the term "architecture" we scarcely think of such a gigantic scale. Soleri calls his cities "arcologies." "Arcology" comes from a combination of "architecture" and "ecology." Architecture suggests a unified structural design. Ecology suggests basic patterns of life for vast populations—new human ecologies.

What has Soleri accomplished with his visionary arcologies? There is no simple answer. Soleri is so sure that others' visions will surpass his own that he refers to his city plans as "model T's." His plans may dazzle contemporaries, but he feels one day they will be obsolete. Soleri said, "What you see is a phantom, the beginning of a process."

Soleri's arcologies:

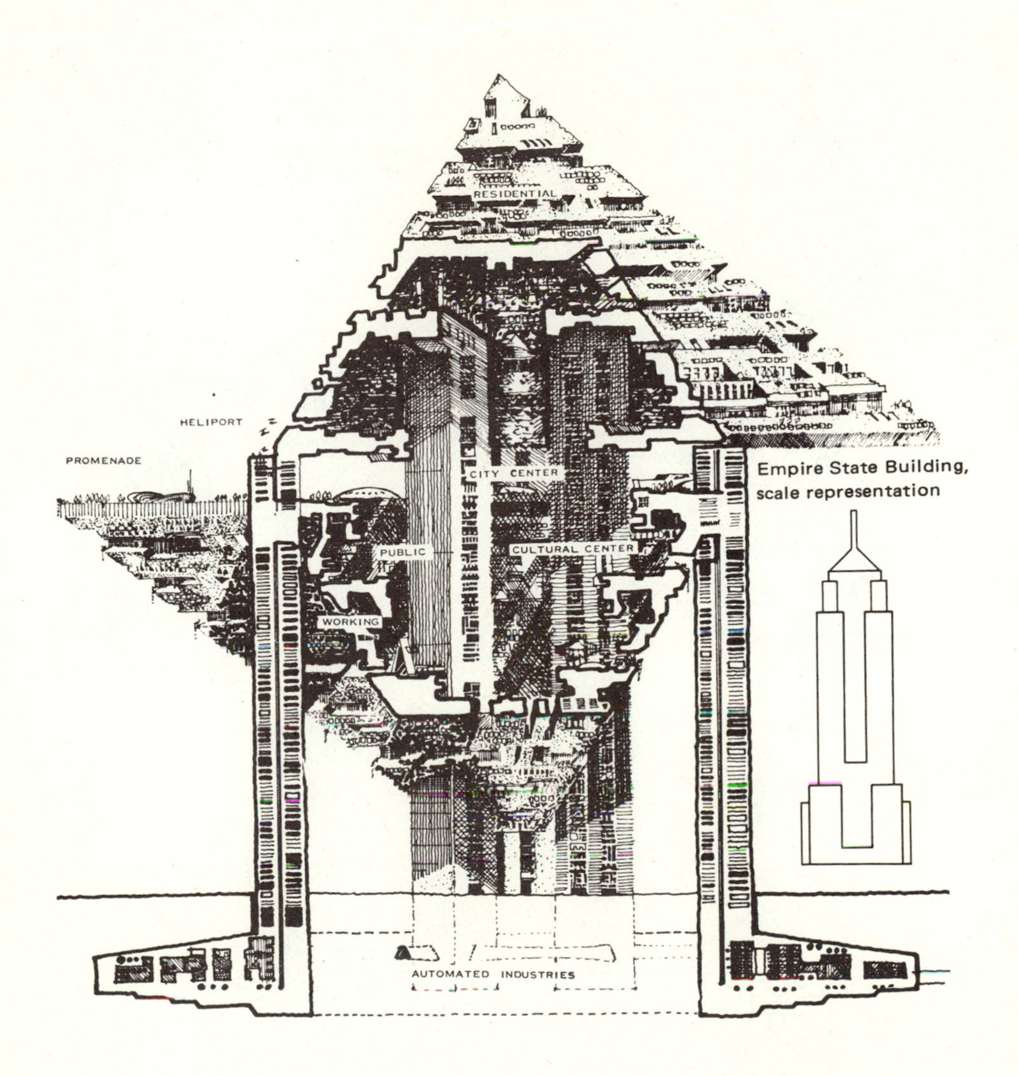

Hexahedron

A city on stilts. "Hexahedron" is a Soleri arcology so fully three-dimensional that to speak of its population density per square mile (forty-six times that of Chicago) would be meaningless. As shown in Soleri's scale model, left, and drawing, below, Hexahedron consists chiefly of two three-sided pyramids, one of them with its apex facing earthward. The city center is the vertical core of the megastructure, which means that every resident of the city is within half a mile of the downtown facilities a supreme virtue of compression in Soleri's view. An outline of the Empire State Building indicates the scale.

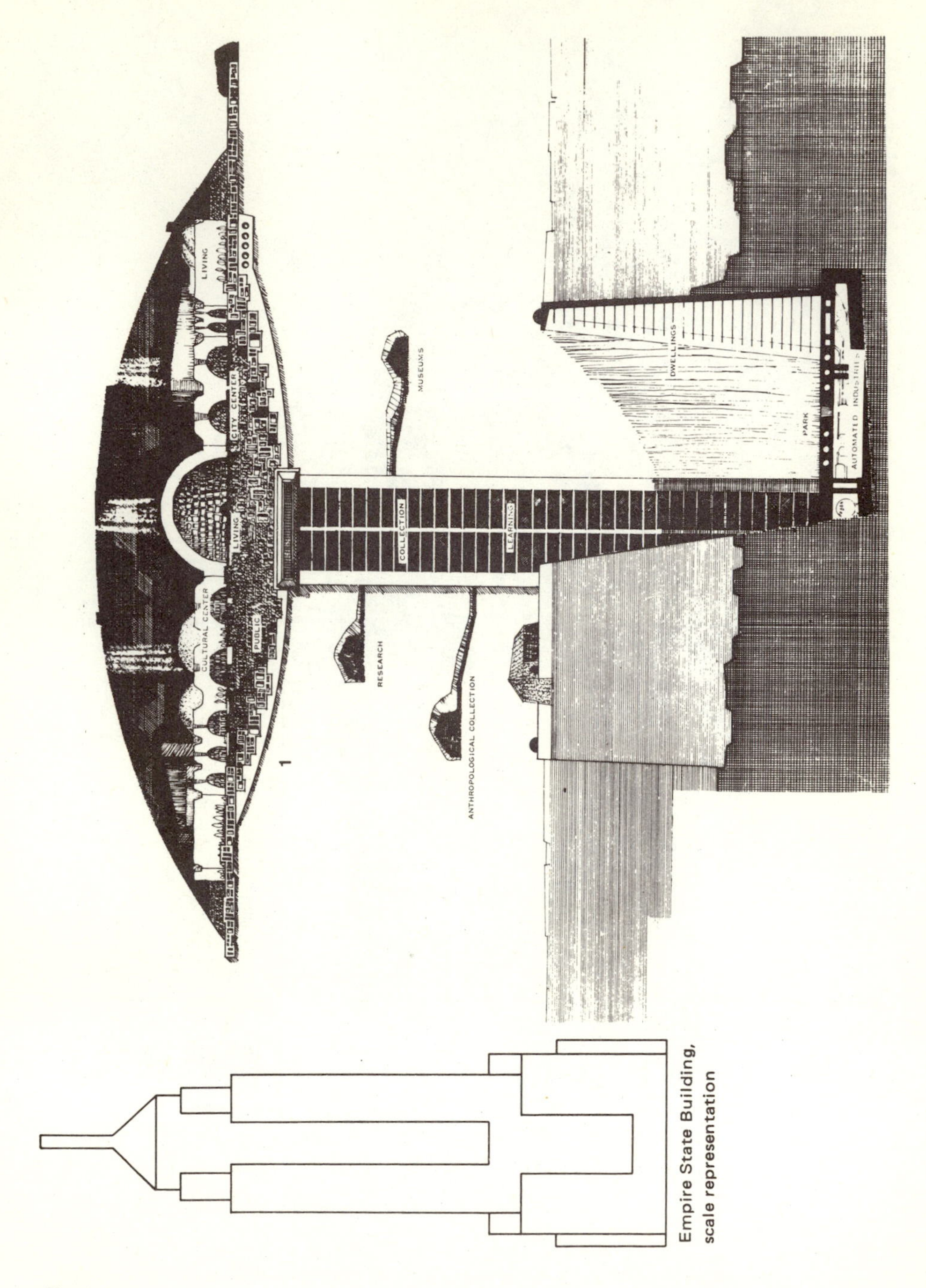

Theology

Set in the sheer rock face of a cliff, right, "Theology" is Soleri's proposal for a community of scholars. Physically, it would be a man-made cave dwelling capable of housing thirteen thousand people. Conceptually, it closely parallels Francis Bacon's visionary "Solomon's House," being a unified center of learning, a repository of useful collections, and a permanent residential area that is set apart from the ordinary, workaday world.

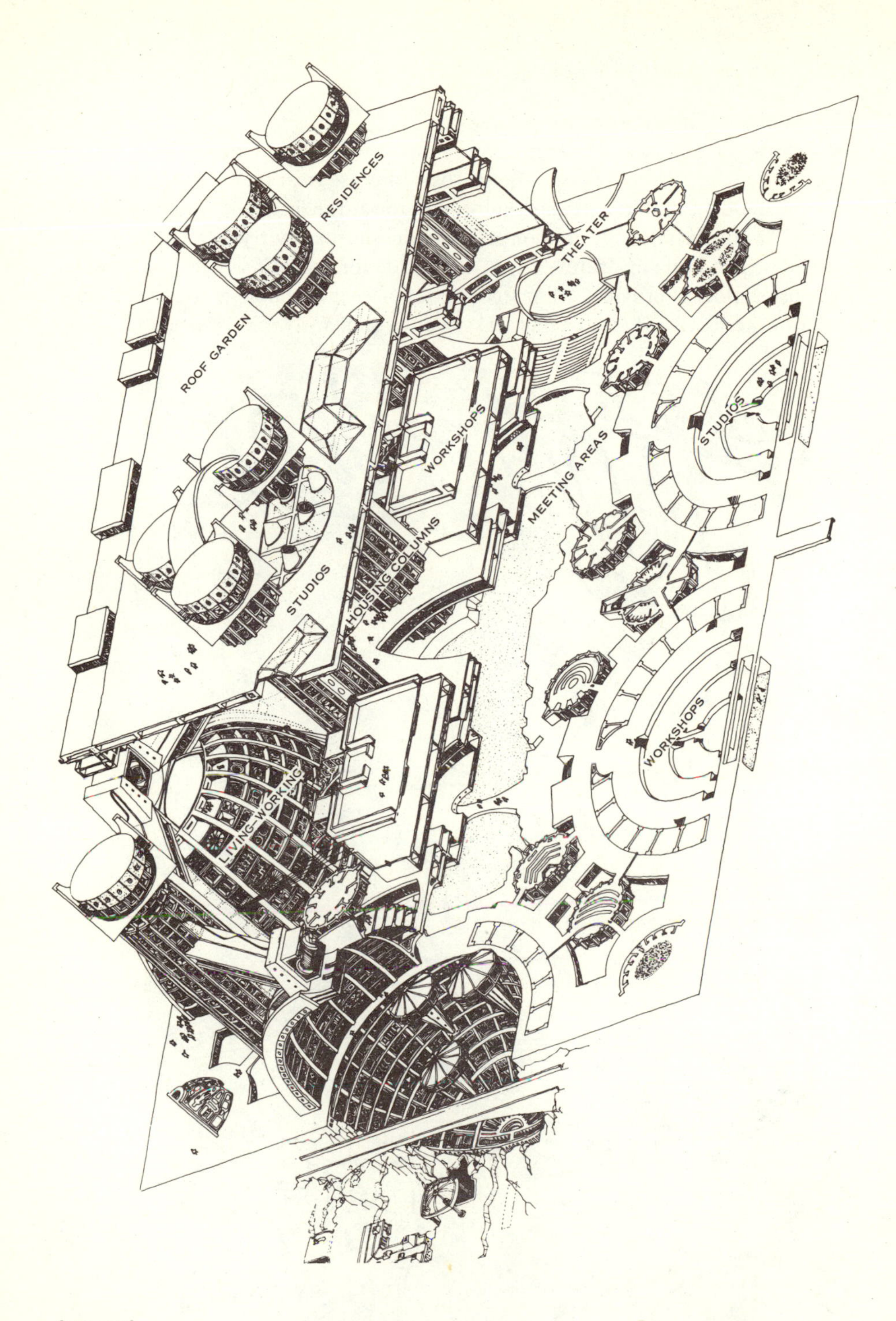

Arcosanti

Arcosanti features such compressing devices as building columns that serve as residences. Just how compressed an urban environment can be and still remain livable the student-builder-residents of Arcosanti will presumably discover for themselves and for the rest of us.

Future cities: Science fiction or reality

The following cartoons and science fiction short story portray amazing and cynical pictures of life in our future cities. Both artists forecast great technological advances but question the attitudes of future individuals toward their city and society in general. As you examine the cartoon and read the short story try to imagine what it would be like living in a future city. Then decide for yourself whether you think man's psychological progress will match the advances in technology. Note that the author of the short story uses a physical structure similar to Soleri's structure.

ONCE A YEAR ALL THE OLD STUFF WILL BE GATHERED UP AND PUT INTO HUGE MACHINES WHICH WILL GRIND IT UP AND MAKE IT INTO NEW STUFF!

THE BED AS WE KNOW IT WILL BE REPLACED BY A SOFT, WARM, MOIST FOAM PLASTIC BLOB THAT YOU JUST DIVE INTO AND FALL ASLEEP WHILE IT UNDULATES SLOWLY IN AND OUT AND SOOTHING, SWEET MUSIC PLAYS.
ZZZZ

BABY SITTING WILL BE DONE BY ROBOTS WITH TV HEADS THAT PLAY VIDEO TAPES OF MOM AND DAD. PARENTS WILL NO LONGER BE TIED TO THEIR CHILDREN!
SUCH CUTE LITTLE DARLINGS!
HEY GIMME A NICKEL MOM!
ME SOME TOO WOW

MANY NEW SPORTS WILL BE INVENTED! KIDS WILL RISK THEIR LIVES IN DANGEROUS ROCKET DRAG RACES. SOME OF THESE JOBS WILL GO AS FAST AS 25,000 MPH!!

THERE'LL ALWAYS BE THE SEARCH FOR THE BIGGER KICK! GUYS WILL PLAY "CHICKEN" WITH SUICIDAL SOUPED-UP BODY ROCKETS!

Robert Silverberg's future city

. . . He enters the dropshaft and programs for the 185th floor. Down he goes to Pittsburgh. He sinks, inertia-free, through the cities that make up Urbmon 116. Down he goes through Chicago, through Edinburgh, through Nairobi, through Colombo.

Forty floors constitute one city. The twenty-five cities of Urbmon 116 comprise the successive layers of a single great urban monad, a tower of super-stressed concrete three kilometers high, a self-contained unit housing more than 800,000 human beings. Most cities within the urbmon have between 30,000 and 40,000 people but there are exceptions. Louisville, the high-prestige abode of the urban administrators, is sparsely populated; luxury is the compensation one is given for the burdens of such responsibility. Reykajavik, Warsaw and Prague, the three bottom cities where the maintenance workers and other humble grubbers live, are overpopulated. Crowding is considered beneficial there. Everything is conceived for the greater good.

Urbmon 116 looks after itself. Its central service core provides light, fresh air, heating, cooling, and other essentials. Central kitchens handle most of the food-processing chores. Below ground level, 400 meters down, is found the utilities substructure: refuse compactors, the plants for the reprocessing of wastes, the heat-sink, the power generators and everything else on which the life of the urbmon depends. Food is the only thing that must come from outside. The agricultural communes lie beyond the urban area. Jason's building is one of fifty-odd identical structures making up the Chipitts urban constellation, which in this year of 2383 has a population of close to 41,000,000. There are many other such urban constellations in the world–Boshwash, Sansan, Shankong, Bocarac, Wienbud. The aggregate human population of Earth has risen well past 75,000,000,000. Because of the new verticality of urban housing patterns, there is ample land for meeting the food requirements of that many people and more.

He feels the comforting solidity of the building about him as he descends. The urbmon is his world. He has never been outside it. Why should he go out? His friends, his family, his whole life, are here. His urbmon is adequately supplied with theaters, sports arenas, schools, hospitals, houses of worship. His data terminal gives him access to any work of art that is considered blessworthy for human consumption. No one he knows has ever left the building, except for the people who were chosen by lot to settle in the newly opened Urbmon 158 a few months ago. They, of course, will never come back. There are rumors that urban administrators sometimes go from building to building on business but Jason is not sure that this is true. He does not see why such travel would be necessary or desirable. Are there not systems of instantaneous communication linking the urbmons, capable of transmitting all relevant data?

It is a splendid system. As a historian, privileged to explore the records of the pre-urbmon world, he knows more fully than most people how splendid it is. He understands the awful chaos of the past. The terrifying freedoms; the hideous necessity of making choices. The insecurity. The confusion. The lack of plan. The formlessness of contexts.

He reaches the 185th floor. He makes his way through the sleepy corridors of Pittsburgh to his office. A modest room but he loves it. Five small glistening cubes lie on his desk. Each holds the contents of several libraries. He has been working with these cubes for two years, now. His theme is *The Urban Monad as Social Evolution: Parameters of the Spirit Defined by Community Structure.* He is attempting to show that the transition to an urbmon society has brought about a fundamental transformation of the human soul. Of the soul of western man, at any rate. Formerly aggressive people accept the yoke of the new environment. A more pliant, more acquiescent mode of response to events; a turning away from the old expansionist-individualist philosophy, as marked by territorial ambition, the conqueror mentality and the pioneering way. People have turned toward a kind of communal expansionism centered in the orderly and unlimited growth of the human race. Definitely a psychic evolution of some sort, a shift toward graceful acceptance of hive-life. The dissatisfied people bred out of the system generations ago. We who have not gone down the chute accept the unalterable society. Yes. Yes. Jason believes that he has struck upon a significant subject. His wife laughed at him when he announced his subject: "You mean you're going to write a book showing that people who live in different kinds of cities are different? That urbmon people have a different attitude than jungle people? Some scholar. I could prove your point in six sentences." Nor was there much enthusiasm for the subject when he proposed it at a staff meeting, although he did manage to get clearance for it. His technique so far has been to steep himself in the images of the past, to turn himself, so far as is possible, into a citizen of the pre-urbmon society. He hopes that this technique will give him the essential perspective on his own society that he will need when he begins to write his study. He expects to start writing in two or three years.

He consults a memorandum, chooses a cube.

A kind of excitement comes over him as scenes out of the ancient world materialize. He leans close to his input speaker and begins to dictate. Frantically, Jason sets down notes on the way it used to be.

The past. Houses and streets. A horizontal world. Individual family shelter units: this is my house, this is my castle. Fantastic! Three people taking up maybe a thousand square meters of surface. Roads. Concept of road hard for us to understand. Like a hallway going on and on. Private vehicles. Where are they all going? Why so fast? Why not stay home? Crash! Blood. Head goes through glass. Crash again! In the rear. Dark fluid flows in street. Middle of day, springtime, major city. Street scene. Which city? Chicago, New York, Instanbul, Cairo. People walking about IN THE OPEN. Paved streets. This for walkers, this for drivers. Filth. Estimated grid reading: 10,000 pedestrians this sector alone, in strip 8 meters wide and 80 meters long. Is that figure right? Check it. Elbow to elbow. And they'd think our world was overcrowded? At least we don't impinge on each other like that. We know how to keep our distances within the overall structure of urbmon life. Vehicles move down middle of street. The good old chaos. Chief activity: the purchase of goods. Private consumption. Cube 11Ab8 shows interior of a shop. Exchanging of money for merchandise. Not much difference there except random nature of transaction. Do they need what they buy? Where do they PUT it all?

This cube holds nothing new for him. Jason has seen such city scenes many times before. Yet the fascination is ever fresh. He is tense, sweat flowing freely, as he strains to comprehend a world in which people may live where they please. A world where they move about on foot or in vehicles in the open, where there is no planning, no order, no restraint. He must perform a double act of imagination. It is necessary for him to see that vanished world from within, as though he lived in it. Then he must try to see the urbmon society as it might seem to someone from the twentieth century. The magnitude of the task dismays him. He knows roughly how an ancient would feel about Urbmon 116. It is a hellish place, the ancient would say. A place where people live hideously cramped and brutal lives, in which every civilized philosophy is turned on its head. A place where uncontrolled breeding is nightmarishly encouraged to serve some incredible concept of a god eternally demanding more worshipers. A place where dissent is ruthlessly stifled and dissenters are destroyed. Jason knows the right phrases, the sort of words an intelligent liberal American would use. But the inner spirit is missing. He tries to see his own world as a kind of hell but he fails. To him it is not hellish. He is a logical man. He knows why the vertical society had to evolve out of the old horizontal one. The new vertical society had to eliminate—preferably before they were old enough to reproduce—all those who would not adapt or could not be adapted to the fabric of society. How could troublemakers be allowed to remain in the tight, intimate, carefully balanced structured of an urbmon? He knows that the probable result of tossing flippos down the chute has been, over a couple of centuries, the creation of a new style of human being through selective breeding. Is there now a *Homo urbmonensis*, adjusted, fully content? These are topics he means to explore intensively when he writes his book. But it is so hard, so absurdly hard, to grasp them from the viewpoint of ancient man!

Jason struggles to understand the uproar over overpopulation in the ancient world. He has drawn from the archives scores of tracts directed against indiscriminate human spawning. These tracts are angry arguments composed at a time when less than 4,000,000,000 people inhabited the world. He is aware, of course, that humans can choke a whole planet quickly when they live spread out horizontally the way they did. But why were they so worried about the future? Surely they could have foreseen the beauties of the vertical society!

No. No. That's just the point, he tells himself unhappily. They did *not* foresee any such thing. Instead they talked about limiting fertility, if necessary by imposing a governmental authority to hold population down. Jason shivers. Don't you see, he asks his cubes, that only a totalitarian regime could enforce such limits? You say that we're a repressive society. But what kind of society would you have built if the urbmons hadn't developed?

The voice of ancient man replies I'd rather take my chances on limiting births and allowing complete freedom otherwise. You've accepted the freedom to multiply but it's cost you all the other freedoms. Don't you see—

You're the one who doesn't see, Jason answers. A society must sustain its momentum through the exploitation of god-given fertility. We've found a way to make room for everybody on Earth, to support a population ten or twenty times greater than what you imagined was the absolute maximum. You see it merely as suppression and authoritarianism. But what about the billions of lives that could never have come into being at all under your system? Isn't that the ultimate suppression: forbidding humans to exist in the first place?

The ancient replies: But what good is letting them exist if the best they can hope for is a box inside a box? What about the quality of life?

Jason argues: I see no defects in the quality of our life. We find fulfillment in the interplay of human relationships. Do I need to go to China or Africa for my pleasures when I can find them within a single building? Isn't it a sign of inner dislocation to feel compelled to roam all over the world? In your day everybody traveled, I know, and in mine no one does. Which is a more stable society? Which is the happier one?

Which is more human? Which exploits man's potential more fully? Isn't it our nature to seek, to strive, to reach out?

What about seeking within? Exploring the inner life?

But don't you see—

But don't you see—

If only you would listen—

If only you would listen—

Jason does not see. Ancient man's spokesman does not see. Neither will listen. There is no communication . . . .

For thought and discussion

What other alternative for future cities can you envision?

Individual and small group activities

1. Work with several of the other members of class to plan a panel discussion on the year 2000. The members of the panel should briefly describe one day of their lives in the year 2000. Each member should make comments on his or her occupation, social relationships, leisure activities as well as a physical description of the city. The members should state their attitudes toward their lifestyles in the year 2000. The members should then debate their reasons for their different perceptions of the future city. Other members of the class may ask the panel to explain their positions more fully.
2. Go to your library and locate information about other future cities such as Cesar Pelli's megastructures and the future city of Tapiola in Finland. You may also choose another science fictions writer's view of future cities such as Arthur C. Clarke's *The City and the Stars* and Ray Bradbury's "The Pedestrian." Describe the author's picture of future urban life to class and compare the description with the alternatives you examined in Assignments 35 and 36.

Bibliography

Urban geography

Berry, Brian. *City Classification Handbook.* New York: John Wiley & Sons, 1972.

Bourne, Larry, ed. *Internal Structure of the City: Readings on Space and Environment.* New York: Oxford University Press, 1971.

Hoyt, Homer. *One Hundred Years of Land Values in Chicago: The Relationship of the Growth of Chicago to the Rise in Its Land Values, 1830–1933.* New York: Arno Press, 1970.

Johnson, James. *Urban Geography,* 2d ed. New York: Pergamon Press, 1973.

Jones, Emrys. *Towns and Cities.* New York: Oxford University Press, 1966.

Urban sociology

Halebsky, Sandor, ed. *The Sociology of the City.*

Hatt, Paul, & Reiss, Albert, eds. *Cities and Society.* New York: Free Press, 1957.

Hauser, Philip, & Schnore, L. *The Study of Urbanization.* New York: John Wiley & Sons, 1965.

Merton, Robert. *Social Theory and Social Structure.* New York: Free Press, 1968.

Urban economics

Hoover, Edgar, & Vernon, Raymond. *Anatomy of a Metropolis.* Garden City, N.Y.: Doubleday, 1962.

Jacobs, Jane. *The Economy of Cities.* New York: Random House, 1970.

Kohler, Heinz. *Economics and Urban Problems.* Lexington, Md.: D.C. Heath, 1973.

Thompson, Wilbur. *A Preface to Urban Economics.* Baltimore: Johns Hopkins Press, 1968.

Urban politics

Banfield, Edward. *The Unheavenly City: The Nature and Future of Our Urban Crisis.* Boston: Little, Brown, 1970.

Banfield, Edward, & Wilson, James. *City Politics.* Cambridge: Harvard University Press, 1963.

Callow, Alexander, Jr. *The Tweed Ring.* New York: Oxford University Press, 1969.

Dahl, Robert. *Who Governs: Democracy and Power in an American City.* New Haven: Yale University Press, 1961.

Haeger, John and Weber, Michael. *The Bosses*, St. Charles, Missouri: Forum Press, 1974.

Herzog, Steve. *Minority Group Politics: A Reader.* New York: Holt, Rinehart and Winston, 1971.

Holli, Melvin. *Reform in Detroit.* New York: Oxford University Press, 1973.

Mandelbaum, Seymour. *Boss Tweed's New York.* New York: John Wiley & Sons, 1968.

Miller, Zane. *Box Cox's Cincinnati: Urban Politics in the Progressive Era.* Richard C. Ward, ed. New York: Oxford University Press, 1968.

Stedman, Murray, Jr. *Urban Politics.* Cambridge: Winthrop, 1972.

Tarr, Joel. *A Study in Boss Politics: William Lorimer of Chicago.* Urbana: University of Illinois Press, 1971.

The walking city

Bridenbaugh, Carl. *Cities in Revolt.* New York: Knopf, 1955.

Bridenbaugh, Carl. *Cities in the Wilderness: The First Century of Urban Life.* New York: Oxford University Press, 1971.

Lane, Roger. *Policing the City: Boston, 1822–1885.* New York: Atheneum, 1971.

Reps, John. *Town Planning in Frontier America.* Princeton, N.J.: Princeton University Press, 1969.

Wade, Richard. *The Urban Frontier: The Rise of Western Cities, 1780–1830.* Chicago: University of Chicago Press, 1964.

The streetcar city

Ginger, Ray. *Altgeld's America: The Lincoln Ideal vs. Changing Realties.* New York: Franklin Watts, 1965.

Hays, Samuel. *The Response to Industrialism.* Chicago: University of Chicago Press, 1957.

Schlesinger, Arthur. *The Rise of the City, 1878–1898.* Dixon R. Fox, ed. New York: Franklin Watts, 1971.

Thernstrom, Stephen, & Sennett, Richard. eds. *Nineteenth-Century Cities: Essays in the New Urban History.* New Haven: Yale University Press, 1969.

Wiebe, Robert. *Search for Order: 1877–1920.* New York: Hill & Wang, 1967.

Urban biography

Chudacoff, Howard. *Mobile Americans: Residential and Social Mobility in Omaha, 1880–1920.* New York: Oxford University Press, 1972.

Clark, Dennis. *The Irish in Philadelphia: Ten Generations of Urban Experience.* Philadelphia: Temple University Press, 1974.

Davis and Haler. *The Peoples of Philadelphia.* Philadelphia: Temple University Press, 1974.

Dykstra, Robert. *Cattle Towns.* New York: Atheneum, 1970.

Frisch, Michael. *Town into City: Springfield, Massachusetts and the Meaning of Community, 1840–1880.* Cambridge: Harvard University Press, 1972.

Green, Constance. *The Secret City: A History of Race Relations in the Nation's Capital.* Princeton, N.J.: Princeton University Press, 1967.

Lubove, Roy. *Twentieth Century Pittsburgh: Government, Business and Environmental Change.* New York: John Wiley & Sons, 1969.

Mayer, Harold, & Wade, Richard. *Chicago: Growth of a Metropolis.* Chicago: University of Chicago Press, 1973.

McKevey, Blake. *Rochester: An Emerging Metropolis.* Rochester: Christopher Press, 1962.

Still, Bayrd. *Mirror for Gothem: New York As Seen by Contemporaries from Dutch Days to the Present.* New York: New York University Press, 1956.

Thernstrom, Stephen. *The Other Bostonians: Poverty and Progress in the American Metropolis, 1880–1970.* Cambridge: Harvard University Press, 1973.

Warner, Sam, Jr. *The Private City: Philadelphia in Three Periods of Its Growth.* Philadelphia: University of Pennsylvania Press, 1968.

Warner, Sam, Jr. *Streetcar Suburbs: The Process of Growth in Boston, 1870–1900.* New York: Atheneum, 1969.

Race and ethnicity

Binzen, Peter. *White Town U.S.A.* New York: Random House, 1970.

Bodnar, John, ed. *The Ethnic Experience in Pennsylvania.* Lewisburg, Pa.: Bucknell University Press, 1973.

Clark, Kenneth. *Dark Ghetto.* New York: Harper & Row, 1965.

Cole, Donald. *Immigrant City: Lawrence, Massachusetts.* Chapel Hill: University of North Carolina Press, 1963.

Duff, John. *The Irish in the United States.* Belmont, Ca.: Wadsworth, 1971.

Gans, Herbert. *The Urban Villagers.* New York: Free Press, 1962.

Glazer, Nathan, & Moynihan, Daniel. *Beyond the Melting Pot: The Negroes, Puerto Ricans, Jews, Italians and Irish of New York City.* Cambridge: MIT University Press, 1970.

Handlin, Oscar. *The Uprooted.* New York: Grosset & Dunlap, 1957.

Handlin, Oscar. *Boston's Immigrants.* New York: Atheneum, 1968.

Higham, John. *Strangers in the Land.* New York: Atheneum, 1963.

Liebow, Elliot. *Talley's Corner.* Boston, Little, Brown, 1967.

Meister, Richard. *The Black Ghetto: Promised Land or Colony.* Lexington, Md.: D.C. Heath, 1972.

Nelli, Humbert. *The Italians in Chicago, 1880–1930: A Study in Ethnic Mobility.* New York: Oxford University Press, 1973.

Novak, Michael. *The Rise of the Unmeltable Ethnics.* New York: MacMillan, 1972.
Osofsky, Gilbert. *Harlem: The Making of a Ghetto, 1890–1930.* New York: Harper & Row, 1966.
Rischin, Moses. *The Promised City: New York's Jews, 1870–1914.* New York: Harper & Row, 1970.
Rudwick, Elliot. *Race Riot at East St. Louis July 2, 1917.* New York: Atheneum, 1972.
Spear, Allan. *Black Chicago: The Making of a Negro Ghetto, 1890–1920.* Chicago: University of Chicago Press, 1967.
Taeuber, Karl, & Taeuber, Alma. *Negroes in Cities: Residential Segregation and Neighborhood Change.* New York: Atheneum, 1969.
Tuttle, William, Jr. *Race Riot: Chicago in the Red Summer of 1919.* New York: Atheneum, 1970.

Index

†